T0400991

IMPROVING COLLEGE STUDENT RETENTION

IMPROVING COLLEGE STUDENT RETENTION

New Developments in Theory, Research, and Practice

Edited by Robert D. Reason and John M. Braxton

Foreword by Laura W. Perna

Routledge
Taylor & Francis Group

NEW YORK AND LONDON

First published in 2023 by Stylus Publishing, LLC.

Published in 2023 by Routledge
605 Third Avenue, New York, NY 10017
4 Park Square, Milton Park, Abingdon, Oxon OX14 4RN

Routledge is an imprint of the Taylor & Francis Group, an informa business.

© 2023 Taylor & Francis Group

Library of Congress Cataloging-in-Publication-Data
Names: Reason, Robert Dean, editor. | Braxton, John M., editor.
Title: Improving college student retention : new developments in theory,
    research, and practice / Edited by Robert D. Reason and John M. Braxton ;
    Foreword by Laura W. Perna.
Description: First edition. | Sterling, Virginia : Stylus Publishing, LLC, 2023. |
    Includes bibliographical references and index.
Identifiers: LCCN 2023014891
    ISBN 9781642672176 (paperback) | ISBN 9781642672169 (cloth)
Subjects: LCSH: College attendance--United States. | College dropouts--
    United States--Prevention. | College students--United States--Social
    conditions. | Education, Higher--Research--United States. | College
    attendance--Social aspects--United States. | Universities and colleges--United
    States--Administration.
Classification: LCC LC148.2 .I47 2023
LC record available at https://lccn.loc.gov/2023014891

ISBN: 978-1-64267-216-9 (hbk)
ISBN: 978-1-64267-217-6 (pbk)
ISBN: 978-1-00344-525-8 (ebk)

DOI:10.4324/9781003445258

CONTENTS

FOREWORD

College student retention is one of the most common topics in higher education research, policy, and practice. Even with past attention, however, the field needs the information that this book provides. College student retention is a large, costly, persisting problem. In fall 2015, 2.3 million students enrolled for the first time in a U.S. college or university seeking a credential. Six years later, 30% of these students—680,000 individuals—were no longer enrolled and had no credential (Lee et al., 2022). Less than half (46%) of students who enrolled full time for the first time in fall 2015 at a public 4-year institution completed a credential within 4 years, and only 72% completed within 6 years (Lee et al., 2022). Completion rates are even lower for students who first enroll part-time, with 21% of those who first enrolled part time at a public 4-year institution earning a credential in 4 years and 37% earning a credential in 6 years (Lee et al., 2022). Four-year and 6-year completion rates are lower for those who first enroll in a public 2-year institution (37% and 49% for those who first enroll full time and 20% and 31% for those who first enroll part time) and higher for those who first in a private, not-for-profit 4-year institution (63% and 79% for those who first enroll full time and 24% and 38% for those who first enroll part time). Regardless of institutional type, the conclusion is the same: Too many students who start college seeking a degree do not achieve their goal even after 6 years.

For every student who enrolls and does not finish, there are real costs. Colleges and universities lose the tuition revenue they would have received if the student had reenrolled each semester until degree completion. Institutions also incur the costs of recruiting new students to fill enrollment seats (rather than filling those seats with persisting students) in order to meet tuition targets. Our communities, states, and nation lose the learning, productivity, civic engagement, tax revenue, and other public benefits that come with greater college completion (Ma et al., 2019).

Students who enroll but do not receive a degree lose access to the higher earnings that typically come with degree completion. Among full-time, full-year workers age 25 and older, median earnings in 2018 were 61% higher for those with a bachelor's degree than for those with a high school diploma. For those with some college and no degree, median earnings were only 14% higher (Ma et al., 2019).

Students who enroll in college but do not finish also incur real costs. For each semester of enrollment, students must pay tuition, fees, and other costs, including books and supplies. They may have to pay financial and emotional costs for caregivers to mind their children (and perhaps their parents and other loved ones) while they attend class and study. Students also lose the earnings they would have received if they had devoted their time to paid employment instead of college-related activities.

The many students who leave without a credential and use loans to pay college costs face even greater costs. Students who borrow to pay college costs and complete their educational programs tend to gain access to jobs with the higher paying salaries that enable them to repay their loans. But, students who borrow and do not receive a credential generally do not secure those higher paying jobs—and they still have a loan to repay. Rates of defaulting on a federal student loan are more than twice as high for those who do not complete their educational programs than for those who do complete (24% versus 9% among borrowers entering repayment in 2011–2012; College Board, 2016).

With the rising costs of attendance and the declining purchasing power of the Federal Pell Grant (Cahalan et al., 2022), students without the family wealth and other personal financial resources often have little choice but to borrow to pay college costs. Black students are especially dependent on student loans. Only 14% of Black bachelor's degree recipients in 2015–2016 had no debt, compared with 41% of Asians, 33% of Hispanics, and 30% of Whites (Davis et al., 2020). One in five (21%) Black bachelor's degree recipients in 2015–2016 had $50,000 or more in student loan debt, compared with 6% of Asian, 7% of Hispanic, and 10% of White bachelor's degree recipients (Davis et al., 2020).

Our students deserve better. We cannot blame students if they do not complete our higher education programs. We cannot expect that, simply because a student has been granted admission, they will be able to navigate institutional processes, find the financial resources required to pay college costs, and engage in academic and other aspects of the college experience the way that we expect. Especially with the high financial costs for students who do not complete, we, as higher education policymakers, administrators, and scholars, need to critically examine how our systems, processes, and practices are failing to enable all students to succeed.

We also cannot assume that what worked in the past will continue to work into the future. The characteristics of college students are changing. As just one example, the percentage of undergraduates identifying as

Hispanic increased from 6% in 1990 to 14% in 2010, to 22% in 2020 (National Center for Education Statistics, 2021, Table 306.10). The world in which students attend college is also changing, as dramatically illustrated by the COVID-19 pandemic. Nearly all (87%) of undergraduates experienced enrollment disruptions due to the COVID-19 pandemic (e.g., movement of classes online), 40% experienced financial disruptions (e.g., loss of job or income), and 27.5% experienced housing disruptions (e.g., changed addresses; Cameron et al., 2021).

This volume recognizes the need for renewed and ongoing commitment from higher education policymakers, administrators, and researchers to improve college student retention. Chapter authors establish what we know and don't know from existing theory and research, and they identify what public policymakers and institutional leaders can do to help students complete their programs.

Chapters in the first part of this three-part volume remind us of the value of theoretical and conceptual models that can explain observed college student retention patterns. With the heterogeneity of today's students and institutional contexts, it is critical that higher education policymakers, practitioners, and researchers understand the diversity of the lived experiences, perceptions, and backgrounds of individual students. At the same time, theoretical and conceptual models help us understand the forces that contribute to more general patterns and point to actions that policymakers and practitioners can take to improve experiences and outcomes for different groups of students attending different types of institutions in different places. No single model or theory is sufficient to explain the experiences of all students at all institutions. But, as demonstrated in this volume, different models and theories can help us understand how to better serve and support different groups of students.

While all chapters in this volume reflect commitment to advancing research-based policies and practices, chapters in the volume's second part delve into what is known, what is not known, and what we need to know if we are to enable all who enroll to complete. Prior research has addressed important questions and more research is needed to address persisting and emerging questions. Chapter authors offer useful guidance on the questions that need to be addressed and methodological approaches for addressing them.

Chapters in the third and final part of the volume focus on practice, including program implementation. Creating meaningful improvements in college student retention is more difficult than simply adopting a policy or practice that has been found to be effective elsewhere. Colleges and universities enroll students that vary in number, enrollment intensity, personal resources, academic interests and preparation, and other characteristics. Colleges and universities vary in the financial and other supports they provide to students, the pressures they experience to advance other institutional goals and priorities, and the extent to which state government policies and resources help or hinder their efforts to improve college student retention.

Given the importance of retention to individual students, higher education institutions, and our communities, states, and nation, higher education institutions and states can and must do more to improve college student retention. This volume offers useful insights and guidance for higher education policymakers, practitioners, and researchers about where we have been, where we are now, and what we need to do into the future.

Laura W. Perna
GSE Centennial Presidential Professor of Education and
Vice Provost for Faculty
University of Pennsylvania

References

Cahalan, M., Addison, M., Brunt, N., Patel, P., Vaughan, T., Genao, A., & Perna, L.W. (2022). *Indicators of higher education equity in the United States: 2022 historical trend report.* The Pell Institute of the Council for Opportunity in Education and Penn AHEAD.

Cameron, M., Lacy, T.A., Siegel, P., Wu, J., Wilson, A., Johnson, R., Burns, R., & Wine, J. (2021, June). *2019-20 National Postsecondary Student Aid Study (NPSAS:20): First look at the impact of the coronavirus (COVID-19) pandemic on undergraduate student enrollment, housing, and finances.* Institute of Education Sciences. https://nces.ed.gov/pubs2021/2021456.pdf

College Board (2016). *Trends in student aid.* https://research.collegeboard.org/media/pdf/trends-student-aid-2016-full-report.pdf

Davis, C. H. F., Bishop, J. M., King, K., & Jama, A. (2020). *Legislation, policy and Black student debt crisis.* NAACP. https://drive.google.com/file/d/1vr0w7y YIXIv5r60up-gQ7P2xv7sPZQ--/view

Lee, S., Ryu, M., & Shapiro, D. (2022, July). *Yearly success and progress rates: Fall 2015 beginning postsecondary student cohort.* National Student Clearinghouse Research Center. https://nscresearchcenter.org/wp-content/uploads/YearlySuccess Progress2022.pdf

Ma, J., Pender, M., & Welch, M. (2019). *Education pays.* College Board. https://research.collegeboard.org/media/pdf/education-pays-2019-full-report.pdf

National Center for Education Statistics. (2021). *Digest of education statistics.* https://nces.ed.gov/programs/digest/d21/tables/dt21_306.10.asp?current=yes

I

IMPROVING COLLEGE STUDENT PERSISTENCE

New Developments in Theory, Research, and Practice

Robert D. Reason and John M. Braxton

Most higher education institutions have already begun to see decreasing enrollment numbers (Snyder et al., 2019), even as higher education enrollment is predicted to drop precipitously starting in 2025 (Grawe, 2018). According to Grawe, much of the decrease in enrollment will be driven by demographic trends (e.g., a decrease in birth rates) about which higher education institutions can do little, making the retention of students who do enroll in our institutions that much more important. Even with considerable scholarly and public policy attention on student retention in higher education, overall retention rates have stagnated and differential retention rates by race and ethnicity have persisted (Snyder et al., 2019). If higher education institutions, researchers, and policymakers are to improve retention rates, we must engage in a critical examination of the current state and future directions of retention theory, research, and practice. This edited volume begins that examination by addressing several major questions. What are the needed directions in theory and research on college student persistence and how do we translate new theory and research into effective practices? Are we asking the right questions, looking in the right places, or trying to apply incongruous theories to new populations? Overall, how do we—as a collective community of scholars—refocus our attention on matters of student persistence for the 21st century?

The Need for New Directions in Theory and Research

Tinto's theory enjoyed paradigmatic status for well over 30 years (Braxton et al., 2004). A significant challenge to its paradigmatic stature took place when Braxton et al. (1997) undertook an empirical assessment of the internal consistency of this theory. Based on this assessment, Braxton et al. concluded that Tinto's theory needed serious revision. As a result, Braxton et al. (2004) studied retention issues at residential colleges and commuter colleges, positing a revision of Tinto's original theory specific to these different types of institutions. Empirical testing of these two theories resulted in support for the revised theory of student persistence in residential colleges and universities and partial support for the theory of student persistence in commuter colleges and universities (Braxton et al., 2014). Given the passage of 7 years since the publication of this book, three questions emerge: Are these theories in need of revision to account for recent research on student persistence? Are these theories based on students in predominantly White colleges and universities suitable for use with minoritized students enrolled in them? Have new theories, for other types of institutions and minoritized students, been promulgated and tested?

In addition to these efforts in theory development, Reason (2009) posited another approach to advancing the conversation. As part of a comprehensive literature review, Reason organized empirical research on student persistence into the categories of student precollege characteristics, organizational characteristics, student peer environments, and individual student experiences. Based on his review of research findings for each of these categories, Reason identified four specific areas for future research. These four specific areas include continued study of students' sociodemographic characteristics, the role of organizational behavior, student environments nested within different institutional settings, and the effects of student subclimates. Again, over a decade later, we are left to ponder if retention research in each of these areas has advanced. What, if anything, new is known about how these four areas affect student persistence?

In addition to future directions in theory and research on college student persistence, a need exists for approaches to the translation of theory and research into actionable terms that inform policies and practices to increase student retention rates. Such a need finds expression in Tinto's (2006–2007) contention that "most institutions have not been able to translate what we know about student retention into forms of action that have led to substantial gains in student persistence and graduation" (p. 5). In his 2012 book *Completing College: Rethinking Institutional Action*, Tinto built on his assertion by positing a framework for institutional action composed of four components: expectations, support, assessment and feedback, and involvement. Have others worked to guide institutional actions to improve institutional retention rates? What future research is needed to guide communities of practice in their efforts to increase student retention? We assert there may be much left to be discovered about what institutions can do to improve retention rates and student success.

Format and Content of Book

In order to address these concerns and update our understanding of theory, research, and practice, we organize the volume around three broad topics: theories and models, research, and practice. Within each of these broad topics, authors focus on updating our understandings, using Reason's (2009) and Braxton et al.'s (2014) work as a starting point. Each chapter attends to the "new majority" students—students from social identity groups that have been traditionally underserved by higher education but who are attending higher education institutions at greater rates than ever before. In so doing, this volume provides an up-to-date understanding of theory, research, and practice as it applies to today's college student.

Theories and Models

Part One reviews new theories and models of persistence published after 2014, when Braxton et al. offered their models related to commuter and residential campuses. In chapter 2, Willis Jones reviews, analyzes, and critiques seven theories or models introduced to the higher education literature since 2014. The chapter ends with recommendations for future theory development and ways of utilizing college student retention theory.

In chapter 3, Robert Palmer and Larry Walker focus attention on the harmful effects of the misapplication of extant persistence theories to the understanding of the persistence of students of color at predominantly White institutions of higher education. The authors challenge both researchers and practitioners to question assumptions, borne of existing theory and research, and point to more culturally appropriate understandings to help maximize persistence among minoritized students.

In chapter 4, Robert D. Reason and John M. Braxton review and revise, in light of empirical research published recently, two theories previously proposed by Braxton et al. (2004, 2014). The chapter highlights a process by which theoreticians and researchers can engage in theory revision and improvement. The process results in the proposal of two new theories for students at commuter and residential institutions that take into account recent research on college student persistence. Although the authors use published evidence to revise these two models, they also acknowledge and encourage researchers to test these models with new data.

Research

Part Two reviews recent empirical research findings and research methods related to student persistence. Its purpose is to present a snapshot of the current state of published research, particularly related to the topical areas Reason (2009) identified, and to explore methodological considerations for persistence research with new students.

In chapter 5, Ann Gansemer-Topf, Rachel Smith, Jodi Wilson, and Maggie Bell inventory persistence articles published in the leading higher education journals in the past decade. Their systematic review of published articles highlights trends in the persistence research, while also providing insight into what researchers are missing and identifying important holes in our understanding of persistence among contemporary college students.

Chapters 6 through 8 update our understanding of the effects on student persistence of three broad topical areas often identified in the research. In chapter 6, Darris Means and Dena Kniess explore the most up-to-date research related to student demographic characteristics and persistence. In chapter 7, Maria Javiera de los Ríos and Leticia Oseguera explore the effects of organizational characteristics and behaviors on student persistence. In chapter 8, KC Culver and Nick Bowman dive deeply into how student peer environments and engagement affect persistence behaviors.

Jungmin Lee explores the methodological concerns that emerge when studying persistence in contemporary college students in chapter 9. Specifically, Lee focuses on the student swirl to highlight the methodological difficulties, and opportunities, when studying student persistence in what she calls the age of student mobility.

Practice

Part Three of this book focuses on the process of translating theories/models and research into institutional and state action. The authors in this part focus on what keeps institutions from acting and processes for improving the translation to action. The part ends with an exploration of how research informs public policy and how that translates into institutional action.

The first two chapters in this part provide an overview of good practices and a conceptual framework. In chapter 10, Kristen A. Renn and Brandon R. G. Smith use the experiences of institutions participating in the University Innovation Alliance, a consortium of 11 research-oriented institutions, to demonstrate how the sharing of data across institutions can inform good practices and improve student retention. In chapter 11, Ezekiel Kimball and Garrett Gowen review a breadth of social science literature, with particular focus on models addressing the intentional translation of theory and research to practice. The result is a proposed new conceptual model for the development of evidence-informed retention practices for higher education institutions.

The next two chapters of this part focus specifically on the application of theory and research to strategic enrollment management (SEM) practices on college campuses. In chapter 12, P. Jesse Rine and Joshua T. Brown focus attention on how SEM practices have changed as a result of advances in policy, technology, data, and market competition. SEM as a field of practice continues to develop as a result of attention to data-informed decision-making that allows for new, and nuanced, approaches to retaining students. Alexandra Wendt, John Braxton, Donald Hossler, Wendy Kilgore, and Heather Zimar, in chapter 13, use their own research to highlight the importance of the communication between practitioners and researchers in SEM.

In the final chapter of this section, Will Doyle examines how theory and research can, and should, inform state-level policies related to student persistence. Doyle explores the data related to some of the most well-known and widely implemented state-level interventions intended to improve student retention, often revealing that little evidence exists to support the efficacy of such interventions.

Reason and Braxton chart future directions for theory, research, and practice for college student persistence in the final chapter of this volume. They propose these future directions to assure the continued vibrancy of college student persistence as a focus of attention by the communities of research and practice of higher education.

Audience and Need

At the risk of trying to be all things to all people, we assembled this book in a way intended to meet the needs of scholars and practitioners alike. The primary audience for this volume will likely be faculty members and graduate students in higher education programs in the United States. Most, if not all, graduate programs in higher education cover the topic of student retention either through a dedicated course or as part of a larger course on student outcomes. The presentation of the most up-to-date understanding of theory, research, and practice will benefit graduate students about to enter faculty careers focused on the study of student persistence and retention or about to enter professional positions that have as part of their responsibility to improve the retention rates of students. Chapter authors calling for exploration and development of new theories and models, exploring the misapplication of existing theories to new populations, and providing frameworks for the analysis of the comprehensiveness of existing theories will push researchers to delve deeper into unexplored areas of inquiry.

Finally, we believe the focus on translation of theory and research into practice and policy will make this book particularly attractive to a practitioner audience. The current emphasis on strategic enrollment management, prompted by the declining enrollments in higher education, have elevated attention on issues of retention and persistence. The specific evidence-informed examples employed by the authors in the practice section of the book allow practitioners to adapt and translate high-quality practices to their local institutional contexts, while reinforcing the importance of data and communication between researchers and practitioners.

References

Braxton, J., Hirschy, A., & McClendon, S. (2004). *Understanding and reducing college student departure.* Jossey-Bass.

Braxton, J., Sullivan, A. S., & Johnson, R. M. (1997). Appraising Tinto's theory of college student departure. In J. Smart (Ed.), *Higher education: Handbook of theory and research* (Vol. 12, pp. 107–164). Springer.

Braxton, J. M., Doyle, W. R., Hartley, H. V., Hirschy, A. S., Jones, W. A., & McClendon, M. K. (2014). *Rethinking college student retention.* Jossey-Bass.

Grawe, N. D. (2018). *Demographics and the demand for higher education.* Johns Hopkins University Press.

Reason, R. D. (2009). An examination of persistence research through the lens of a comprehensive conceptual framework. *Journal of College Student Development, 50*(6), 659–682. https://muse.jhu.edu/article/364959

Snyder, T. D., de Brey, C., & Dillow, S. A. (2019). *Digest of education statistics, 2017.* U.S. Department of Education.

Tinto, V. (2006–2007). Research and practice of student retention: What next? *Journal of College Student Retention, 8*(1), 1–19. https://doi.org/10.2190/4YNU-4TMB-22DJ-AN

Tinto, V. (2012). *Completing college: Rethinking institutional action.* University of Chicago Press.

PART ONE

THEORIES AND MODELS

REIMAGINING STUDENT PERSISTENCE, RETENTION, AND SUCCESS

An Exploration of New Theories and Models

Willis A. Jones

In 2009, President Barack Obama, while offering remarks at McComb Community College, described what his administration called the American Graduation Initiative. This initiative's goal was to return America to first in the world in the proportion of its population with a college degree. To accomplish this goal, 60% of Americans aged 25–34 needed to complete an associate degree or higher by 2020 (Obama, 2009).

Unfortunately, as we approached 2020, America was a bit behind schedule in its degree-attainment goals. In 2010, 42% of Americans age 25–34 had a college degree. By 2018, that number crept up to around 49% (Organisation for Economic Co-Operation and Development [OECD], 2019). At this pace, America would not reach its college graduation percentage goal until 2041 (Marcus, 2019).

This slow growth in college graduates and increased recognition of the need for more college-educated workers has resulted in colleges and universities being forced to put renewed focus on preventing students from leaving school before degree completion. The work of these colleges and universities is being supported by a dynamic new group of higher education scholars who are reimagining the college student departure puzzle and proposing new ways of understanding why many people who start college fail to earn their degree. Unfortunately, these newer frameworks for understanding student retention are scattered across a wide variety of books and journal articles.

This chapter reviews theories of college student retention, persistence, and success proposed since the publication of the Braxton et al. (2014) book *Rethinking College Student Retention*. The chapter begins with a brief review of theories historically used to study college student retention, followed by a discussion of Braxton et al.'s revised theories of student persistence at residential and commuter colleges and universities. The chapter then offers a review and analysis of recently proposed theories of college student retention, persistence, and success.[1] The chapter ends with recommendations for future theory development and suggestions for how practitioners and policymakers can utilize college student retention theory.

Brief History of Research on College Student Retention and Persistence

Academic interest in better understanding student failure to remain in college until graduation dates back to the early 1930s. Much of the early research in this area involved single-institution studies such as the study from Edgerton and Toops (1929). John McNeely published one of the first multi-institutional studies of student dropout[1] prior to graduation in 1937. McNeely's (1937) work used data from 25 colleges and universities across the United States to investigate various questions related to student dropout. He found that across institutions, around 45% of students permanently withdrew from university before graduating. This percentage varied somewhat based on institutional type and student demographics.

The comprehensiveness of McNeely's work served as a precursor to research on student dropout published in the 1940s, 1950s, and 1960s. Papers from Gekoski and Schwartz (1961), Grace (1957), Mercer (1941), Panos and Astin (1968), and Summerskill (1962) looked to identify factors that influenced student persistence. By the 1970s, college dropouts had become an extensively researched area (Spady, 1970).

Up to the early 1970s, however, much of the college student dropout literature lacked a strong theoretical foundation (Spady, 1970, 1971;

---

[1] *Retention, persistence, success, dropout, attrition,* and *degree completion* are often used interchangeably in higher education. Scholars have noted, however, that each of these terms can have slightly different meanings (Hagedorn, 2005). For example, *dropout* is a term that was common for many years but is seldom used today. In this chapter, I use the term employed by the authors of the respective models reviewed. A theoretical model described as a retention model by the model's authors is described as a retention model in this chapter. A theoretical model described as a persistence model by the model's authors is described as a persistence model in this chapter, etc.

Tinto, 1975). Scholars responded to this dearth of theoreticalization by initiating what Berger et al. (2012) called the era of building retention theory. The first model proposed was Spady's (1971) sociological student retention model. Spady's model was followed by Tinto's (1975) model of dropout behavior, Bean's (1980) student attrition model, Bean and Metzner's (1985) model of nontraditional undergraduate student attrition, and Cabrera et al.'s (1993) overlapping model of college persistence. These models were built largely on theories from the fields of sociology, social anthropology, and human resources (Aljohani, 2016).

Braxton et al.'s Theories of Student Persistence

One of the most widely cited models of college student persistence/retention is Tinto's (1993) interactionist theory of student departure. Some argue that Tinto's model has reached paradigmatic status within the field of higher education (Braxton et al., 2004). Given its popularity, Braxton et al. (1997) were interested in assessing the empirical support for Tinto's theory. While they found partial support for Tinto's theory within residential colleges, they found little to no support for the theory within commuter colleges. Given the unique characteristics of residential and commuter institutions (e.g., differences in available social communities for students and differences in the heterogeneity of students), Braxton et al. (2004) proposed two new frameworks to account for student persistence. These frameworks were slightly revised in Braxton et al. (2014).

Figure 2.1 depicts the Braxton et al. (2014) revised theory of student persistence at residential universities. The theory posits that students' background characteristics such as family socioeconomic status, race, and academic achievement help shape students' initial commitment to the institution and their initial commitment to the goal of graduation. Students' initial institutional commitment impacts subsequent institutional commitment and students' perception of their institution's commitment to student welfare, institutional integrity, and psychosocial engagement. Students' perception of their institution's commitment to student welfare, institutional integrity, and psychosocial engagement directly influences students' degree of social integration. Social integration has a direct impact on students' persistence decisions. Subsequent institutional commitment also has a direct influence on student persistence in the model.

Cultural capital (defined as student involvement in cultural activities such as reading, attending plays, museums, etc.) plays an important role in

Figure 2.1. Braxton et al. revised theory of student persistence in residential colleges and universities.

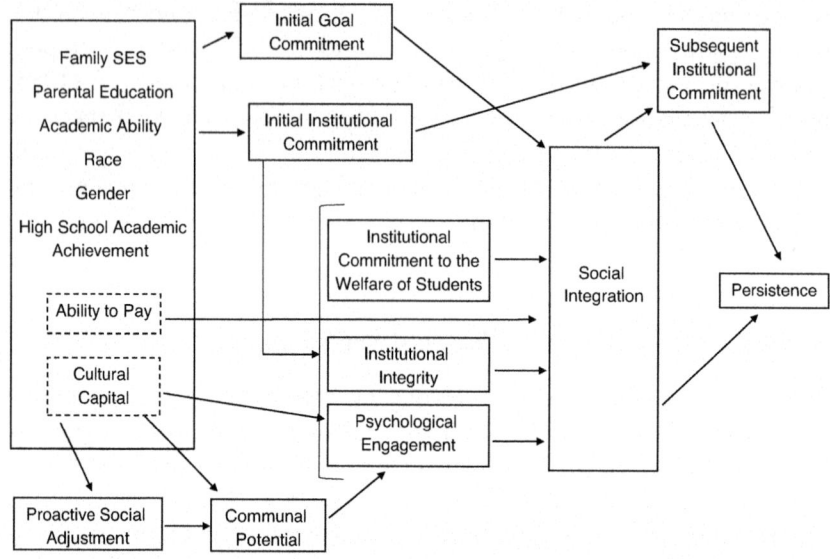

the Braxton et al. (2014) theory. The model posits that students' cultural capital directly affects psychosocial engagement and has an indirect effect on psychosocial engagement through proactive social adjustment and communal potential. Psychosocial engagement directly influences social integration, which in turn impacts student persistence.

Figure 2.2 displays Braxton et al's (2014) revised theory of student persistence in commuter colleges and universities. This framework consists of seven major dimensions: (a) entry characteristics, (b) initial institutional commitment, (c) the external environment, (d) perceived organizational characteristics, (e) academic and intellectual development, (f) subsequent institutional commitment, and (g) persistence in the college or university. The framework argues that students' entry characteristics such as parental education, motivation to attend college, and their sense of self-efficacy have a direct impact on students' persistence and levels of initial institutional commitment. Initial institutional commitment interacts with characteristics of the external environment and organizational characteristics of the campus environment. Perceived external environmental support in the form of family support or lower felt costs of attendance increases the likelihood of persistence. Students' perceptions of organizational characteristics such as institutional integrity and institutional commitment to student welfare influence students' academic/intellectual development and

Figure 2.2. Braxton et al. revised theory of student persistence in commuter colleges and universities.

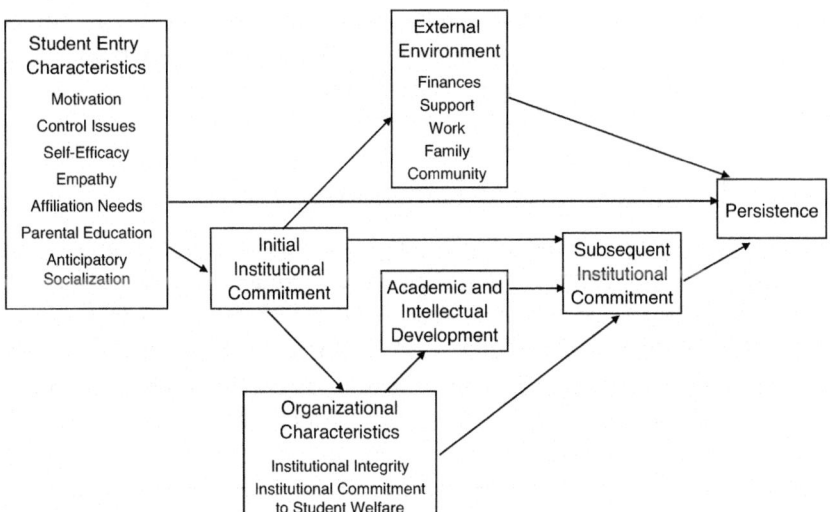

their subsequent institutional commitment. Higher levels of subsequent institutional commitment lead to a higher likelihood of persistence.

Chapter Methodology

Since the publication of Braxton et al. (2014), other researchers have proposed theoretical frameworks to better understand student persistence, retention, and success. In the remainder of this chapter, I provide an overview of these frameworks. To identify frameworks for inclusion in this chapter, I engaged in a systematic review of several major higher education publications. First, I reviewed every chapter published since 2014 in *Higher Education: Handbook of Theory and Research*. Next, I reviewed every article published since 2014 in five peer-reviewed higher education journals— *Journal of College Student Retention: Research, Theory & Practice, Journal of College Student Retention, Research in Higher Education, Review of Higher Education*, and *Journal of Higher Education*. Finally, I engaged in a Google Scholar search for books and articles published since 2014 using the search terms *student retention theory, college student dropout theory, student persistence theory*, and *student success theory*. This review identified seven newly proposed frameworks related to college student retention, persistence, and success. The frameworks reviewed here are unlikely to be a complete list of student persistence frameworks proposed since 2014. In particular, frameworks presented in dissertations and theses are not included in this review. However, I am confident that the frameworks discussed in this chapter offer a comprehensive summary of recently proposed theoretical frameworks related to student retention, persistence, and success.

Culturally Engaged Campus Environment Model

Museus (2014) proposed the culturally engaged campus environment (CECE) model of college student success. Racially diverse students are the focus of the model. Museus defined racially diverse student populations as inclusive of both White students and students of color. Museus acknowledged, however, that the majority of empirical research used to justify the model's constructs come from work that examined the experiences of undergraduates of color. Museus argued that a new theoretical framework was needed because of the inability of dominant theoretical perspectives of college success to account for the racial and cultural bias experienced by populations of color.

The CECE model, displayed in Figure 2.3, posits that external influences such as family support and financial resources shape the individual influences and college success of racially diverse students. Precollege characteristics such as gender, academic preparation, and initial academic disposition also directly affect both individual influences and college success.

However, the focal point of the model is on the role of culturally engaging campus environments on individual influences and student success.

Figure 2.3. Museus culturally engaging campus environment model.

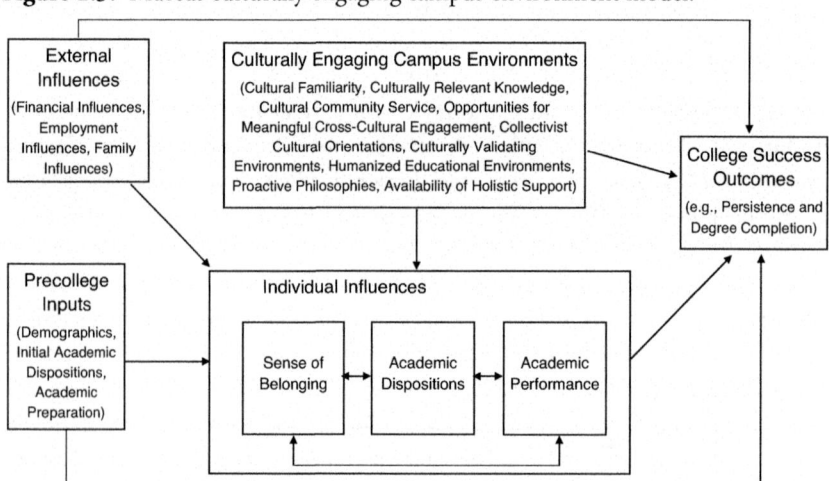

Specifically, the more a college campus engages in activities that create culturally engaging environments, the more students develop positive individual influences and the greater the likelihood of student success. Museus (2014) highlighted nine activities colleges and universities can offer to create a culturally engaged campus:

- cultural familiarity (offering students the opportunity to connect with people with whom they share a common background)
- culturally relevant knowledge (offering students the opportunity to cultivate, sustain, and increase knowledge of their culture and community)
- cultural community service (offering students spaces and tools to give back to and positively transform their cultural communities)
- opportunities for meaningful cross-cultural engagement (offering students access to opportunities for cross-cultural engagement)
- collectivist cultural orientations (offering students institutional environments based on collectivist cultural orientations)
- culturally validating environments (surrounding students with educators who validate their cultural backgrounds and identities)
- humanized educational environments (offering students environments that care about, are committed to, and develop meaningful relationships with students)
- proactive philosophies (surrounding students with educators who make extra efforts to bring information and support)
- availability of holistic support (surrounding students with educators who provide them the information they seek, offer required help, or connect them with the information or support they need)

These activities focus on ways campus environments can promote diverse student populations' success rather than focus on the negative pressures that might hinder students' success.

A final key construct in the CECE model is individual influences (defined as the academic and psychosocial factors that influence success among racially diverse students). As mentioned earlier, the model suggests that various factors shape individual influences. These influences, in turn, impact student persistence. For Museus (2014), three individual influences exhibit significant impact over persistence decisions—sense of belonging, academic dispositions (e.g., self-efficacy and motivation), and academic performance. The various individual influences also interact with each other.

Museus (2014) did not intend the CECE model to replace other existing frameworks. The model should instead be seen as a complement to existing frameworks of student success and retention. Museus believed the CECE framework can best be used in conjunction with models focused on exploring the impact of factors such as finances and student behavior on student success in college.

Theoretical Model of Momentum for Community College Student Success

Wang (2017) advanced a new holistic theory of community college student success. The concept of momentum anchors this theory. Typically, the idea of momentum is used in disciplines like mechanics and physics to highlight the fact that a still object will remain still and a moving object will retain its speed and motion in the same direction until an external force acts upon it. Educational researchers have adopted this idea as a way of understanding student academic progress. Scholars such as Adelman (2006) and Doyle (2011) contended that various forces can collectively build students' momentum toward positive educational outcomes, or create friction that reduces momentum. Wang argued that momentum can be a unifying framework for disparate and often unorganized research on community college students.

Figure 2.4 visually outlines the model of momentum for community college student success proposed by Wang (2017). The model is predicated

Figure 2.4. Wang theoretical model of momentum for community college student success.

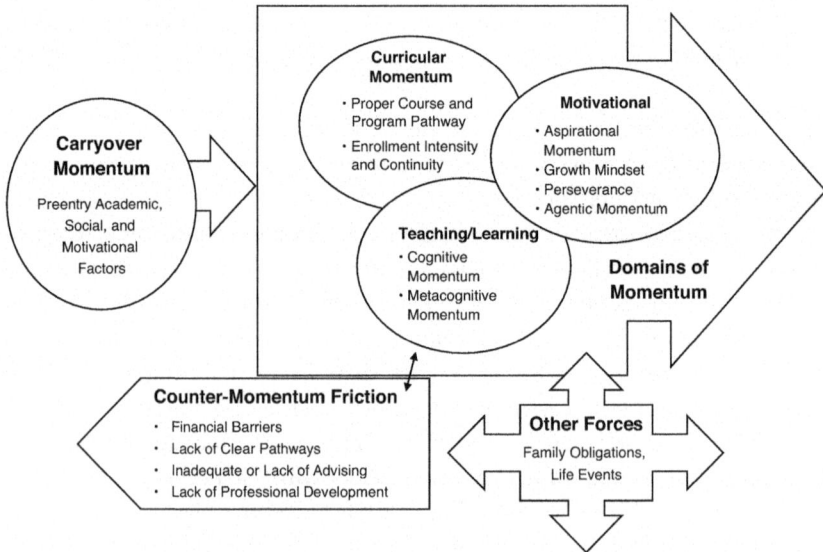

on the argument that to assist students in pursuing fruitful educational experiences and positive educational outcomes (like persistence), community colleges must create environments that foster momentum. Three domains of momentum are particularly important: curricular momentum, motivational momentum, and teaching/learning momentum. Curricular momentum refers to students' progress and efforts in course-taking. Students can maintain curricular momentum through enrolling in a higher number of courses, enrolling uninterruptedly, and following a well-scaffolded and aligned course sequence. Students with more curricular momentum are more likely to reach their educational goals.

Teaching/learning momentum features two key subareas: cognitive momentum and metacognitive momentum. Wang (2017) defined *cognitive momentum* as students' progress toward the goal of learning complex subject matter. Metacognitive momentum is developing skills such as planning, problem-solving, and self-regulation that influence student learning. The theory argues that community colleges can enhance student success by engaging in practices that promote cognitive and metacognitive momentum within classroom spaces. When used appropriately, active learning strategies can be one approach used to help students learn course content (cognitive momentum) and learn how to learn (metacognitive momentum).

Motivational momentum speaks to the "development of aspirations, mindsets, perseverance, and agency that allow community college students to stay on track of their educational journey despite setbacks and counter-momentum" (Wang, 2017, p. 285). Wang highlighted four types of motivation key to the momentum model: aspirational, growth mindset, perseverance, and agentic. Aspirational momentum refers to students' definition of and commitment to their educational goals. Growth mindset refers to students' belief that academic performance is changeable through hard work. Perseverance refers to students' ability to remain focused and engaged despite barriers and constraints. Agentic momentum refers to students' drive to seek help and resources by their own action. These various types of momentum are not necessarily innate and are continually interacting with each other.

A second important concept in the model of momentum for community college student success is counter-momentum friction. The model argues that while various domains of momentum can move community college students toward academic success, there can exist counterforces that deter or redirect student positive momentum. Community colleges must reduce this counter friction faced by students. In particular, four factors can create friction for community college students: financial barriers, lack of clear course or program pathways, inadequate advising, and lack of faculty adoption of active learning or teaching approaches.

Two other concepts are important within the model of momentum. The first is carryover momentum. This is momentum obtained before attending community college that contributes to later momentum developed by students. Students can bring carryover momentum from high school, life experiences, work experiences, and so on. The second concept is other forces. Compared to their peers at 4-year universities, community college students often have significant life responsibilities outside of college. These life circumstances can either push or pull students on their academic trajectory.

In summary, Wang's (2017) model argues that momentum is the key to understanding community college student success (e.g., persistence and degree completion). Students enter community colleges with various degrees of carryover momentum. This carryover momentum combines with three domains of momentum that help students proceed toward goal achievement. Various types of counter-momentum friction, however, can stifle students' momentum toward success. Wang argued that this model can provide researchers and policymakers with a holistic approach and structure for helping community college students combat the various barriers to college success they face.

Structural Model of Predicting Undergraduate Student Retention

Sass et al. (2018) proposed a model for predicting student retention. Sass et al. argued that a new structural model for predicting student retention was needed to address the lack of integration of educational and psychological literature on student success. Therefore, Sass et al. presented and tested a model in hopes of determining how the interrelations of different variables can help us better understand undergraduate student success.

The Sass et al. (2018) model is presented in Figure 2.5. The model centers on socioeconomic, psychosocial, and student success variables. Socioeconomic status variables such as first-generation status and Pell Grant eligibility are hypothesized to have an indirect relationship with student retention through SAT scores and several psychosocial variables. Four psychosocial variables, in particular, are prominent in this model: academic efficacy, problem-solving skills, professor connectedness, and connectedness to the college. Academic efficacy is the confidence students have in their ability to complete an academic task. Academic efficiency is presumed to be a direct predictor of student problem-solving skills. Problem-solving skills are predicted to impact academic performance (student GPA) via professor and college connectedness. Sass et al. defined professor connectedness as student perceptions of professor availability, belief in students' ability, and

Figure 2.5. Sass et al. structural model of predicting undergraduate student retention.

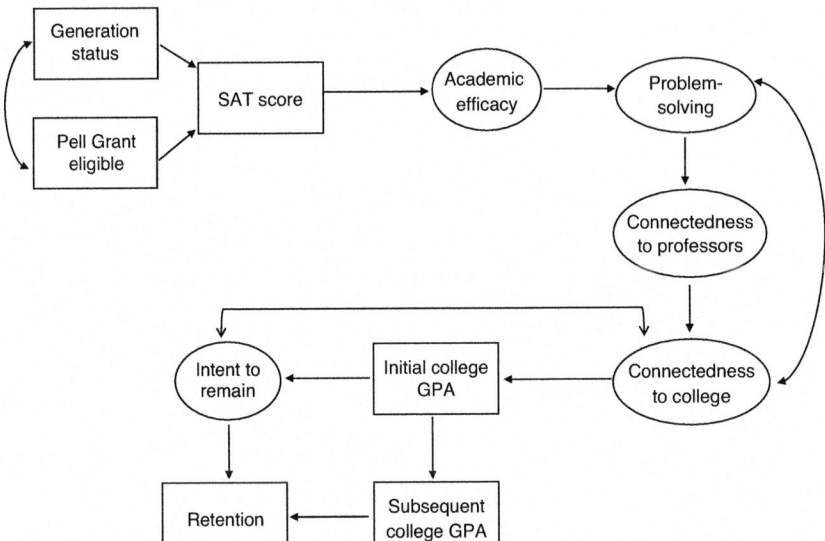

quality of relationships. College connectedness is defined as students' sense of belonging or connection to a school. The model predicts that students who seek greater professor and college connectedness will earn higher college GPAs. Higher college grades in turn predict students' intent to remain at a college and, ultimately, student retention.

Sass et al. (2018) tested their retention model on data from 1,470 students at a large, Hispanic-serving research university. Using Bayesian structural equation modeling, findings from their estimations generally showed support for their hypothesized model. Adding additional direct paths in the model improved model fit, but in general, the researchers felt their model offered promise and guidance to institutions seeking to improve their retention initiatives.

American Indian/Alaska Native Millennium Falcon Persistence Model

The Lopez (2018) American Indian/Alaska Native Millennium Falcon persistence model is presented in Figure 2.6. This model was developed out of a comprehensive review of peer-reviewed articles on the persistence and retention of American Indian/Alaska Native undergraduates. After reviewing

Figure 2.6. Lopez American Indian/Alaska Native Millennium Falcon persistence model.

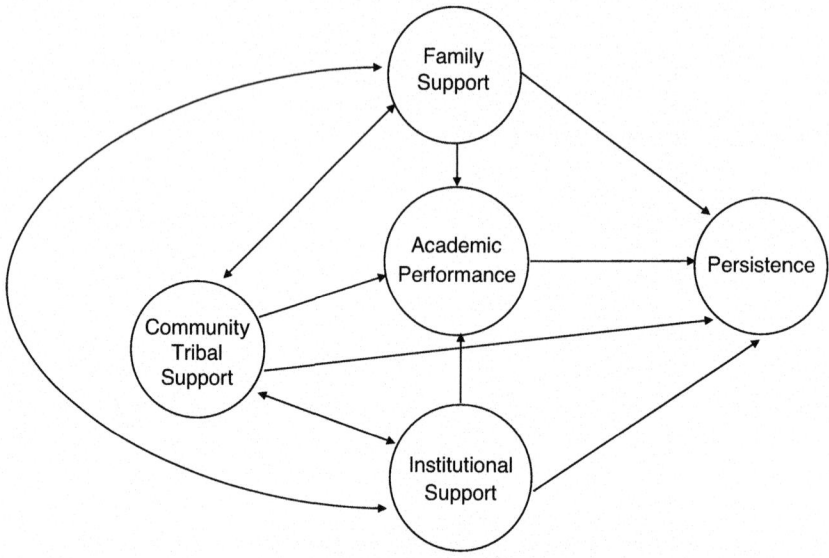

19 qualitative and 25 qualitative articles, Lopez identified several themes related to American Indian/Alaska Native student persistence. These themes are the building blocks for the model.

The Millennium Falcon model argues that four factors impact American Indian/Alaska Native student persistence: family support, institutional support, tribal community support, and academic performance. Family support occurs through encouragement and personal motivation for students to be role models for their families. Family support, however, is not always a positive predictor of student persistence. Often family support can create obligations that interfere with the academic work of American Indian/Alaska Native students. For example, feeling obligated to return home to attend ceremonies/funerals or using financial aid to support families instead of educational expenses can interfere with academic work. Institutional support focuses on the ways colleges and universities can support American Indian/Alaska Native students through support services, impactful faculty, and financial aid. Tribal support highlights the importance of interdependence in American Indian/Alaska Native communities (as opposed to the individualism emphasized in many American communities). The support of tribal communities along with the desire of American Indian/Alaska Native students to give back to their community can be important motivating factors for success. Finally, academic performance highlights the role of academic preparation and skill development in the persistence of American Indian/ Alaska Native students.

Each of the four factors are predicted to have a direct impact on student persistence. Each factor also indirectly impacts retention through the other factors. For example, the impact of community tribal support on persistence is moderated by family support and institutional support. Academic performance is influenced by family support, institutional support, and community tribal support. The model also argues that institutional supports interact with family support to influence persistence. Overall, the model provides a first attempt to present a holistic understanding of American Indian/Alaska Native college student persistence.

Theory of Planned Behavior

Past and present work on student dropout has been guided mainly by the concepts related to social integration. Dewberry and Jackson (2018), however, argued that sociologically based concepts do not explain many of the factors shown to significantly influence student persistence. Expanding on the approach proposed by Bean (1990) and Eaton and Bean (1995), Dewberry and Jackson proposed that the theory of planned behavior might provide more explanatory power than concepts related to social integration. The theory of planned behavior is based on subjective utility theory. Subjective utility theory assumes that individuals make decisions based on a rational evaluation of the probabilities and values of the outcomes of various choices (Savage, 1972). People are believed to make choices that maximize positive outcomes and minimize negative ones.

The theory of planned behavior argues that a primary driver of individuals' action is their intent to perform that action. Three factors influence intent to act: attitude toward the behavior, subjective norms toward a behavior (the social pressure one faces to perform or not perform a behavior), and the extent to which a person believes they can act successfully (Ajzen & Fishbein, 2005).

Theory of planned behavior as it is related to student retention is presented in Figure 2.7. Having a positive attitude toward graduating, receiving encouragement and support toward the goal of graduating, and students' belief about their ability to fulfill graduation requirements are each predicted to have a direct impact on intent to graduate. Students with higher intent to graduate have a higher likelihood of persisting. Dewberry and Jackson (2018) tested this framework in two studies at a nonresidential university in the United Kingdom. They found that variables associated with the theory of

Figure 2.7. Theory of planned behavior for college student retention.

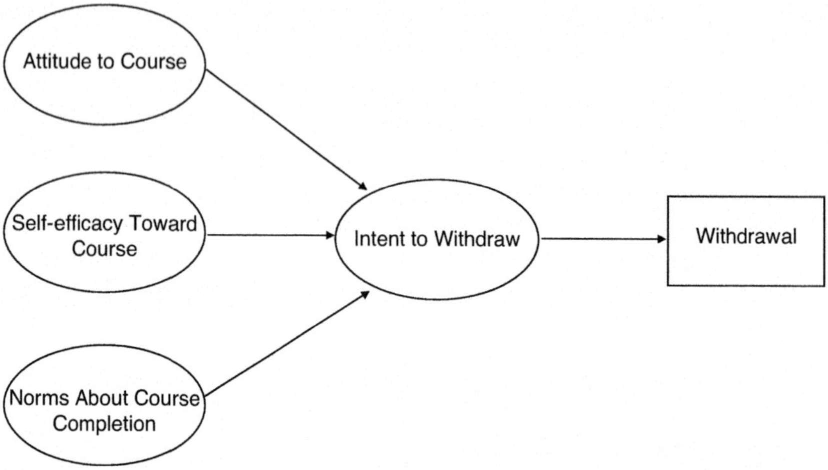

planned behavior often predicted more variance in students' intent to gradu-ate than variables related to social integration theory. Dewberry and Jackson argued that the theory of planned behavior offers the foundation for novel approaches to improving student persistence.

Frameworks Around Student Sense of Belonging

Two frameworks found in the literature did not attempt to predict student persistence directly, but focused instead on a critical concept within many student persistence models—sense of belonging. Vaccaro et al. (2015) pro-posed a theoretical model of belonging for college students with a disability (Figure 2.8). They argued that, although sense of belonging is considered a key variable for enhancing student success and persistence, very little work has focused on sense of belonging for students with disabilities. After inter-viewing eight students, the authors proposed three factors tied to sense of belonging for college students with disabilities. First, sense of belonging was tied to students' ability to self-advocate inside and outside the classroom. Students who were aware of their disability and able to identify ways to address their needs had higher levels of belonging. Second, students who were able to better master the demands of being a college student were able to feel a greater sense of belonging. These demands of being a college student included earning good grades, blending in with peers, being viewed as a legit-imate student, and gaining recognition for academic success. Third, having supportive relationships improved students' sense of belonging. Being able

Figure 2.8. Vaccaro et al. theoretical model of belonging for college students with disabilities.

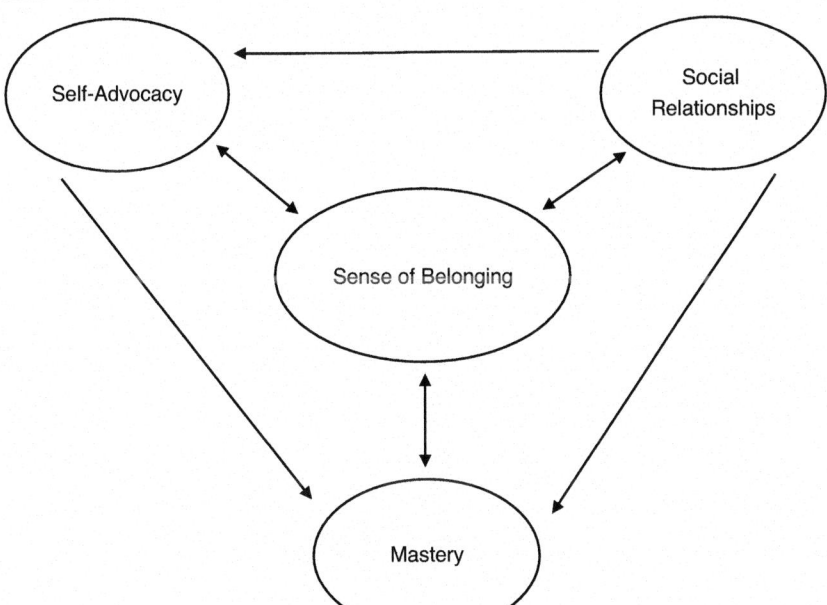

to form relationships with peers helps students with disabilities feel more socially connected. Vaccaro et al. noted that each of these three factors are interrelated. Sense of belonging is impacted by and impacts self-advocacy, mastery, and social relationships. By better understanding the processes students with disabilities use to develop belonging, Vaccaro et al. argued that this framework can help institutions provide better accommodations to support students.

Vaccaro and Newman (2016) used a grounded theory approach to develop another model of college student sense of belonging. This model focuses on the experiences of privileged and minoritized students. Vaccaro and Newman defined *minoritized students* as students who self-identify as belonging to at least one historically unrepresented social identity group by race, sexual orientation, ability, or religion. Through their interviews with first-year students at a midsized public residential university, the authors identified three themes that shaped sense of belonging for all college students: environmental perception, involvement, and relationships. Minoritized and privileged students, however, made meaning of these three themes very differently.

Figure 2.9. Vaccaro and Newman model of belonging for privileged and minoritized students.

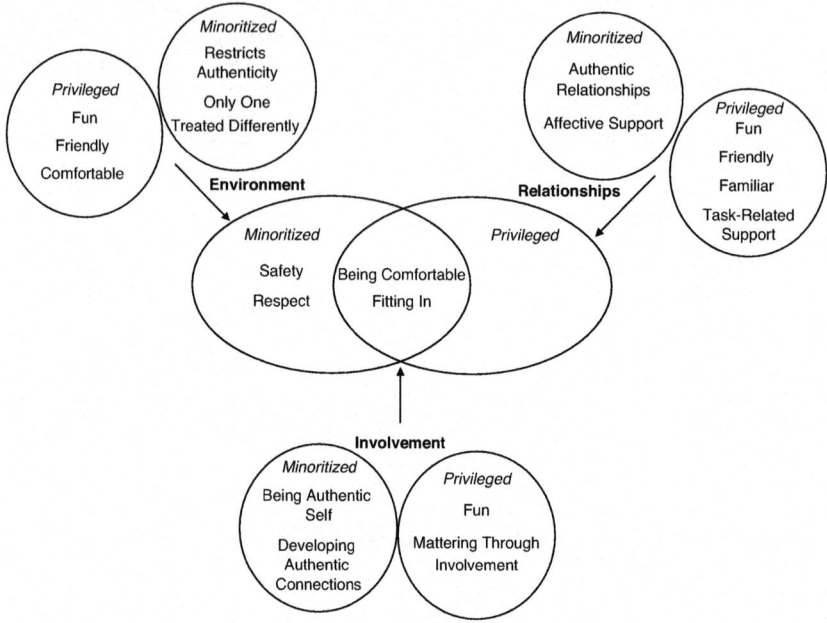

Figure 2.9 presents the Vaccaro and Newman (2016) model of belonging for privileged and minoritized students. The model argues that while both privileged and minoritized students define sense of belonging in terms of being comfortable and fitting in, minoritized students also need safety and respect to feel like they belong. Sense of belonging in the model is influenced by student involvement in extracurricular activities. For privileged students, involvement meant having fun and doing things to increase their sense of accomplishment. For minoritized students, involvement refers to activities that allow them to be their authentic selves and help them make authentic connections. Perceptions of the external environment also shape sense of belonging. For privileged students, campus environments that are fun, friendly, and comfortable increase their sense of belonging. For minoritized students, environments that are diverse enough to promote authenticity, reduce tokenism, and increase minoritized students' feelings of being judged positively influence sense of belonging. Finally, the model argues that relationships are critical to students' sense of belonging. For privileged students, relationships that offer fun, task-related support, and the chance to create familiarity positively influence students' sense of belonging. Minoritized

students, on the other hand, need relationships that are authentic and provide affective support. Vaccaro and Newman hoped their model "would add to the toolkit of perspectives that educators can draw upon when developing programs and services aimed at increasing the sense of belonging for diverse first-year students" (p. 941).

Analysis of Frameworks

Patterson (1983) proposed eight criteria for judging the quality of theoretical models developed in applied fields like education. These eight criteria are importance, precision/clarity, parsimony/simplicity, comprehensiveness, operationality, empirical validation/verification, fruitfulness, and practicality. I collapsed these eight criteria into four themes that served as my framework for providing commentary on the recently proposed models of college student persistence, retention, and success described in the chapter. The first theme is testability. A good theory must contain concepts and relationships that can be operationalized and tested. Testability is key to assessing whether the predicted consequences and relationships in a framework are valid.

I believe each of the models described in this chapter identifies measurable concepts and relationships. In instances where the concepts presented by the models give greater measurement challenges, the authors of the models offer some guidance for the reader. For example, in the CECE model (Museus, 2014) it is crucial to identify ways of operationalizing the nine indicators of a culturally engaged campus environment. Given the nature of those nine indicators, measurement (especially quantitative measurement) might be difficult. While Museus did not offer much guidance on how the various indicators of the CECE model might be measured in his 2014 paper, his subsequent work (Museus et al., 2016) developed and validated a scale designed to measure campus environments. The three domains of momentum proposed by Wang (2017) might also present unique measurement challenges. Given the interdisciplinary nature of defining and measuring momentum, it could be challenging for individuals to operationalize. Wang offered several suggestions for how one might approach developing measurement models for teaching/learning, motivation, and curricular momentum such as drawing from scholarship across multiple disciplines and attending to heterogeneities among community college students.

The second theme of a good theoretical framework is that it is stated as simply and concisely as possible (Patterson, 1983). A good framework makes clear what a researcher needs to do to test it. Some of the frameworks presented in this chapter are indeed parsimonious with minimal complexity.

The theory of planned behavior, for example, provides a concise framework for predicting college student retention. The theoretical model of belonging for college students with disabilities is also relatively noncomplex and presents researchers with clear, testable relationships.

Most student retention, persistence, and success frameworks, however, are complex. This complexity should be expected when dealing with a phenomenon as complicated as students' decisions to remain in college through graduation. Rarely can complex human affairs be captured in simple, parsimonious models. This complexity should not be viewed as a limitation. While parsimony can be good in some cases of theory building, in other cases it can limit our understanding. In the case of student retention, persistence, and success, complex but narratively rich models may be preferable to parsimonious models that fail to fully capture key constructs.

A third theme when assessing the utility of theoretical models is comprehensiveness. Patterson (1983) argued that theory should be complete and include all known data in a field. Theories should be data-driven and hypothesized relationships should be consistent with the data. The frameworks discussed in this chapter largely meet these criteria for good theory. The authors of these newer theories of retention, persistence, and success provided extensive evidence and documented support for their concepts and hypotheses. Given the nature of student persistence and the wide variety of factors involved with persistence decisions, it is unlikely that a single theory can be truly complete, as suggested by Patterson. Within a given context, however, the theories presented in this chapter can be informative and comprehensive. For example, Museus (2014) offered a framework to be considered within the context of campus environments. Concepts related to college costs or student behavior, while undoubtedly important, are outside the scope of the CECE model. Museus rightly argued that the CECE model is best used in conjunction with other frameworks. We should keep in mind that the frameworks discussed in this chapter do not attempt to be grand theories of retention. Instead, these frameworks should be viewed as mid-range or substantive theories that offer explanations in a restricted setting or limited scope (Creswell, 1994).

Finally, Patterson (1983) argued that a good theoretical framework must be important and practical. Importance refers to a theory having some relevance to life or real behavior. Practicality refers to a theory being useful to practitioners for organizing their thinking and practice. As noted earlier in this chapter, student retention, persistence, and success have become increasingly important in higher education. For colleges and universities, retention and graduation rates are important parts of performance funding formulas and other accountability matrixes. For students, persistence and degree/credential completion is a key to future job attainment and higher salaries. Each of the frameworks discussed in this chapter offers a deeper understanding of institutional or student behaviors that influence retention, persistence, and success. A better understanding of these behaviors is vital for the higher education community.

These frameworks also offer valuable ways of organizing institutional action around retention, persistence, and success. For example, institutional efforts around diversity could be viewed as ways of making campuses more culturally engaged, as Museus (2014) highlighted. Efforts around curriculum formalization and articulation at community colleges can be viewed from the perspective of curricular momentum, as proposed by Wang (2017). Efforts to help students with disabilities identify resources and supports on campus can be viewed as a way of encouraging self-advocacy, as discussed by Vaccaro et al. (2015). The frameworks presented in this chapter are both important and practical.

One potential drawback of these frameworks from a practicality perspective may be their complication. Some might find the frameworks, especially the more complex frameworks from Wang (2017), Museus (2014), and Lopez (2018), challenging to utilize in practice given the abstraction of individual concepts within the model. If efforts are made to understand these models deeply, however, I believe practitioners will see them as solid foundations for developing new strategies that create meaningful change in students' pursuit of a degree.

We should commend theoretical models of retention, persistence, and success published since 2014 for centering the voices of those often excluded in earlier theoretical models. The models discussed in this chapter are grounded in work examining the experiences of students of color, community college students, students with disabilities, and other minoritized students. Given the unique challenges to persistence faced by these subsets of students, frameworks must address ways to improve the experiences of what are often our most vulnerable students. As theoretical work on student retention, persistence, and dropout continues, we must maintain the focus on students across a broader spectrum of postsecondary education.

Moving Forward

This chapter's goal was to review theoretical frameworks related to college student retention, persistence, and success published since 2014. This chapter offers one of the first comprehensive reviews of theoretical models recently published in high-profile higher education books and journals. I hope this review can be a tool used by policymakers, practitioners, scholars, and others in the higher education community interested in learning about various theoretical lenses that can be applied to the college student departure puzzle.

Moving forward, I believe three things should happen with the information provided in this chapter. First, scholars should work on empirically validating the theoretical models discussed in this chapter. The work of Braxton et al. (1997) offers a model for how to identify and test hypotheses within a proposed theoretical model. Researchers should be careful to accurately measure the various concepts within the proposed models. Second, as evidence builds supporting these models, practitioners should utilize these frameworks in support of their student success efforts. These efforts will take the coordination of multiple offices and support from upper-level administration. However, as noted earlier, one theoretical model should not be viewed as a grand theory of student success. Thrid, practitioners should develop knowledge of multiple frameworks, both newer and older, and utilize these multiple perspectives to better understand the various factors associated with retention, persistence, and success.

Scholars should build off the frameworks presented in this chapter and continue theoretical work on college student retention, persistence, and success. In particular, focus should continue to be placed on student subpopulations at highest risk of dropout. For example, according to data from the National Center for Education Statistics, female students in the 2014 cohort had about a 7% higher 6-year graduation rate than male students (De Brey et al., 2021). This graduation rate gender gap is even larger for Black and Hispanic students. I could find no newer theoretical models of student retention that were intentionally grounded in work on male student success, especially the success of underrepresented males. Continued theoretical work centering vulnerable student subpopulations would be a valuable addition to the retention, persistence, and success literature.

References

Adelman, C. (2006). *The toolbox revisited: Paths to degree completion from high school through college.* https://www2.ed.gov/rschstat/research/pubs/toolboxrevisit/toolbox.pdf

Ajzen, I., & Fishbein, M. (2005). The influence of attitudes on behavior. In D. Albarracín, B. T. Johnson, & M. P. Zanna (Eds.), *The handbook of attitudes* (pp. 173–221). Erlbaum.

Aljohani, O. (2016). A comprehensive review of the major studies and theoretical models of student retention in higher education. *Higher Education Studies, 6*(2), 1–18. http://dx.doi.org/10.5539/hes.v6n2p1

Bean, J. (1980). Dropouts and turnover: The synthesis and test of a causal model of student attrition. *Research in Higher Education, 12*(2), 155–187. https://doi.org/10.1007/BF00976194

Bean, J. (1990). Understanding why students stay or leave. In D. Hossler & J. Bean (Eds.), *The strategic management of college enrollments* (pp. 617–645). Jossey-Bass.

Bean, J., & Metzner, B. (1985). A conceptual model of nontraditional undergraduate student attrition. *Review of Educational Research, 55*(4), 485–540. https://doi.org/10.2307/1170245

Berger, J. B., Ramirez, G. B., & Lyons, S. (2012). Past to present: A historical look at retention. In A. Seidman (Ed.), *College student retention: Formula for student success* (pp. 7–34). Rowman & Littlefield.

Braxton, J., Doyle, W. R., Hartley, H. V., III, Hirschy, A. S., Jones, W. A., & McLendon, M. K. (2014). *Rethinking college student retention.* Jossey-Bass.

Braxton, J., Hirschy, A., & McClendon, S. (2004). *Understanding and reducing college student departure.* Jossey Bass.

Braxton, J., Sullivan, A. S., & Johnson, R. M. (1997). Appraising Tinto's theory of college student departure. In J. Smart (Ed.), *Higher education: Handbook of theory and research* (Vol. 12, pp. 107–164). Springer.

Cabrera, A. F., Nora, A., & Castaneda, M. B. (1993). College persistence: Structural equations modeling test of an integrated model of student retention. *Journal of Higher Education, 64*(2), 123–139. https://doi.org/10.2307/2960026

Creswell, J. W. (1994). *Research design: Qualitative and mixed methods approaches.* SAGE.

De Brey, C., Snyder, T. D., Zhang, A., & Dillow, S. A. (2021). *Digest of Education Statistics 2019* (*NCES 2021-009*). National Center for Education Statistics, Institute of Education Sciences, U.S. Department of Education. https://nces.ed.gov/pubs2021/2021009.pdf

Dewberry, C., & Jackson, D. J. (2018). An application of the theory of planned behavior to student retention. *Journal of Vocational Behavior, 107*, 100–110. https://doi.org/10.1016/j.jvb.2018.03.005

Doyle, W. R. (2011). Effect of increased academic momentum on transfer rates: An application of the generalized propensity score. *Economics of Education Review, 30*(1), 191–200. https://doi.org/10.1016/j.econedurev.2010.08.004

Eaton, S. B., & Bean, J. P. (1995). An approach/avoidance behavioral model of college student attrition. *Research in Higher Education, 36*(6), 617–645. https://doi.org/10.1007/BF02208248

Edgerton, H. A., & Toops, H. A. (1929). *Academic progress: A follow-up study of the freshmen entering the university in 1923.* Ohio State University Press.

Gekoski, N., & Schwartz, S. (1961). Student mortality and related factors. *Journal of Educational Research, 54*(5), 192–194. https://doi.org/10.1080/00220671.1961.10882710

Grace, H. A. (1957). Personality factors and college attrition. *Peabody Journal of Education, 35*(1), 36–40. https://www.jstor.org/stable/1490539

Hagedorn, L. S. (2005). How to define retention. In A. Seidman (Ed.), *College student retention formula for student success* (pp. 90–105). Praeger.

Lopez, J. D. (2018). Factors influencing American Indian and Alaska Native post-secondary persistence: AI/AN Millennium Falcon persistence model. *Research in Higher Education, 59*(6), 792–811. https://doi.org/10.1007/s11162-017-9487-6

Marcus, J. (2019, January 14). *10 years later, goal of getting more Americans through college is way behind schedule.* The Hechinger Report. https://hechingerreport.org/10-years-later-goal-of-getting-more-americans-through-college-is-way-behind-schedule/

McNeely, J. H. (1937). *College student mortality.* U.S. Government Printing Office.

Mercer, M. (1941). A study of student mortality in a home economics college. *Journal of Educational Research, 34*(7), 531–537. https://doi.org/10.1080/00220671.1941.10881027

Museus, S. D. (2014). The culturally engaging campus environments (CECE) model: A new theory of success among racially diverse college student populations. In M. B. Paulsen (Ed.), *Higher education: Handbook of theory and research* (Vol. 29, pp. 189–227). Springer.

Museus, S. D., Zhang, D., & Kim, M. J. (2016). Developing and evaluating the culturally engaging campus environments (CECE) scale: An examination of content and construct validity. *Research in Higher Education, 57*(6), 768–793. https://doi.org/10.1007/s11162-015-9405-8

Obama, B. (2009, July 14). *Investing in education: The American Graduation Initiative* [Speech audio recording]. White House Archives. https://obamawhitehouse.archives.gov/blog/2009/07/14/investing-education-american-graduation-initiative

Organisation for Economic Co-operation and Development. (2019). *Population with tertiary education.* https://data.oecd.org/eduatt/population-with-tertiary-education.htm

Panos, R. J., & Astin, A. W. (1968). Attrition among college students. *American Educational Research Journal, 5*(1), 57–72. https://doi.org/10.2307/1161701

Patterson, C. H. (1983). *Theories of counseling and psychotherapy.* Harper & Row.

Sass, D. A., Castro-Villarreal, F., Wilkerson, S., Guerra, N., & Sullivan, J. (2018). A structural model for predicting student retention. *Review of Higher Education, 42*(1), 103–135. https://doi.org/10.1353/rhe.2018.0035

Savage, L. J. (1972). *The foundations of statistics.* Wiley.

Spady, W. (1970). Dropouts from higher education: An interdisciplinary review and synthesis. *Interchange, 1*(1), 64–85. https://doi.org/10.1007/BF02214313

Spady, W. (1971). Dropouts from higher education: Toward an empirical model. *Interchange, 2*(3), 38–62. https://doi.org/10.1007/BF02282469

Summerskill, J. (1962). Dropouts from college. In N. Sanford (Ed.), *The American college: A psychological and social interpretation of the higher learning* (pp. 627–657). Wiley.

Tinto, V. (1975). Dropouts from higher education: A theoretical synthesis of the recent literature. *Review of Educational Research, 45*(1), 89–125. https://doi.org/10.3102/00346543045001089

Tinto, V. (1993). *Leaving college: Rethinking the causes and cures of student attrition* (2nd ed.). The University of Chicago Press.

Vaccaro, A., Daly-Cano, M., & Newman, B. M. (2015). A sense of belonging among college students with disabilities: An emergent theoretical model. *Journal of College Student Development, 56*(7), 670–686. http://dx.doi.org/10.1353/csd.2015.0072

Vaccaro, A., & Newman, B. M. (2016). Development of a sense of belonging for privileged and minoritized students: An emergent model. *Journal of College Student Development, 57*(8), 925–942. https://doi.org/10.1353/csd.2016.009

Wang, X. (2017). Toward a holistic theoretical model of momentum for community college student success. In M. B. Paulsen (Ed.), *Higher education: Handbook of theory and research* (Vol. 32, pp. 259–308). Springer.

3

A CRITICAL ASSESSMENT OF THEORIES OF RETENTION AND PERSISTENCE FOR BLACK STUDENTS IN PREDOMINANTLY WHITE INSTITUTIONS

Robert T. Palmer and Larry J. Walker

Historically and presently, racism has been deeply ingrained into the fabric of America. This is reflected in deplorable incidents in this country, such as slavery and the promulgation of Jim Crow laws. This is also noticeable in many of this country's institutions, such as the criminal justice system that has demonstrated little regard for Black and Brown lives (Dunham & Petersen, 2017). Historically Black colleges and universities (HBCUs) were established due to racist practices, primarily in the South, to provide a pathway for Black students to access higher education (Palmer & Gasman, 2008). Since institutions of higher education do not operate in a vacuum and represent a microcosm of society, research has contextualized how racism, which has become more covert in recent years, has impacted and shaped the experiences of Black students at predominantly White institutions (PWIs; George Mwangi et al., 2018; Harper & Hurtado, 2007; Rankin & Reason, 2005; Yosso et al., 2009).

According to many scholars, Black students have consistently described the campus climate at PWIs as racist, chilly, and alienating (Fries-Britt & Turner, 2002). Research has shown Black students experience psychological stress as a consequence of the racial microaggressions they endure on a daily basis at PWIs. For example, Black men have adopted a "prove-them-wrong syndrome" to combat the perceptions among White faculty that Black students are not as equally committed and invested in their academics as their White counterparts (Moore et al., 2003). Palmer and Walker (2020) indicated that Black Americans are subjected to a Black tax. This is not a monetary tax, but a psychological burden manifesting from the socially constructed way in which Blackness has been characterized in America by those in power. In the context of PWIs, the tax can include racial profiling of Black students by campus police and White students questioning the legitimacy of Black student enrollment. The tax has also created stressors that impact Black faculty, including forcing them to commit to extra service activities at the expense of earning tenure (Hartlep & Ball, 2019; Moody, 2012). This further contributes to the marginalization of Black students because it limits the number of Black faculty on campus to serve as role models and supporters.

Given the experiences of Black students at PWIs, some have transferred to HBCUs in search of a better institutional fit (Williams et al., 2021). Increasingly, scholars in higher education have conceptualized theories to help institutions increase the retention and persistence rates of students. However, these theories may have unintentional consequences for Black students. For this reason, this chapter discusses these theories and highlights the ways in which they may not meet the needs of Black students enrolled in PWIs. This chapter aims to direct higher education scholars and practitioners to theories and strategies that may improve Black students' college experiences and academic outcomes.

Tinto's Theory of Student Departure

One of the first theories this chapter will focus on is Tinto's theory of student departure. Tinto (1975) proposed a longitudinal model that explained the "processes of interaction between the individual and the institution that lead differing individuals to drop out from institutions of higher education" (p. 90). In this model, Tinto argued students enter college with a variety of background factors, experiences, and attributes, which influences their goal of pursuing higher education. Central to his model was the idea of academic and social integration. Specifically, borrowing from Durkheim's theory of suicide, which asserted that an individual's risk of committing suicide was based on their level of integration into the social fabric of society, Tinto posited colleges comprise both academic and social systems. He postulated that a student's integration into these domains is directly related to their commitment to the institution and, ultimately, their persistence.

Academic integration is demonstrated by a student's grade performance and intellectual development during college (Tinto, 1975). In this regard, academic integration is reflective of a student's formal interaction with the institution, which consists of attending classes, studying, and formal interaction with faculty and staff. Conversely, social integration is facilitated by "informal peer group associations, semi-formal extracurricular activities and interaction with faculty and administrative personnel within the college" (p. 107). Tinto noted successful social integration includes various levels of social communication, friendship and faculty support, and group affiliation.

Tinto (1988) further developed his theory of student departure by using Van Gennep's work on rites of passage to explain the process students must go through as they transition from their former communities and become integrated into the college environment. Specifically, with Van Gennep's work, Tinto (1988) underscored three stages including separation, transition, and incorporation. During the first stage, separation, students must physically and socially remove themselves from their former communities to integrate into the college community. Doing this creates the potential for success in college because students will be able to adopt the norms and behaviors of the college environment while rejecting prior norms. After the separation stage, students enter in the second stage in Tinto's (1988) theory, transition. Tinto characterized this stage as a period of uncertainty. He noted this stage as being "between associations of the past and hope for associations with the communities of the present" (p. 444). Tinto described the transition stage as stressful and, without support, many students may limit their time on campus, which will hinder opportunities for campus engagement and learning college norms, thus increasing the likelihood they will drop out. In the last stage of Tinto's (1988) theory of student departure, he argued students seek to become socially and academically integrated within the university by establishing contact with institutional officials.

Some scholars have criticized certain aspects of Tinto's theory as it relates to minoritized students (Guiffrida, 2006; Kuh & Love, 2000; Rendón et al., 2000; Tierney, 1992). Tierney (1992), for example, argued that Tinto's (1988) use of Van Gennep's model of transition, from which Tinto derived the notion that students must separate from their communities, is not applicable to minoritized students because the model was intended to describe the progression within a culture as opposed to the assimilation from one culture to another. Given that the cultural backgrounds of minoritized students differ substantially from the Eurocentric norms and values upon which Tinto's (1988) framework is based, Tierney argued that "Tinto has misinterpreted the anthropological notions of ritual, and in doing so he has created a theoretical construct with practical implications that hold potentially harmful consequences for racial and ethnic minorities" (p. 603).

Other scholars (e.g., Guiffrida, 2005; Hurtado, 1997; Tierney, 1999) have argued that the emphasis on students separating from their former communities to help facilitate their integration into the college environment is particularly problematic for minoritized students because their support systems lie outside of the institutional environment (Gonzalez, 2002; Guiffrida, 2004a; Rosas & Hamrick, 2002). While Tinto (2006) later acknowledged this criticism and delineated the importance of students maintaining connections with their communities, another aspect of his theory that is worthy of critique is the notion that students must academically and socially integrate within the campus community in order to establish meaningful relationships with campus constituents to increase their commitment to the institution.

While Braxton et al. (1997) have argued that Tinto's (1975) theory of student departure has achieved near paradigmatic stature in higher education, they noticed that the literature has yielded mixed results when testing Tinto's theory. To this end, Braxton et al. (2004) have proposed revisions to Tinto's (1975) theory of student departure. Similar to Braxton et al., who recommended critical revisions to Tinto's theory, as well as other scholars, who called out the applicability of Tinto's theory to minoritized students, we will examine the academic and social integration aspect of Tinto's theory.

Specifically, we seek to argue that these aspects are a misfit for Black students on the campuses of PWIs. First, regarding academic integration, to be successful in college, students must attend class, study, and use the academic resources on campus. However, academic integration is an issue for Black students attempting to foster relationships with faculty and other institutional agents at PWIs. Most of the faculty in postsecondary education are White. In fact, Palmer (2019) noted 73.2% of full-time faculty and administrators in higher education are White. Given the lack of diversity among faculty at PWIs, and how the literature has characterized the experiences of Black students with White faculty (George Mwangi et al., 2018; Harper & Hurtado, 2007; Yosso et al., 2009), it seems problematic to emphasize the importance of Black students establishing relationships with faculty or other campus agents who may not have the cultural competence to best support Black students.

Research has shown that White faculty are likely to harbor stereotypical views about Black students and to have low expectations for their academic performance (Brooms, 2017; Fries-Britt & Turner, 2002; Yosso et al., 2009). Therefore, encouraging Black students to engage with faculty who may have racial bias could potentially be harmful to the psychological development of Black college students and manifest in racial battle fatigue (Smith, 2008). According to Smith, racial battle fatigue is defined as a "physiological, psychological, and behavioral strain exacted on racially marginalized and stigmatized groups and the amount of energy they expend coping with and fighting against racism" (p. 617). Not only does racial battle fatigue impose a psychological burden among Black students and faculty, but it can also result in physical ailments, such as high blood pressure and mental health problems. In his book *Being Black, Being on Campus: Understanding and Confronting Black Male Collegiate Experiences*, Brooms (2017) contextualized the experiences, perceptions, and interactions of Black males with White faculty at PWIs. Specifically, Brooms's book is based on 40 in-depth interviews with Black male college students across two PWIs. The students in his book provided compelling narratives about their interactions and experiences with White faculty. For example, one of the participants, Terrance, expressed frustration when he discussed how White faculty denigrated his academic abilities. Specifically, he shared:

> I feel like the majority of teachers outside of Black Studies class have been White. A lot of them I've been talked down on until I had to prove to them that I could do the work. I had a couple of teachers look down on me like I was a boy, but I am a grown man. I haven't gotten any stares downs or anything like that, but if there's anything going on my focus and motivation just block those things out automatically. (p. 104)

Similarly, Deondre, another participant in Brooms's (2017) study, reflected on some of the challenges he encountered with White faculty. He explained:

> I mean, it's just kinda it is what it is. I just go to class, I don't really talk to teachers after class that often and I don't think they want to talk to me after class. I'm a guy on campus. . . . There are some professors that I have been cool with. I had this one White professor and I told him that I was interested in astronomy and he told me that I wasn't smart enough for astronomy. He told me that I would have to take higher-level math and I'm pretty good at math. Instead of you telling me about the program you're telling me that I can't do the classes. It pisses me off a little. After that, I was just like, "It's whatever; I don't really care. I'll just do me." (p. 105)

These narratives from Terrance and Deondre provide a powerful illustration of some of the racialized encounters that Black students have with White faculty. To this end, in the context of Tinto's theory of student departure, when he underscored the value of academic integration, he did not take into consideration the experiences of Black students.

In addition to academic integration, Tinto's social integration was not conceptualized with a focus on Black students at PWIs. More specifically, the problem with social integration is that it encourages Black students to become integrated into a psychologically toxic climate. In his book *Leaving College*, Tinto (1993) indicated that if students cannot become integrated into the dominant culture of the college environment, they must become socially integrated into a subculture of the college in order to help increase their commitment to the university and to help facilitate their success. Given that Black students have always been at the margin of the institutions at PWIs, they have never been able to integrate into the dominant culture of these institutions. Their social integration into PWIs has primarily been through counterpart spaces such as Black cultural centers (Patton, 2006), Black Greek letter organizations (Palmer et al., 2014), and athletics (Harper, 2018). As noted, Black students have generally described the environment of PWIs as alienating. Because of this, they are not fully able to make the most of their college experience at PWIs, unlike many of their White counterparts. For example, Fred, a participant in Brooms's (2017) study on Black men at PWIs, described the climate at the institution he attended as segregated, which engendered a sense of isolation. Specifically, he reflected:

> It's kinda segregated for the most part. For events, it is segregated. Say like an organization is having a forum for marriage or something and only people of that ethnicity is going to be there. Or say there's a party, really only people of that ethnicity that's throwing the party will be there. But, socially, people get along. So, you can say the campus is diverse but as far as mingling, it's not. (p. 96)

Similar to Fred, Sean, another participant in Brooms's (2017) study, expressed how racism contributes to the segregation of campus, preventing meaningful cross-racial interactions and dialogue. Specifically, he explained:

> It's like, it's diverse but you can tell people don't want you there. I have an elevator and I live on the 9th floor—that's all the way on the top. We're on the elevator and say there's a group of White girls talking and they just get quiet. They stop talking [when we get on] and pull out their phones and act like they're messaging. It's like they're scared and they don't want to talk to you sometimes . . . and we're on a college campus. (p. 99)

Both Fred and Sean provide powerful narratives about how the racialized climate of PWIs hinders Black students from fully participating and enjoying the college experience.

Without a doubt, Tinto's (1975) theory of student departure has made a significant contribution to the field of higher education. While his theory is widely cited, it has garnered some criticism. Nevertheless, when it comes to Black students at PWIs, the notion to academically and socially integrate into an environment that research has described as racist, toxic, and isolating is problematic. While aspects of his theory, such as social integration, seem to serve as harbingers to student success, especially for those attending residential institutions (Braxton et al., 2014; Braxton & McClendon, 2001), without considerations to improve the campus climate of PWIs, Tinto's theory is insensitive to the lived realities of the experiences of Black students.

Astin's Theory of Student Involvement

Tinto's theory of student departure is not the only theory that raises concerns about its appropriateness for Black students at PWIs. Another such theory is Astin's (1999) theory of student involvement. According to Astin, *involvement* "refers to the amount of physical and psychosocial energy that the student devotes to the academic experience" (p. 518). A student who is highly involved on campus is one who devotes significant time to preparing for class, participates in organizations, and engages with faculty and other institutional agents. A student who is not involved on campus has a schedule that is the antithesis of a student who is involved. For example, this student does not dedicate sufficient time to preparing for class, is hardly involved on campus, and has minimum interaction with faculty and other institutional agents.

Astin (1999) indicated that there are five postulates or tenets to his conceptualization of student involvement. The first postulate underscores the amount of physical and psychological energy students devote to various aspects of the college experience. The second postulate indicates that involvement in the campus experience varies by student. For example, some students may be more involved in a certain aspect of the campus experience, such as studying and preparing for class, than others at a given time. The third postulate denotes "involvement has both quantitative and qualitative features" (p. 519). More specifically, the degree of a student's involvement in their academic work can be measured quantitatively and qualitatively. For example, quantitatively, it can be measured by the number of hours a student devotes to preparing for class, whereas qualitatively, it can be measured by the quality of a student's class preparation. The fourth postulate of Astin's theory of student involvement emphasizes that "the amount of student learning and personal development associated with any educational program is directly proportional to the quality and quantity of student involvement in that program" (p. 519). The final postulate of Astin's theory indicates the effectiveness of any educational policy or practice implemented on campus can be determined by the impact on student involvement.

Research has supported the relationship between student involvement and retention for college students in general (Berger & Milem, 1999; Kuh et al., 1994; Pascarella & Terenzini, 2005), and Black students specifically (DeSousa & Kuh, 1996; Flowers, 2004; Harper & Quaye, 2007; Palmer & Young, 2009; Patton, 2006; Strayhorn, 2011). Generally, research has shown that student involvement is linked to academic success and persistence (Pascarella & Terenzini, 2005). For example, Kuh et al. (1994) explained that creating a balance in a variety of in-class and out-of-classroom activities maximizes positive outcomes among college students. They pointed out that out-of-classroom experiences contribute directly or indirectly to persistence and other "valued skills and competencies considered important outcomes for attending colleges" (p. 43). Moreover, using data from the 2008 National Survey of Student Engagement at one research university, Webber et al. (2013) found that student engagement in curricular and cocurricular activities contributed significantly to students' cumulative GPA and their perception of the overall academic experience.

Regarding research on Black students and Astin's theory of student involvement, using data from the College Student Experiences Questionnaire, in which 7,923 Black students across 192 institutions participated between 1990 and 2000, Flowers (2004) found that involvement in class and out of class facilitated student development for Black students. The results from his study showed that student involvement in academic and social development was more impactful for some student involvement experiences than it was for others. As result of being involved, Flowers found students had more library, course-learning, and personal experiences compared to other experiences. Specifically, he noted that student involvement contributed to developmental gains for Black students in academic domains, such as arts and humanities, science and technology, thinking and writing skills, and vocational preparation. Flowers explained that results from his study complemented findings from other scholars (e.g., Littleton, 2002), who found that student involvement was linked to persistence in college for a number of Black students. Given that Flowers found that student involvement among Black students seemed low to moderate for certain measures in his study, he emphasized the need for student affairs professionals to work continuously to promote the involvement of Black students on campus.

As indicated previously, research has shown that most Black students tend to be involved in Black student organizations (Guiffrida, 2004b). In fact, using Astin's theory of student involvement, Guiffrida (2004b) conducted a study on 84 Black students at one PWI to understand whether involvement in Black student organizations could be an asset or a liability. In his study, which consisted of high- and low-achieving Black students,

Guiffrida found that involvement for Black students was critical to helping students feel connected to the institutions. Nevertheless, he found that some of the low-achieving students were overinvolved in Black student organizations at the expense of their academic work. Conversely, he found that many of the high-achieving students tended to be more involved in their academic work. To this end, Guiffrida noted while the low-achieving students were "physically and psychologically invested into college life, many of them were not living up to their academic potential and some were in danger of being academically dismissed" (p. 94). He explained that this finding stood in contrast to Astin's (1999) of student involvement, which posited that the more involved students are in college activities, the more they would learn and be retained. Guiffrida acknowledged the limitation that Astin pointed out in his theory by explaining that the findings from his study shined light on a recommendation Astin observed about the need for more research to understand the possible "limits beyond which increasing involvement ceases to produce desirable results" (Astin, 1984, as cited in Astin, 1999, p. 528).

While Guiffrida (2004b) pointed out one limitation to Astin's theory, another limitation when it comes to Black students at PWIs is that Astin's encourages Black students to become involved in the hostile, racist environment of PWIs. According to Reason (2009), Tinto's notion of integration is closely aligned to Astin's involvement theory. Thus, it is not surprising that Astin's theory of student involvement does not consider the lived realities of Black students at PWIs, much like Tinto's theory of student departure. As noted with Tinto's theory, a bevy of research has firmly supported the relationship between Astin's theory of student involvement and retention, persistence, and other skills and competencies for college students in general and Black students in particular (Berger & Milem, 1999; DeSousa & Kuh, 1996; Flowers, 2004; Pascarella & Terenzini, 2005). To this end, while the impact that student involvement has on the success of college students cannot be discounted, what needs further consideration in Astin's theory is the environment that Black students are being asked to engage.

Thus far, this chapter has criticized the applicability of theories, such as Tinto's theory of student departure and Astin's theory of involvement, as it relates to their relevance for Black students attending PWIs. Criticism without a probable solution does little to help advance research and practice for Black students in higher education. For this reason, we will devote the subsequent section of this chapter to highlight theories and concepts that could be used when working with Black students on the campuses of PWIs to help facilitate their retention and persistence. These theories are Rendón's (1994) theory of validation, Schlossberg's (1989) theory of marginality and mattering, and Yosso's (2005) concept of community cultural wealth. Scholars who have used these approaches to investigate the experiences of minoritized students in higher education and research suggest that these theories and concepts are most appropriate for students of color. In delineating these theories and concepts, we are proposing that a bricolage approach be used to help PWIs be more intentional in facilitating the retention and persistence of Black students on college campuses. For example, one or more of the aforementioned frameworks can be used to positively facilitate academic and social outcomes for Black students.

Validation Theory

This notion of validation emerged from a larger project based on Astin's work on student involvement and Pascarella and Terenzini's comprehensive review of literature. The goal of this project was to understand how student learning was impacted "by student involvement in academic and nonacademic experiences in college" (Rendón, 1994, p. 34). Participants for this research study consisted of 132 racially and ethnically diverse first-year students from a constellation of institutional types, such as a community college, a liberal arts institution, a predominantly White research university, and a predominantly Black, comprehensive state university. One of the aspects that became apparent in this study was how some nontraditional students at community colleges came to college with thoughts of not being successful, but what helped to facilitate their success was an innate belief in their capacity to learn. This finding, along with other findings, such as students encountering faculty at 4-year institutions who were distant or cold, led to the conceptualization of validation.

According to Rendón (1994), "Validation is an enabling, confirming and supportive process initiated by in- and out-of-class agents that foster academic and interpersonal development" (p. 44). When students are validated, they not only feel capable of achieving but they experience a sense of self-worth. Validation also helps students to feel that all aspects they bring to college with them are accepted and valuable. Validation can occur inside as well as outside the classroom. Rendón posits the following examples of in-class academic validation:

- faculty displaying genuine care for teaching students
- faculty being personable and approachable
- faculty treating students equally
- faculty structuring the learning environment to allow students to understand their capacity to learn

- faculty working one-on-one with students who need extra help
- faculty providing meaningful feedback to students

Aside from faculty, classmates, teaching assistants, and lab instructors can serve as agents of in-class validation. Conversely, family members, classmates, friends on and off campus, significant others, and institutional agents such as resident advisors, faculty, and student affairs professionals can serve as out-of-class validating agents. According to Rendón and Muñoz (2011), "at the core of validation is authentic caring and concern" (p. 24). Specifically, Noddings (1984), as cited in Rendón and Muñoz (2011), explained that caring is a fundamental aspect of human life: "Simple actions such as calling students by name, expressing concern, and offering assistance can go a long way toward building caring, validating relationships with students" (p. 25). The conditions engendered by validation, which makes students feel valued and cared for within an institutional community, help to promote persistence (Strayhorn, 2012). Researchers have used validation to design student success initiatives to impact their persistence. For example, Ekal et al. (2011) discussed how the University of Texas at El Paso, which serves a large population of Mexican American students, has incorporated Rendón's (1994) theory of validation into several areas of their access programming in order to be more intentional in facilitating the persistence of newly admitted students. In addition to being instrumental in framing and guiding programs that help to facilitate student persistence, Rendón and Muñoz (2011) posited that validation can help to improve teaching and learning and has the propensity for creating liberatory classrooms.

Rendón's (1994) conceptualization of validation is appropriate for Black students at PWIs for several reasons. First, validation emphasizes that faculty display an ethic of care when interacting with students. In Rendón's (1994) theory of validation, she recognizes that faculty can be inequitable in their treatment of students; therefore, she posits this can lead to feelings of invalidation. To this end, she encourages faculty to treat all students equally and to create learning environments that support the capacity of student learning and success. Second, validation is about faculty and other institutional agents empowering students to believe in themselves and their innate potential to learn. Third, validation also highlights a communal approach to helping students be successful by noting that students can experience a sense of validation by those on campus and those in the students' communities who they interacted with before enrolling in college. Finally, and perhaps, most importantly, validation underscores the importance of the university working to provide an affirming and empowering experience for college students as opposed to encouraging them to engage in a college environment that could potentially be toxic for their physical and psychological health.

Schlossberg's Theory of Marginality and Mattering

In addition to validation, another theory that is suitable to Black students at PWIs is Schlossberg's (1989) theory of marginality and mattering. Schlossberg's work is premised on transitional phases in life. Specifically, Schlossberg posited that an individual transitioning into a new role in life may experience a lack of belonging, which could manifest in feelings of self-consciousness. She noted that the more dissimilar the new role is from the former, the more likely a person may experience a sense of marginality, especially if there are no role models for the new role. While Schlossberg noted that, in many cases, marginality can be transitory, in some cases, it can be permanent. She explained that is the case for a person who identities as bicultural, as they may feel committed to two worlds. According to Schlossberg mattering is distinctly different from marginalization because it makes one feel valued, important, and relevant, which is in opposition to marginality.

Mattering, which is based on the work of Morris Rosenberg, involves feelings of belonging and mattering to others. Mattering includes several tenets: (a) attention—creating positive relationships with others that promote feelings of personal worth; (b) importance—feeling valued and cared about; (c) ego extension—feeling that our success or failures matter to someone; (d) dependence—knowing that there is a reciprocal process between the positive contribution that one makes to the community and what they receive in return from the community; and (e) appreciation—feeling appreciated and valued by others (Schlossberg, 1989).

Similar to Rendón's (1994) validation theory, Schlossberg's theory of marginality and mattering is directly applicable to Black students at PWIs because it encourages the university community to create an environment where students feel important and valued. Given that this theory is rooted in phrases of transition, marginality and mattering hold particular relevance to Black students because they are often transitioning into a new culture, which is largely Eurocentric. This theory stands in contrast to Tinto's and Astin's theories that largely encourage the university to provide resources to facilitate student involvement into the campus community and for students to engage in those resources to get the most out of their college experience.

With Schlossberg's theory, the onus is on the university to create conditions that help students to feel a sense of belonging. Given how Black students experience and perceive the campus climate of PWIs, this theory is critical. When universities work proactively to create an environment where all students feel as if they matter, especially those who are at the margin of the institutions, this will manifest in a powerful academic and social experience for all students. One of the ways universities can do this is by being more intentional to improve the campus climate for Black students at PWIs.

Community Cultural Wealth

The final theory is Yosso's (2005) concept of community cultural wealth (CCW). The theory is centered within critical race theory (CRT; Delgado & Stefancic, 2001) and Bourdieu and Passeron's (1977) capital framework. The capital framework focuses on three areas including obligations, connections, and networks. According to Delgado and Stefancic (2001) CRT is "a collection of activists and scholars interested in studying and transforming the relationship among race, racism, and power" (p. 2). Research from Solórzano and Villalpando (1998) and Villalpando and Solórzano (2005) have also impacted Yosso's concept of CCW by underscoring the nurturing and empowering experiences minoritized students draw from communities of color.

Yosso's (2005) theory differs from other frameworks because it places value on students of color. It focuses on student's assets, not their weaknesses. This is critical considering our critique of Tinto's and Astin's concepts as it relates to Black students. According to Yosso (2005), "Community cultural wealth is an array of knowledge, skills, abilities and contacts possessed and utilized by Communities of Color to survive and resist macro and microforms of oppression" (p. 77). This distinction from Tinto and Astin's work is notable. As previously explained, Black students encounter an array of challenges at PWIs (Jones & Reddick, 2017). Yosso chose to center the experiences of students of color when developing the theory.

There are six essential elements of CCW. They include (a) aspirational capital—dreaming of future opportunities regardless of current challenges; (b) linguistic capital—this relates to intellectual and social skills gained through utilizing other languages; (c) familial capital—with Yosso suggesting that family bonds can apply to nontraditional members of the community while acknowledging the role family plays in the lives of students of color; (d) social capital—this relates to relationships with peers and other networks that can provide socio-emotional support; (e) navigational capital—the ability to navigate spaces which were not created for students of color; and (f) resistant capital—a tenet embracing the concept of a resistor (Yosso, 2005).

Some researchers have used CCW in various ways. For example, Kouyoumdjian et al. (2017) conducted a mixed-methods study to understand the challenges to the retention and persistence of Latinx students enrolled in a Hispanic-serving institution. Using CCW, Kouyoumdjian et al. underscored how different aspects of CCW helped the students to be successful despite some of the obstacles. Moreover, Preston and Palmer (2018) used CCW to understand the diverse forms of capital that HBCUs impart to Black students in order to help maximize their holistic growth and development.

CCW is a better option as it relates to the lived experiences of Black students. It focuses on strengths including familial bonds, navigating challenges, community, resisting, language, and the importance of being connected. Utilizing a strength-based framework would allow postsecondary institutions to understand and develop curriculums and initiatives that value their abilities. In contrast to Tinto and Astin, it is rooted in CRT, which seeks to disrupt and dismantle systems of oppression. Further, it places value on students who disproportionally encounter barriers at PWIs.

Incorporating CCW tenets would also allow PWIs to see the value of external factors in the lives of Black students. Far too often, colleges, including PWIs, allow deficit narratives to obscure how peers and family help Black students to succeed. Postsecondary institutions can learn to focus on areas including social and familial capital to support Black students. Investing in support systems could increase student retention rates and provide a return on investment. Additionally, schools could fund on-campus initiatives that mimic the nurturing that students seek from confidantes during difficult times in the classroom and residence halls. Providing more scaffolding could dramatically alter the academic and social trajectory of Black students at PWIs.

Conclusion

Racism is firmly entrenched in American society, which has contextualized the experiences of Black students at PWIs. While some scholars have proposed theories of retention and persistence to help higher education officials increase social and academic outcomes for college students in general, some of these are not applicable to Black students because they do not consider the lived realities of Black students enrolled in PWIs. Consequently, in this chapter, we provided higher education scholars and leaders with guidance to identify theories that are compatible with the experiences of Black students. As previously discussed, Tinto's theory of student departure and Astin's theory of student involvement are popular frameworks but have flaws. We argued there are other frameworks that should be considered when examining the experiences of Black students. These include Rendón's (1994) validation theory, Schlossberg's (1989) theory of marginality and mattering, and Yosso's (2005) community cultural wealth theory. Rendón's framework focuses on students feeling valued and accepted. According to Rendón (1994), this occurs inside and outside of academic settings. Schlossberg (1989) contended that transitional phases can contribute to a lack of belonging. Using this concept is a vital lens considering the cultural transition that Black students experiences at PWIs.

Lastly, Yosso's (2005) framework acts as a counterweight to Tinto's and Astin's theories. It is an asset-based framework that acknowledges the experiences of Black students. Utilizing the tenets from Yosso can help college leaders understand and provide support systems that increase retention. Focusing on concepts that value Black students, first-generation students, and individuals from underserved communities is critical. Overall, we believe this chapter provides scholars and practitioners guidance for PWIs to ensure they become inclusive environments that support Black students.

References

Astin, A. W. (1999). Student involvement: A developmental theory for higher education. *Journal of College Student Development, 40*(5), 518–529.

Berger, J. B., & Milem, J. F. (1999). The role of student involvement and perceptions of integration in a causal model of student persistence. *Research in Higher Education, 40*(6), 641–664.

Bourdieu, P., & Passeron, J. (1977). *Reproduction in education, society and culture.* SAGE.

Braxton, J. M., Doyle, W. R., Hartley, H. V., Hirschy, A. S., Jones, W. A, & McLendon, M. K. (2014). *Rethinking college student retention.* Jossey-Bass.

Braxton, J. M., Hirschy, A. S., & McClendon, S. A. (2004). Understanding and reducing college student departure (ASHE-ERIC Higher Education Report, Vol. 30, no. 3). Jossey-Bass.

Braxton, J. M., & McClendon, S. A. (2001). The fostering of social integration through institutional practice. *Journal of College Student Retention, 3*(1), 57–71.

Braxton, J. M., Sullivan, A. S., & Johnson, R. (1997). Appraising Tinto's theory of college student departure. In J. Smart (Ed.), *Higher education: Handbook of theory and research* (Vol. 12, pp. 107–164). Springer.

Brooms, D. R. (2017). *Being Black, being male on campus: Understanding and confronting Black male collegiate experience.* SUNY Press.

Delgado, R., & Stefancic, J. (2017). *Critical race theory: An introduction* (Vol. 20). NYU Press.

DeSousa, D. J., & Kuh, G. D. (1996). Does institutional racial composition make a difference in what Black students gain from college? *Journal of College Student Development, 37*(3), 257–267.

Dunham, R., & Petersen, N. (2017). Making Black Lives Matter: Evidence-based policies for reducing police bias in the use of deadly force. *Criminology & Public Policy, 16*(1) 341–348. https://doi.org/10.1111/1745-9133.12284

Ekal, E. D., Rollins Hurley, S., & Padilla, R. (2011). Validation theory and student success: The UTEP way. *Enrollment Management Journal: Student Access, Finance, and Success in Higher Education, 5*(2), 138–147.

Flowers, L. A. (2004). Examining the effects of student involvement on African American college student development. *Journal of College Student Development, 45*, 633–654.

Fries-Britt, S. L., & Turner, B. (2002). Uneven stories: Successful Black collegians at a Black and a White campus. *Review of Higher Education, 25*, 315–330.

George Mwangi, C. A., Thelamour, B., Ezeofor, I., & Carpenter. A. (2018). "Black elephant in the room": Black students contextualizing campus racial climate within US racial climate. *Journal of College Student Development, 59*(4), 456–474.

Gonzalez, K. P. (2002). Campus culture and the experiences of Chicano students in a predominantly White university. *Urban Education, 37*(2), 193–218.

Guiffrida, D. A. (2004a). Friends from home: Asset or liability to African Americans students attending a predominantly White institution. *NASPA Journal, 24*(3), 693–708.

Guiffrida, D. A. (2004b). How student involvement in African American organization supports and hinders academic achievement. *NACADA Journal, 24*(1–2), 88–98.

Guiffrida, D. A. (2005). To break away or strengthen ties to home: A complex question for African American students attending a predominantly White institution. *Equity and Excellence in Education, 38*(1), 49–60.

Guiffrida, D. A. (2006). Toward a cultural advancement of Tinto's theory. *Review of Higher Education, 29*(4), 451–472.

Harper, S. R. (2018). *Black male student-athletes and racial inequities in NCAA Division I college sports.* University of Southern California, Race and Equity Center.

Harper, S. R., & Hurtado, S. (2007). Nine themes in campus racial climates and implications for institutional transformation. In S. R. Harper & L. D. Patton (Eds.), *Responding to the Realities of Race on Campus* (New Directions for Student Services, no. 120, pp. 7–24). Jossey-Bass.

Harper, S. R., & Quaye, S. J. (2007). Student organizations as venues for Black identity expression and development among African American male student leaders. *Journal of College Student Development, 48*(2), 127–144.

Hartlep, N. D., & Ball, D. (2019). *Racial battle fatigue in faculty: Perspectives and lessons from higher education.* Routledge.

Hurtado, A. (1997). Understanding multiple group identities: Inserting women into cultural transformations. *Journal of Social Issues, 53*(2), 299–328.

Jones, V. A., & Reddick, R. J. (2017). The heterogeneity of resistance: How Black students utilize engagement and activism to challenge PWI inequalities. *The Journal of Negro Education*, *86*(3), 204–219.

Kouyoumdjian, C., Guzmán, B. L., Garcia, N. M., & Talavera-Bustillos, V. (2017). A community cultural wealth examination of sources of support and challenges among Latino first- and second-generation college students at a Hispanic serving institution. *Journal of Hispanics in Higher Education*, *16*(1), 61–76.

Kuh, G. D., Douglas K. B., Lund J. P., & Ramin-Gyurnek, J. (1994). *Student learning outside the classroom: Transcending artificial boundaries*. The George Washington University, Graduate School of Education and Human Development.

Kuh, G. D., & Love, P. G. (2000). A cultural perspective on student departure. In J. M. Braxton (Ed.), *Reworking the student departure puzzle* (pp. 196–212). Vanderbilt University Press.

Littleton, R. A. (2002). Campus involvement among African American students at small, predominately white colleges. *College Student Affairs Journal*, *21*(2), 53–67.

Moody, J. (2012). *Faculty diversity: Removing the barriers* (2nd ed.). Routledge.

Moore, J. L., III, Madison-Colmore, O., & Smith, D. (2003). The prove-them-wrong syndrome: Voices from unheard African American males in engineering disciplines. *Journal of Men's Studies*, *12*(1), 61–73.

Palmer, R. T. (2019, October). Are you serious about diversifying your faculty and staff? *Inside Higher Ed*. https://www.insidehighered.com/views/2019/10/21/recommendations-institutions-diversifying-their-faculty-and-staff-opinion

Palmer, R. T., & Gasman, M. (2008). "It takes a village to raise a child": The role of social capital in promoting academic success for African American men at a Black college. *Journal of College Student Development*, *49*(1), 52–70.

Palmer, R. T., & Walker, L. J. (2020, July). *Proposing a concept of the Black tax to understand the experiences of Blacks in America*. Diverse Issues in Higher Education. https://diverseeducation.com/article/182837/

Palmer, R. T., Wood, J. L., Dancy, T. E., & Strayhorn, T. (2014). *Black male collegians: Increasing access, retention, and persistence in higher education* (ASHE Higher Education Report, Vol. 40, No. 3). *Jossey-Bass*.

Palmer, R. T., & Young, E. M. (2009). Determined to succeed: Salient factors that foster academic success for academically unprepared Black males at a Black college. *Journal of College Student Retention*, *10*(4), 465–482.

Pascarella, E. T., & Terenzini, P. T. (2005). *How college affects students: A third decade of research* (Vol. 2). Jossey-Bass.

Patton, L. D. (2006). The voice of reason: A qualitative examination of Black student perceptions of Black culture centers. *Journal of College Student Development*, *47*(6), 628–646.

Preston, D. C., & Palmer, R. T. (2018). When relevance is no longer the question. *Journal of Black Studies*, *48*(9), 782–800.

Rankin, S. R., & Reason, R. D. (2005). Differing perceptions: How students of color and White students perceive campus climate for underrepresented groups. *Journal of College Student Development*, *46*(1), 43–61.

Reason, R. (2009). An examination of persistence research through the lens of a comprehensive conceptual framework. *Journal of College Student Development*, *50*(6), 659–682.

Rendón, L. I. (1994). Validating culturally diverse students: Toward a new model of learning and student development. *Innovative Higher Education*, *19*(1), 33–50.

Rendón, L. I., Jalomo, R. E., & Nora, A. (2000). Theoretical considerations in the study of minority student retention in higher education. In J. M. Braxton (Ed.), *Reworking the student departure puzzle* (pp. 127–156). Vanderbilt University Press.

Rendón, L. I., & Munoz, S. M. (2011). Revisiting validation theory: Theoretical foundations, application, and extensions. *Enrollment Management Journal: Student Access, Finance, and Success in Higher Education*, *5*(2), 12–33.

Rosas, M., & Hamrick, F. A. (2002). Postsecondary enrollment and academic decision making: Family influences on women college students of Mexican descent. *Equity and Excellence in Education*, *35*(1), 59–69.

Schlossberg, N. K. (1989). Marginality and mattering: Key issues in building community. In D. C. Roberts (Ed.), *Designing Campus Activities to Foster a Sense of Community* (New Directions for Student Services, no. 48, pp. 1–15). Jossey-Bass.

Smith, W. A. (2008). Higher education: Racial battle fatigue. In R. T. Schaefer (Ed.), *Encyclopedia of race, ethnicity, and society* (pp. 615–618). SAGE.

Solórzano, D., & Villalpando, O. (1998). Critical race theory, marginality, and the experience of minority students in higher education. In C. Torres & T. Mitchell (Eds.), *Emerging issues in the sociology of education: comparative perspectives* (pp. 211–224). SUNY Press.

Strayhorn, T. L. (2011). Singing in a foreign land: An exploratory study of gospel choir participation among African American undergraduates at a predominantly White institution. *Journal of College Student Development*, *52*(2), 137–153. https://doi.org/10.1353/csd.2011.0030

Strayhorn, T. L. (2012). *College students' sense of belonging: A key guide to educational success for all students*. Routledge.

Tierney, W. G. (1992). An anthropological analysis of student participation in college. *Journal of Higher Education*, *63*(6), 603–618.

Tierney, W. G. (1999). Models of minority college-going and retention: Cultural integrity versus cultural suicide. *Journal of Negro Education*, *68*(1), 80–91.

Tinto, V. (1975). Dropout from higher education: A theoretical synthesis of recent research. *Review of Educational Research*, *45*, 89–125.

Tinto, V. (1988). Stages of student departure: Reflections on the longitudinal character of student leaving. *Journal of Higher Education*, *59*(4), 438–455.

Tinto, V. (1993). *Leaving college: Rethinking the causes and curses of student attrition* (2nd ed.). The University of Chicago Press.

Tinto, V. (2006). Research and practice of student retention: What next? *Journal of College Student Retention: Research, Theory, & Practice*, *8*(1), 1–19.

Villalpando, O., & Solórzano, D. (2005). The role of culture in college preparation programs: A review of the literature. In W. Tierney, Z. Corwin, & J. Kolyar (Eds.), *Preparing for college: Nine elements of effective outreach* (pp. 13–28). SUNY Press.

Webber, K. L., Krylow, R. B., & Zhang, Q. (2013). Does involvement really matter? Indicators of college student success and satisfaction. *Journal of College Student Development, 54*(6), 591–611. https://doi.org/10.1353/csd.2013.0090

Williams, J. L., Palmer, R. T., & Jones, B. (2021, August 19). "Where I can breathe": Examining the impact of the current racial climate on Black students' choice to attend historically Black colleges and universities. *Journal of Black Studies.* Advance online publication.

Yosso, T. J. (2005). Whose culture has capital? A critical race theory discussion of community cultural wealth. *Race Ethnicity and Education, 8*(1), 69–91.

Yosso, T. J., Smith, W. A., Ceja, M., & Solórzano, D. G. (2009). Critical race theory, racial microaggressions, and campus racial climate for Latina/o undergraduates. *Harvard Educational Review, 79,* 659–690.

4

TOWARD A REVISION OF TWO EMPIRICALLY SUPPORTED THEORIES OF COLLEGE STUDENT PERSISTENCE

Robert D. Reason and John M. Braxton

Two theories of college student persistence initially presented in 2004 by Braxton et al. and then empirically tested by Braxton et al. in 2014 represented perhaps the first substantive step forward in theory development since Tinto presented his original models (Tinto, 1975, 1993). These revisions of Tinto's theory for students in residential colleges and universities and for students in in commuter colleges and universities encompass economic, organizational, psychological, and sociological perspectives (Braxton et al., 2004, 2014). Moreover, empirical research exploring both theories support continued use of them in future research (Braxton et al., 2014). These two theories wielded a substantial impact on the literature of college student retention, with over 2,000 citations to the combination of Braxton et al. (2004) and Braxton et al. (2014) recorded by Google Scholar in August 2021.

These two factors, coupled with an elapsed time of over 15 years since the publication of Braxton et al. (2004) and over 7 years since the publication of Braxton et al. (2014), strongly indicate a need for review and revision of these two theories. Moreover, good theories consider current extant research findings in their formulations (Chafetz, 1978). Consequently, revisions to both theories that use research findings on college student persistence help assure the continued viability of these two theories.

Revisions to the theory of student persistence in residential colleges and universities and the theory of student persistence in commuter colleges and universities constitute the primary purpose of this chapter. We array this chapter into four sections. The first section describes the formulations of the two theories. The second section consists of a summary of research findings pertinent to the relationship between student persistence and students' pre-college characteristics and experiences, the organizational context, students' peer environments, and students' individual experiences. Revisions to both theories based on the research findings summarized in the second section provide the focus of the third section. The last section of this chapter offers recommendations for theory and research.

Description of the Two Theories

Braxton et al. (2014) identified the role of social communities and the role of the external environment, two differentiating dimensions between residential and commuter colleges and universities. The differing influence these two dimensions have on the persistence of students provides a cogent rationale for the need for separate theories to account for student persistence in these two types of institutions of higher education.

Compared to residential colleges and universities, commuter institutions often lack well-defined and structured social communities for students to affiliate with and within which to establish membership (Braxton et al., 2004). Moreover, the external environments in commuter colleges and universities play a defining role in the college student experience that substantially differs from the role of the external environment for students at residential institutions (Braxton & Hirschy, 2005). To elaborate, commuter institutions enroll a wide variety of students such as traditional-age students who live at home with their parents, older students, students with family obligations, working students, part-time students, and full-time students (Bean & Metzner, 1985; Stewart & Rue, 1983). In addition, many adult students attending a commuter college or university have other day-to-day commitments and obligations, such as family and work responsibilities (Tinto, 1993). These obligations shape the daily activities of commuter students (Webb, 1990) as well as their collegiate experiences.

Despite these distinctions, Braxton et al.'s (2004) two theories share some of the same concepts. They both situate student persistence as a longitudinal process. In their construction they accounted for empirical research findings on college student persistence (Braxton et al., 2004, 2014). In this section, we first describe the formulations of the theory of student persistence in residential colleges and universities because it includes concepts that reflect the existence of well-defined and structured social communities in residential institutions. In doing so, the stark contrasts between these two theories become more evident. Social integration plays a predominant role in residential colleges and universities, whereas student perceptions of their academic and intellectual development play a more central role in commuter colleges and universities.

The Theory of Student Persistence in Residential Colleges and Universities

This theory posits gender, race/ethnicity, parental education, family socioeconomic status, academic ability, and average grades in high school as student entry characteristics that influence initial commitments to the institution. Initial commitments, in turn, influence the students' degree of social integration. Social integration signifies the students' perception of their degree of social affiliation with others and their degree of congruence with the attitudes, beliefs, norms, and values of the social communities of a college or university (Tinto, 1975). Increases in social integration lead to greater degrees of subsequent levels of commitment to an institution (Tinto, 1975). The greater the students' degree of subsequent institutional commitment, the more likely students persist in a residential college (Braxton et al., 2004, 2014; Tinto, 1975).

Social integration constitutes a key concept in this theory given that six antecedents shape students' degree of social integration. These six antecedents include ability to pay, commitment of the institution to student welfare, institutional integrity, communal potential, proactive social adjustment, and psychosocial engagement (Braxton et al., 2014).

Ability to Pay
Students who have an ability to pay for college tend to experience fewer barriers to their participation in the social communities of their college or university because they have fewer financial concerns about paying for college (Cabrera et al., 1990).

Commitment of the Institution to Student Welfare
Three dimensions that speak to the commitment of the institution to the welfare of its students define this antecedent to social integration. An abiding concern for the growth and development of its students expressed by a given college or university constitutes the first, and primary, dimension. The second dimension takes the form of the high value the institution places on

its students. The treatment of each student with respect as an individual as well as equitable treatment of students is the third dimension (Braxton et al., 2004, 2014; Braxton & Hirschy, 2005).

Institutional Integrity

This antecedent of social integration pertains to students' perceptions of the congruency between the espoused mission and goals of a college or university and the actions of its administrators, faculty, and staff (Braxton et al., 2004, 2014; Braxton & Hirschy, 2005).

Communal Potential

This antecedent of social integration involves the extent to which students perceive that a subgroup of students exists within the various communities of their college or university that holds values, beliefs, and goals similar to their own (Braxton et al., 2004, 2014; Braxton & Hirschy, 2005).

Proactive Social Adjustment

Proactive social adjustment entails the recognition by first-year students that they need to adjust to the social challenges of their interactions with student peers. Students may view such interactions as stressful (Braxton et al., 2014). Students who cope positively with such stress through positive reinterpretation and growth demonstrate proactive social adjustment (Carver et al., 1989).

Psychosocial Engagement

The amount of psychological energy students invest in their social interactions with peers and in their participation in extracurricular activities (Braxton et al., 2004, 2014) defines this antecedent of social integration. Peer social interactions and participation in extracurricular activities require investment of psychological energy by students.

The Theory of Student Persistence in Commuter Colleges and Universities

Braxton et al (2014) regarded this theory as applicable to both 4- and 2-year commuter colleges and universities. In the case of 2-year colleges, this theory applies to students enrolled in degree programs (Braxton et al., 2004). This theory consists of six major dimensions that seek to account for the persistence of students in commuter colleges and universities: entry characteristics, the external environment, the campus environment, student academic and intellectual development, subsequent institutional commitment, and student persistence in the college or university.

Student Entry Characteristics

Student entry characteristics such as the record of high school academic achievement, gender, and race or ethnicity play an important part in the persistence decisions of students enrolled in commuter colleges and universities (Braxton et al., 2014). Other entry characteristics, including students' motivation to attend college, parental educational level, and the need for social affiliation, directly influence student persistence in a commuter college or university (Braxton et al., 2014). These various student entry characteristics also affect the initial commitment to the institution held by the student.

Student entry characteristics such as the need for control, sense of self-efficacy, empathy, and anticipatory socialization were initially posited in both theories. However, the researchers elected not to include them in the theory of student persistence in commuter colleges and universities because of the difficulties in their measurement. In particular, their measurement requires the use of specifically designed instruments that are not readily available for use by other researchers.

The External Environment

Support from significant others and finances comprise two salient aspects of the external environment of commuter colleges and universities. To elaborate, commuter students frequently have obligations distinct from attending college, including work and family (Tinto, 1993). Conflicts between the commitments of both work and attending college may negatively affect the families of such commuter students (Braxton et al., 2014). As a result, support and encouragement to attend college from significant others becomes important to their continued attendance. In turn, support for attending college from students' significant others positively influences their persistence decisions (Cabrera et al., 1999; Okun et al., 1996).

Financial aid reduces the actual price that students must pay to attend college, especially financial aid in the form of grants that do not need to be repaid. As a consequence, financial aid lessens the negative effects of college attendance on families. Thus, the lower the costs of college attendance incurred by students, the greater their likelihood of persisting in college (St. John & Starkey, 1995).

The Campus Environment

Organizational characteristics such as the commitment of the institution to student welfare and institutional integrity constitute important aspects of the campus environment, functioning as antecedents to students' perceptions of their academic and intellectual development (Braxton et al., 2004, 2014).

We previously defined these two organizational characteristics. These two organizational characteristics also wield a positive influence on the level of students' commitment to their college or university formed during their attendance (subsequent institutional commitment) at the institution (Braxton et al., 2004, 2014).

Academic and Intellectual Development

Students' perceptions of their academic and intellectual development also act as precursors to subsequent institutional commitment. The greater the degree of academic and intellectual development perceived by students, the greater their degree of subsequent commitment to their commuter college or university (Braxton et al., 2004, 2014).

Subsequent Institutional Commitment

Greater levels of subsequent institutional commitment develop in students who perceive that their college or university exhibits institutional integrity as well as a commitment to the welfare of its students (Braxton et al., 2004, 2014).

Student Persistence

The greater the students' degree of subsequent commitment to their college or university, the greater the students' likelihood of persistence in a commuter college or university (Braxton et al., 2004, 2014; Tinto, 1975).

Summary of Recent Persistence Research

We move now to a review of existing research taking Reason's (2009) review of empirical research on persistence as a starting point and using Terenzini and Reason's (2005) comprehensive model of influences on student learning and persistence as a framework to organize findings. The comprehensive framework incorporated variables related to students' precollege characteristics and experiences, the organizational context, students' peer environments, and students' individual experiences as influences on student outcomes, including persistence. In this section, we revisit Reason's (2009) findings incorporating research published subsequently to provide an up-to-date comprehensive understanding of influences on student persistence in college. We then use these findings to begin a revision process of Braxton et al.'s college persistence theories presented in the previous section.

Precollege Characteristics and Experiences

In his initial review, Reason (2009) considered two primary groups of precollege characteristics and experiences: sociodemographic traits and academic preparation and performance.

Sociodemographic Factors

Gender, race, ethnicity, and socioeconomic status (SES) are common sociodemographic traits included in persistence research. Even though findings of differences in persistence differences based on these sociodemographic traits can be difficult to interpret and "almost useless in practice" (Reason, 2009, p. 663), Reason concluded that including sociodemographic characteristics in research studies remained "important, however, because between-group difference in persistence rates remain" (p. 663). Recent research reinforces this conclusion.

In their review of recent research on demographic characteristics in chapter 6 of this volume, Means and Kniess find that gender, race and ethnicity, and SES continue to be common variables in persistence research. They also conclude that findings related to these variables are difficult to interpret and their statistical significance varies based on other variables, particularly variables related to experiences, included in the studies.

Gender/sex. Research from the National Student Clearinghouse (2020) indicates that, in general, women persist to graduation at higher rates than men, although understanding student persistence based on gender binary is problematic. Both Renn and Reason (2021) and Mayhew et al. (2016) suggested, after extensive reviews of literature, that an understanding of interactions between gender identity and other characteristics or experiences is necessary to fully understand the effects on persistence. Further, the study of the experiences of gender nonbinary students is almost nonexistent in our empirical understanding. To fully understand the effects of gender on persistence, researchers must include nongender-binary students in their research studies, and theorists must include these students' experiences in their theories.

Race. The general understanding of persistence differences by race and ethnicity is that Asian American/Pacific Islander (AAPI) students and White students persist at greater rates than do other students of color (National Student Clearinghouse, 2020; Renn & Reason, 2021; see also chapter 6). Black, Latinx, and Native American students persist at lower rates. Although true, these simple findings do not convey the nuances associated with differential persistence rates by race and ethnicity. In chapter 6,

Means and Kniess, for example, report that although AAPI students have the highest persistence rates of any racial or ethnic group, differences in persistence rate exist between the multiple groups that fall within the larger AAPI category.

In highly controlled studies, particularly those that include several pre-college experiences related to education, poverty, and family, race drops out as a statistically significant predictor of retention (Reason, 2009), indicating that these experiences rather than race may be more influential (see chapter 6). Noncollege life events both prior to college and during college affect student persistence differently for different racial and ethnic groups (Cox et al., 2016). Black students in the Cox et al. study were more likely than White students to experience financial struggles and major life changes that interfered with persistence. Finally, welcoming campus racial climates and a perceived sense of belonging may also improve persistence rates among students of color (see chapter 6).

Socioeconomic status. A student's SES may mediate many of the direct relationships between other demographic variables and persistence in college (Mayhew et al., 2016; Reason, 2009; see also chapter 6). Indicators of lower SES, such as Pell Grant eligibility and first-generation student status, remain predictors of lower persistence rates in many retention studies (Mayhew et al., 2016), although the effects of SES on students' persistence seem to differ by institutional type. In chapter 6, Means and Kniess cite studies based at small, private liberal arts colleges and at community colleges in which no statistically significant relationships existed between socioeconomic back-grounds and college student persistence.

Academic Experiences and Preparation
Given the obvious relationship between academic success, measured often by grades, and persistence in college, it makes sense that academic prepara-tion and experiences in high school are also related to college persistence. According to Allensworth and Clark (2020), the combination of high school grades, curriculum, and admissions test scores is the strongest predictor of persistence early in a college student's career. Precollege academic experiences and preparation are highly correlated with first-year college grades, which are the strongest predictor of persistence to graduation in college (Pascarella & Terenzini, 2005).

Organizational Factors
With few exceptions, traditional measures of institutions do not predict persistence in well-controlled studies (Reason, 2009). Institutional size,

source of support (public/private), and institutional mission (liberal arts/ research) do not normally statistically significantly predict student persistence when other factors are accounted for in a study. When organization variables reflect or influence students' experiences, however, they often become significant predictors of persistence. Attending historically Black colleges and universities (HBCUs) positively influences the likelihood of persistence to graduation for African American men, for example (Wilson, 2007).

In chapter 7, de los Ríos and Oseguera suggest that when institutional type predicts persistence, those effects are likely indirect through other characteristics like campus climate. This assertion reflects an understanding of decades worth of research reported first by Pascarella and Terenzini (1991, 2005) and then by Mayhew et al. (2016). In chapter 6, Means and Kniess explore the effects of a perceived lack of community and lack of a sense of belonging for traditionally underrepresented and underserved student groups at predominantly White institutions (PWIs) as a mediator of persistence.

Similarly, institutional policies and practices influence how students perceive the campus environment and are ultimately related to student persistence (Reason, 2009; see also chapter 7). Rigid adherence to policies and practices that reflect a bureaucratic organizational style (Berger, 2000, 2001; see also chapter 7), for example, can serve as an obstacle to persistence, whereas policies and practices that encourage student engagement in institutional decision-making or improve students' socialization to the institution often positively influence persistence.

The relationship between organizational characteristics (e.g., size, source of support, and mission) and the organizational style of policy implementation is not direct, although certainly the size and complexity of a large research-oriented institution makes rigid bureaucracy more likely. Similarly, the smaller size and mission of a small, private liberal arts college may allow for greater student opportunities for engagement with institutional decision-making, which is related to higher persistence rates. Finally, clear policies and practices, which are indicative of bureaucratic systems, have been related to higher persistence of students at community colleges (Scott-Clayton, 2011). In chapter 7, de los Ríos and Oseguera suggest that for students who may have limited knowledge of how to navigate a bureaucratic system of higher education well-defined and clearly articulated policies and practices might be beneficial to success.

Student Peer Environments

According to Terenzini and Reason (2005) and Reason (2009) the "peer environment is a 'sense of place' that conveys to students what others value and expect behaviorally, in the social and academic world" (Reason, 2009, p. 670). According to some authors, the influence of peer environments is subtle, gradual, and invisible (Astin, 1993; Astin & Panos, 1969), whereas for other authors the influence of peer environments is primary (Renn & Arnold, 2003).

Racial Climate

Compositional diversity on a college campus matters to student persistence. In chapter 8, Culver and Bowman cite findings from Bowman and Denson (2021) when they conclude that "graduation rates among Black, Latinx, and White students were nearly identical when students attended an institution where same-race peers comprised at least half of the undergraduate population" (p. 156). It is widely understood that the positive effects of compositional diversity are mediated through the sense of belonging and support students feel when around students who share similar racial and ethnic identities (Mayhew et al., 2016; Renn & Reason, 2021). A positive perception of the campus racial climate leads to greater institutional commitment among students of color, which, in turn, results in a greater likelihood of persistence to graduation (Museus et al., 2008).

Academic Climate

Reason (2009) suggested that although research was just beginning to emerge related to the effects of campus academic climate on students' persistence, the existing evidence at the time suggested that campus climates that supported academic engagement and standards were likely indirectly related to student persistence. Mayhew et al. (2016) reinforced the importance of academic engagement when interpreting the positive relationship between traditional measures of institutional quality and persistence rates. Hallett et al. (2019) reported the positive effects on low-income students of a comprehensive intervention intended to increase academic expectations and support. Students reported a perception within the program of high academic expectations and responded with a desire to meet those expectations.

Individual Experiences

Terenzini and Reason (2005), based on previous work by Pascarella et al. (1996), sorted individual student experiences into three categories: classroom experiences, out-of-class experiences, and curricular experiences. Reason (2009) used these three categories to organize his presentation of research findings, ultimately concluding that engagement in these three overlapping areas of student life generally and positively affect students' likelihood of persistence in college. Although these categories are instructive, for the purposes of this chapter thinking about engagement in students' experiences more broadly might be just as effective. Therefore, this section explores overall findings related to students' experiences related to academic areas of campus life and out-of-classroom areas of student life.

Academic Experiences

It makes intuitive sense to most higher education researchers that academic experiences, and the level of achievement in academic areas of a student's life, are predictors of the likelihood of persistence through college. If students do well in courses and receive positive feedback on their achievement from faculty members, they are more likely to persist. Students who do not do well academically are less likely to persist. Research bears out this intuition (Mayhew et al., 2016; Renn & Reason, 2021).

According to Culver and Bowman (see chapter 8) academic achievement in college is both directly and indirectly related to persistence. Directly, of course, most institutions of higher education require students to maintain minimum GPAs to maintain eligibility for enrollment. If a student falls below the minimum GPA, they enter a process that could ultimately lead to dismissal from the institution. Similarly, many institutions require students to maintain a trajectory toward graduation, often understood as a minimum number of credits earned over the course of time. These are both direct influences of academic achievement on a student's persistence in college.

Formal faculty feedback on assignments, informal feedback on academic performance, and grades allow students to assess their academic fit at an institution (see chapter 8). These relationships belie the role faculty and other academic staff at institutions of higher education have in socializing students into the academic culture (Terenzini & Reason, 2005; Weidman, 1989; see also chapter 8). Mayhew et al. (2016) concluded that "students view their grades as a source of feedback about their learning and 'ability,' so may choose to switch majors, transfer, or drop out if they come to believe that they are not well-suited for their intended degree" (p. 416).

Institutions of higher education have several forms of academic intervention that have been shown to mediate the negative direct and indirect effects of low academic engagement. These interventions are often focused early in a college student's career in order to build a foundation for success (Renn & Reason, 2021), although recent research on multiyear comprehensive student support programs suggests efficacy of these interventions increases with the length of time students are engaged with them (Hallett et al., 2019). In chapter 8, Culver and Bowman highlight the importance of these comprehensive transition programs for students from traditionally underserved and underrepresented populations, especially as these programs facilitate the interactions between these students and faculty and staff members at an institution.

Out-of-Classroom Engagement

The positive effects of out-of-classroom engagement on student persistence have been well studied for several decades. Living on campus, for example, has been linked to higher persistence rates (Mayhew et al., 2016; see also chapter 8). Living on campus and engaging in educationally purposeful campus activities outside of the classroom positively influence student persistence through increases in opportunities to interact with supportive faculty and staff members, greater knowledge of and access to campus resources, and a stronger sense of belonging (Mayhew et al., 2016; Reason, 2009). Obviously, not every college or university offers students the option of on-campus living (Braxton et al., 2004).

Revisions of the Two Theories

In this section of this chapter, we delineate revisions to the theory of student persistence in residential colleges and universities and to the theory of student persistence in commuter colleges and universities previously described in this chapter based on the summary of recent persistence research provided in the previous section. We make two types of revisions to these two theories. One type entails additions to an extant component or concept of the theory whereas the addition of a new component or concept to the theory constitutes the other type of revision.

Revisions to Extant Components and Concepts of Both Theories

Student entry characteristics stand as one existing component of both theories. These characteristics include gender, race/ethnicity, parental education, family SES, academic ability, and average grades in high school. We posit additions to gender, race/ethnicity, family SES, academic ability, and average grades in high school. The summary of recent persistence research pertinent to the category of precollege characteristics and experience supplies the basis for these additions. First, and importantly, we highlight the need to explicitly expand the original operationalization of gender, race/ethnicity, and family SES based on contemporary understanding of these constructs and recent literature. A contemporary understanding of gender must include nonbinary students. Similarly, an understanding of race and ethnicity must acknowledge the differential experiences of AAPI, Black, Latinx, Native American, and White students, as well as students who identify as multiracial. We highlight

Pell Grant eligibility as a factor of family SES. Recent research also indicates we must add either the student's ACT or SAT scores, high school experiences, and the quality of students' high school curricula to the original list of entry characteristics.

Commitment of the institution to student welfare and institutional integrity stand as two concepts common to both theories for which we recommend a nominal change. This change takes the form of renaming them as characteristics of institutional culture. The rationale for this nominal change emanates from the conclusion advanced by Braxton et al. (2014) that organizational culture plays an indirect role in student persistence. This conclusion suggests a need for consistency in the naming of these concepts across the two theories.

Revisions as New Concepts to Both Theories

We advance three new concepts as revisions to both the theory of student persistence in residential colleges and universities and the theory of student persistence in commuter colleges and universities. We present these three new concepts and the source of their derivation from the review of recent persistence research presented in this chapter.

Based on the review of recent persistence research centered on organizational factors, we posit a new concept titled "institutional policies and practices" as an antecedent to commitment of the institution to student welfare and institutional integrity in both theories. The research reviewed pertinent to organizational factors points to organizational style of policy implementation as a relevant institutional practice. In chapter 7, de los Ríos and Oseguera find that when policies and practices are implemented in a manner that is overly bureaucratic or overly political, students' persistence is likely to suffer. But when policies are implemented in a manner that is collaborative and includes students as part of the decision-making process, students are likely to feel valued and included, which should result in greater likelihood of persistence. So, as the style of policy implementation increases students' sense that the institution cares about their welfare, students' persistence should increase.

The concepts of compositional diversity and campus racial climate spring from the peer environment category of the review of recent persistence research. Together these two concepts comprise the new broader concept of "institutional racial dynamics." We place institutional racial dynamics as an antecedent of both commitment of the institution to student welfare and institutional integrity in both theories. Braxton et al. (2014) found that students in residential colleges and universities who perceive racial prejudice and discrimination on their campus also perceive lower commitments of the institution to student welfare and institutional integrity. Accordingly, we posit institutional racial dynamics as an antecedent of these two characteristics of institutional culture. By extension, we posit the same pattern of influence for the theory of student persistence in commuter colleges and universities.

"Institutional expectations for high academic achievement" constitutes the third new concept. We derive this concept from two different sources. From peer environments and the subcategory of academic climate, we delineate high expectations for academic achievement as one aspect of this concept. The other concept takes the form of two types of faculty feedback on student academic achievement: feedback on assignments and informal feedback on academic performance. We derived these two types of faculty feedback from the subcategory of academic expectations and support of the category of individual experiences. We place institutional expectations for high academic achievement and its specific aspects of high expectations for academic achievement and faculty feedback on student academic performance as antecedents of commitment of the institution to student welfare in both theories. Research reported by Braxton et al. (2014) provides the justification for this location in residential colleges and universities and commuter colleges and universities. Specifically, they found a positive association between student reports of good teaching by faculty and commitment of the institution to student welfare in residential institutions. In commuter colleges and universities also, a positive relationship exists between a perception that faculty exhibit an interest in students and commitment of the institution to student welfare (Braxton et al., 2014).

In the theory of student persistence in commuter colleges and universities we also position institutional expectations for academic achievement as antecedent to academic and intellectual development, stemming from the two causes noted previously. Research reported by Braxton et al. (2014) provides the rationale for this placement as a positive relationship exists between students who perceive that faculty have an interest in students and academic and intellectual development.

We graphically depict these revisions in Figures 4.1 and 4.2. Figure 4.1 displays the theory of student persistence in residential colleges and universities with the revisions we made, and Figure 4.2 exhibits the revised theory of student persistence in commuter colleges and universities. We henceforth refer to these theories as the revised theory of student persistence in residential colleges and universities and the revised theory of student persistence in commuter colleges and universities.

Figure 4.1. Revised theory of student persistence at a residential college or university.

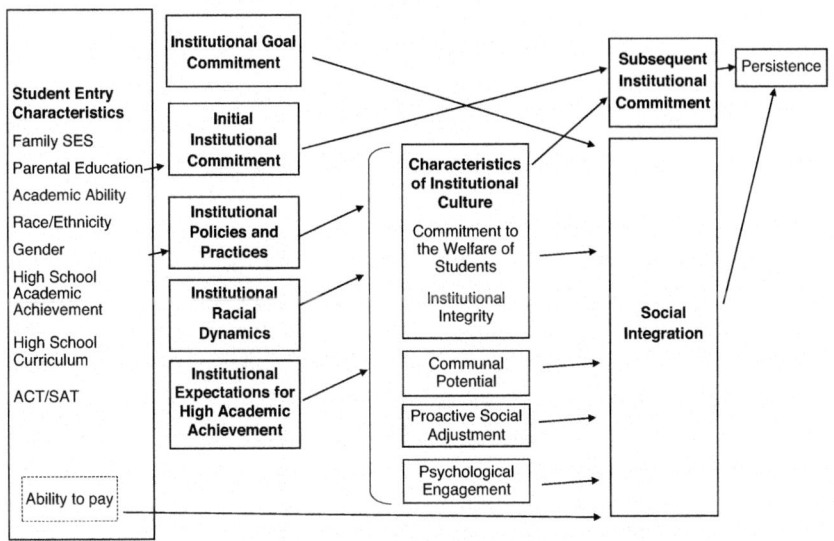

Figure 4.2. Revised theory of student persistence at a commuter college or university.

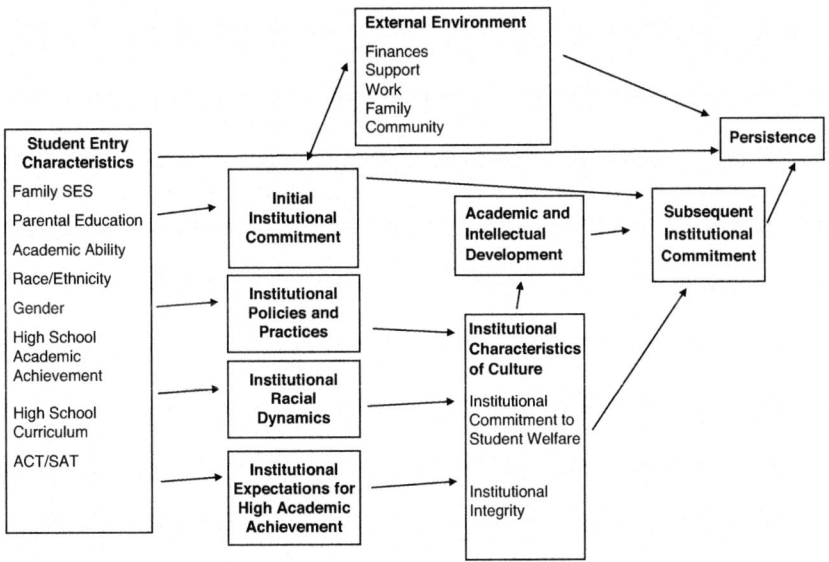

Recommendations for Theory and Research

Our primary recommendation for theory and research pertains to the suitable use of the two revised theories to understand the college persistence of students of various racial or ethnic groups other than White, such as AAPI,

Black, Latinx, and Native American. Two suitable uses and one unsuitable use of these two theories exist.

The first suitable use entails the testing of both theories on an entire class, such as first-time, full-time, first-year students, without regard to specific racial/ethnic groups. Our previously delineated recommendation for the expansion of the entry characteristics of students to include AAPI, Black, Latinx, Native American, and White students provides reinforcement for the suitability of this use of both revised theories.

The second suitable use involves a test of both theories focused on only one of these four different racial or ethnic groups in institutional settings in which the focal group of students comprise the majority of the students enrolled. Such institutional settings include HBCUs, Hispanic-serving institutions (HSIs), and tribal colleges and universities. Baker et al. (2020, 2021) provided a strong rationale for the suitability of these theories to HBCUs. They contended that Black students attending these institutions do not face the same campus climate as Black students attending PWIs. This rationale also extends to HSIs and tribal colleges and universities.

An unsuitable use of both theories involves institutional settings in which White students comprise the majority of the students enrolled (PWI) and Asian American, Black, Latinx, and Native American students comprise a minority of students enrolled. This minoritized situation constitutes a misuse of these two theories given the problematic application of PWI-based theories to study the persistence of Black students raised by Palmer and Walker in chapter 3. Specifically, they note that scholars consistently described the campus climate at PWIs as racist, chilly, and alienating (Fries-Britt & Turner, 2002). Asian American, Latinx, and Native American students may also experience the campus climate at PWIs as racist, chilly, and alienating.

Closing Thoughts

Systematic theory revision that incorporates new empirical understanding into existing theories and models is a process that we rarely engage in as scholars. This is unfortunate because the process in which we engaged to revise Braxton et al.'s theories for residential colleges and universities and community colleges and universities both improved the articulation of the theories and highlighted some larger themes that can inform theory development into the future. We identified at least four interrelated themes that we share in this closing section.

Increasingly Diverse Student Body Must Change How We Use Theory

The increasing sociodemographic diversity represented among college students means that, as scholars and practitioners, we need more nuanced and targeted theories. The two theories we reviewed and revised in this chapter were built upon the proposition that different types of institutions enrolled students with different needs and circumstances, so this realization was present at the advent of these two theories. Recent research, however, reinforces this understanding. At a minimum, we must understand that no single theory describes persistence experiences for all students, particularly when those students' sociodemographic characteristics are not fully accounted for in the theory. Further, we must be cautious when attempting to use a theory developed for a specific type of institution at other types of institutions. Braxton et al. (2004) highlighted the importance of the difference between residential and commuter institutions in their theories, but we must also understand the importance of generating theories designed particularly for HBCUs, HSIs, and other institutions with missions to serve specific students.

The Role of Campus Climates

Research about the role of students' perceptions of campus climates, particularly students' perceptions of racial climates, is abundant over past decades. Campus climate research often situates individual students within a broader context and assumes that both student and climate exert influence on the other (Strange & Banning, 2015). In conceptualizing a campus climate, we often use anthropomorphic terms to describe how a place feels (e.g., friendly, welcoming, hostile) to individuals or groups of students who share similar characteristics.

In the process of revising Braxton et al.'s (2004) two theories, we concluded that students' perceptions of multiple climates (e.g., racial climates, academic climates, policy climates) should be included in our understanding of persistence decisions as these climates affect how students experience college. Renn and Arnold (2003) used Urie Bronfenbrenner's (1993, 2005) concepts of climates to explore how the influence of peer groups affects students' learning. These authors, in essence, posited how a peer group climate that reinforces the importance of academic achievement can facilitate students' learning, a finding reinforced by Hallett et al. (2019). Finally, in chapter 7, de los Ríos and Oseguera, drawing from Berger's (2000, 2001) organizational styles, indicate that the messages sent by an institution's policy climate can influence students' persistence decisions through a sense of belonging and engagement. The ways in which students perceive the multiple climates with which they interact on a college campus likely affect persistence in direct and indirect ways; they should be accounted for in persistence theories.

Institutional Type Matters

Reason (2009) concluded that traditional measures of institutional type (size, source of support, mission) generally do not reach levels of statistical significance when studying persistence in well-designed research studies. On the other hand, institutional type difference—residential compared to commuter—was the basis for Braxton et al.'s (2004) initial development of the two theories under consideration in this chapter. The importance of institutional difference was reinforced in Braxton et al.'s (2014) empirical validation of the original theories and our current revision process.

Based on our revision process, we conclude that even though traditional measures of institutional type are not statistically significant in well-designed studies, institutional type must be accounted for in persistence theories. Institutional type affects which components of a theory might be most applicable to improving persistence at an institution. When comparing residential and commuter institutions, a primary distinction, the presence or absence of residential facilities, directly relates to both social integration and access to academic support resources (Mayhew et al., 2016). Social integration is a key component in persistence of students at residential colleges and universities, but not at commuter institutions (Braxton et al., 2014). We must not assume a theory developed at one type of institution fully describes persistence at another type of institution.

Instrumentation and Measurement of Concepts Pose Challenges

Institutional policies and practices and institutional expectations for high academic achievement present measurement challenges because of the level of abstraction and complexity of their constituent concepts. Bureaucratic, political, and collaborative styles of policy implementation compromise the abstract and complex concepts subsumed under institutional policies and practices. Subsumed under institutional expectations for high academic achievement, the concepts of high expectations for student academic achievement, faculty feedback on course assignments, and informal feedback from faculty also stand as abstract and complex. The constructs and their constituent components must be clearly and consistently operationalized in research in order to fully understand their influences on student persistence.

Aside from the operationalization of these concepts, the unit of analysis for their measurement stands as another issue. In particular, the measurement of the style of policy implementation should occur using those individuals of a college or university best able to observe such styles. Students, the standard unit of analysis for student persistence research, would be unable to observe styles affecting administrative officers, faculty, and staff.

Fortunately, some approaches to the measurement of these concepts exist in the literature. For example, Berger (2000) developed an instrument to measure five core dimensions of organizational behavior, including the bureaucratic, collegial, and political dimensions. Researchers interested in the testing of the influence of institutional policies and practices on the characteristics of institutional culture and institutional commitment to institutional integrity and student welfare should consider using the measures developed by Berger (2000).

Moreover, a vehicle for the measurement of high expectations for student academic achievement also exists in the literature. Academic rigor in the form of the type of examination questions written by faculty affords researchers a way to measure the conveyance to students of the high expectations for their academic achievement held by faculty. Course examination questions that require a higher order understanding of course content (e.g., compare and contrast questions) offer a measure of the academic rigor of a course (Nordvall & Braxton, 1996). Braxton and Francis (2018) used such a measure of academic rigor in a study of student persistence in both residential and commuter colleges and universities. In this research, just like in our revisions to the two theories, academic rigor was placed as an antecedent to institutional commitment to student welfare and institutional integrity. Braxton and Francis (2018) reported empirical affirmation for the influence of academic rigor on these two characteristics of institutional culture in both commuter and residential colleges. Our confidence in academic rigor as an indicator of high expectations for academic achievement increases with these findings as well as its posited role as an antecedent of the two characteristics of institutional culture.

In closing, our revision process demonstrated the malleability of the two theories, as indicated by the additions of previously unaccounted for concepts to their formulations. Accordingly, we urge vigilance by researchers for studies that provide empirical support for concepts previously not included in research on student persistence in either residential colleges and universities or in commuter colleges and universities. Such vigilance ensures the continued viability of these theories through revisions to either or both of them that include such empirically supported concepts. Thus, a cycle of research to revisions and then revisions to research transpires. Such a cycle sustains the vibrancy of the theory and research process dedicated to understanding and improving college student persistence.

References

Allensworth, E. M., & Clark, K. (2020). High school GPAs and ACT scores as predictors of college completion: Examining assumptions about consistency across high schools. *Educational Researcher, 49*(3), 198–211. https://doi.org/10.3102/001389X20902110

Astin, A. W. (1993). *What matters in college? Four critical years revisited.* Jossey-Bass.

Astin, A. W., & Panos, R. J. (1969). *The educational and vocational development of college students.* U.S. Department of Education.

Baker, D. J., Arroyo, A. T., Braxton, J. M., & Gasman, M. (2020). Understanding student persistence in commuter historically Black colleges and universities. *Journal of College Student Development, 61*(1), 34–50. https://muse.jhu.edu/article/747303

Baker, D. J., Arroyo, A. T., Braxton, J. M., Gasman, M., & Francis, C. H. (2021). Expanding the student persistence puzzle to minority serving institutions: Residential historically Black college and university context. *Journal of College Student Retention: Research, Theory, and Practice, 22*(4), 676–698. https://doi.org/10.1177/1521025118784030

Bean, J. P., & Metzner, B. S. (1985). A conceptual model of nontraditional student attrition. *Review of Educational Research, 55*, 485–540. https://doi.org/10.2307/1170245

Berger, J. B. (2000). Organizational behavior at colleges and student outcomes: A new perspective on college impact. *Review of Higher Education, 23*(2), 177–198. https://doi.org/10.1353/rhe.2000.0001

Berger, J. B. (2001). Understanding the organizational nature of student persistence: Empirically-based recommendations for practice. *Journal of College Student Retention: Research, Theory & Practice, 3*(1), 3–21. https://doi.org/10.2190/3K6A-2REC-GJU5-8280

Bowman, N. A., & Denson, N. (2021, September 10). Institutional racial representation and equity gaps in college graduation. *Journal of Higher Education.* Advance online publication. https://doi.org/10.1080/00221546.2021.1971487

Braxton, J. M., Doyle, W. R., Hartley, H. V., Hirschy, A. S., Jones, W. A., & McLendon, M. K. (2014). *Rethinking college student retention.* Jossey-Bass.

Braxton, J. M., & Francis, C. H. (2018). The influence of academic rigor on factors related to college student persistence. In C. M. Campbell (Ed.), *Reframing Rigor: New Understandings for Equity and Student Success* (New Directions for Higher Education, no. 181, pp. 73–87). Jossey-Bass.

Braxton, J. M., & Hirschy, A. S. (2005). Theoretical developments in college student departure. In A. Seidman (Ed.), *College student retention: Formula for student success* (pp. 61–87). Praeger.

Braxton, J. M., Hirschy, A. S., & McClendon, S. A. (2004). *Understanding and reducing college student departure* (ASHE-ERIC Higher Education Report, Vol. 30, No. 3). Jossey-Bass.

Bronfenbrenner, U. (1993). The ecology of cognitive development: Research models and fugitive findings. In R. H. Wozniak & K. W. Fischer (Eds.), *Examining lives in context: Perspectives on the ecology of human development* (pp. 619–647). American Psychological Association.

Bronfenbrenner, U. (2005). *Making human beings human: Biological perspectives on human development*. SAGE.

Cabrera, A., Nora, A., Pascarella, E. T., Terenzini, P. T., & Hagedorn, L. S. (1999). Campus racial climate and the adjustment of students to college: A comparison between White students and African-American students. *Journal of Higher Education, 70*(2), 134–160. https://doi.org/10.2307/2649125

Cabrera, A., Stampen, J. O., & Hansen, W. (1990). Exploring the effects of ability to pay on persistence in college. *Review of Higher Education, 13*(3), 303–336. https://doi.org/10.1353/rhe.1990.0020

Carver, C. S., Scheier, M. F., & Weintraub, J. K. (1989). Assessing coping strategies: A theoretically based approach. *Journal of Personality and Social Psychology, 56*(2), 267–283. https://doi.org/10.1037/0022-3514.56.2.267

Chafetz, J. S. (1978). *A primer on the construction and testing of theories in sociology.* F. E. Peacock.

Cox, B. E., Reason, R. D., Nix, S., & Schwab, M. (2016). Life happens (outside of college): Non-college life-events and students' likelihood of on-time graduation. *Research in Higher Education, 57*(7), 823–844. http://dx.doi.org/10.1007/s11162-016-9409-z

Fries-Britt, S. L., & Turner, B. (2002). Uneven stories: Successful Black collegians at a Black and a White campus. *Review of Higher Education, 25*, 315–330. https://doi.org/10.1353/rhe.2002.0012

Hallett, R. E., Reason, R. D., Tocoli, J., Kitchen, J. A., & Perez, R. J. (2019). The process of academic validation within a comprehensive college transition program. *American Behavioral Scientist, 64*(3), 253–275. https://doi.org/10.1177/0002764421986419

Mayhew, M. J., Rockenbach, A. N., Bowman, N. A., Seifert, T. A., Wolniak, G. C. (with Pascarella, E. T., & Terenzini, P. T.). (2016). *How college affects students: Vol. 3. 21st century evidence that higher education works*. Jossey-Bass.

Museus, S. D., Nichols, A. H., & Lambert, A. D. (2008). Racial differences in effects of campus racial climate on degree completion: A structural equation model. *Review of Higher Education, 32*(1), 107–134. http://doi.org/10.1353/rhe.0.0030

National Student Clearinghouse Research Center. (2020, March 2). *Completing college: 2019 national report*. https://nscresearchcenter.org/completing-college/

Nordvall, R. C., & Braxton, J. M. (1996). An alternative definition of quality of undergraduate college education: Toward usable knowledge for improvement. *Journal of Higher Education, 67*(5), 483–497. https://doi.org/10.2307/2943865

Okun, M. A., Benin, M., & Brandt-Williams, A. (1996). Staying in college: Moderators of the relation between intention and institutional departure. *Journal of Higher Education, 67*(5), 577–596. https://doi.org/10.2307/2943869

Pascarella, E. T., & Terenzini, P. T. (1991). *How college affects students: Findings and insights from two decades of research*. Jossey-Bass.

Pascarella, E. T., & Terenzini, P. T. (2005). *How college affects students. Vol. 2: A third decade of research*. Jossey-Bass.

Pascarella, E., Whitt, E., Nora, A., Edison, M., Hagedorn, L., & Terenzini, P. (1996). What have we learned from the first year of the national study of student learning? *Journal of College Student Development, 37*, 182–192.

Reason, R. D. (2009). An examination of the persistence research through the lens of a comprehensive conceptual framework. *Journal of College Student Development, 50*, 659–682. https://muse.jhu.edu/article/364959

Renn, K. A., & Arnold, K. D. (2003). Reconceptualizing research on peer culture. *Journal of Higher Education, 74*(3), 261–291. https://doi.org/10.1177/0895904804269941

Renn, K. A., & Reason, R. D. (2021). *College students in the United States: Characteristics, experiences, and outcomes* (2nd ed.). Stylus.

Scott-Clayton, J. (2011). *The shapeless river: Does a lack of structure inhibit students' progress at community colleges?* (CCRC Working Paper No. 25). Community College Research Center, Columbia University.

St. John, E. P., & Starkey, J. B. (1995). An alternative to net price: Assessing the influence of prices and subsidies on within-year persistence. *Journal of Higher Education, 66*(2), 156–186. https://doi.org/10.1080/00221546.1995.11774771

Stewart, S. S., & Rue, P. (1983). Commuter students: Definitions and distribution. In S. S. Stewart (Ed.), *Trauma-Informed Practice in Student Affairs: Multidimensional Considerations for Care, Healing, and Wellbeing* (New Directions for Student Services, no. 24, pp. 3–8). Wiley.

Strange, C. C., & Banning, J. H. (2015). *Designing for learning: Creating campus environments for student success*. Wiley.

Terenzini, P. T., & Reason, R. D. (2005, November). *Parsing the first year of college: Rethinking the effects of college on students* [Paper presentation]. Annual Conference of the Association for the Study of Higher Education, Philadelphia, PA, United States.

Tinto, V. (1975). Dropout from higher education: A theoretical synthesis of recent research. *Review of Educational Research, 45*(1), 89–125. https://doi.org/10.2307/1170024

Tinto, V. (1993). *Leaving college: Rethinking the causes and cures of student attrition* (2nd ed.). The University of Chicago Press.

Webb, M. W., II. (1990, April 16–20). *Development and testing of a theoretical model for predicting student degree persistence at four-year commuter colleges* [Paper presentation]. Annual Meeting of the American Educational Research Association, Boston, MA, United States.

Weidman, J. (1989). Undergraduate socialization: A conceptual approach. In J. Smart (Ed.), *Higher education: Handbook of theory and research* (Vol. 5, pp. 289–322). Springer.

Wilson, V. R. (2007). The effect of attending an HBCU on persistence and graduation outcomes of African-American college students. *Review of Black Political Economy, 34*(1), 11–52. https://doi.org/10.1007/s12114-007-9006-7

PART TWO

RESEARCH

5

INVENTORYING THE ARTICLES ON STUDENT RETENTION PUBLISHED IN CORE HIGHER EDUCATION JOURNALS OVER THE PAST 10 YEARS

Ann Gansemer-Topf, Rachel A. Smith, Jodi Wilson, and Maggie Bell

With the assistance of Madeline Topf and Kevin Grady

Ensuring students' persistence toward graduation remains a focal point for postsecondary policy, practice, and research. At the institutional level, retention and graduation rates are critical metrics used to assess institutions' quality and value and are often proxies for student learning and success (Braxton et al., 2014; Seidman, 2012). From the student perspective, persistence to graduation results in significant social, health, civic, economic, and career advantages (Mayhew et al., 2016). Researchers too have focused on this topic with the intent to inform policy and practice.

These research efforts seem to be making a difference. In the past decade, overall retention and graduation rates have increased and, perhaps most promising, these rates have increased regardless of institutional type and student demographics (i.e., race, gender, socioeconomic status; National Center for Education Statistics [NCES], 2018a, 2018b, 2018c). Despite these upward trends, one in three students who begin at a 4-year institution do not graduate, and there remain significant gaps in persistence and graduation among student demographics and institutional types (NCES, 2018b,

2018c). Therefore, although a seemingly overstudied topic, there is more to know. If we have an obligation to accept educational responsibility for opportunity gaps, examining the student populations, institutional contexts, and methods we use to study retention and graduation is essential.

In this chapter, we examine the past decade's retention literature in 10 higher education journals to identify the "who, where, and how" this topic has been studied. Unlike other publications that have addressed "what" we know about retention, we wanted to take a closer look into the contexts and methods that have led to these conclusions. Examining longitudinal patterns of literatures provides insight into the ways retention is theorized, measured, and enacted. Our research investigates the extent to which retention has been conceptualized and empirically studied, and correspondingly, where exclusion is happening and where new theory, focus, or measurement is needed. By looking back, we hope to inform the present and future.

Conceptual Framework

Constructing field and disciplinary knowledge involves social and cognitive processes, which various authors have described in complementary, yet distinct, ways. Leydesdorff (1998) theorized knowledge processes in terms of networks. These networks are formed as individuals and their ideas interact, containing the interrelationships of authors, texts, and groups of authors and texts. Abbott (2001) argued that fractal processes, where divisions in discussion are repeated along branches of inquiry, could be used as a framework for understanding the ways that scholarly conversations developed over time within disciplines, highlighting mechanisms of continued differentiation, reproduction, and reset. Abbott described a field's canon as useful for driving change, in that scholars tend to either develop it or revolt against it. In academia, scholarly literature has historically evolved in a relatively fixed pattern, involving personal communication, scholarly and professional conference presentations, journal publications, and the later packaging of journal articles within monographs and books (Drott, 1995). The speed of this evolutionary process varies by field.

How concepts develop, what counts as knowledge, and how we know about these concepts is contested and political terrain. Authors can potentially build on one another, contributing to research and practice, and concepts can also become overly entrenched and immune to challenge. Journals that disseminate research are also gatekeepers and norm-setters. For example, if a journal predominantly publishes articles featuring newly developed quantitative methodological techniques, those analyses require particular kinds of data, constraining potential research questions and the inclusion of "countable" populations. Looking across publications in a field, because each journal may have its own purposes and foci, is one way to make sense of how researchers and practitioners come to know what they know in terms of which knowledges are centered and which are relegated to the margins.

Analyses of U.S. higher education research have included articles in the *Journal of Higher Education* (*JHE*), *Research in Higher Education* (*ResHE*), *Review of Higher Education* (*RevHE*; Budd, 1990; Budd & Magnuson, 2010), the *Journal of College Student Development* (*JCSD*; Davis & Liddell, 1997; Smith, 2019), and the *Journal of the First-Year Experience and Students in Transition* (Campbell et al., 2013). These analyses have focused on citation patterns, trends in student affairs, and first-year experiences but have not specifically focused on retention and persistence. Methodologically, higher education research has been characterized as largely quantitative with increasingly advanced statistical use (Hutchinson & Lovell, 2004; Johnson et al., 2016; Wells et al., 2015). Relatively more qualitative work was found in *JHE* (Williams et al., 2018) and *JCSD* (Davis & Liddell, 1997). Previous topics of analysis have, for example, included the first-year experience (Campbell et al., 2013), community colleges (Townsend et al., 2005), feminist topics (Hart, 2006), and race (Mitchell et al., 2014). Our analysis of retention-focused studies follows those that examined the prevalence and character of other topics in higher education journals and incorporates analyses of methodology. Our research question is: How can the U.S.-based undergraduate retention literature in the past decade be characterized, particularly in terms of focal student populations, theoretical frameworks, and methodologies engaged?

Methodology

We engaged in a systematic literature review (Fink, 2005) to identify articles on retention, and then we descriptively coded each article's characteristics to construct a quantitative dataset that we used to answer our research questions. We selected 10 focal U.S. higher education–related journals:

Community College Journal of Research and Practice (*CCJRP*)
Community College Review (*CCR*)
Journal of College Student Development (*JCSD*)
Journal of College Student Retention (*JCSR*)
Journal of Diversity in Higher Education (*JDHE*)
Journal of the First-Year Experience and Students in Transition (*JFYESIT*)
Journal of Higher Education (*JHE*)

Journal of Student Affairs Research and Practice (*JSARP*)
Research in Higher Education (*ResHE*)
Review of Higher Education (*RevHE*)

We chose these journals because several come from among the set of "tier one" higher education journals (Bray & Major, 2011), and the group varies by student population or experience, topical focus, institutional type, and readership. We choose the time period of fall 2009–fall 2019 because it was the most recent decade at the time our analysis began. It also coincided with the first year following the U.S. economic recession, an important environmental context for institutions concerned with enrollment and retention (Gansemer-Topf et al., 2018).

Our process included a review of all articles published in each journal during the time span (N = 3,554). We assembled an initial database of all research articles published by all 10 journals, primarily using Web of Science or Scopus, depending on which subscription-based service indexed the journal. In one case we relied on the journal's website for information. The database contained article titles, authors, abstracts, and other publication information. We read all titles and abstracts and manually coded whether each article engaged the topic of undergraduate retention or persistence, in some cases looking to the article itself if the abstract was unclear (e.g., if it used "student success"). We focused narrowly on studies that had retention, persistence, or graduation as a central axis of analysis. We did not include studies that mentioned retention as an indirect outcome. For example, studies that focused solely on grade point averages as a measure of student success or as a proxy for retention or persistence were not included. Similarly, we also excluded studies that focused on topics that are often closely related to retention such as sense of belonging or student engagement. We did include studies focused on graduation rates, as graduation rates represent a 4–6-year retention or persistence rate. Using this screening process, we reduced the 3,554 articles to 608. Table 5.1 contains the percentage of retention-related articles by journal and year. We downloaded all articles identified as centering retention and read them, coding for methodology and methods, participants, samples, data sources, institution types, findings, and author characteristics.

Trends in Retention Publication Rates

Of the 3,553 articles reviewed, 608 (17%) focused on retention or graduation. Colleges and universities are complex organizations that serve a variety of

TABLE 5.1

Percentage of Articles on Retention by Journal and Year

	2009	2010	2011	2012	2013	2014	2015	2016	2017	2018	2019	Total
Community College Journal of Research and Practice	10.0%	23.1%	12.7%	11.8%	28.1%	18.2%	20.5%	5.8%	13.5%	9.1%	16.7%	16.0%
Community College Review	26.7%	0.00%	15.4%	13.3%	37.5%	33.3%	23.5%	7.4%	35.7%	12.5%	15.4%	20.2%
Journal of College Student Development	29.4%	6.3%	6.1%	6.0%	8.2%	3.2%	7.5%	5.3%	11.4%	6.7%	10.3%	7.8%
Journal of College Student Retention	57.1%	77.8%	80.6%	72.0%	67.9%	79.0%	72.7%	75.0%	73.9%	64.0%	62.8%	70.9%
Journal of Diversity in Higher Education	0.0%	0.0%	15.0%	12.5%	5.9%	5.6%	5.9%	0.0%	7.7%	16.1%	4.8%	7.3%
Journal of the First-Year Experience and Students in Transition	20.0%	10.0%	10.0%	40.0%	33.3%	10.0%	18.2%	8.3%	41.7%	8.3%	40.0%	20.2%
Journal of Higher Education	8.3%	10.3%	22.2%	9.4%	3.5%	17.2%	10.0%	6.7%	14.3%	5.6%	16.7%	11.3%
Journal of Student Affairs Research and Practice	14.3%	4.6%	0.0%	0.0%	11.8%	10.7%	6.4%	6.5%	9.4%	3.1%	1.8%	5.7%
Research in Higher Education	25.0%	27.0%	5.0%	10.5%	18.9%	29.1%	18.4%	18.4%	15.8%	22.7%	22.9%	18.9%
Review of Higher Education	12.50%	27.78%	5.26%	7.69%	0.00%	0.00%	11.11%	0.00%	21.05%	12.00%	7.69%	9.13%
Total Number of Articles on Retention	32	62	42	47	69	61	65	40	67	50	73	608
Total Percentage of Articles on Retention	19.4%	20.3%	15.2%	14.6%	22.3%	18.2%	17.9%	11.3%	18.6%	14.6%	17.8%	17.1%

competing goals and purposes. If we assume that journal publications represent topics that are of value to higher education, the finding that almost one fifth of all articles published in the last 10 years have a direct focus on retention suggests this topic has been and remains a critical higher education issue. The number of studies focused on retention has varied from 32 in 2009 to 73 in 2019; the percentage of articles focused on retention each year has ranged from 11% in 2016 to 22% in 2013. There is no consistent trend in the percentage of studies published on retention, persistence, or graduation for each of the journals over the 10-year period (see Table 5.1). Not surprisingly, the *JCSR* published the highest percentage of articles focused on retention (71%). About one fifth of articles published in *CCR, JFYESIT,* and *ResHE* were focused on retention; less than 10% of the articles in *JCSD, JDHE, JSARP,* and *RevHE* centered retention as their primary topic.

Focus of Retention Studies

Understanding student retention should, undoubtedly, focus on the student. Retention articles have examined how policies, institutional contexts, demographics, academic programs, and experiences influence retention. For purposes of our analysis, we examined the primary audience and the implications for that audience or topic. Of the 608 published articles on retention, 92% of the articles included student-level variables or experiences as the primary subject of analysis. In several of these studies, other variables such as institutional characteristics, faculty engagement, or program participation may have been included in the analysis. Approximately 4% of the articles focused on institutions; 3% on faculty, staff, or administration; 1% on programs such as precollege preparation programs; and 0.05% focused on policies or past research and theories.

Institutional Type and Control

Braxton et al.'s (2014) book *Rethinking College Student Retention* emphasized the importance of considering institutional context within discussions of retention. Therefore, a thorough understanding of retention must account for the varied institutional contexts. Our analysis focused on institutional level (2-year and 4-year institutions) and control (private and public).

2-Year and 4-Year Institutions

We examined the percentage of articles that focused on students and institutions at 2-year and 4-year institutions (see Table 5.2). Of the 608 studies reviewed, we could not ascertain the institutional types for 3.3% of the

TABLE 5.2
Percentage of Articles on Retention, by Institutional
Level, Institutional Type, by Journal and Year

	Institutional Level			Institutional Type		
	2-Year	*4-Year*	*Both*	*Public*	*Private*	*Both*
CCJRP	78.2%	6.8%	15.0%	96.5%	0.00%	3.5%
CCR	88.2%	0.0%	11.8%	97.0%	0.00%	3.0%
JCSD	2.4%	81.0%	16.7%	70.3%	0.00%	29.7%
JCSR	12.3%	82.7%	5.0%	85.4%	4.2%	10.4%
JDHE	6.3%	81.3%	12.5%	41.7%	16.7%	41.7%
JFYESIT	10.5%	63.2%	26.3%	94.4%	0.0%	5.6%
JHE	11.1%	63.9%	25.0%	82.8%	0.0%	17.2%
JSARP	11.8%	88.2%	0.0%	78.6%	7.1%	14.3%
ResHE	14.7%	68.0%	17.3%	74.7%	6.7%	18.7%
RevHE	21.7%	65.2%	13.0%	100.00%	0.00%	0.00%
2009–2014	36.3%	51.7%	12.0%	86.6%	3.0%	10.4%
2015–2019	29.2%	57.6%	13.2%	85.6%	2.3%	12.1%
Average	32.8%	54.6%	12.6%	86.1%	2.7%	11.2%

articles (N = 588). Of the 588 studies that described institutional type, 55% focused solely on 4-year, 33% focused on 2-year institutions, and 13% included 2-year and 2-year institutions. Not surprisingly, almost 95% of the articles published in the community college journals (*CCJRP* and *CCR*) included 2-year institutions; 80% of the articles focused solely on 2-year institutions. In comparison, 12% of the articles published in the other journals focused solely on 2-year institutions, 12% included 2-year and 4-year institutions, and 76% only included 4-year institutions. Eighty percent of articles published in *JCSD, JCSR, JDHE,* and *JSARP* included 4-year institutions only.

In 2020–2021, 33% of undergraduate students attended a public 2-year college and 49% of students who completed a 4-year degree had enrolled in a 2-year college in the previous 10 years (Community College Research Center [CCRC], 2022). Given the percentages of students who attend community college and the importance of community colleges in minimizing the opportunity gaps for low-income and racially minoritized students (American Association of Community Colleges, 2017), it is critical that research on the success of community college students continues. The lack of publications may also be the result of the challenges associated with measuring retention in community college settings. Some students attend community colleges with the intent to transfer after 1 year; some are dual enrolled at the community college and high school or even other 4-year institutions. This variety of transfer patterns can make it difficult to measure retention or in some instances, retention of students from year to year may not be the primary goal. Journals that do not focus specifically on community colleges publish a relatively small percentage of research related to the 2-year institution. It is unclear if this lack of publishing is a result of editorial decisions or authors' decisions on where to publish.

Public and Private Institutions

Over 97% of the published studies were conducted within a public institution context. Less than 3% of studies focused solely on private institutions. When we omit community colleges journals, which we assume focus on public community colleges, this percentage increases to 4%. On average, another 15% of studies included private and public institutions. Over our study period, the percentage of studies focused solely on private institutions ranged from zero to 5% (see Table 5.2).

This lack of focus on private institutions is problematic. As private institutions tend to be more heavily tuition dependent, small increases or decreases in retention have significant impacts on revenue (Schuh & Gansemer-Topf, 2012). Although a small percentage of private institutions have high enrollment and retention rates, the majority of private institutions do not (Gansemer-Topf & Schuh, 2006). In the current higher education landscape, these less selective, more tuition-driven institutions increasingly are at risk of closing (National Association of College and University Business Officers [NACUBO], 2019), and this risk likely will be heightened as a result of declining college-going populations (Grawe, 2018) and COVID-19 (Korn et al., 2020). Retention and graduation research focused on these vulnerable institutions may be a scenario of "too little, too late" for some institutions, but can increase the likelihood of survival for others.

Data Sources

Our knowledge of retention has been informed by a variety of data. We often overlook where the data have originated and the value and limitations of these data. Examining data sources by journal also lends insights into the type(s) of data valued by each publication outlet. For this analysis, we identified the various sources of data collected. When, for example, a study utilized institutional data and an institutional survey or when a national data set was followed by individual interviews, we noted each data source. Over a third of the data (36%) used in retention studies is based on data from one institution (see Table 5.3). As mentioned earlier, a majority of the studies focused on retention within public institutions. Of the studies that included institutional data, 83% were based on public institutions and over 60% on 4-year public institutions.

A quarter of the studies utilized data from national datasets or national surveys. Some of the datasets included those collected by the Department of Education's NCES, such as the Integrated Postsecondary Education Data System or Beginning Postsecondary Students, or national surveys, such as the National Survey of Student Engagement or the Wabash Study of Liberal Arts Education. Approximately 20% of studies included data from multiple institutions or data provided by a state (e.g., Tennessee). Less than 20% of the data came from interviews, focus groups, or observations. Other data sources that were utilized less frequently were document analysis, literature and journal reviews, and program surveys.

Journals varied in the types of data sources used in publications. For example, *ResHE* and *JHE* were unlikely to publish articles based on interview, focus group, or observational data. However, over a quarter of articles in *CCJRP*, *JCSD*, *JDHE*, *JSARP*, and *JFYESIT* included these three data sources in their publications.

Within higher education, discussions about methodological legitimacy, research training, and knowledge gatekeeping persist (Renn, 2020). Organizations such as NCES have increased efforts to make their national datasets more accessible by providing trainings such as those cosponsored by the Association of Institutional Research. Given these changes, we investigated differences in the percentages of articles by data source from the first 5 years (2009–2014) to 2015–2019. Table 5.3 illustrates that the percentages have remained fairly consistent. There were small increases in data from national datasets and surveys as well as multi-institutional and state data.

Student Characteristics

Student retention data can yield significant influence over an institution's image and power. Retention data by student characteristics are commonly included in institutional, state, and national reports and in funding decisions, rankings, and accreditation. Although an institution's retention rate can provide some indication of student success, closer examination of

TABLE 5.3
Data Sources by Journal and Year

	Document Analysis	Interview	Focus Group	Institutional Data	Institutional Survey	State Data	National Survey/ Data	Multi- Institutional Data	Instrument/ Scale	Observation	Literature Review
CCJRP	10.2%	16.3%	8.2%	38.1%	10.2%	7.5%	19.0%	8.8%	3.4%	3.4%	5.4%
CCR	11.8%	17.6%	0.0%	26.5%	5.9%	17.6%	44.1%	14.7%	0.0%	5.9%	2.9%
JCSD	4.3%	26.1%	0.0%	23.9%	13.0%	0.0%	21.7%	13.0%	15.2%	0.0%	6.5%
JCSR	4.2%	14.6%	1.6%	44.3%	17.7%	2.1%	17.2%	7.3%	0.5%	2.1%	7.8%
JDHE	6.3%	25.0%	6.3%	6.3%	31.3%	6.3%	12.5%	6.3%	0.0%	12.5%	0.0%
JFYESIT	9.5%	19.0%	4.8%	38.1%	23.8%	0.0%	4.8%	9.5%	4.8%	0.0%	9.5%
JHE	2.8%	2.8%	0.0%	19.4%	8.3%	11.1%	63.9%	11.1%	0.0%	0.0%	5.6%
JSARP	0.0%	27.8%	11.1%	50.0%	11.1%	0.0%	5.6%	5.6%	5.6%	0.0%	5.6%
ResHE	0.0%	0.0%	0.0%	33.3%	13.3%	14.7%	49.3%	60.0%	24.0%	0.0%	0.0%
RevHE	4.3%	13.0%	0.0%	30.4%	13.0%	13.0%	43.5%	56.5%	30.4%	0.0%	0.0%
2009–2014	6.4%	14.1%	2.9%	36.1%	13.4%	5.4%	24.3%	15.3%	6.4%	3.2%	8.0%
2014–2019	4.8%	14.6%	3.4%	35.6%	14.6%	7.8%	28.5%	19.0%	6.8%	1.0%	2.4%
Average	5.6%	14.3%	3.1%	35.9%	14.0%	6.6%	26.3%	17.1%	6.6%	2.1%	5.3%

retention rates by characteristics can often tell a different story. Opportunity gaps in retention and graduation rates by race, socioeconomic status, and academic preparedness emphasize the need for reporting retention by these different characteristics so that administrators and policymakers can provide better support and interrupt the perpetuation of inequality.

Similarly, the retention literature frequently highlights differences in retention rates by student demographics. These differences are not new, but as the college student population becomes increasingly diverse and student success remains a priority, retention research should mirror this diversity. Therefore, we identified some of the common student characteristics included in the retention literature.

As mentioned in the previous section, over one third of the studies used institutional data and one quarter included national surveys or datasets (see Table 5.3). We then examined, where applicable, the percentages of students by race that were included in each sample (see Table 5.4). In reviewing these studies, we found that 60% of studies using institutional samples and 56% of studies using national surveys or datasets had "samples" that were overwhelming White. In some instances, students of color were analyzed by racial/ethnic categories, and when sample sizes were too small, researchers created a binary category of "White/non-White." We also noted the prevalence of the use of the term *representative sample*. This term is often used to reflect the larger target population. When this larger population is predominantly White, the representative sample is largely White. Subsequently, conclusions based on the studies of these "representative samples" must also acknowledge the lack of racially diverse students. These categorizations point to the ways that countability renders (in)visibility and (il)legitimacy in neoliberal institutional environments and can undermine student success efforts when students with marginalized identities are not included in "data" (Taylor, 2020).

Table 5.4 includes an overview of the student characteristics studied. When studies focused on two or more demographics—for example, Latinx men in community colleges—we identified all three populations. Academic programs included precollege programs such as Upward Bound, college-sponsored programs or initiatives such as learning communities or orientation, or specific majors such as STEM. We recognize that several studies may include these demographic and program variables in their analysis. However, for purposes of this analysis, we identified the characteristics that were the primary focus of the research.

We also looked for patterns or trends by years and journals. We noted a few, nonsurprising patterns. The highest percentage of articles on first-year students was found in *JFYESIT*, and the highest percentages of articles focused on community college students were in *CCR* and *CCJRP*. Studies

TABLE 5.4
Student Characteristics as the Primary Focus of Journal Articles

Student Characteristic	Percentage
Community College	34.9%
Institutional Sample—White	21.7%
Academic Program	15.6%
First-Year Students	15.3%
Institutional Sample—Diverse	14.3%
National Sample—White	7.2%
Transfer	5.9%
National Sample—Diverse	5.6%
Latinx	4.6%
Low Income	4.1%
African American	3.8%
Men	3.5%
First Generation	3.0%
State Sample—Diverse	2.6%
Women	2.4%
Students of Color	2.1%
Military Connected	1.3%
Second-Year Students	1.0%
State Sample—White	1.0%
Disability/Ability	0.8%
Seniors	0.7%
Asian American	0.5%
Native Pacific Islander	0.5%
Upper Class	0.3%
LGBTQ	0.3%
Third-Year Students	0.2%
Other (e.g., athletes, nontraditional, international, Indigenous)	3.5%

focused on military-connected/veteran students and low-income students
were more commonly published after 2013. Although it is beyond the scope
of our analysis to know why we have seen this increase, it may likely be due to

the timing of the influx of veteran students as a result of the availability of the Post-9/11 Veterans Educational Assistance Act in 2009 and the recession of 2008. The variety of student characteristics studied in the past decade illustrates that although the retention literature has accounted for the diversity of student populations, there is work to be done.

Methodologies, Methods, Analyses

We examined the methodologies used to study retention, overall and by journal (see Table 5.5). Overall, 71% of articles used quantitative methodologies. The distribution ranged across journals, with some featuring quantitative methodologies about half the time (*JSARP* and *CCJRP*), and others contained almost exclusively quantitative methodologies (*JHE*, *ResHE*, and *RevHE*). *ResHE* specifically states it will only publish quantitative methodologies. As such, the type of data required and type of questions that can be answered may be limited. *JDHE* published the highest percentage of qualitative work (44%) and *CCJRP* published the most program descriptions, which featured no specific research methodology (16%). Results from the qualitative studies can offer insights into questions of "why" and "how" that may not be possible with quantitative methods. Mixed methods did

TABLE 5.5
Methodologies Used to Study Retention, by Journal, 2009–2019 (N = 608)

Journal	Quantitative	Qualitative	Mixed Methods	Theoretical or Scholarly	Program Descriptions
CCJRP	53.7%	16.3%	2.0%	11.6%	16.3%
CCR	67.6%	17.6%	5.9%	8.8%	0.0%
JCSD	65.2%	26.1%	0.0%	8.7%	0.0%
JCSR	74.0%	14.6%	1.6%	8.9%	1.0%
JDHE	56.3%	43.8%	0.0%	0.0%	0.0%
JFYESIT	66.7%	23.8%	0.0%	9.5%	0.0%
JHE	91.7%	2.8%	0.0%	5.6%	0.0%
JSARP	50.0%	22.2%	11.1%	5.6%	11.1%
ResHE	100.0%	0.0%	0.0%	0.0%	0.0%
RevHE	87.0%	13.0%	0.0%	0.0%	0.0%
All Journals Combined	71.4%	14.8%	1.6%	7.6%	4.6%

not feature widely (1.6% overall). We also compared the percentages of methodologies in the first half of the decade to the second. The percentage of quantitative methods increased from 65% during 2009–2014 to 76% during 2015–2019. Qualitative studies saw a small percentage increase (14% to 16%), and studies dedicated to theoretical or scholarly discussion on retention decreased from 11% to 3%. Unlike other empirical articles that may attempt to test a theory, this category of articles sought to use past research and scholarly work to critique or propose new theories. Some articles interrogated the variables and research methods used to understand retention while other articles proposed new models and frameworks for specific populations (i.e., community college, African Americans, Native Americans, Latinx). We noted that the theoretical frameworks used to understand retention have not significantly changed in the past decade, but they have been altered and refined to better reflect changing student demographics and institutional environments.

Quantitative Research Designs

Studying retention can utilize a variety of designs. Of the 428 quantitative articles, causal-comparative designs made up almost two thirds of the retention studies, followed by correlational designs examining relationships between variables without controls (15%) and quasi-experimental designs that aimed to provide evidence of causation (13%). The journals with the highest percentage of quasi-experimental studies included *JHE, RevHE, ResHE,* and *JFYESIT.* Regression analysis, specifically logistic regression, was the most commonly used analysis method among causal-comparative studies, as the majority of outcomes were binary retained/persisted/graduated or not. Analyses showed an increasing percentage of more advanced statistical analyses such as structural equation modeling, event history modeling, and propensity score matching, consistent with previous studies of methodology (Wells et al., 2015).

Table 5.6 illustrates the types of research designs found in each journal. Of note, over 50% of articles in each journal included studies that used more complex research designs such as quasi-experimental and causal-comparative. Some journals appear to only publish articles using more complex designs. *JHE, JCSD, JSARP, ResHE,* and *RevHe* rarely, if ever, publish articles in which descriptive statistics such as means, percentages, and frequencies are the primary means of analysis. In most of the complex design studies, descriptive statistics may be included, but these statistics are often followed by additional inferential statistics. Authors looking to publish retention studies that use descriptive or correlational analysis may be best served by submitting to

TABLE 5.6

Types of Quantitative Designs and Analysis Methods Used to Study Retention, by Journal, 2009–2019 (N = 428)

Journal	Descriptive	Correlational	Quasi-Experimental	Experimental	Causal Comparative (N = 278)				
					Regression	Multilevel	SEM	Other	Combined
CCJRP	16.7%	26.9%	10.3%	0.0%	80.6%	8.3%	8.3%	2.8%	46.2%
CCR	4.3%	13.0%	13.0%	0.0%	81.3%	6.3%	12.5%	0.0%	69.6%
JCSD	0.0%	17.9%	7.1%	0.0%	81.0%	9.5%	9.5%	0.0%	75.0%
JCSR	7.0%	21.8%	5.6%	0.0%	81.7%	6.5%	10.8%	1.1%	65.5%
JDHE	22.2%	0.0%	0.0%	0.0%	71.4%	0.0%	28.6%	0.0%	77.8%
JFYESIT	7.7%	15.4%	23.1%	0.0%	100.0%	0.0%	0.0%	0.0%	53.8%
JHE	0.0%	0.0%	24.2%	3.0%	58.3%	16.7%	20.8%	4.2%	72.7%
JSARP	0.0%	12.5%	0.0%	12.5%	100.0%	0.0%	0.0%	0.0%	75.0%
ResHE	1.4%	2.7%	23.0%	1.4%	58.5%	5.7%	20.8%	15.1%	71.6%
RevHE	0.0%	0.0%	25.0%	0.0%	73.3%	0.0%	26.7%	0.0%	75.0%
All Journals Combined	6.5%	15.2%	12.6%	0.7%	75.2%	6.8%	14.0%	4.0%	65.0%

journals such as *JDHE*, *JCSR*, *CCJRP*, and *JFYESIT*. However, over the past decade, the number of studies using these analyses have declined. Between 2009–2014 and 2015–2019, we noted a 22% increase in the percentage of quantitative studies using more complex research designs and a 31% decrease in studies using descriptive or correlational designs.

Sample Size

Because of the high percentage of articles relying on quantitative methodologies, we examined sample sizes and quantitative design and method by journal (see Table 5.7). We grouped sample sizes into four categories (0 = unknown, 1 = 1–200; 2 = 201–1,000; 3 = 1,001–5,000; 4 = 5,001 and above). Over half (58.5%) of the quantitative studies examined had sample sizes of over 1,001 students, but these percentages varied by publication outlet. Over 70% of the articles published in *CCR*, *JHE*, *ResHE*, and *RevHe* had sample sizes over 1,001. Over 60% of the articles published in *JFYESIT* and *JDHE* used sample sizes of fewer than 1,000. *JDHE* and *CCJRP* were most likely to publish quantitative articles having sample sizes fewer than 200 students. The appropriateness of the sample size should be determined in the context of the research purpose, but these data illustrate that the likelihood of getting a quantitative-focused study with a small sample size varies by journal.

TABLE 5.7
Sample Size by Journal, 2009–2019 (N = 434)

	Unknown	*1–200*	*201–1,000*	*1,001–5,000*	*5,001 and Above*
CCJRP	3.8%	20.3%	26.6%	26.6%	22.8%
CCR	0.0%	0.0%	26.1%	39.1%	34.8%
JCSD	0.0%	10.0%	33.3%	36.7%	20.0%
JCSR	0.7%	14.1%	33.1%	33.8%	18.3%
JDHE	0.0%	44.4%	22.2%	33.3%	0.0%
JFYESIT	7.1%	14.3%	42.9%	21.4%	14.3%
JHE	6.1%	12.1%	9.1%	42.4%	30.3%
JSARP	0.0%	0.0%	44.4%	33.3%	22.2%
ResHE	1.3%	5.3%	18.7%	30.7%	44.0%
RevHE	0.0%	0.0%	30.0%	40.0%	30.0%
Journals Combined	1.8%	12.2%	27.4%	32.9%	25.6%

Qualitative Research Designs

Of the 89 qualitative studies identified, 40% did not discuss a specific methodological approach as part of their research design, but did use interviews or focus groups as the method of data collection. Generally, a lack of methodological approach specification can be problematic, because those discussions help the reader understand the study's grounding and congruence across researcher choices, which influence methodological goodness (Jones et al., 2013). Those that did explain their methodological approach included mostly phenomenology (17%), case studies (12%), and grounded theory (8%). A few studies utilized ethnography, critical discourse, and narrative inquiry. In the past 5 years, researchers also used visual methods such as photo elicitation, sharing circles, and participant action research to explore retention.

Author Characteristics

In addition to capturing the data sources and institutional context, we examined the institutional contexts and roles of authors at the time of publication. This analysis was limited as we only had author information for 60% of the articles. Because author positionality and experience play a significant role in what is studied and how it is studied, we were surprised that 40% of the articles contained little readily available information about the authors. Of those studies that included author information, we noted a diversity in authorship. Although not surprising that over half of the articles were authored by faculty members, almost a quarter of the articles were written by staff or administrators and 10% by individuals not affiliated with an institution. Graduate students accounted for 9% of the publications. We found that three fourths of articles on retention had two or more authors and commonly included coauthors with varying positions. This collaboration points to a strength in the retention literature—blending expertise of researchers, administrators, and policymakers, while training future leaders to more comprehensively understand this topic. The study of retention is not limited to faculty within higher education; practitioners also empirically examine ways in which we can improve student success.

Summary of Findings

We inventoried articles on student retention that were published in 10 higher education journals during 2009–2019 (N = 3,554). The percentage of articles focused on retention in each journal ranged from 11% to 22%. A majority of the retention articles (N = 608) were written by faculty members and focused on public 4-year institutions and analyzed institutional data using quantitative methodologies. There has been an increased focus on racially minoritized student populations, although White students continue to be the most represented in the research.

Additional analysis by journal type showed differences in these overall trends. Community college journals, for instance, focused primarily on 2-year institutions, and although quantitative was consistently the most common methodological approach, almost half of the retention articles in *CCJRP*, *JDHE*, and *JSARP* used an alternative methodology. The use of large datasets and complexity of statistical methods have increased and so has the variety of data sources and methodologies. Our study did not focus on the results of these studies; we leave that to the authors of the other chapters in this book. Nevertheless, by examining what has been published, how knowledge was generated, and by whom, we provide a foundation on which to further understand the retention literature landscape.

Looking Back to Inform Future Research

Retention-related studies have maintained a prominent place in the broad higher education literature. Sorting through and making sense of the retention literature can be overwhelming but necessary as we strive to align our policies and practices to meet the needs of our current students. Building on Braxton et al.'s (2014) work, our research examines the approaches, subjects, and ways of knowing that inform our knowledge of retention. Through this examination, our values as researchers, practitioners, and policymakers can be identified, celebrated, or questioned. Our study focused specifically on empirical research published in 10 higher education journals during 2009–2019. Given the current social, political, economic, and health-related environment, knowing what we know about retention, locating and rectifying gaps, and applying the knowledge we have are especially paramount. Looking at the past and considering our present, we identify future areas of inquiry necessary to continue to inform our understanding of retention and, subsequently, the policies and practices that can improve student success for all students within different institutional types.

- *Examination of institutional types.* The campus environment is a critical factor in retention, yet not all campus environments have received equal attention in our focus. Small, private liberal arts institutions are some of the most vulnerable institutional types but have not been at the forefront of retention inquiries.

- *Examination of the influence of online learning.* COVID-19 has forced all institutions to offer courses and services online, therefore disrupting the ways in which students and faculty interact with one another. Since these interactions have long been a significant hallmark of retention theories and research, examination of these new online ways of engagement can influence our understanding of the importance of interactions and their role in retention.

- *Examination of the role of "big data."* We have seen a dramatic increase in the use of predictive analytics designed to offer an individualized, institutional approach to understanding and improving retention. These approaches examine past data and use algorithms with varying levels of transparency to "predict" the future and encourage institutions to focus on those students most likely to need assistance to be retained. Research examining the ethics of such approaches and the influence of these approaches on access, admissions, and student success is warranted.

- *Examination of students.* Historically, retention data has focused on the experiences of students. This work must continue. As our student populations continue to diversify and change, our research must capture their distinctive identities and experiences.

- *Examination of methods.* We have seen new and innovative approaches to studying retention. A significant amount of retention research relies on analysis of quantitative datasets. Data analysis can only include variables that can be counted. Datasets that lack details regarding critical factors such as mental health and wellness, campus climates, racial and sexual identities, and intersections of identities and climates will continue to misrepresent or ignore key retention issues. We encourage the continued application of novel data collection techniques and methods of inquiry and analysis that examine retention as a way to make visible the invisible and to uncover previously hidden understandings.

- *Examination of frameworks.* As we continue to expand and decipher retention, we must also revisit the frameworks in which we work. Students, institutions, and the external environmental influences may necessitate a reenvisioning of the importance of retention, its goals, and the ways in which these goals can be realized.

Closing Thoughts

Although retention has long been studied, external factors remind us that this work must continue. Expanding on Abbott's (2001) fractal processes, the field of higher education studies has grappled with retention in ways that show differentiation in methodologies, reproduction, and advancing sophistication of those methodologies, and the field is potentially heading for a reset in terms of conceptualization and data use, given future conditions. Most critically, our work challenges the assumptions of who is included in our research, which work gets published, and how our concepts of "rigor" may perpetuate notions of Whiteness. By looking back, we can build on a strong trajectory, complicate it, and explore new ways to build knowledge.

References

Abbott, A. (2001). *Chaos of disciplines*. The University of Chicago Press.

American Association of Community Colleges. (2017). *Community college enrollment crisis? Historical trends in community college enrollment*. https://www.aacc.nche.edu/wp-content/uploads/2019/08/Crisis-in-Enrollment-2019.pdf

Braxton, J. M., Doyle, W. R., Hartley, H. V., III, Hirschy, A. S., Jones, W. A., & McLendon, M. K. (2014). *Rethinking college student retention*. Jossey-Bass.

Bray, N., & Major, C. (2011). Status of journals in the field of higher education. *Journal of Higher Education, 82*(4), 479–503. https://doi.org/10.1080/00221546.2011.11777213

Budd, J. M. (1990). Higher education literature: Characteristics of citation patterns. *Journal of Higher Education, 61*(1), 84–97. https://doi.org/10.1080/00221546.1990.11775093

Budd, J. M., & Magnuson, L. (2010). Higher education literature revisited: Citation patterns examined. *Research in Higher Education, 51*, 294–304. https://doi.org/10.1007/s11162-009-9155-6

Campbell, R., Saltonstall, M., & Buford, B. (2013). The scholarship of a movement: A 24-year content analysis of the *Journal of the First-Year Experience and Students in Transition*. *Journal of the First-Year Experience and Students in Transition, 25*(1), 13–34. https://www.ingentaconnect.com/contentone/fyesit/fyesit/2013/00000025/00000001/art00002

Community College Research Center. (2022). *Community college enrollment and completion*. Teachers College Columbia University. https://ccrc.tc.columbia.edu/community-college-faqs.html

Davis, T. L., & Liddell, D. L. (1997). Publication trends in the *Journal of College Student Development*: 1987–1995. *Journal of College Student Development, 38*(4), 325–332.

Drott, M. C. (1995). Reexamining the role of conference papers in scholarly communication. *Journal of the American Society for Information Science, 46*(4), 299–305. https://doi.org/10.1002/(SICI)1097-4571(199505)46:4%3C299::AID-ASI6%3E3.0.CO;2-0

Fink, A. (2005). *Conducting research literature reviews: From the internet to paper* (2nd ed.). SAGE.

Gansemer-Topf, A. M., Downey, J., Thompson, K., & Genschel, U. (2018). Did the recession impact student success? Relationships of finances, staffing and institutional type on retention. *Research in Higher Education, 59*(2), 174–197. https://doi.org/10.1007/s11162-017-9462-2

Gansemer-Topf, A. M., & Schuh, J. H. (2006). Institutional selectivity and institutional expenditures: Examining organizational factors that contribute to retention and graduation. *Research in Higher Education, 47*(6), 613–642. https://doi .org/10.1007/s11162-006-9009-4

Grawe, N. D. (2018). *Demographics and the demand for higher education.* Johns Hopkins University Press.

Hart, J. (2006). Women and feminism in higher education scholarship: An analysis of three core journals. *Journal of Higher Education, 77*(1), 40–61. https://doi.org/ 10.1080/00221546.2006.11778918

Hutchinson, S., & Lovell, C. (2004). A review of methodological characteristics of research published in key journals in higher education: Implications for graduate research training. *Research in Higher Education, 45*(4), 383–403. https://doi .org/10.1023/B:RIHE.0000027392.94172.d2

Johnson, M., Wagner, N., & Reusch, J. (2016). Publication trends in top-tier journals in higher education. *Journal of Applied Research in Higher Education, 8*(4), 439–454. https://doi.org/10.1108/JARHE-01-2015-0003

Jones, S. R., Torres, V., & Arminio, J. (2013). *Negotiating the complexities of qualitative research in higher education: Fundamental elements and issues* (2nd ed.). Routledge.

Korn, M., Belkin, D., & Chung, J. (2020, April 30). Coronavirus pushes colleges to the breaking point, forcing "hard choices" about education. *The Wall Street Journal.* https://www.wsj.com/articles/coronavirus-pushes-colleges-to-the-breaking-point-forcing-hard-choices-about-education-11588256157

Leydesdorff, L. (1998). Theories of citation? *Scientometrics, 43*(1), 5–25. https://doi .org/10.1007/bf02458391

Mayhew, M. J., Rockenbach, A. N., Bowman, N. A., Seifert, T. A., & Wolniak, G. C. (2016). *How college affects students: 21st century evidence that higher education works.* Jossey-Bass.

Mitchell, D., Jr., Hardley, J., Jordan, D., & Couch, M. (2014). Journals in the field of higher education: A racial analysis. *Journal of Research Initiatives, 1*(2), 1–10. https://digitalcommons.uncfsu.edu/jri/vol1/iss2/2

National Association of College and University Business Officers. (2019). *2018 tuition discounting study.*

National Center for Education Statistics. (2018a). *Digest of education statistics, 2018* (Table 326.10). https://nces.ed.gov/programs/digest/d18/tables/dt18_326.10.asp

National Center for Education Statistics. (2018b). *Digest of education statistics, 2018* (Table 326.20). https://nces.ed.gov/programs/digest/d18/tables/dt18_326.20.asp

National Center for Education Statistics. (2018c). *Digest of education statistics, 2018* (Table 326.30). https://nces.ed.gov/programs/digest/d18/tables/dt18_326.30.asp

Renn, K. A. (2020). Reimagining the study of higher education: Generous thinking, chaos, and order in a low consensus field. *Review of Higher Education, 43*(4), 917–934. https://doi:10.1353/rhe.2020.0025

Schuh, J. H., & Gansemer-Topf, A. M. (2012). Finances and retention: Trends and potential implications. In A. Seidman (Ed.), *College student retention: Formula for student success* (pp. 101–118). Rowman & Littlefield.

Seidman, A. (2012). *College student retention: Formula for student success* (2nd ed.). Rowman & Littlefield.

Smith, R. A. (2019). Structuring the conversations: Using co-citation networks to trace 60 years of the *Journal of College Student Development. Journal of College Student Development, 60*(6), 695–717. https://doi.org/10.1353/csd.2019.0063

Taylor, L. D. (2020). Neoliberal consequence: Data-driven decision making and the subversion of student success efforts. *Review of Higher Education, 43*(4), 1069–1097. https://doi.org/10.1353/rhe.2020.0031

Townsend, B. K., Donaldson, J., & Wilson, T. (2005). Marginal or monumental? Visibility of community colleges in selected higher-education journals. *Community College Journal of Research and Practice, 29*(2), 123–135. http://doi.org/10.1080/10668920590524265

Wells, R. S., Kolek, E. A., Williams, E. A., & Saunders, D. B. (2015). "How we know what we know": A systematic comparison of research methods employed in higher education journals, 1996–2000 v. 2006–2010. *Journal of Higher Education, 86*(2), 171–198. https://doi.org/10.1080/00221546.2015.11777361

Williams, E. A., Kolek, E. A., Saunders, D. B., Remaly, A., & Wells, R. S. (2018). Mirror on the field: Gender, authorship, and research methods in higher education's leading journals. *Journal of Higher Education, 89*(1), 28–53. https://doi.org/10.1080/00221546.2017.1330599

SOCIODEMOGRAPHIC CHARACTERISTICS AND COLLEGE STUDENT PERSISTENCE, RETENTION, AND GRADUATION

Darris R. Means and Dena R. Kniess

While persistence, retention, and graduation rates of undergraduate students have increased in the United States since 2000, only 62% of undergraduate students who began their bachelor degree programs in fall 2012 earned a degree within 6 years (National Center for Education Statistics [NCES], 2020). In addition, for first-time, full-time degree-seeking undergraduate students who enrolled in 2-year institutions in 2017, only 62% were retained from 2017 to 2018 (NCES, 2020). Persistence, retention, and graduation rates differ across social identities, revealing students minoritized by their race, ethnicity, economic circumstances, and first-generation college student status have higher college departure rates (e.g., Cabrera et al., 2013; D'Allegro & Kerns, 2010–2011; Kopp & Shaw, 2016; NCES, 2020; Pratt et al., 2019; Shamsuddin, 2016; Spangler & Slate, 2015). Researchers have pointed to academic factors (e.g., grade point average, academic preparation) and sociodemographic characteristics (e.g., parental income and education level, racial and ethnic identities) to explain inequities in college student persistence, retention, and graduation (D'Allegro & Kerns, 2010–2011; D'Amico & Dika, 2013–2014; Kim, 2015; Mendoza & Mendez, 2012–2013; Mooring & Mooring, 2016). However, researchers, higher education leaders, and policymakers must understand racial and class inequities in persistence, retention, and graduation as systemic and perpetuated by racism, classism, and other forms of oppression (Simpfenderfer, 2019; Teranishi & Bezbatchenko, 2015). Thus, researchers, higher education leaders, and policymakers must go beyond examining individual-level contexts or blaming individuals and families for educational inequities and seek to understand and address how systemic challenges, racism, classism, and other forms of oppression hinder persistence, retention, and graduation for individual students (Teranishi & Bezbatchenko, 2015; Yosso, 2005).

In this chapter, we will examine literature on sociodemographic characteristics (economic background and circumstances, first-generation college student status, and race and ethnicity) and college student persistence, retention, and graduation from the past 10 years (What is known?). We integrated literature on individual-level factors *and* institutional and macro-level factors to discuss disparities in college student persistence, retention, and graduation across sociodemographic characteristics. We then discuss scholarship and research from the past decade that offer critical perspectives on college student persistence, retention, and graduation across sociodemographic characteristics (What is known, and how could this knowledge continue to disrupt and transform practice and policy?). Critical perspectives and approaches help institutional agents, policymakers, and researchers "to identify the causes and causalities of inequitable access to higher education, as well to craft a view of the discriminatory and unjust experiences of actors in higher education" (Martínez-Alemán et al., 2015, p. 2). In addition, critical perspectives and approaches challenge deficit-oriented perspectives about minoritized student populations and their families; recognize the assets, resources, and networks of minoritized student populations as being critical to their success; and seek to disrupt systemic challenges rooted in racism, classism, and other forms of oppression (Harper, 2012a; Simpfenderfer, 2019; Yosso, 2005). In this chapter, we specifically focus on asset-based, intersectional, and structural perspectives and approaches to scholarship and research on college student persistence, retention, and graduation over the past decade and how this body of research could address educational inequities.

Given the magnitude of literature from the past decade on college student persistence, retention, and graduation, we chose to focus this chapter on social class, race and ethnicity, and the intersection of these and other identities at multiple institutional types (e.g., community colleges, bachelor degree–granting institutions, minority-serving institutions) due to the significant amount of scholarship that continues to highlight how racism and classism hinder persistence, retention, and graduation in higher education. We recognize our choice leaves out critical perspectives in this chapter about how to address inequities in college student persistence, retention, and graduation for students who are minoritized due to ableism, cisgenderism, sexism, and heterosexism. Other books and special journal issues, fortunately, have recently taken up important discussions related to how other forms of oppression hinder college student persistence, retention, and graduation. For example, in 2020, Jason Garvey published an edited special issue in the *Journal of College Student Retention: Research, Theory & Practice* on queer and trans college student retention. We hope this chapter builds upon previous work to call higher education researchers, leaders, and policymakers to address inequities in higher education related to multiple forms of oppression.

Positionality of the Authors

We, Dena and Darris, bring our positionalities and subjectivities to this book chapter, and our positionalities and subjectivities shape our approaches to research, teaching, and service. As the contributors of this chapter, we believe it is important for readers to understand how our positionalities and subjectivities shape our understanding of college student persistence, retention, and graduation. Darris is a higher education faculty member and has studied topics related to college student persistence, retention, and graduation for over a decade. In addition to studying these topics, Darris's understanding of persistence, retention, and graduation are shaped by his social identities, personal experiences, and professional experiences. Darris is a cisgender, queer Black man from a low-income background and was a first-generation college student. Darris found himself navigating classism, racism, heterosexism, and the intersection of these forms of oppression during his time as a student in higher education. While Darris was marginalized by his race, social class, and sexuality, he had access and continues to have access to privilege as a cisgender, able-bodied man in higher education. Darris also worked for almost 8 years with a college access and success program that supported access to and persistence through higher education for students who identity as first-generation college students and/or students from low-income and working-class backgrounds. Darris's scholarship, social identities, and personal and professional experiences have shaped his critical approach to studying college student persistence and retention. He believes that for far too long college and university leaders, policymakers, and researchers have placed blame for educational inequities on students and families instead of understanding these inequities as systemic and pervasive.

Dena is a cisgender, heterosexual White woman from a middle-class background and was a first-generation college student. Dena found herself navigating sexism and classism during her time as a student, practitioner, and now faculty member in higher education. While her parents' financial background was middle class, Dena's felt social class was working class as her family members worked in factories and mines in the Western Pennsylvania region. Her first experiences in and impressions of higher education left her feeling "out of place" due to the terminology or jargon used to describe various processes pertaining to enrollment and financial aid. For 11 years, Dena worked as a practitioner in student affairs in the areas of residence life and student transition programs. During her time working in student affairs, she noticed college environments mirrored the inequities present in society, specifically in how opportunities were created to mirror White, middle-class values without affirming students' social identities. She believes deficit-based approaches to programs and policies in higher education have significantly impacted minoritized students' ability to persist and graduate from colleges and universities.

Methods

We conducted a review of higher education peer-reviewed articles to examine scholarship on college student persistence, retention, and graduation across sociodemographic characteristics. The field of higher education has numerous journals that focus on diverse topics—student affairs, community colleges, retention, and policy. Harper (2012b) and Harris and Patton (2019) conducted systemic analyses on higher education scholarship, using journals that are viewed as primary venues for higher education scholarship. Between Harper (2012b) and Harris and Patton (2019), they selected the following peer-reviewed higher education journals to include in their systemic analysis: *Review of Higher Education, Journal of Higher Education, Research in Higher Education, Journal of College Student Development, Journal of Student Affairs Research and Practice, Community College Journal of Research and Practice,* and *Community College Review.* Using Harper (2012b) and Harris and Patton (2019) as a guide, we included these listed journals for our systemic analysis. Given our focus on college student persistence and retention, we also included the following journals: *Journal of College Student Retention: Research, Theory & Practice, Journal of the First-Year Experience and Students in Transition,* and the *Journal of Critical Scholarship on Higher Education and Student Affairs.* We delimited the selection of published articles to a 10-year period beginning January 2010 and ending December 2019 to identify the most recent scholarship on college student persistence, retention, and graduation. The time period also marks 10 years since Reason (2009) provided a review of research on college student persistence. In addition, we examine persistence and retention only for undergraduate students.

We searched for articles in the journals using electronic databases and/ or went directly to the websites of the journals. Our chapter focuses on sociodemographic characteristics and college student retention and persistence, and specifically on social class, racial, ethnic, and first-generation college student social identities. Thus, we used *persistence, retention,* and *graduation* as search terms, with the following social identity categories: race, social class, ethnicity, and first-generation college student. We also included articles that did not show up in our search but that we were aware of, focusing on sociodemographic characteristics and college student retention and persistence. We then reviewed the abstracts for the articles to ensure they focused on college student persistence, retention, and graduation and sociodemographic characteristics. Our final sample included 113 peer-reviewed articles.

We developed a coding scheme to understand higher education literature on college student persistence and retention and sociodemographic characteristics. Our coding scheme included social identities focused on for the article (e.g., race, class, and first-generation status, as well as the intersection of these and other identities), individual and familial assets that support persistence and retention and sociodemographic characteristics, institutional resources and practices that support and/or hinder persistence and retention and sociodemographic characteristics, and macro-level factors that support and/or hinder persistence and retention and sociodemographic characteristics. We applied the coding scheme to the 113 articles in our final sample.

What Is Known From the Past Decade About Sociodemographic Characteristics and College Student Persistence, Retention, and Graduation?

For this section, we examine the literature about college student persistence, retention, and graduation from the past decade based on the following sociodemographic characteristics: economic background and circumstances, first-generation college student status, and racial and ethnic minoritized and Indigenous student populations. While we recognize these social identities intersect, we want to begin with an examination of what is known about each of these sociodemographic characteristics and the individual, institutional, and macro-level contexts and factors that shape college student persistence, retention, and graduation. We acknowledge some of the literature discussed in the following sections does not take a critical, nuanced perspective to examine how power, privilege, and oppression have and continue to uphold racial and class inequities in college student persistence, retention, and graduation.

Economic Background and Circumstances

In our review of scholarship from the past decade, researchers have used multiple definitions to define a student's economic background and circumstances: recipient of need-based federal aid (e.g., Pell Grant; Cabrera et al., 2013; Kim, 2015; Ocean, 2017), expected family contribution through the financial aid application process (Davidson, 2015; Roksa & Kinsley, 2019), family/parental income (Cox et al., 2016; Gershenfeld et al., 2016; Kopp & Shaw, 2016; N. D. Martin et al., 2017; Mendoza & Mendez, 2012–2013; Newton et al., 2013–2014; Wirt & Jaeger, 2014), and student income and savings (Wirt & Jaeger, 2014). Our review of literature on economic background and circumstances included all the previously listed definitions due to how they have been used in higher education scholarship over the past decade to focus on the experiences of poor and working-class students related to college student persistence, retention, and graduation.

Some researchers have not found students' economic backgrounds and circumstances to be statistically significant factors for persistence and retention (Dika, 2014–2015; Windham et al., 2014). While several studies did not find a student's economic background and circumstances to be statistically significant factors for persistence and retention (Dika, 2014–2015; Windham et al., 2014), researchers have found that poor and working-class students reported academic, social, and emotional challenges in navigating postsecondary education (Cabrera et al., 2013; Kopp & Shaw, 2016; Ocean, 2017; Soria et al., 2013–2014).

Poor and working-class students often had work and family responsibilities that sometimes interfered with their academic and social integration in college (Ocean, 2017; Soria et al., 2013–2014). Poor and working-class students also had challenges developing academic habits (e.g., study skills, study behaviors) and finding a conducive environment for studying (Soria et al., 2013–2014). Soria et al. (2013–2014) found "working-class students were more likely to report feeling depressed, stressed, or upset, and that these mental health concerns were obstacles to their academic success" (p. 228).

These academic, social, and emotional challenges may lead to poorer academic outcomes, such as grade point average (Cabrera et al., 2013) and departure because of academic jeopardy (Kopp & Shaw, 2016). For example, in a study on college departure for students in academic jeopardy, Kopp and Shaw (2016) found "students with low parental income levels were also more likely to leave in academic jeopardy" (p. 23). Researchers have also studied the experiences of food-insecure (FI) students and students who have been or are homeless (Silva et al., 2017). For example, Silva et al. (2017) found

> those who had been homeless were 13 times more likely to have failed courses and were 11 times more likely to have withdrawn or failed to register for more courses. Students who had experienced severe FI were nearly 15 times more likely to have failed courses and were 6 times more likely to have withdrawn or failed to register for more courses. (pp. 293–294)

While some researchers have noticed academic outcome gaps between poor and working-class students and their more affluent peers (Cabrera et al., 2013; Kopp & Shaw, 2016), it is critical for researchers, practitioners, and policymakers to consider how the effects of classism have led to inequitable collegiate experiences for poor and working-class students (e.g., a financial aid system that leaves poor and working-class students needing to take on student debt to pursue postsecondary education).

First-Generation College Students

First-generation college students and students who are from poor and working-class backgrounds are often conflated in higher education scholarship (Davis, 2010). While first-generation college students are more likely to also be from poor and working-class backgrounds, first-generation college students reflect a distinct student population on college and university campuses (Davis, 2010). First-generation college students had a higher rate of college departure compared to continuing-generation college students (D'Allegro & Kerns, 2010–2011; Kopp & Shaw, 2016; H. Lee & Schneider, 2018; Pratt et al., 2019). While most scholarship from the past decade has contended that first-generation college students are less likely to persist and be retained by colleges and universities (D'Allegro & Kerns, 2010–2011; Kopp & Shaw, 2016; H. Lee & Schneider, 2018; Pratt et al., 2019), some scholars have not found statistically significant differences between first-generation and continuing-generation college students and their first-to-second-year retention, college persistence, and/or graduation (D'Amico & Dika, 2013–2014; Dika, 2014–2015; Gansemer-Topf et al., 2014).

While findings from the past decade are mixed about how being a first-generation college student influences retention, persistence, and graduation, researchers have found first-generation college students experience more academic, social, and financial barriers compared to continuing-generation college students (D'Allegro & Kerns, 2010–2011; D'Amico & Dika, 2013–2014; Kopp & Shaw, 2016; Pratt et al., 2019). First-generation college students were more likely to doubt their academic abilities and expect more academic challenges compared to their continuing-generation peers (Pratt et al., 2019). First-generation college students also earned fewer academic credits in the first semester of college (D'Allegro & Kerns, 2010–2011) and lower first-semester and first-year grade point averages compared to continuing-generation college students (D'Allegro & Kerns, 2010–2011; D'Amico & Dika, 2013–2014). In addition, Kopp and Shaw (2016) found that first-generation college students were more likely to leave college when "in academic jeopardy" compared to continuing-generation college students (p. 23).

First-generation college students had more financial concerns while in college and had a need to maintain employment throughout college compared to continuing-generation college students (Pratt et al., 2019). The need for first-generation students to maintain their employment throughout college may explain some social challenges faced by first-generation college students. First-generation college students had more challenges with social integration at their institutions, finding it more difficult to make new friends compared to continuing-generation college students (Pratt et al., 2019). Students who had a more difficult experience getting involved at their college or university were less likely to persist in college (Pratt et al., 2019). Over the past decade, researchers have provided insights into the financial, social, and academic barriers for first-generation college students, which should be considered and addressed by higher education practitioners, policymakers, and researchers (D'Allegro & Kerns, 2010–2011; D'Amico & Dika, 2013–2014; G. L. Martin, 2015; Kopp & Shaw, 2016; Pratt et al., 2019).

Racially and Ethnically Minoritized and Indigenous Students

While race and ethnicity are often conflated, they are related but different socially constructed concepts (Cokley, 2007; Harris, 2020; Johnston-Guerrero, 2016). According to Johnston-Guerrero (2016), "No consensus has been reached on defining race and ethnicity within the United States—let alone considering global perspectives—complicating conceptions of racial identity and ethnic identity" (p. 44). *Ethnicity* often refers to "a pattern of culture, traditions, customs, and norms unique to, but also shared within, an ethnic community" (Patton et al., 2016, p. 127), and *race* often refers to "a characterization of a group of people believed to share physical characteristics" and has and continues to be an important construct to examine how people "construct their identities in response to an oppressive and highly racialized society" (Cokley, 2007, p. 225). A student, for example, may identify their race as Black and identify their ethnicity as Jamaican American, African American, Brazilian, or Nigerian.

In this chapter, we focus on higher education literature from the past 10 years on the following student populations: Black students, Latinx students, Indigenous students, Asian American, and Pacific Islander students. We recognize the challenges of not discussing college student persistence, retention, and graduation for biracial and multiracial college students, but these identities have not always been acknowledged or discussed in the higher education literature on persistence, retention, and graduation over the past decade. In addition, it is critical to recognize there is not a universal experience for Black, Latinx, Indigenous, Asian American, and Pacific Islander student populations, and there is much diversity across these groups related to ethnicity, language, and even race (Porter, 2020). While some researchers did not find a statistically significant relationship between race and ethnicity and persistence and retention in their studies (e.g., Gansemer-Topf et al., 2014; Windham et al., 2014), numerous researchers have found in their studies that racially and ethnically minoritized students and Indigenous students experience racism on their college and university campuses, which may explain inequities in persistence, retention, and graduation (Bingham & Solverson, 2016; Gloria et al., 2017).

Black Students
Black students at 4-year institutions are likely to experience higher departure rates and more academic challenges compared to White students and other racially minoritized students (Cox et al., 2016; Farruggia et al., 2018). For example, Cox et al. (2016) conducted a study on how noncollege life events (e.g., financial struggles, the death of a family member or friend) affected likelihood of graduation, and they found Black students experiencing noncollege life events were less likely to graduate from college. Black students also had lower grade point averages in the first year compared to White students and other racially and ethnically minoritized student populations (Cabrera et al., 2013; N. D. Martin et al., 2017), but the gaps narrowed as students persisted through college and integrated into their academic major (N. D. Martin et al., 2017). However, Black students "were not only more likely to experience a major change, but also were more likely to change due to academic challenges" (p. 633).

Black students' graduation, persistence, and retention may be related to institutional context (Mooring & Mooring, 2016). For example, Mooring and Mooring (2016) studied degree attainment for racially minoritized community college transfer students and found Black students had a higher likelihood of graduating from nonprofit private institutions and public institutions compared to for-profit institutions. While Flores and Park (2015) did not find a significant relationship between Black students' enrollment at a minority-serving institution and graduation, Nyirenda and Gong (2009–2010) found at one HBCU that White students were less likely to be retained by their institution compared to Black students. Black students at community colleges also have higher departure rates or a higher likelihood of not planning to return to their institution (Hatch & Garcia, 2017; Spangler & Slate, 2015; Wolfle & Williams, 2014). The higher departure rates of Black students may also be a reflection of the campus climate at some predominantly White institutions (Strayhorn, 2013).

Latinx Students
Researchers have found several factors influence college student persistence and retention for Latinx students, including institutional type (e.g., for-profit, public, private, nonprofit; Mooring & Mooring, 2016), attendance at an institution where they are "undermatched" (i.e., when a student attends an institution where their academic profile is stronger than the average at the institution; Kang & García Torres, 2021), and financial aid (Gross et al., 2013; Museus, 2009–2010). For example, Latinx students' access to need-based state aid supported college persistence (Gross et al., 2013), while student loans had a negative effect on degree completion for Latinx students (Museus, 2009–2010). Gershenfeld et al.'s (2016) study on graduation rates for racially minoritized students found Latinx students were less likely to graduate compared to African American students. However, H. Lee and Schneider (2018) found "Hispanic transfer students have a 1.87 times better chance to persist or attain a bachelor's degree than their White counterparts" (p. 87).

While there are conflicting findings about college persistence, retention, and graduation for Latinx students, Gloria et al. (2017) found Latino men experience racism and feelings of loneliness and being academically underprepared. These experiences may contribute to the academic gaps between Latinx students and Asian American and White students (Farruggia et al., 2018; N. D. Martin et al., 2017). Similar to Black students, N. D. Martin et al. (2017) found the "Latino-White GPA gaps were largest during the first college year and narrowed as students selected final majors and settled into campus life" (p. 633). However, Latinx students were more likely to change their major "due to academic challenges" (p. 633).

Indigenous Students
Similar to Lopez (2018), we found the literature on Indigenous students and college student persistence, retention, and graduation to be limited. The existing literature from the past decade has revealed that Indigenous student populations were less likely to persist at their higher education institutions and to have lower first-year grade point averages (Cabrera et al., 2013;

J. Lee et al., 2010–2011). However, academic challenges may be related to challenges concerning experiences with racism and invalidation on college and university campuses and financial difficulties (J. Lee et al., 2010–2011; Motl et al., 2018; Tachine et al., 2017). For example, Motl et al. found that Indigenous students who experienced fair treatment by others at their institution were more likely to persist. Additionally, Indigenous students' persistence, retention, and graduation were supported by personal goals and dreams, family support, and spaces on a college campus (e.g., Native American Student Center; Makomenaw, 2014; Motl et al., 2018; Tachine et al., 2017; Waterman, 2012).

Asian American and Pacific Islander Students

While Asian American and Pacific Islander individuals have the highest college attainment and retention rates across racial groups (Bingham & Solverson, 2016; Cabrera et al., 2013; Lumina Foundation, 2019), researchers, educators, and policymakers often fail to acknowledge the differences in attainment by ethnicity and social class (Museus & Kiang, 2009; Museus & Vue, 2013). The failure to acknowledge and address differences across ethnicity and social class for Asian American and Pacific Islander students perpetuates the model minority myth, the notion that Asian American students "achieve universal and unparalleled academic and occupational success" (Museus & Kiang, 2009, p. 6). For example, the NCES (2020) differentiates Asian and Pacific Islander students when reporting graduation rates from bachelor-awarding institutions, finding approximately 74% of Asian students who began college in 2012 graduated within 6 years and approximately 49% of Pacific Islander students who began college in 2012 graduated within 6 years.

Over the past decade, while the persistence, retention, and graduation rates for Asian American and Pacific Islander students are higher compared to other racially minoritized student populations (Bingham & Solverson, 2016; Cabrera et al., 2013; Lumina Foundation, 2019), researchers have discussed challenges experienced by Asian American and Pacific Islander students related to college student persistence, retention, and graduation (Hatch & Garcia, 2017; Lui, 2013). For example, Hatch and Garcia conducted a study on community college students' persistence intentions at the start of the semester, and they found Asian American and Pacific Islander students were more likely to have plans not to return compared to White and Latinx students. In addition, researchers over the past decade have discussed how Asian American and Pacific Islander students experience cultural shock and challenges with academic and social integration (Lui, 2013; Uehara et al., 2018). For instance, Uehara et al. (2018) found Pacific Islander college students experienced academic challenges (not feeling prepared for higher education) and social challenges (not feeling like they fit in with peers).

Commonalities and Differences Across Racially and Ethnically Minoritized Student Populations

Across racially and ethnically minoritized student populations, structural and systemic conditions were shown to hinder college persistence, retention, and graduation of Black, Latinx, Indigenous, Asian American, and Pacific Islander students. For example, in each of the previous sections, scholars have discussed in their research how unwelcoming campus environments and feelings of not belonging hindered college persistence, retention, and graduation of racially and ethnically minoritized student populations. However, unwelcoming campus environments and feelings of not belonging are not by happenstance and are rooted in how pervasive racism and other forms of oppression are in society, limiting and shaping opportunities in the broader society and on college and university campuses. We will provide further context about structural and systemic conditions in the next section. There are also differences across racially and ethnically minoritized student populations related to grade point averages and rate of college departure. For example, researchers found Black students at community colleges had a higher departure rate (Spangler & Slate, 2015; Wolfle & Williams, 2014). This points to the need for researchers, policymakers, and educators to better understand how historical and current context, policies, and practices and other forms of oppression, such as anti-Black racism, may lead to different experiences and outcomes in college student persistence, retention, and graduation across racially and ethnically minoritized student populations.

Summary of What Is Known From the Past Decade About Sociodemographic Characteristics and College Student Persistence, Retention, and Graduation

In this section, we provide a brief summary of the previous sections on college student persistence, retention, and graduation and economic background and circumstances, first-generation college student status, and racial and ethnic minoritized and Indigenous student populations.

- *Economic background and circumstances.* Research findings varied on whether economic background and circumstances directly impacted college persistence, retention, and graduation. However, researchers have documented how poor and working-class students experienced academic, social, emotional, and financial challenges in higher education that may lead to college departure.

- *First-generation college student status.* Research findings varied on whether being a first-generation college student directly impacted college persistence, retention, and graduation. However, researchers documented how first-generation college students have to navigate more social, academic, and financial barriers compared to their continuing–college generation peers that may lead to college departure.

- *Racial and ethnic minoritized and Indigenous student populations.* In this section, we emphasized the need to recognize the diversity across racial and ethnic minoritized and Indigenous student populations and also within these student populations. The findings across racial and ethnic minoritized and Indigenous students point to how campus environment and institutional context, financial aid, and a sense of belonging do shape student outcomes.

What Is Known About Asset-Based, Intersectional, and Structural Perspectives That Can Disrupt and Transform Practice and Policy?

In this section, we examine the same 113 articles from the past decade to understand how scholars have applied critical perspectives and approaches to study college student persistence, retention, and graduation across sociodemographic characteristics. Critical perspectives and approaches encourage researchers, policymakers, and practitioners to identify and address systemic and structural barriers in higher education that lead to racial and class inequities (Martínez-Alemán et al., 2015). We specifically focus on asset-based, intersectional, and structural perspectives and approaches to scholarship and research on college student persistence, retention, and graduation. While we discuss these approaches (asset-based, intersectional, and structural) separately, we encourage researchers, policymakers, and higher education leaders to consider all three approaches together to examine and address college student persistence, retention, and graduation inequities. As we discuss each approach, we will also offer how each approach could enhance practice, policy, and research in higher education related to sociodemographic characteristics and college student persistence, retention, and graduation.

Asset-Based Approaches: Findings and Implications for Practice, Policy, and Research

Much of higher education scholarship continues to use deficit-oriented perspectives to describe college student retention, persistence, and graduation for poor and working-class students and racially and ethnically minoritized student populations, placing blame on students and their families for educational inequities (Harper, 2012a; Simpfenderfer, 2019; Yosso, 2005). Instead, an asset-based approach seeks to understand the assets, resources, and networks of poor and working-class students and racially and ethnically minoritized students and their families that support their success in educational settings, while recognizing and naming how forms of oppression (e.g., racism, classism) lead to educational inequities (Harper, 2012a; Simpfenderfer, 2019; Yosso, 2005). From the analysis of scholarship on college student persistence, retention, and graduation from the past decade, researchers have framed their studies to better understand the critical assets, resources, and networks of first-generation college students, poor and working-class students, and racially and ethnically minoritized students in the following areas: (a) family, community, and institutional networks; (b) individual determination and goals; and (c) institutional networks.

Challenging deficit-oriented perspectives about the families of first-generation college students, poor and working-class students, and racially and ethnically minoritized students, researchers have identified families as being a critical source of support and encouragement for first-generation college students (Mobley & Brawner, 2019), students from poor and working-class backgrounds (Hlinka, 2017; Roksa & Kinsley, 2019), racially and ethnically minoritized students (Chavez, 2015; Gloria et al., 2017; Palmer et al., 2011; Perez, 2017; Sáenz et al., 2018), and Indigenous students (Makomenaw, 2014; Waterman, 2012). For example, Palmer et al. (2011) found family support and encouragement were critical for the success and achievement of Black men at a historically Black university. First-generation college students, poor and working-class students, and racially and ethnically minoritized students across multiple studies focused on how their success in higher education could positively impact their families and communities (Makomenaw, 2014; Mobley & Brawner, 2019; Pyne & Means, 2013; Uehara et al., 2018). For example, Uehara et al. (2018) did a study on the perceptions of Pacific Islander students in higher education and found students had a goal to support their families by being successful in their educational pathways and careers.

Based on the literature covered, we know first-generation college students, poor and working-class students, and racially and ethnically minoritized students experience racism, classism, and other forms of oppression that can hinder their college persistence, retention, and graduation (e.g., Gloria et al., 2017; Motl et al., 2018; Pyne & Means, 2013; Strayhorn, 2013). Despite these challenges, in addition to encouragement from family and motivation to give back to their families and communities, first-generation college students, poor and working-class students, and racially and ethni-cally minoritized students used resiliency (Chavez, 2015), self-determination and initiative (Chavez, 2015; K. Martin et al., 2014; Mobley & Brawner, 2019; Perez, 2017; Pyne & Means, 2013), coping (Gloria et al., 2017), self-efficacy (Chun et al., 2016), and spirituality and religion (Gloria et al., 2017) to persist through higher education. Minoritized student populations also focus on their goals as a way to persist through higher education (Chavez, 2015; Makomenaw, 2014; K. Martin et al., 2014). For example, Chavez's (2015) study on Hispanic women who spoke English as a second language found they were able to navigate their experiences at a community college by remaining focused on and dedicated to their goals. Practitioners should build upon the critical role of family and students' aspirations and dreams to support their persistence, retention, and graduation in higher education. For example, instead of developing a program for first-generation college stu-dents based on what one believes that they lack, practitioners and practice-focused scholars could first survey students about their current knowledge and learn about their goals and aspirations and use the information to build upon the strengths of first-generation college students.

First-generation college students, poor and working-class students, and racially and ethnically minoritized students across studies also discussed critical networks of faculty and staff (Chavez, 2015; Luedke, 2017; Ocean, 2017; Perez, 2017) and peers (Druery & Brooms, 2019; Mobley & Brawner, 2019; Ocean, 2017; Perez, 2017) who supported their persistence through higher education. For example, Perez (2017) found that the peers of Latino men in college reinforced their goals for the future. Practitioners have an opportunity to build upon the critical networks that support student suc-cess in higher education. For instance, practitioners can consider ways to create and sustain identity-based student organizations and campus offices and centers designed to provide support for students who are minoritized by their economic background and circumstances, first-generation college student status, and race and ethnicity, which could in turn be critical for student persistence, retention, and graduation. Of course, it is not enough for these student organizations and campus offices and centers to exist on college and university campuses. Higher education leaders must find ways to make the focus on advancing racial and class equity and embedding justice on college and university campuses. For instance, implementing diversity/culture audits at the institutional level and the departmental level as a part of 5-year or 10-year review processes could help departments and institutions identify deficit-based approaches and interactions and implement initiatives and programs that affirm Students of Color with the outcome of increasing persistence and retention (McCoy et al., 2017).

Intersectional Approaches: Findings and Implications for Practice, Policy, and Research

Much has been written about how college students have multiple, intersecting identities that must be considered to enhance student learning and development in higher education (e.g., Jones & Abes, 2013). We, as contributors, argue researchers need to also consider students' multiple, intersecting identities to improve college student persistence, retention, and graduation and how these multiple, intersecting identities are connected to multiple, intersecting forms of oppression (i.e., intersectionality; Crenshaw, 1991). From the analysis of scholarship on college student persistence, retention, and graduation from the past decade, researchers have conducted research on the intersection of multiple minoritized social identities (e.g., Students of Color, Indigenous students, poor and working-class students, and/or first-generation college students) as students navigate issues related to college persistence, retention, and graduation (Aguinaga & Gloria, 2015; D'Amico & Dika, 2013–2014; Pyne & Means, 2013; Talusan & Franke, 2019).

A significant amount of scholarship from the past decade examined the intersection of gender and race/ethnicity with a particular focus on Men of Color in higher education, specifically Latino men (Gloria et al., 2017; Perez, 2017; Sáenz et al., 2018) and Black men (Druery & Brooms, 2019; Palmer et al., 2011). There are significant persistence, retention, and graduation challenges for Men of Color in higher education (Gloria et al., 2017; Spruill et al., 2014–2015; Strayhorn, 2013). For example, Spruill et al. (2014–2015) conducted a study on college persistence of men and found Black men were less likely to persist to a degree. In addition, Latino and Black men can experience college and university campuses as lonely and filled with issues related to racism (Druery & Brooms, 2019; Gloria et al., 2017). However, institutional agents, peers, and spaces that encourage, support, and affirm Latino and Black men can enhance educational environments that promote persistence and retention (Druery & Brooms, 2019; Perez, 2017).

While we found fewer published articles on college student persistence, retention, and graduation for Women of Color, we found a few articles from the past decade focused on Latina women (Chavez, 2015; Muñoz, 2013) and Black women (Henry et al., 2011–2012). These researchers have documented how Women of Color experience the intersection of racism and sexism in higher education (Chavez, 2015; Henry et al., 2011–2012). For example, Chavez (2015) found Hispanic women in their study experienced racism and sexism during their educational experiences, but the participants in the study discussed how the classmates who became friends and faculty mentors supported their persistence at their community college. Not only has research focused on Women of Color but also other intersecting identities of Women of Color (Chavez, 2015; Muñoz, 2013). For instance, Muñoz (2013) examined the challenges that Mexican women who are undocumented navigate in response to the systemic denial of financial aid opportunities, xenophobia, and racism they experience as they pursue their degrees.

Practitioners, policymakers, and researchers must consider intersectional approaches to study and address issues related to college student persistence, retention, and graduation. State policymakers and higher education leaders must employ intersectional approaches when enacting programs, services, and policies. For example, research has often highlighted how students who live on college and university campuses during their first year of college are more successful than students who live off campus (e.g., Schudde, 2011). Thus, residence life and housing departments across the United States have instituted live-on policies for first-year students. However, these policies may be an extra burden for poor and working-class students who are also undocumented and do not have access to federal and state financial aid programs. Researchers should consider intersectional approaches to study student persistence, retention, and graduation to better understand how the intersection of multiple forms of oppression leads to college departure for minoritized student populations.

Structural Approaches: Findings and Implications for Practice and Policy

Based on the studies we reviewed, as researchers we identified two primary structural challenges for minoritized students at colleges and universities—finances (Gloria et al., 2017; Muñoz, 2013; Uehara et al., 2018) and unsupportive campus environments (Hlinka, 2017). These studies revealed the challenges minoritized students navigated in their pursuit of a college degree. Yet there are larger or macro-level systems of higher education including institutional context, policies, and practices that support or hinder student persistence and retention.

Urie Bronfrenbrenner's (1981) work described the importance of the ecological system on individual behavior and agency. Bronfrenbrenner posited "the ecological system as extending far beyond the immediate situation directly affecting the developing person" (p. 7). Bronfrenbrenner's (1981) ecological systems model contains four components: the microsystem, mesosystem, exosystem, and macrosystem. The microsystem consists of the individual's close networks (i.e., family, school, work, and peer groups). The mesosystem level consists of the interaction between two or more microsystems, and the exosystem considers the impact of the local environment and shared networks and services on the individual. For the purposes of this section, we focused on the macrosystem level, or the shared customs, values, beliefs, and laws shaping marginalized students' ability to effectively navigate and persist in higher education.

The cost of college is a recurring issue for students. While support for higher education grew slightly, the price of college has increased rapidly while household incomes did not and subsequent increases in federal grants and institutional grant aid were not enough to cover college costs (College Board, 2019). Scholars have noted the challenges undocumented students face in pursuing and completing their college degree due to their immigration status or the immigration status of their family members (Muñoz, 2013; Pyne & Means, 2013). Undocumented students do not have access to federal and state financial aid and consequently have to pay full tuition costs. The uncertainty of federal government support for the Deferred Action for Childhood Arrivals program leaves undocumented students fearful of deportation due to their immigration status. Silva et al. (2017) found homeless and food-insecure students either withdrew from classes or failed classes at higher rates than their peers. Additionally, student activities, study abroad opportunities, and leadership opportunities come with costs low-income students may not be able to afford. Students of Color and poor and working-class students experience unwelcoming campus climates, limiting their ability to not only navigate but persist in higher education (Gloria et al., 2017; Soria et al., 2013–2014).

Local community programs do support minoritized students with grant aid and helping with food insecurity. Using validation theory as a framework, Baber (2018) studied underrepresented students in the One Million Degrees (OMD) program in Chicago, Illinois. The OMD program provided academic support and resources for students in 2-year colleges in the Chicago area. The OMD program also offered tuition assistance and a $500 stipend per semester for academic expenses. OMD alumni reported the attentive relationships from the staff in the program validated their identities and provided them with a sense of belonging and place in their respective college environments (Baber, 2018). Although community-based partnerships, such as the OMD program, may not be possible in every local community where 2-year and 4-year institutions exist, these programs provide validation for minoritized students in addition to financial support. Mendez et al.'s (2011) study revealed the importance of federal financial aid policies and state aid policies for Native American students through federal Pell Grants and the Oklahoma Promise Grant.

Food pantries have also emerged to help students secure their basic needs. According to statistics published on the College and University Food Bank Alliance (CUFBA, n.d.) website, 30% of college students are food insecure, 56% of food-insecure students are working, and 75% of food-insecure students have financial aid. Studying the effects campus food pantries have for food-insecure students is another avenue for action-oriented research that could contribute to persistence. Also, auditing campus activities in terms of fees and costs or sociodemographic characteristics of those participating and not participating in fee-based activities could be a beginning point for discussions on equity related to involvement opportunities (McClure & Ryder, 2017).

Closing Thoughts

In this chapter, we examined higher education literature over the past decade on college student persistence, retention, and graduation across the following sociodemographic characteristics: economic background and circumstance; first-generation college student status; and race, ethnicity, and Indigenous student identity. We then examined the higher education literature over the past decade, providing asset-based, intersectional, and structural approaches and insights into college student persistence, retention, and graduation across sociodemographic characteristics, offering implications for practice and policy. Overall, there are a few main areas in which colleges and university administrators can address persistence and retention on college campuses. Campus culture and equity audits should be conducted to identify and remove structural barriers to persistence for minoritized students. Additionally, implementing asset-based approaches to retention programs and initiatives aids in persistence and retention. Lastly, the costs of college and food insecurity should be addressed through local, state, and federal initiatives and approaches. We hope our chapter serves as a continued call to researchers, policymakers, and higher education leaders to examine and address college student persistence, retention, and graduation through asset-based, intersectional, and structural approaches.

References

Aguinaga, A., & Gloria, A. M. (2015). The effects of generational status and university environment on Latina/o undergraduates' persistence decisions. *Journal of Diversity in Higher Education, 8*(1), 15–29. http://dx.doi.org/10.1037/a0038465

Baber, L. D. (2018). "Living in the along": Validating experiences among urban community college students in a college transition program. *Community College Review, 46*(3), 316–340. https://doi.org/10.1177/009155211877

Bingham, M. A., & Solverson, N. W. (2016). Using enrollment data to predict retention rate. *Journal of Student Affairs Research and Practice, 53*(1), 51–64. https://doi.org/10.1080/19496591.2016.1110035

Bronfrenbrenner, U. (1981). *The ecology of human development: Experiments by nature and design.* Harvard University Press.

Cabrera, N. L., Miner, D. D., & Milem, J. F. (2013). Can a summer bridge program impact first-year persistence and performance?: A case study of the new start summer program. *Research in Higher Education, 54*(4), 481–498. https://doi .org/10.1007/s11162-013-9286-7

Chavez, M. A. (2015). Community college journeys of Hispanic ESL women. *Community College Journal of Research and Practice, 39*(3), 207–221. https://doi .org/10.1080/10668926.2013.795506

Chun, H., Marin, M. R., Schwartz, J. P., Pham, A., & Castro-Olivo, S. M. (2016). Psychosociocultural structural model of college success among Latino/a students in Hispanic-Serving Institutions. *Journal of Diversity in Higher Education, 9*(4), 385–400. https://doi.org/10.1037/a0039881

Cokley, K. (2007). Critical issues in the measurement of ethnic and racial identity: A referendum on the state of the field. *Journal of Counseling Psychology, 54*(3), 224–234. https://doi.org/10.1037/0022-0167.54.3.224

College and University Food Bank Alliance. (n.d.). *Resources.* https://cufba.org/ resources/

College Board. (2019). *Trends in college pricing.*

Cox, B. E., Reason, R. D., Nix, S., & Gillman, M. (2016). Life happens (outside of college): Non-college life-events and students' likelihood of graduation. *Research in Higher Education, 57*(7), 823–844. https://doi.org/10.1007/s11162-016-9409-z

Crenshaw, K. (1991). Mapping the margins: Intersectionality, identity politics, and violence against women. *Stanford Law Review, 43*(6), 1241–1299.

D'Allegro, M. L., & Kerns, S. (2010–2011). Is there such a thing as too much of a good thing when it comes to education? Reexamining first generation student success. *Journal of College Student Retention: Research, Theory & Practice, 12*(3), 293–317. https://doi.org/10.2190/CS.12.3.c

D'Amico, M. M., & Dika, S. L. (2013–2014). Using data known at the time of admission to predict first-generation college student success. *Journal of College Student Retention: Research, Theory & Practice, 15*(2), 173–192. https://doi .org/10.2190/CS.15.2.c

Davidson, J. C. (2015). Examining zero expected family contribution as a new criterion for "low income": Comparing the impact on student persistence at two- and four-year institutions. *Community College Journal of Research and Practice, 39*(5), 442–460. https://doi.org/10.1080/10668926.2013.837414

Davis, J. (2010). *The first-generation student experience: Implications for campus practice, and strategies for improving persistence and success.* Stylus.

Dika, S. L. (2014–2015). The role of socioeconomic factors in the prediction of persistence in Puerto Rico. *Journal of College Student Retention: Research, Theory & Practice, 16*(1), 111–125. https://doi.org/10.2190/CS.16.1.f

Druery, J. E., & Brooms, D. R. (2019). "It lit up the campus": Engaging Black males in culturally enriching environments. *Journal of Diversity in Higher Education, 12*(4), 330–340. http://dx.doi.org/10.1037/dhe0000087

Farruggia, S. P., Han, C-w., Watson, L., Moss, T. P., & Bottoms, B. L. (2018). Noncognitive factors and college student success. *Journal of College Student Retention, Theory & Practice, 20*(3), 308–327. https://doi.org/10.1177/1521025116666539

Flores, S. M., & Park, T. J. (2015). The effect of enrolling in a minority-serving institution for Black and Hispanic students in Texas. *Research in Higher Education, 56*(3), 247–276. https://doi.org/10.1007/s11162-014-9342-y

Gansemer-Topf, A. M., Zhang, Y., Beatty, C. C., & Paja, S. (2014). Examining factors influencing attrition at a small, private, selective liberal arts college. *Journal of Student Affairs Research & Practice, 51*(3), 270–285. https://doi.org/10.1515/jsarp-2014-0028

Garvey, J. C. (2020). Queer and trans college student retention [Special issue]. *Journal of College Student Retention: Research, Theory & Practice, 21*(4).

Gershenfeld, S., Hood, D. W., & Zhan, M. (2016). The role of first-semester GPA in predicting graduation rates of underrepresented students. *Journal of College Student Retention: Research, Theory & Practice, 17*(4), 469–488. https://doi.org/10.1177/1521025115579251

Gloria, A. M., Castellanos, J., Delgado-Guerrero, M., Salazar, A. C., Nieves, C. M., Mejia, A., & Martinez, V. L. (2017). El ojo en la meta: Latino male undergraduates' coping processes. *Journal of Diversity in Higher Education, 10*(1), 11–24. http://dx.doi.org/10.1037/a0040216

Gross, J. P. K., Torres, V., & Zerquera, D. (2013). Financial aid and attainment among students in a state with changing demographics. *Research in Higher Education, 54*(4), 383–406. https://doi.org/10.1007/s11162-012-9276-1

Harper, S. R. (2012a). *Black male student success in higher education: A report from the National Black Male College Achievement Study.* University of Pennsylvania, Center for the Study of Race and Equity in Education.

Harper, S. R. (2012b). Race without racism: How higher education researchers minimize racist institutional norms. *Review of Higher Education, 36*(1), 9–29. https://doi.org/10.1353/rhe.2012.0047

Harris, J. C. (2020). Ethnicity, acculturation, and student development. In J. C. Garvey, J. C. Harris, D. R. Means, R. J. Perez, & C. J. Porter (Eds.), *Case studies for student development theory: Advancing social justice and inclusion in higher education* (pp. 39–41). Routledge.

Harris, J. C., & Patton, L. D. (2019). Un/doing intersectionality through higher education research. *Journal of Higher Education, 90*(3), 347–372. https://doi.org/10.1080/00221546.2018.1536936

Hatch, D. K., & Garcia, C. E. (2017). Academic advising and the persistence intentions of community college students in their first weeks in college. *Review of Higher Education, 40*(3), 353–390. https://doi.org/10.1353/rhe.2017.0012

Henry, W. J., Butler, D. M., & West, N. M. (2011–2012). Things are not as rosy as they seem: Psychosocial issues of contemporary Black college women. *Journal of College Student Retention: Research, Theory & Practice, 13*(2), 137–153. https://doi.org/10.2190/CS.13.2.a

Hlinka, K. R. (2017). Tailoring retention theories to meet the needs of rural Appalachian community college students. *Community College Review, 45*(2), 144–164. https://doi.org/10.1177/0091552116686403

Johnston-Guerrero, M. P. (2016). Embracing the messiness: Critical and diverse perspectives on racial and ethnic identity development. In E. S. Abes (Ed.), *Critical Perspectives on Student Development Theory* (New Directions for Student Services, no. 154, pp. 43–55). Jossey-Bass.

Jones, S. R., & Abes, E. S. (2013). *Identity development of college students: Advancing frameworks for multiple dimensions of identity.* Jossey-Bass.

Kang, C., & García Torres, D. (2021). College undermatching, bachelor's degree attainment, and minority students. *Journal of Diversity in Higher Education, 14*(2), 264–277. http://dx.doi.org/10.1037/dhe0000145

Kim, J. (2015). Predictors of college retention and performance between regular and special admissions. *Journal of Student Affairs Research & Practice, 52*(1), 50–63. https://doi.org/10.1080/19496591.2015.995575

Kopp, J. P., & Shaw, E. J. (2016). How final is leaving college while in academic jeopardy? Examining the utility of differentiating college leavers by academic standing. *Journal of College Student Retention: Research, Theory & Practice, 18*(1), 2–30. https://doi.org/10.1177/1521025115579670

Lee, H., & Schneider, T. (2018). Does posttransfer involvement matter for persistence of community college transfer students? *Community College Journal of Research and Practice, 42*(2), 77–94. https://doi.org/10.1080/10668926.2016.1251351

Lee, J., Donlan, W., & Brown, E. F. (2010–2011). American Indian/Alaskan Native undergraduate retention at predominantly White institutions: An elaboration of Tinto's theory of college student departure. *Journal of College Student Retention: Research, Theory & Practice, 12*(3), 257–276.

Lopez, J. D. (2018). Factors influencing American Indian and Alaska Native postsecondary persistence: AI/AN Millennium Falcon persistence model. *Research in Higher Education, 59*(6), 792–811. https://doi.org/10.1007/s11162-017-9487-6

Luedke, C. L. (2017). Person first, student second: Staff and administrators of color supporting students of color authentically in higher education. *Journal of College Student Development, 58*(1), 37–52. https://doi:10.1353/csd.2017.0002

Lui, J. (2013). Grades of the not so modeled: Asian American and Pacific Islander transfer students at middle university. *Community College Journal of Research and Practice, 37*(3), 205–215. https://doi.org/10.1080/10668926.2013.740385

Lumina Foundation. (2019). *A stronger nation: Learning beyond high school builds American talent.* https://www.luminafoundation.org/stronger-nation/report/2020/#nation

Makomenaw, M. (2014). Goals, family, and community: What drives tribal college transfer student success. *Journal of Student Affairs Research & Practice, 51*(4), 380–391. https://doi.org/10.1515/jsarp-2014-0039

Martin, G. L. (2015). "Tightly wound rubber bands": Exploring the college experiences of low-income, first-generation White students. *Journal of Student Affairs Research and Practice, 52*(3), 275–286. https://doi.org/10.1080/19496591.2015.1035384

Martin, K., Galentino, R., & Townsend, L. (2014). Community college student success: The role of motivation and self-empowerment. *Community College Review, 42*(3), 221–241. https://doi.org/10.1177/0091552114528972

Martin, N. D., Spenner, K. I., & Mustillo, S. (2017). A test of leading explanations for the college racial-ethnic achievement gap: Evidence from a longitudinal case study. *Research in Higher Education, 58*(6), 617–645. https://doi.org/10.1007/s11162-016-9439-6

Martínez-Alemán, A. M., Pusser, B., & Bensimon, E. M. (2015). Introduction. In A. M Martínez-Alemán, B. Pusser, & E. M. Bensimon (Eds.), *Critical approaches to the study of higher education: A practical introduction* (pp. 1–6). Johns Hopkins University Press.

McClure, K., & Ryder, A. J. (2017). The costs of belonging: How spending money influences social relationships in college. *Journal of Student Affairs Research and Practice, 55*(2), 196–209. https://doi.org/10.1080/19496591.2017.1360190

McCoy, D. L., Luedke, C. L., & Winkle-Wagner, R. (2017). Encouraged or weeded out: Perspectives of students of color in the STEM disciplines on faculty interactions. *Journal of College Student Development, 58*(5), 657–673. https://doi.org/10.1353/csd.2017.0052

Mendez, J. P., Mendoza, P., & Malcolm, Z. (2011). The impact of financial aid on Native American students. *Journal of Diversity in Higher Education, 4*(1), 12–25. https://doi.org/10.1037/a0021202

Mendoza, P., & Mendez, J. P. (2012–2013). The Oklahoma's Promise program: A national model to promote college persistence. *Journal of College Student Retention: Research, Theory & Practice, 14*(3), 397–421.

Mobley, C., & Brawner, C. E. (2019). "Life prepared me well for succeeding": The enactment of community cultural wealth, experiential capital, and transfer student capital by first-generation engineering transfer students. *Community College Journal of Research and Practice, 43*(5), 353–369. https://doi.org/10.1080/10668926.2018.1484823

Mooring, R. D., & Mooring, S. R. (2016). Predictors of timely baccalaureate attainment for underrepresented minority community college transfer students. *Community College Journal of Research and Practice, 40*(8), 681–694. https://doi.org/10.1080/10668926.2015.1070775

Motl, T. C., Multon, K. D., & Zhao, F. (2018). Persistence at a tribal university: Factors associated with second year enrollment. *Journal of Diversity in Higher Education, 11*(1), 51–66. http://dx.doi.org/10.1037/dhe0000034

Muñoz, S. M. (2013). "I just can't stand being like this anymore": Dilemmas, stressors, and motivators for undocumented Mexican women in higher education. *Journal of Student Affairs Research & Practice, 50*(3), 233–249. https://doi .org/10.1515/jsarp-2013-0018

Museus, S. D. (2009–2010). Understanding racial differences in the effects of loans on degree attainment: A path analysis. *Journal of College Student Retention: Research, Theory & Practice, 11*(4), 499–527. https://doi.org/10.2190/CS.11.4.d

Museus, S. D., & Kiang, P. N. (2009). Deconstructing the model minority myth and how it contributes to the invisible minority reality in higher education research. In S. Museus (Ed.), *Conducting Research on Asian Americans in Higher Education* (New Directions for Institutional Research, no. 142, pp. 5–15). Wiley.

Museus, S. D., & Vue, R. (2013). Socioeconomic status and Asian American and Pacific Islander students' transition to college: A structural equation modeling analysis. *Review of Higher Education, 37*(1), 45–76. http://dx.doi.org/10.1353/ rhe.2013.0069

National Center for Education Statistics. (2020). *Undergraduate retention and graduation rates.* https://nces.ed.gov/programs/coe/indicator_ctr.asp

Newton, B. C., Ghee, K. L., & Langmeyer, D. (2013–2014). Correlates of African-American undergraduate student achievement: Implications for the prize initiative. *Journal of College Student Retention: Research, Theory & Practice, 15*(4), 605–631. https://doi.org/10.2190/CS.15.4.g

Nyirenda, S. M., & Gong, T. (2009–2010). The squishy and stubborn problem of retention: A study of a mid-Atlantic historically Black institution with a land-grant mission. *Journal of College Student Retention: Research, Theory & Practice, 11*(4), 529–550. https://doi.org/10.2190/CS.11.4.e

Ocean, M. (2017). Financially eligible Pell Grant community college students' perceptions of institutional integration. *Journal of College Student Retention: Research, Theory & Practice, 19*(3), 333–356. https://doi.org/10.1177/1521025116630757

Palmer, R. T., Davis, R. J., & Maramba, D. C. (2011). The impact of family support on the success of Black men at an Historically Black University: Affirming the revision of Tinto's theory. *Journal of College Student Development, 52*(5), 577–597. http://dx.doi.org/10.1353/csd.2011.0066

Patton, L. D., Renn, K. A., Guido, F. M., & Quaye, S. J. (2016). *Student development in college: Theory, research, and practice* (3rd ed.). Wiley.

Perez, D., II. (2017). In pursuit of success: Latino male college students exercising academic determination and community cultural wealth. *Journal of College Student Development, 58*(2), 123–140. https://doi.org/10.1353/csd.2017.0011

Porter, C. J. (2020). Students' racial identity development. In J. C. Garvey, J. C. Harris, D. R. Means, R. J. Perez, & C. J. Porter (Eds.), *Case studies for student development theory: Advancing social justice and inclusion in higher education* (pp. 23–26). Routledge.

Pratt, I. S., Harwood, H. B., Cavazos, J. T., & Ditzfeld, C. P. (2019). Should I stay or should I go? Retention in first-generation college students. *Journal of College Student Retention: Research, Theory & Practice, 21*(1), 105–118. https://doi .org/10.1177/1521025117690868

Pyne, K. B., & Means, D. R. (2013). Underrepresented and in/visible: A Hispanic first-generation student's narratives of college. *Journal of Diversity in Higher Education, 6*(3), 186–198. https://doi.org/10.1037/a0034115

Reason, R. D. (2009). An examination of persistence research through the lens of a comprehensive conceptual framework. *Journal of College Student Development, 50*(6), 659–682. https://doi.org/10.1353/csd.0.0098

Roksa, J., & Kinsley, P. (2019). The role of family support in facilitating academic success of low-income students. *Research in Higher Education, 60*(4), 415–436. https://doi.org/10.1007/s11162-018-9517-z

Sáenz, V. B., García-Louis, C., Drake, A. P., & Guida, T. (2018). Leveraging their family capital: How Latino males successfully navigate the community college. *Community College Review, 46*(1), 40–61. https://doi.org/10.1177/0091552117743567

Schudde, L. T. (2011). The casual effect of campus residency on college student retention. *Review of Higher Education, 34*(4), 581–610. http://dx.doi.org/10.1353/rhe.2011.0023

Shamsuddin, S. (2016). Berkeley or bust? Estimating the causal effect of college selectivity on bachelor's degree completion. *Research in Higher Education, 57*(7), 795–822. https://doi.org/10.1007/s11162-016-9408-0

Silva, M. R., Kleinert, W .L., Sheppard, A. V., Cantrell, K. A., Freeman-Coppadge, D. J., Tsoy, E., Roberts, T., & Pearrow, M. (2017). The relationship between food security, housing stability, and school performance among college students in an urban university. *Journal of College Student Retention: Research, Theory & Practice, 19*(3), 284–299. https://doi.org/10.1177/1521025115621918

Simpfenderfer, A. J. D. (2019). Higher education: Path or barrier to opportunity? *Journal of Critical Scholarship on Higher Education and Student Affairs, 5*(2), 23–38.

Soria, K. M., Stebleton, M. J., & Huesman, R. L., Jr. (2013–2014). Class counts: Exploring differences in academic and social integration between working-class and middle/upper-class students at large, public research universities. *Journal of College Student Retention: Research, Theory & Practice, 15*(2), 215–242. https://doi.org/10.2190/CS.15.2.e

Spangler, J. M., & Slate, J. R. (2015). Texas community college graduation and persistence rates as a function of student ethnicity. *Community College Journal of Research and Practice, 39*(8), 741–753. https://doi.org/10.1080/10668926.2013.878261

Spruill, N., Hirt, J., & Mo, Y. (2014–2015). Predicting persistence to degree of male college students. *Journal of College Student Retention: Research, Theory & Practice, 16*(1), 25–48. https://doi.org/10.2190/CS.16.1.b

Strayhorn, T. L. (2013). Measuring race and gender differences in undergraduate students' perceptions of campus climate and intentions to leave college: An analysis in black and white. *Journal of Student Affairs Research and Practice, 50*(2), 115–132. https://doi.org/10.1515/jsarp-2013-0010

Tachine, A. R., Cabrera, N. L., & Yellow Bird, E. (2017). Home away from home: Native American students' sense of belonging during their first year in college. *The Journal of Higher Education, 88*(5), 785–807. https://doi.org/10.1080/00221546.2016.1257322

Talusan, L., & Franke, R. (2019). (Un)fulfilling requirements: Satisfactory academic progress and its impact on first-generation, low-income, Asian American students. *Journal of Critical Scholarship on Higher Education and Student Affairs*, 5(1), 15–28.

Teranishi, R. T., & Bezbatchenko, A. W. (2015). A critical examination of the college completion agenda: Advancing equity in higher education. In A. M. Martínez-Alemán, B. Pusser, & E. M. Bensimon (Eds.), *Critical approaches to the study of higher education: A practical introduction* (pp. 241–256). Johns Hopkins University Press.

Uehara, D. L., Chugen, J., & Staley Raatior, V. (2018). Perceptions of Pacific Islander students in higher education. *Journal of Diversity in Higher Education*, 11(2), 182–191. http://dx.doi.org/10.1037/dhe0000057

Waterman, S. (2012). Home-going as a strategy for success among Haudenosaunee college and university students. *Journal of Student Affairs Research and Practice*, 49(2), 193–209. https://doi.org/10.1515/jsarp-2012-6378

Windham, M. H., Rehfuss, M. C., Williams, C. R., Pugh, J. V., & Tincher-Ladner, L. (2014). Retention of first-year community college students. *Community College Journal of Research and Practice*, 38(5), 466–477. https://doi.org/10.1080/10668926.2012.743867

Wirt, L. G., & Jaeger, A. J. (2014). Seeking to understand faculty-student interaction at community colleges. *Community College Journal of Research and Practice*, 38(11), 980–994. https://doi.org/10.1080/10668926.2012.725388

Wolfle, J. D., & Williams, M. R. (2014). The impact of developmental mathematics courses and age, gender, and race and ethnicity on persistence and academic performance in Virginia community colleges. *Community College Journal of Research and Practice*, 38(2–3), 144–153. https://doi.org/10.1080/10668926.2014.851956

Yosso, T. J. (2005). Whose culture has capital? A critical race theory discussion of community cultural wealth. *Race Ethnicity and Education*, 8(1), 69–91. https://doi.org/10.1080/1361332052000341006

ORGANIZATIONAL BEHAVIOR AND STUDENT PERSISTENCE IN COLLEGE

Maria Javiera de los Ríos and Leticia Oseguera

For the United States, it has been challenging to increase the share of college graduates. While the number of the population enrolling in college has increased, the proportion of students graduating has not increased and in some years, it has even declined slightly (Carey, 2004; Shapiro et al., 2016). Sixty percent of first-time, full-time students at U.S. 4-year colleges complete their degree within 6 years (Bound et al., 2010; Shapiro et al., 2016), and only about 30% of those who enter a 2-year program as full-time students graduate within 5 years (Shapiro et al., 2016). Nationally, only 49% of 25- through 34-year-olds hold an associate or bachelor's degree (Organisation for Economic Co-Operation and Development [OECD], 2019). Organizational behavior's role in these student completion rates is the focus of this chapter.

Specifically, this chapter focuses on how actors in higher education organizations behave while serving organizational interests and connects organizational behavior to student persistence in college. Organizational behavior encompasses the "actions of organizational agents (faculty, administrators, and staff) at a college or university" (Berger, 2001, p. 4) that contribute to (or thwart) successful degree completion. We open with a description of how organizational behavior was missing from early retention theory and move to what changes have occurred since early retention theories and calls for attention to organization behavior concerns were raised.

This chapter also includes recent literature about the effects of organizational behavior framings on practices that have been linked to student persistence utilizing Berger's (2001) summary of five organizational frames and their relationship to undergraduate student persistence within higher education. The often overlooked characteristics embedded within an organizational behavior framing shape student outcomes in more subtle or indirect ways than other factors that affect these outcomes more directly (i.e., peer environments and student demographic characteristics and school background; Lambert et al., 2006). For this reason, we also incorporate literature that indirectly links organizational behavior framings to student persistence. Finally, the chapter will summarize existing multidimensional organizational frameworks that can be adopted to promote student success. Special attention will be paid to multidimensional frameworks that center diversity and inclusion as key components of comprehensive organizational change strategies for student success.

Early Retention Theory—Missing Organizational Behavior

Understanding which factors can explain college students' retention and departure decisions has been the object of academic research for more than 90 years (Braxton, 2000), and its major theoretical development took place in the late 1970s.[1] Since then, the theoretical framework that dominated the empirical research on retention was Tinto's (1975) interactionalist theory of college student departure (Braxton et al., 2011). Tinto (1975) proposed a Durkheimian model for studying dropout. According to Tinto, the conditions for a person's social integration proposed by Durkheim (2005), normative congruence and collective affiliation, are the connecting points between suicide and student dropout. Although dropping out is undoubtedly a less radical form of rejecting social life than suicide, the elements affecting the former are analogous to those producing the latter. Tinto (1975, 1993) also incorporated relevant concepts from Van Gennep's (1960) theory of the rites of passage in his theoretical framework. In his study of tribal societies, Van Gennep (1960) described three stages of a successful ritual transition process: separation, transition, and incorporation. According to Tinto (1993), these three stages explain "the longitudinal process of student persistence in college" (p. 94). In the first stage, students have to detach themselves from their communities of origin. Then, in the second stage of transition, students

---

[1] In this section of the chapter, we use the terms *retention* and *dropout* instead of *persistence* and *degree completion* to highlight how early work in this field framed the persistence issue negatively. The traditional use of the term *dropout* shows how early retention researchers focused on what made students leave college instead of focusing on what makes them stay. In the remaining sections of the paper, we go back to using the terms *persistence* and *degree completion* to highlight that our work uses an asset frame to understand what makes students persist toward degree completion.

have to accept the cultural norms and behaviors of the new community, and finally, in the third stage, after detaching themselves from the culture of their previous communities, students become fully integrated into the academic and social college system. Therefore, according to Tinto (1993), students who fail to "physically as well as socially dissociate from the communities of the past" (p. 96) and who are not integrated into the academic and social culture of their campuses are more likely to drop out.

Despite Tinto's (1975, 1993) relevance in systematizing the study of dropout in the United States by understanding this issue through a theoretical model that enhanced future researchers' study of it, his focus on how the entry characteristics, integration, and subsequent commitments of students affect the likelihood of persistence in college overlooked how other factors also influence student persistence decisions. The paradigmatic status of Tinto's initial theory explains, in part, that much of the research on college persistence has focused primarily on a subset of students' characteristics, traits, and college experiences. However, by the second half of the 1980s, Tinto (1986) himself altered his initial departure theory. In *Theories of Student Departure Revisited*, Tinto (1986) acknowledged that one of the limitations of his early departure theory was its failure to take explicit account of the formal organizational forces that also impact students' departure decisions. Echoing these amendments, other higher education researchers, like Berger (2001) and Berger and Milem (2000), reacted to the limitations of Tinto's (1975, 1993) early theory and the research using it by proposing new ways to address dropout that included previously unobserved factors, such as the institution's organizational behavior.

Berger (2001) posited that the mainstream organizational behavior literature in higher education did not focus on "how organizational behavior at colleges affects students, and even fewer [researchers] investigated the effects of organizational behavior on student persistence" (p. 5), a limitation still not entirely overcome. Twenty years after Berger's publication, it is still pressing to deepen and broaden our understanding of the relationship of organizational behavior to student persistence as an institution's organizational behavior, unlike strategies that target specific student populations or programs, can have consequences on the entire student population (Berger, 2001).

Berger and Milem's Conceptual Model of Organizational Impact on Student Outcomes

Berger (2000, 2001) and Berger and Milem's (2000) foundational work describing the relationship between organizational behavior and student outcomes acknowledges that the latter are determined by multiple factors. Some of these factors, like students' precollege characteristics, student experiences (behavioral and perceptual), and peer group characteristics, have a direct effect on students' outcomes. On the other hand, factors like the organizational environment, which is composed of the structural/demographic characteristics of the campus and the organizational behavior of the institution, have indirect effects on students' outcomes, because their effects are mediated by the students' experiences and their peer group characteristics.

The authors define colleges and universities' *organizational behavior* as a multidimensional construct composed of five core dimensions: bureaucratic, collegial, political, symbolic, and systemic. The bureaucratic dimension emphasizes rational goals and adherence to rules and is driven by formal structures such as regulations, hierarchy, and institutional goals. The collegial dimension captures the alignment between the interests of the organization and the individuals within it, and thus this dimension emphasizes collaboration and consensus to establish goals and make decisions. The political dimension refers to the competition for limited resources among various groups within the institution. The symbolic dimension focuses on the role of symbols (e.g., stories, ceremonies, traditions) in creating meaning. Finally, the systemic dimension acknowledges the university as an open system that interacts with other systems in the external environment. All colleges and universities exhibit aspects of all dimensions to some extent, but the strengths that each of these five dimensions exhibit vary among different campuses.

Along with defining these core concepts, Berger (2000, 2001) and Berger and Milem (2000) described the ways in which the organizational environment at a college or university impacts both students' psychological and behavioral outcomes and explained that organizational behavior refers to how the actions of organizational agents (faculty, administrators, and staff) are congruent with the dominant organizational behavior dimension. So, organizational environments that are dominated by one of the organizational dimensions exert effects on students' outcomes that are also congruent with that dominant dimension.

Review of Empirical Studies

While some scholars have embraced the ideas of Berger (2001) and Berger and Milem (2000), agreeing that their work changed the agenda regarding the study of persistence by introducing the organizational dimension of the university into the equation (Oseguera & Rhee, 2009; Ro et al., 2013; Tinto, 2010), others have criticized Berger's (2001) and Berger and Milem's (2000) work due to its inclusion of components that are too abstract to effectively guide policymakers in developing change strategies (Lambert et al., 2006; Ro et al., 2013). While the works of Berger (2001) and Berger and Milem

(2000) have been scarcely cited since their publication 2 decades ago (Kim et al., 2020; Miller, 2019; Nuñez, 2009; Ro et al., 2013; Zhou & Okahana, 2019), shaping little of the current conversation around the study of student persistence, there is a small body of literature that provides direct and indirect empirical evidence regarding the effects of organizational behavior on student persistence. These studies are reviewed in the following paragraphs and are organized further along the five organizational frames.

The Effects Of Bureaucratic Organizational Behavior On Persistence

According to Berger (2001), the *bureaucratic* mechanisms of an organization are its rules, regulations, policies, chain of command, and formal procedures. Therefore, bureaucracy within colleges/universities provides identifiable goals and expectations to its members, and it also provides the framework that formally defines what the fair and just procedures are within the organization. According to Berger's (2001) review of research, in the literature there is less clarity about the effects of bureaucratic organizational behavior on student persistence than about the effects of the other four types of organizational behavior.

Berger (2001) explained that, generally, students consider that dealing with the bureaucratic mechanisms is an expected part of being a college student. However, as Berger explained, if the bureaucratic mechanisms create a problem for students or do not work properly, then the institution's bureaucracy can have a negative impact on student persistence. High levels of bureaucracy tend to depersonalize the college experience, reducing students' opportunities of having meaningful contact with faculty and administrators. This reduction in opportunities for connecting in turn decreases the social and academic integration of students, which decreases their likelihood of persisting in college.

In his revision of literature that studies how bureaucracy affects persistence, Berger (2001) found limited agreement among researchers. This lack of agreement is presumably due to the curvilinear nature of the relationship between levels of bureaucratic behavior on campus and student persistence. Berger (2001) posited that "while some level of bureaucratic organizational behavior appears to be necessary for student persistence, it appears that more is not always better" (p. 12).

Over the last 20 years, except for some investigations (Gansemer-Topf & Schuh, 2006), few scholars have researched the effect of university bureaucratic behavior on persistence. The Gansemer-Topf and Schuh (2006) study of college money allocation provides partial evidence supporting Berger and Milem's (2000) claims. In this research, which assumed that adding more resources for institutional support increases the bureaucratic dimension of the university, the researchers found that increasing these types of expenditures in universities does little to improve graduation rates. The study concludes that creating another faculty position, rather than adding more administrative personnel, may be more effective in enhancing student persistence.

While organizational behavior researchers have not focused on the impact of bureaucratic behavior on persistence, scholars studying first-generation, undocumented, and community college students' persistence have provided meaningful insights about this topic. For instance, the research about community college students' persistence suggests that the lack of bureaucratic structure in community colleges negatively impacts students' intentions to persist toward obtaining a credential. On the other hand, in highly bureaucratized programs with relatively little room for individuals to deviate, community college students are more likely to persist (Scott-Clayton, 2011). However, similarly to what happens with the 4-year programs, bureaucratic obstacles for community college students also prevent them from persisting (Scott-Clayton, 2011). While these results apply for community college students in general, when researchers studied persistence in diverse subpopulations of community college students, they found that Hispanic students often lack the know-how skills to navigate the bureaucracy of the community college system, which in turn reduces their odds of persisting (Deil-Amen & Rosenbaum, 2003; Zell, 2010). According to the community college literature, advisors can become key actors in helping students navigate some of the bureaucratic difficulties they may encounter within the community college environment (Cuseo, 2004). Despite this, Mozella Garcia's (2010) qualitative work interviewing community college staff revealed that most of the interviewees were barely aware of the difficulties faced by those students without the social expertise that is needed to navigate community colleges' bureaucratic mechanisms.

Research on first-generation college students' persistence has also considered how bureaucratic mechanisms relate to persistence. Regardless of the institution type, large higher education institutions tend to have a complex system of bureaucratic requirements, which tends to depersonalize the student experience. First-generation students attending large institutions do not get the individual attention they need to overcome their lack of familiarity with the college experience (Darling & Smith, 2007). First-generation students tend to lack this particular know-how, because they have fewer familial role models who attended college and they are less exposed to the information needed to successfully navigate the bureaucratic mechanism of the institution (Engle & Tinto, 2008; Thayer, 2000). However, research about the negative effects of large campuses on nontraditional students' persistence is not conclusive (Davis, 2012), as researchers have also posited that first-generation students thrive at large institutions because they give students a broader spectrum of engagement opportunities.

Researchers have also worked to understand how college policies and bureaucratic regulations affect undocumented students' persistence. Marrow (2009), for instance, found that inclusive policies enhance the flexibility and service roles of bureaucrats who deal directly with students more often, such as counselors, academic advisors, and other college administrators, while restrictive policies enhance their regulatory role. Higher education professionals are critical for undocumented students' educational success, because their college persistence is affected by being able to interpret policies and navigate bureaucratic processes (Contreras, 2009; Nienhusser, 2014; Pérez & Rodríguez, 2012). Undocumented youth tend to come from families with little college know-how and low levels of social capital, so the bureaucrats who deal directly with students have the potential to affect them by complying with those policies that involve sharing support, opportunities, and information in order to facilitate persistence and degree completion (Marrow, 2009).

The research on college students' relationship with the college system of bureaucratic requirements shows that, when students perceive that bureaucracy is more important to college staff than supporting students, they can disengage from the institution (Roberts & Styron, 2010). Similarly, students become equally disengaged with an institution when they feel they have been misinformed or given the runaround (Bean, 2005), developing negative attitudes toward that institution, which in turn will affect their likelihood to graduate. These findings suggest that the relation between the institution's bureaucratic requirements and student persistence is not direct, but mediated by student engagement.

An important area of research related to bureaucratic organizational behavior was outlined in Berger's original piece. He asserted that perceiving the institution's administrative actions as just and fair can positively affect students' persistence (Berger, 2001). Braxton et al. (2014) found evidence supporting this claim when revising this relationship, although noting that it is an indirect relationship, mediated by students' perception of the commitment of their college or university to their welfare. Therefore, "the more the student perceives that their college or university fairly administers its rules and regulations, the more favorable the student's perception of the commitment of their college or university to the welfare of its students" (p. 175), a perception that is, in turn, associated with students' persistence in residential colleges and universities.

Scholars studying gender-based violence in college have examined how perceived procedural justice in college and universities is relevant for affecting students' behaviors, like cooperation on maintaining a safe community (Rizzo et al., 2020). Although most students are likely not directly involved in justice procedures on campus, they still have perceptions of those processes that take place on their campuses, and these perceptions may affect their behavior. Students' perceptions of institutional responsiveness and procedural fairness in reaction to acts of violence on campus evolve into attitudes about the institution, which eventually determine a student's sense of belonging to the institution. Thus, students' perceptions of the fairness of institutional policies and the responsiveness of faculty and staff to violence on campus presumably affect their decisions to persist or leave the institution. The perceived procedural justice of the university in its relation to students' persistence has not been central to the persistence research agenda, but given the frequency with which particular groups of college students—such as women and LGBTQ communities—experience situations of violence and aggression, it is relevant to include in this agenda more research correlating persistence with the organizational features of the university.

The Effects of Collegial Organizational Behavior on Persistence

Berger's (2001) conceptualization of the *collegial* dimension describes the university's organizational behavior in terms of cooperation, focus on human resources, and the equal participation of diverse university stakeholders in defining goals and making other important decisions. Students participating in official committees and/or other collegial efforts where decisions are reached largely through consensus-building processes is one of the indicators signaling high levels of collegiality. High levels of student participation in instances of university governance are in turn associated with higher persistence rates.

According to Berger (2001), it is not clear through which path high levels of collegiality positively affect persistence. It may be that modeling collegiality on these campuses positively benefits student persistence, or it may be that high collegiality in the college administration results in a strong focus on students' well-being, which in turn leads to decreased attrition rates. Kezar (2005) explained, "Students bring an essential perspective for creating a success-oriented learning environment to the policymaking process and on committees, task forces, and governance groups in which they participate" (p. 2). Conversely, a hierarchical approach to the university administration, a traditional characteristic of highly bureaucratic institutions, is considered to negatively affect the administration's level of concern for students, which leads to increased attrition rates. Therefore, institutions with high levels of collegiality provide a more caring and humane environment for students, and this kind of environment promotes and facilitates students' persistence.

Berger's (2001) revision of literature shows relevant findings supporting his claims. He posited that the existing research (Astin & Scherrei, 1980; Berger & Braxton, 1998; Cameron & Ettington, 1988; Ewell, 1989) suggests that student participation in institutional decision-making and using higher levels of collegial administration styles within the university have positive indirect and total effects on student satisfaction and student persistence (Berger, 2001; Berger & Milem, 2000). During the last 20 years, however, the research around this particular topic has been a relatively neglected area of inquiry. In this sense, due to the lack of institutions practicing shared leadership that can serve as sites for research, empirical studies of student participation in governance, distributed leadership, and shared governance instances are limited and tend to be conceptual (Trowler & Trowler, 2010).

Despite limited research in this area, there are relevant pieces in the persistence research that provide evidence to support Berger's (2001) suggestions about the influence of collegiality on persistence. Research modeling collegiality on college campus effects on student persistence provide relevant insights. One of the most important and distinctive findings from Wolniak et al.'s (2012) work on persistence is that the more students demonstrated socially responsible leadership capabilities by the end of their first year of college, the more likely they were to enroll during the fall of their second college year. Thus, persistence decisions are influenced by the extent to which students possess values such as equity, social justice, self-knowledge, citizenship, and commitment toward social change as measured by the socially responsible leadership construct these authors used in their research.

Collegial organizational behaviors may also influence students' intentions to persist by promoting a caring culture within the university. Evidence suggests that caring institutions foster and support persistence (O'Keefe, 2013). Similarly, the qualitative work of Wagner et al. (2019) shows how students' perceptions of institutional care decrease their considerations about leaving college and encourage them to persist. Related to how high levels of collegiality can promote caring college cultures and consequently improve persistence rates, researchers studying community colleges explored how faculty participation in campus decision-making and faculty satisfaction relate to students' persistence. Miller (2019) found that only faculty job satisfaction was positively associated in a statistically significant way with student persistence rates in the community college context.

A shared governance structure and/or shared leadership can also be described as an indicator of strong collegial organizational behaviors. Thirty years ago, Birnbaum (1992) asserted that "when leadership is shared, a college has multiple ways of sensing environmental change, checking for problems, and monitoring campus performance. Shared leadership is likely to provide a college with a more complex way of thinking" (p. 187). More complex ways of institutional thinking are likely to produce more complex and holistic interventions to increase persistence. Given the limitations in conducting empirical studies about distributed leadership in entire systems, the most common type of research in this area focuses on cross-functional leadership teams as a proxy for distributed leadership (Kezar & Holcombe, 2017). Findings in this research field suggest that cross-functional campus teams of faculty and administration were more prone to identifying performance gaps between subpopulations and developing more integral solutions and interventions for particular groups of students (Bauman, 2005). Along with this, scholars have also shown that participants in cross-functional collaboration programs or projects consider cooperation between students and academic affairs personnel as a critical component to student success strategies aimed at increasing persistence, and that these participants were also more likely to focus holistically on student success (Schlam, 2018). These findings suggest that the adoption of shared leadership approaches within the campus administration may be an essential step toward cultivating inclusive environments that tap into the unique perspectives and experiences of diverse student subpopulations.

The Effects of Political Organizational Behavior on Persistence

According to Berger (2001), organizations often hold multiple and changing interest groups, each following their own agenda in a battle for control over limited resources. Hence, an important dimension of organizational behavior emerges from the competition for scarce resources among groups within an organization—the *political* dimension of organizational behavior. Since political behavior is a central dimension of organizational behavior, it implies that power and conflict are central to a higher education institution's organizational dynamic.

Berger's (2001) review of the scant literature produced until 2000 around this topic suggests that highly political organizational behavior has negative indirect effects on student persistence, as it is negatively associated with participation in campus life and academic satisfaction, which may lead to decreases in student persistence. For example, Berger posited that organizationally competitive campuses, described as institutions with higher levels of political behavior, coupled with lower levels of collegial behavior, have lower rates of student involvement in cocurricular activities. Since students' involvement in cocurricular activities has been shown to be a significant predictor of persistence (Astin, 1985; Berger & Milem, 2000; Milem & Berger, 1997), following Berger's argument, it can be reasonably suggested that higher levels of political organizational behavior may negatively affect persistence.

Berger (2001) warned, however, that student attrition from institutions with higher levels of political behavior may be the result of resource scarcity rather than the result of political behavior within the organization. Institutions with scarce resources are more likely to be highly political as individuals and interest groups compete for such limited resources. Berger (2001) concluded that more evidence is needed before certainly describing the path through which the political behavior of an organization influences student persistence.

Despite Berger's (2001) call to better understand how the political behavior of a higher education organization influences student persistence, this research area remains underdeveloped. According to Bastedo (2012), higher education organizational scholarship has been slow to embrace the concepts of conflict and power. It was only 2 decades ago that the critical political approach—which focuses on issues of power—emerged within higher education scholarship. But, as Bastedo (2012) explained, this critical approach has not been used by the higher education organizational scholarship. Moreover, the absence of this critical approach has become a weakness of higher education organizational scholarship (Bastedo, 2012; Pusser, 2008). Bastedo (2012) speculated that that this is partially caused by the dominance of neoliberal models in the study of higher education organizations, models that usually evade the question of power by using rational choice and interest-driven approaches.

Similarly, scholars have argued that the dominant literature on higher education student experiences has led researchers to neglect the study of the role of the organization's political behavior, by mainly focusing on the psycho-educational context of the college student experience (Chen, 2012; Mann, 2008). This psycho-educational approach tries to understand why students approach their college education in the ways they do, by investigating the relation between students' characteristics and their perceptions of their educational context. In this way, this research approach is primarily an individual-centered approach, which gives priority to data from students' accounts of their own experiences. This scholarship has made a significant contribution to the understanding of the college student experience and how students' diverse perceptions are related to educational outcomes, such as persistence. What is not directly addressed in this approach are the ways in which power and conflict permeate the student college experience (Mann, 2008) and how this affects students' persistence. While it is still relevant to hold onto the significance and complexity of the individual student's experience, at the same time it is urgent to adopt a critical approach based on socially informed theory in order to understand how the political behavior of higher education organizations affects students' persistence.

Resource allocation decisions might not be the same as higher education organizations' political behavior, understood as the power dynamics and conflicts within the organization, but they can be considered as one of the direct outcomes of the organization's political behavior, because they are the result of the conflict derived from the competition for scarce resources between different groups within the university. According to Harrison (2013), students suffer multiple consequences resulting from resource allocation decisions. For instance, adjunct professors often combine multiple teaching assignments in order to make a living; when institutions replace full-time faculty with adjuncts, they are also creating a professoriate that is less likely to interact with students (Clay, 2008; June, 2012). Such reduction of the opportunities for faculty–student interactions is likely to affect persistence rates (Harrison, 2013), because students' interactions with faculty are positively associated with greater odds of persisting toward graduation. Researchers have found similar evidence regarding universities' greater investments in student services, which translate into higher persistence rates (Chen, 2012). Moreover, research around student service spending shows that it influences graduation and persistence rates, and that the marginal effects are higher for students at institutions with lower entrance test scores and higher Pell Grant expenditures per student, which tend to be institutions that currently have lower graduation and first-year persistence rates (Webber & Ehrenberg, 2010).

Another way of approaching the understanding of political organizational behavior has been to focus on the extent to which different groups within the university collaborate with each other instead of competing for resources. In this regard, researchers have begun to study how collaboration between faculty and student affairs professionals aids in fostering students' success, and they have found that it has positive effects on students' persistence and degree completion (Commodore et al., 2018).

Since the power dynamics within a higher education organization not only include the conflicts among administrators, faculty, and staff, it is important to understand how other types of groups exert power within the organizational life of the university. For instance, critical race theory researchers challenge claims that all race/ethnic groups within higher education organizations have equal opportunities when competing for resources. Researchers such as Villalpando (2003) and Solórzano et al. (2005) have investigated how power works within higher education organizations, suggesting that there are power differentials and systemic conditions that privilege some and systematically disadvantage others. Therefore, uncovering how power differentials between race/ethnic groups unequally affect the persistence of diverse students would be a considerable contribution to better understanding of how the political dimension of organizational behavior affects persistence rates not only for students in general but for all diverse groups attending college.

Conflict and power differentials between groups are endemic to higher education organizations. Furthermore, unprecedented pressures such as the reduction of public funding for higher education, the expansion of student enrollment, the increasing expectations for external funding, and the increasing tension derived from racial and gender-related conflicts within society in general have made conflict more prevalent within higher education organizations. As a result, higher education leaders spend more than 40% of their time managing within-organization conflicts (Stanley & Algert, 2007). In this sense, understanding how power differentials and conflict between groups for the limited resources within universities affect students' persistence seems to be more urgent than ever before.

The Effects of Symbolic Organizational Behavior on Persistence

According to Berger and Milem (2000), the *symbolic* organizational behavior of colleges and universities is one of the multiple levels of their organizational culture. This organizational culture is composed of the deeply embedded and enduring patterns of behaviors, assumptions, beliefs, attitudes, and values about the nature of the university or college and its functioning that are held by the community members. In particular, symbolic organizational behavior is considered the most superficial and explicit manifestation of the organizational culture. Organizational symbols on campus convey shared institutional values through artifacts (e.g., logos, seals, architectural style), rituals (e.g., orientation, final exams, commemorative weeks), ceremonies (e.g., commencements, convocations), and stories and myths about the founding of the institution or exemplary faculty and campus leaders. Symbols help organizational members deal with the inherent ambiguities and uncertainty of organizational life through the creation of meaning within the university. Therefore, managing this created meaning becomes a central process of the university administration.

Symbolic behavior has three major functions: integration, differentiation, and fragmentation. Symbolic behavior has a powerful socializing effect, and through this socializing effect that creates shared meaning, it integrates the members of the college community. To understand the differentiation function of symbolic behavior, it is important to consider that colleges are rarely monolithically cultured. Colleges have subcultures that engage in and understand symbolic behavior from their own perspectives, and thus the institution's symbols and the meaning that is attached to them becomes differentiated across these groups. Also, the seemingly stable meaning of symbols can be fragmented at the individual level, because not all symbols mean the same to all people.

According to Berger's (2001) revision of the literature, symbolic behavior affects students' college experiences and persistence decisions through different paths. For instance, when the symbolic behavior reduces the ambiguity of the college's values and norms, it facilitates shared meaning, which in turn facilitates socialization and integration into the campus's academic and social subsystems. This integration, as Tinto (1993) implied, is fundamental in explaining students' decisions to persist in the institution. When the symbolic behavior creates shared meaning, it has also been shown to be an effective mean for improving communication throughout the organization. Shared meaning increases the ability of people in different parts of the organization and with different roles within the organization to understand and share information with each other (Bush, 1995).

Also, when the symbolic behavior has created a cohesive and strong shared meaning, colleges tend to exhibit high levels of image potency, which is defined by the strength of the institution's reputation outside of the campus. Generally, image potency produces homogeneity in the student body with high levels of shared characteristics and interests among the students, because in the external societal environment the college's image functions as a cue telling prospective students what the organization values and who may belong to that institution. According to Berger and Milem (2000) this high homogeneity also facilitates students' persistence. A similar mechanism operates among high-prestige colleges. Colleges with higher prestige have higher persistence rates because the degree awarded by that institution has a greater symbolic value in the external societal environment, and therefore students feel more compelled to graduate. This latter characteristic combines the benefits of positive systemic organizational behaviors with those of symbolic behaviors to the benefit of students.

Berger (2001) explained that examining to what extent integration, differentiation, and fragmentation are occurring among students as they make meaning out of organizational symbols is particularly important when researchers understand the college experiences of first-generation students and students who have been traditionally minoritized in higher education settings. Berger asserted that these students may construct meaning in ways that are less congruent with dominant modes of meaning-making on campus. Consequently, relevant efforts to understand the symbolic behavior of a university have been made by scholars whose work focuses on diversity and equity issues in higher education.

Using case studies, diversity and equity researchers documented how flagship universities tried to produce organizational change using symbols but failed to make bureaucratic or political behavior changes around diversity (Berrey, 2011, 2015; Thomas, 2018). Simply creating a narrative around how important diversity is for the university does not necessarily produce the institutional changes needed to dismantle the structural disparities that produce inequities on campus. On the other hand, other scholars documented cases in which systemic and bureaucratic behaviors were not coupled with changes in symbolic behaviors. For instance, Johnson-Bailey et al.'s (2009) case study from the perspective of African American graduate students describes how a flagship university changed over the span of 3 decades. Particularly, they documented the process in which the university enacted desegregation policies during the 1960s that were not observed in its symbolic behavior. The authors explain that organizational symbols derived from a college culture centered on whiteness affected students' perceptions of the college, their satisfaction with the institution, and their academic and social experiences. Examining the relationship between processes of bureaucratic and symbolic change, researchers have described how changes in university policies, including the creation of nondiscrimination policies, serve important symbolic functions for LGBTQ+ populations (Pitcher et al., 2018).

With a few exceptions, the symbolic organizational behavior dimension has not been assessed from a quantitative approach. As a consequence, there is minimal research linking it to educational outcomes like persistence (Hurtado et al., 2008). Also, despite the challenges of comparatively studying the symbolic behavior of organizations through quantitative approaches, scholars who work on diversity and equity issues in higher education have made valuable methodological contributions in an effort to understand the symbolic behavior of multiple institutions. For instance, the Higher Education Research Institute (HERI) and Cooperative Institutional Research Program included in one of its surveys the Diverse Learning Environments Survey, items that capture students' perceptions about the symbolic behavior of their university on issues related to diversity. This inclusion has made available data that capture this organizational behavior dimension, data that were then used by scholars to link to educational outcomes that are related to student persistence. For instance, Hussain and Jones (2019), in their research on the experiences of students of color at a primarily White institution, found that positive perceptions of the university's symbolic behavior on issues related to diversity, captured in the HERI factor Institutional Commitment to Diversity, buffer against the negative effects of having suffered experiences of discrimination and bias in college on students' sense of belonging to the institution, which is a strong predictor of persistence.

In an effort to study the symbolic behavior of multiple institutions, Holland and Ford (2020) employed more innovative methods. The authors analyzed the admission webpages of 278 universities across the United States to understand whether their way of symbolizing diversity in their admission webpages is associated with their other organizational features. The results suggest that more selective institutions are more likely to engage in practices that highlight the presence of their traditionally underrepresented minority student populations when compared to less selective institutions. While Holland and Ford's (2020) work provides insight about the relation between the university's admission selectivity and its image or reputation regarding diversity, an important symbolic resource, there is still a need to better understand the relationship between the latter and persistence rates on campus.

The importance of university symbolic behavior has become a major issue on many campuses across the United States. Several universities have been showcased in the media due to increasing conflict derived from instances of racial insults, graffiti, or social media posts by students or faculty (Bledsoe et al., 2020). Acknowledging the relevance of this trend, Bledsoe et al. (2020) discussed how linguistic violence diminishes equal educational opportunity and creates harmful learning and work environments. Along with this, interest in changing the university's symbolic artifacts has grown among students (Kretsinger-Harries, 2021). Since 2015, many student groups across the United States have called on their colleges and universities to rename buildings and remove monuments that commemorate the Confederacy or people they considered to be White supremacists. Researchers have posited that the protection of Confederate monuments by authorities has negative effects on Black students' sense of belonging (Britt et al., 2020); however, there is no research focusing on how university symbolic behavior relates to college students' sense of belonging or persistence. This trend suggests that future research on symbolic behavior and persistence could be expanded to consider the effects of a broader array of issues, such as the universities' protection of Confederate monuments or its symbolic responses to their media coverage in relation to racism.

The Effects of Systemic Organizational Behavior on Persistence

The *systemic* organizational behavior of a university or college acknowledges the institution as an open system, and therefore considers the impact of external influences in the organization. As Reason (2009) explained, "Systemic organizations behave as interconnected subsystems, recognizing that behavior is influenced by others within and external to the organization" (p. 668); the systemic aspects of the university's organizational behavior have important effects on student outcomes (Berger, 2001).

The literature reviewed by Berger (2001) suggests that understanding students' persistence also requires looking at the college's connections to its external environment. Based on the postulates of resource dependency theory, it can be asserted that organizational success is finally dependent on the ability of an organization to acquire resources. Resources are potentially important influences on the ability of an institution to retain undergraduate students (Berger, 2001).

There have been relevant efforts to examine the relationship between persistence and certain state-level policies (Perna & Thomas, 2008; Perna & Titus, 2004; Titus, 2006; Zhang, 2006). For instance, it has been shown that both 4-year and 2-year college students are positively affected by increases in state appropriations per student during their time of enrollment (Chakrabarti et al., 2020). Similarly, Zhang (2006) found that changing state appropriations by 10 percentage points results in a variation of approximately 0.64 percentage points in public 4-year institutions' graduation rates. This correlation remains the same whether state appropriations increase or decrease, if other individual and institutional variables stay constant.

Similarly, it has been posited that students' persistence may be associated not only with changes in state appropriations but also with changes in the mix of financial resources (Kelly & Jones, 2007; Titus, 2009). Titus's (2020) case study shows how increasing revenues from students via tuition and federal and state governments contribute to increase students' persistence and graduation rates. On the other hand, revenue from the federal government in the form of contracts and grants decreases students' graduation rates (Titus, 2020). Such findings suggest that college graduation rates can be influenced by policymakers through increasing state allotments for financial support, especially if such support benefits populations that are traditionally underrepresented. Researchers' understanding of the impact of state or federal policies on persistence has focused on a rather narrow range of policies, particularly patterns in state appropriations and student financial aid. However, state and federal policy influences on colleges are multidimensional, and therefore researchers should extend their work beyond appropriations and financial aid alone.

According to Berger's (2001) postulates, the ability of any higher educational organization to invite students is a relevant product of the university's systemic behavior. In this regard, the development and/or maintenance of positive external images and reputations to build higher levels of shared meaning with external constituents represents a major challenge. The benefits of having a positive external image, however, are not only restricted to admission selectivity but also influence the university's ability to retain its students.

During the last 20 years, diverse researchers have worked on better understanding how the perceptions of an organization's prestige foster positive self-esteem among the members of the organization, and in turn increase their intentions to remain in the organization (Bamber & Iyer, 2002; Cole & Bruch, 2006; Gautam et al., 2004; Herrbach, 2006; Mael & Ashforth, 1995; Mignonac et al., 2006; Riketta, 2005; Van Dick & Wagner, 2002; Van Dick et al., 2004; Van Knippenberg & Sleebos, 2006; Van Knippenberg & Van Schie, 2000). Also, the perceived external prestige of a higher education institution has an indirect and negative effect on students' intentions to leave college. When students perceive that their institution is valued by the external environment, they develop a stronger group-based self-esteem, which in turn increases students' commitment to the university and their persistence intentions (Ciftcioglu, 2010).

Berger (2001) also suggested that other systemic connections, like the ability of a college or university to successfully allocate students in particular careers, professions, and graduate schools, also enhances the institution's ability to retain its students. Both the theoretical work of Stuart et al. (2014) as well as the empirical work of Stuart (2009) on community college have been important in supporting this claim. The authors proposed a community college persistence model that questions the traditional approach of centering the study of persistence on engagement or integration models that only consider within-college relationships. Specifically, the authors proposed that community college persistence models should incorporate students' considerations regarding the opportunities and risks they may face in the labor market, asserting students think about their employment opportunities and risks when they are making decisions to stay, transfer, or leave community colleges, and this variable should also be incorporated by researchers. There is still a need to conduct more research that connects students' perceptions of the costs and benefits of obtaining their degree (in terms of the labor market) with various broader measures of engagement and success.

Multidimensional Frameworks

Berger and Milem (2000) asserted that organizational frameworks and studies of college students' outcomes, such as persistence, have been surprisingly unconnected. Although frameworks that include organizational variables are relevant for improving students' outcomes, as they provide evidence that can be easily transformed into policies, they are scarcely found in the higher education literature. Since these kinds of frameworks consider the entire organization as one of the central units of analysis, rather than considering individuals only, they have great potential for informing transformative policies (Gonzales et al., 2018; Peterson, 2007). During the last 20 years, not only has the design and implementation of such frameworks been scant in the research but also even the use of organizational variables is diminishing. In this regard, Bastedo (2012) explained that "the study of organizational topics is in sharp decline, owing largely to a lack of perceived connection between organization theory and major contemporary concerns in higher education" (p. 5), such as student persistence and the unequal persistence patterns of diverse student groups. Moreover, as Bastedo (2012) posited, "Scholars of higher education interested in access, [persistence], equity, and social justice often fail to see the usefulness of organization theory" (p. 5).

There are two considerable exceptions to this trend that are important to highlight. These prominent conceptual models are the comprehensive model of influences on student learning and persistence by Terenzini and Reason (2005) and the multicontextual model for diverse learning environments (MMDLE) from Hurtado et al. (2012).

To develop their comprehensive model of influences on student learning and persistence, Terenzini and Reason (2005) revised and adjusted Berger and Milem's (2000) conceptual model. According to Reason (2009), this model was unique in its time, since it explicitly stressed the effects that organizational characteristics have on students' outcomes. The modifications to this model by Terenzini and Reason (2005) consisted of the integration of certain features from Astin's (1985, 1993), Pascarella's (1985), and Tinto's (1975, 1993) models of student persistence. This way, Terenzini and Reason's (2005) completed model combined four different components: students' characteristics and experiences from before college, their individual experiences in college, the context derived from peer interactions, and the organizational environment. Aside from students' precollege experiences and characteristics, the three remaining components composed the holistic student college experience.

One key difference between Terenzini and Reason's (2005) model and Berger and Milem's model (2000) was the way in which the organizational component was characterized. Rather than following the original model's approach of defining different organizational behavior dimensions to complement the organization's demographic and structural aspects, Terenzini and Reason (2005) suggested three main areas to describe the organizational context. These areas were academic and cocurricular programs, faculty culture, and the organization's practices, policies, and internal structures. Terenzini and Reason (2005) argued that such modification of Berger and Milem's (2000) model was necessary because the latter contained organizational behavior dimensions that were too abstract and difficult to observe and study, whereas their new model proposed the more concrete areas that made this kind of research easier. In addition, Terenzini and Reason (2005) also argued that their three suggested organizational domains were closer to students' experiences, thus providing researchers and institutions with clearer guidelines for defining, developing, and implementing institutional practices to improve the student experience.

On the other hand, the MMDLE is a college climate model that seeks to predict student persistence, among other outcomes, such as a student's habits of mind, competencies for a multicultural world, and achievement. Hurtado et al. (2012) considered a multiplicity of factors to create their model. These factors include the broader contexts in which an institution is situated, such as the socio-historical, the community, and the policy contexts. Also, the MMDLE incorporates the curricular and cocurricular contexts within the institution. The curricular context comprises the instructors' identities, curriculum, and teaching methods. The cocurricular context is formed by the staff's identities, practices, and university programming. Another factor in the MMDLE is the students' identities, as well as the processes at the intersection of these identities and the curricular and cocurricular contexts. Finally, Hurtado et al.'s (2012) model includes what they described as the two main dimensions of climate—the institutional-level and the individual-level dimensions. The former includes the institution's historical legacy of inclusion or exclusion, its organizational structures and behaviors, and the diversity of its students, faculty, and staff. The individual-level dimension, on the other hand, includes the behavioral facet encompassing both individual actions and the interactions among different groups, as well as the psychological perceptions that individuals have regarding the institution.

Regarding the organizational structures and behaviors, Hurtado et al. (2012) explained that they comprise the institution's organizational structures and behaviors that ensure the privilege of some groups within it through, for instance, tenure, recruitment and hiring processes, budget allocations, curriculum, and other practices and policies. These are commonly agreed upon and implemented by dominant groups of faculty and administrators within the institution, and scholars have often stated that such structures and processes have played a key role in the generation of barriers preventing underrepresented groups from accessing academia (Hurtado et al., 2012).

Considering the importance of better understanding the unequal patterns of persistence shown by different groups of college students, it is crucial to incorporate organizational frameworks into higher education research that can complement the more individual-based models commonly used to study student persistence. In this sense, Hurtado et al. (1998) asserted that conventional conceptualizations of persistence models have failed to consider how students from marginalized backgrounds are affected by the university's organizational behavior, and these considerations need to be taken into account in order to improve the persistence rates of minoritized groups. One effective path that higher education research can take to aid in this goal is the inclusion of organizational theory into the models used to study student persistence in such a way that the systemic and structural inequities of college institutions can be considered when attempting to understand, and correct, the inequalities in persistence among different students.

Conclusion

In light of the multiple and well-studied negative effects, both social and personal, of students leaving college before graduating (Faas et al., 2018; Heckman et al., 2014; Hoeschler & Backes-Gellner, 2019; Hout, 2012), and the diverse benefits for both individuals and society at large of having more college graduates in the United States (Hout, 2012; Koropeckyj et al., 2017; Schneider & Yin, 2011), this chapter sought to suggest alternative paths of inquiry that would enhance and complement currently existing research methods and frameworks in higher education scholarship about student persistence specifically focused on organizational behavior. The chapter engaged in a revision of how the path that Berger (2001) initiated 2 decades ago to better understand the many times the indirect, yet not to be overlooked, influence of organizational behavior on college students' outcomes (e.g., persistence) has evolved since he first circulated his ideas on the importance of understanding this relation to improve, among other outcomes, student persistence. Taking Berger's (2001) ideas into account is important considering the noticeable lack of research making such connections since his work came out, and how neglecting this agenda has led to overlooking important factors that shape not only an individual's but also multiple, and often underserved, social groups' chances of persisting until graduation, factors that, due to their direct connection to institutional practices and policies, can be more easily transformed by each college in order to improve their student persistence rates.

After introducing the concept of organizational behavior, this chapter unpacked Berger's (2001) description of the five overarching organizational behavior frames in higher education (bureaucratic, collegial, political, symbolic, and systemic), and explored how his revision of the literature addressed the connections between each of these dimensions and student persistence, as well as offered newer scholarship that updated such connections after 2001. For each of the aforementioned five dimensions, there are different, yet not particularly abundant, research endeavors that support Berger's (2001) claim that increasing or decreasing the prevalence or strength of any specific organizational behavior dimension within a higher education institution has consequences that, although indirect, affect students' persistence decisions. Most of the time, as found in the literature reviewed here, the impact of organizational behavior on students is not directly related to student persistence, but to other more direct predictors of student persistence instead, such as the amount of participation by students and/or faculty in institutional decisions, the amount of student–faculty and student–staff interactions, students' perceptions of the university's values and reputation, students' sense of belonging to their college, or resource allocation and overall access and opportunities for different social groups within campuses, among others. By connecting to these predictors, organizational behavior can also be linked to student persistence, and thus it would be an important contribution to keep expanding the research focusing on this particular aspect of colleges and universities.

The scholarship reviewed here also establishes how this research agenda could be particularly beneficial for historically minoritized and underserved student populations, as it may serve to help in the design and development of transformative practices at the institutional level that can overcome how individual-based research that dominates the student persistence field has failed to acknowledge the systemic and structural inequities that affect entire groups of students' persistence decisions, rather than those of individuals alone. With this in mind, this chapter also offered a review of two important multidimensional frameworks that acknowledge and include, in different ways, the influence of the organizational behavior component of college institutions on the persistence decisions of their students: the comprehensive model of influences on student learning and persistence by Terenzini and Reason (2005), and the MMDLE from Hurtado et al. (2012). In particular, the MMDLE centers diversity and inclusion as key components of comprehensive organizational change strategies for student success. However, these two endeavors are not enough to overcome the considerable lack of higher education organizational scholarship embracing concepts of power and conflict and how these relate to the unequal college experiences and persistence rates of diverse social groups within higher education institutions (Bastedo, 2012; Gonzalez et al., 2018). Considering how pressing it is to produce more research that can thoroughly unveil the structures and practices behind such inequities, incorporating Berger's (2001) ideas would be a significant contribution to the development and application of transformative changes in U.S. higher education.

References

Astin, A. W. (1985). Involvement the cornerstone of excellence. *Change: The Magazine of Higher Learning, 17*(4), 35–39. https://doi.org/10.1080/00091383.1985 .9940532

Astin, A. W. (1993). *What matters in college: Four critical years revisited.* Jossey-Bass.

Astin, A. W., & Scherrei, R. A. (1980). *Maximizing leadership effectiveness: Impact of administrative style on faculty and students.* Jossey-Bass.

Bamber, E. M., & Iyer, V. M. (2002). Big 5 auditors' professional and organizational identification: Consistency or conflict? *Auditing: A Journal of Practice & Theory*, *21*(2), 21–38. https://doi.org/10.2308/aud.2002.21.2.21

Bastedo, M. N. (Ed.). (2012). *The organization of higher education: Managing colleges for a new era*. Johns Hopkins University Press.

Bauman, G. L. (2005). Promoting organizational learning in higher education to achieve equity in educational outcomes. In A. Kezar (Ed.), *Organizational Learning in Higher Education* (New Directions for Higher Education, no. 131, pp. 23–35). Wiley. https://doi.org/10.1002/HE.184

Bean, J. P. (2005). Nine themes of college student retention. In A. Seidman (Ed.), *College student retention: Formula for student success* (pp. 215–240). Praeger.

Berger, J. B. (2000). Organizational behavior at colleges and student outcomes: A new perspective on college impact. *Review of Higher Education*, *23*(2), 177–198. https://doi.org/10.1353/RHE.2000.0001

Berger, J. B. (2001). Understanding the organizational nature of student persistence: Empirically-based recommendations for practice. *Journal of College Student Retention: Research, Theory & Practice*, *3*(1), 3–21. https://doi.org/10.2190/3K6A-2REC-GJU5-8280

Berger, J. B., & Braxton, J. M. (1998). Revising Tinto's interactionalist theory of student departure through theory elaboration: Examining the role of organizational attributes in the persistence process. *Research in Higher Education*, *39*(2), 103–119. https://doi.org/10.1023/A:1018760513769

Berger, J. B., & Milem, J. F. (2000). Organizational behavior in higher education and student outcomes. In J. C. Smart (Ed.), *Higher education: Handbook of theory and research* (Vol. 15, pp. 268–338). Agathon.

Berrey, E. C. (2011). Why diversity became orthodox in higher education, and how it changed the meaning of race on campus. *Critical Sociology*, *37*(5), 573–596. https://doi.org/10.1177/0896920510380069

Berrey, E. (2015). *The enigma of diversity: The language of race and the limits of racial justice*. The University of Chicago Press.

Birnbaum, R. (1992). *How academic leadership works: Understanding success and failure in the college presidency*. Jossey-Bass.

Bledsoe, C. L., Dowd, A. C., & Ward, L. W. (2020). Silence is complicity: Why every college leader should know the history of lynching. *Change: The Magazine of Higher Learning*, *52*(2), 22–25. https://doi.org/10.1080/00091383.2020.1732755

Bound, J., Lovenheim, M. F., & Turner, S. (2010). Why have college completion rates declined? An analysis of changing student preparation and collegiate resources. *American Economic Journal: Applied Economics*, *2*(3), 129–157. https://doi.org/10.1257/APP.2.3.129

Braxton, J. M. (Ed.). (2000). *Reworking the student departure puzzle*. Vanderbilt University Press.

Braxton, J. M., Hirschy, A. S., & McClendon, S. A. (2011). *Understanding and reducing college student departure* (ASHE-ERIC Higher Education Report, Vol. 30, No. 3). Wiley.

Britt, L., Wager, E., & Steelman, T. (2020). Meanings and impacts of Confederate monuments in the U.S. South. *Du Bois Review: Social Science Research on Race, 17*(1), 1–19. https://doi.org/10.1017/S1742058X2000020X

Bush, T. (1995). *Theories of educational management.* Paul Chapman.

Cameron, K. S., & Ettington, D. R. (1988). The conceptual foundations of organizational culture. In J. C. Smart (Ed.), *Higher education: Handbook of theory and research* (Vol. 4, pp. 429–447). Agathon.

Carey, K. (2004). *A matter of degrees: Improving graduation rates in four-year colleges and universities.* Education Trust.

Chakrabarti, R., Gorton, N., & Lovenheim, M. F. (2020). *State investment in higher education: Effects on human capital formation, student debt, and long-term financial outcomes of students* (No. w27885). National Bureau of Economic Research. https://doi.org/10.2139/ssrn.3696679

Chen, R. (2012). Institutional characteristics and college student dropout risks: A multilevel event history analysis. *Research in Higher Education, 53,* 487–505. https://doi.org/10.1007/S11162-011-9241-4

Ciftcioglu, A. (2010). The relationship between perceived external prestige and turnover intention: An empirical investigation. *Corporate Reputation Review, 13*(4), 248–263. https://doi.org/10.1057/CRR.2010.22

Clay, R. (2008). The corporatization of higher education. *APA Monitor, 39*(11), 50–52. https://doi.org/10.1353/DSS.2012.0087

Cole, M. S., & Bruch, H. (2006). Organizational identity strength, identification, and commitment and their relationships to turnover intention: Does organizational hierarchy matter? *Journal of Organizational Behavior: The International Journal of Industrial, Occupational and Organizational Psychology and Behavior, 27*(5), 585–605. https://doi.org/10.1002/JOB.378

Commodore, F., Gasman, M., Conrad, C., & Nguyen, T. H. (2018, May 31). Coming together: A case study of collaboration between student affairs and faculty at Norfolk State University. *Frontiers in Education.* Advance online publication. https://doi.org/10.3389/feduc.2018.00039

Contreras, F. (2009). Sin papeles y rompiendo barreras: Latino students and the challenges of persisting in college. *Harvard Educational Review, 79*(4), 610–632. https://doi.org/10.17763/HAER.79.4.02671846902GL33W

Cuseo, J. (2004). *Academic advisement and student retention: Empirical connections and systematic interventions.* Jossey-Bass.

Darling, R. A., & Smith, M. S. (2007). First-generation college students: First-year challenges. *Academic Advising: New Insights for Teaching and Learning in the First Year, 14,* 203–211.

Davis, J. (2012). *The first generation student experience: Implications for campus practice, and strategies for improving persistence and success.* Stylus.

Deil-Amen, R., & Rosenbaum, J. E. (2003). The social prerequisites of success: Can college structure reduce the need for social know-how? *The Annals of the American Academy of Political and Social Science, 586*(1), 120–143. https://doi.org/10.1177/0002716202250216

Durkheim, E. (2005). *Suicide: A study in sociology*. Routledge.

Engle, J., & Tinto, V. (2008). *Moving beyond access: College success for low-income, first-generation students*. Pell Institute for the Study of Opportunity in Higher Education.

Ewell, P. T. (1989). Institutional characteristics and faculty/administrator perceptions of outcomes: An exploratory analysis. *Research in Higher Education, 30*(2), 113–136. https://doi.org/10.1007/BF00992715

Faas, C., Benson, M. J., Kaestle, C. E., & Savla, J. (2018). Socioeconomic success and mental health profiles of young adults who drop out of college. *Journal of Youth Studies, 21*(5), 669–686. https://doi.org/10.1080/13676261.2017.1406598

Gansemer-Topf, A. M., & Schuh, J. H. (2006). Institutional selectivity and institutional expenditures: Examining organizational factors that contribute to retention and graduation. *Research in Higher Education, 47*(6), 613–642. https://doi.org/10.1007/S11162-006-9009-4

Garcia, M. (2010). When Hispanic students attempt to succeed in college, but do not. *Community College Journal of Research and Practice, 34*(10), 839–847. https://doi.org/10.1080/10668926.2010.485003

Gautam, T., Van Dick, R., & Wagner, U. (2004). Organizational identification and organizational commitment: Distinct aspects of two related concepts. *Asian Journal of Social Psychology, 7*(3), 301–315. https://doi.org/10.1111/J.1467-839X.2004.00150.X

Gonzales, L. D., Kanhai, D., & Hall, K. (2018). Reimagining organizational theory for the critical study of higher education. In M. Paulsen (Ed.), *Higher education: Handbook of theory and research* (Vol. 33, pp. 505–559). Springer. https://doi.org/10.1007/978-3-319-72490-4_11

Harrison, L. M. (2013). Faculty and student affairs collaboration in the corporate university. *Journal of College and Character, 14*(4), 365–372. https://doi.org/10.1515/jcc-2013-0046

Heckman, J. J., Humphries, J. E., Veramendi, G., & Urzua, S. S. (2014). *Education, health and wages* (No. w19971). National Bureau of Economic Research. https://doi.org/10.3386/W19971

Herrbach, O. (2006). A matter of feeling? The affective tone of organizational commitment and identification. *Journal of Organizational Behavior: The International Journal of Industrial, Occupational and Organizational Psychology and Behavior, 27*(5), 629–643. https://doi.org/10.1002/JOB.362

Hoeschler, P., & Backes-Gellner, U. (2019). *Shooting for the stars and failing: College dropout and self-esteem* (Economics of Education Working Paper Series, no. 100). University of Zurich, Department of Business Administration. https://doi.org/10.5167/UZH-173560

Holland, M. M., & Ford, K. S. (2020). Legitimating prestige through diversity: How higher education institutions represent ethno-racial diversity across levels of selectivity. *Journal of Higher Education, 92*(1), 1–30. https://doi.org/10.1080/00221546.2020.1740532

Hout, M. (2012). Social and economic returns to college education in the United States. *Annual Review of Sociology, 38*, 379–400. https://doi.org/10.1146/ANNUREV.SOC.012809.102503

Hurtado, S., Alvarez, C. L., Guillermo-Wann, C., Cuellar, M., & Arellano, L. (2012). A model for diverse learning environments. In J. C. Smart & M. B. Paulsen (Eds.), *Higher education: Handbook of theory and research* (Vol. 27, pp. 41–122). Springer. https://doi.org/10.1007/978-94-007-2950-6_2

Hurtado, S., Clayton-Pedersen, A. R., Allen, W. R., & Milem, J. F. (1998). Enhancing campus climates for racial/ethnic diversity: Educational policy and practice. *Review of Higher Education, 21*(3), 279–302. https://doi.org/10.1353/RHE.1998.0003

Hurtado, S., Griffin, K. A., Arellano, L., & Cuellar, M. (2008). Assessing the value of climate assessments: Progress and future directions. *Journal of Diversity in Higher Education, 1*(4), 204–221. https://doi.org/10.1037/A0014009

Hussain, M., & Jones, J. M. (2019). Discrimination, diversity, and sense of belonging: Experiences of students of color. *Journal of Diversity in Higher Education, 14*(1), 63–71. https://doi.org/10.1037/DHE0000117

Johnson-Bailey, J., Valentine, T., Cervero, R. M., & Bowles, T. A. (2009). Rooted in the soil: The social experiences of Black graduate students at a southern research university. *Journal of Higher Education, 80*(2), 178–203. https://doi.org/10.1353/jhe.0.0040

June, A. W. (2012). Adjuncts build strength in numbers. *Chronicle of Higher Education, 59*(11), 17.

Kelly, P. J., & Jones, D. P. (2007). *A new look at the institutional component of higher education finance: A guide for evaluating performance relative to financial resources.* National Center for Higher Education Management Systems.

Kezar, A. (2005). *Promoting student success: The importance of shared leadership and collaboration* (Occasional Paper No. 4). National Survey of Student Engagement.

Kezar, A. J., & Holcombe, E. M. (2017). *Shared leadership in higher education.* American Council on Education.

Kim, J., Ott, M., & Dippold, L. (2020). University and department influences on scientists' occupational outcomes. *Research in Higher Education, 61*(2), 197–228. https://doi.org/10.1007/s11162-019-09584-6

Koropeckyj, S., Lafakis, C., & Ozimek, A. (2017, November). *The economic impact of increasing college completion.* American Academy of Arts and Sciences.

Kretsinger-Harries, A. C. (2021). Teaching public memory through analysis of Confederate monument controversies on college campuses. *Communication Teacher, 35*(1), 55–60.

Lambert, A. D., Terenzini, P. T., & Lattuca, L. R. (2006). More than meets the eye: Curricular and programmatic effects on student learning. *Research in Higher Education, 48*(2), 141–168. https://doi.org/10.1007/S11162-006-9040-5

Mael, F. A., & Ashforth, B. E. (1995). Loyal from day one: Biodata, organizational identification, and turnover among newcomers. *Personnel Psychology, 48*(2), 309–333. https://doi.org/10.1111/J.1744-6570.1995.TB01759.X

Mann, S. (2008). *Study, power and the university.* McGraw-Hill Education.

Marrow, H. B. (2009). Immigrant bureaucratic incorporation: The dual roles of professional missions and government policies. *American Sociological Review, 74*(5), 756–776. https://doi.org/10.1177/000312240907400504

Mignonac, K., Herrbach, O., & Guerrero, S. (2006). The interactive effects of perceived external prestige and need for organizational identification on turnover intentions. *Journal of Vocational Behavior, 69*(3), 477–493. https://doi.org/10.1016/J.JVB.2006.05.006

Milem, J. F., & Berger, J. B. (1997). A modified model of college student persistence: Exploring the relationship between Astin's theory of involvement and Tinto's theory of student departure. *Journal of College Student Development, 38*(4), 387.

Miller, L. (2019). The level of decision-making, perceived influence, and perceived satisfaction of faculty and their impact on student retention in community colleges. *Community College Journal of Research and Practice, 43*(7), 515–529. https://doi.org/10.1080/10668926.2018.1504700

Nienhusser, H. K. (2014). Role of community colleges in the implementation of postsecondary education enrollment policies for undocumented students. *Community College Review, 42*(1), 3–22. https://doi.org/10.1177/0091552113509837

Nuñez, A. M. (2009). Organizational effects on first-year students' academic outcomes at a new public research university. *Journal of College Student Retention: Research, Theory & Practice, 10*(4), 525–541. https://doi.org/10.2190/CS.10.4.g

O'Keeffe, P. (2013). A sense of belonging: Improving student retention. *College Student Journal, 47*(4), 605–613.

Organisation for Economic Co-operation and Development. (2019). *Education at a glance 2019: OECD indicators.* www.oecd.org/education/education-at-a-glance-19991487.htm

Oseguera, L., & Rhee, B. S. (2009). The influence of institutional retention climates on student persistence to degree completion: A multilevel approach. *Research in Higher Education, 50*(6), 546–569. https://doi.org/10.1007/S11162-009-9134-Y

Pascarella, E. T. (1985). College environmental influences on learning and cognitive development: A critical review and synthesis. In J. Smart (Ed.), *Higher education: Handbook of theory and research* (Vol. 1, 1–62). Agathon Press.

Perez, P. A., & Rodriguez, J. L. (2012). Access and opportunity for Latina/o undocumented college students: Familial and institutional support factors. *Journal of the Association of Mexican American Educators, 5*(1), 14–21.

Perna, L.W., & Thomas, S.L. (2008). Theoretical Perspectives on Student Success: Understanding the Contributions of the Disciplines. *ASHE Higher Education Report, 34*, 1-87.

Perna, L. W., & Titus, M. A. (2004). Understanding differences in the choice of college attended: The role of state public policies. *Review of Higher Education, 27*(4), 501–525. https://doi.org/10.1353/rhe.2004.0020

Peterson, M. W. (2007). The study of colleges and universities as organizations. In P. J. Gumport (Ed.), *Sociology of higher education: Contributions and their contexts* (pp. 147–186). Johns Hopkins University Press.

Pitcher, E. N., Camacho, T. P., Renn, K. A., & Woodford, M. R. (2018). Affirming policies, programs, and supportive services: Using an organizational perspective to understand LGBTQ+ college student success. *Journal of Diversity in Higher Education, 11*(2), 117. https://doi.org/10.1037/dhe0000048

Pusser, B. (2008). The state, the market and the institutional estate: Revisiting contemporary authority relations in higher education. In J. C. Smart (Ed.), *Higher education: Handbook of theory and research* (Vol. 23, pp. 105–139). Springer. https://doi.org/10.1007/978-1-4020-6959-8_4

Reason, R. D. (2009). An examination of persistence research through the lens of a comprehensive conceptual framework. *Journal of College Student Development, 50*(6), 659–682. https://doi.org/10.1353/csd.0.0098

Riketta, M. (2005). Organizational identification: A meta-analysis. *Journal of Vocational Behavior, 66*(2), 358–384. https://doi.org/10.1016/J.JVB.2004.05.005

Rizzo, A. J., Demers, J. M., Howard, M. E., & Banyard, V. L. (2020, February 11). Perceptions of campus authorities: Institutional responses, fairness, and bystander action. *Journal of American College Health.* Advance online publication. https://doi.org/10.1080/07448481.2020.1711762

Ro, H. K., Terenzini, P. T., & Yin, A. C. (2013). Between-college effects on students reconsidered. *Research in Higher Education, 54*(3), 253–282. https://doi.org/10.1007/S11162-012-9269-0

Roberts, J., & Styron, R., Jr. (2010). Student satisfaction and persistence: Factors vital to student retention. *Research in Higher Education, 6*, 1.

Schlam, E. (2018). *Academic and student affairs collaboration to impact undergraduate persistence in the Jesuit university context: A phenomenological study* [Unpublished doctoral dissertation]. UCLA.

Schneider, M., & Yin, L. (2011). *The high cost of low graduation rates: How much does dropping out of college really cost?* American Institutes for Research. https://doi.org/10.1037/e537282012-001

Scott-Clayton, J. (2011). *The shapeless river: Does a lack of structure inhibit students' progress at community colleges?* (CCRC Working Paper No. 25). Community College Research Center, Columbia University. https://doi.org/10.7916/D8183FRG

Shapiro, D., Dundar, A., Wakhungu, P. K., Yuan, X., Nathan, A. & Hwang, Y. (2016, November). *Completing college: A national view of student attainment rates—Fall 2010 cohort (Signature report No. 12)*. National Student Clearinghouse Research Center.

Sólorzano, D. G., Villalpando, O., & Oseguera, L. (2005). Educational inequities and Latina/o undergraduate students in the United States: A critical race analysis of their educational progress. *Journal of Hispanic Higher Education, 4*(3), 272–294. https://doi.org/10.1177/1538192705276550

Stanley, C. A., & Algert, N. E. (2007). An exploratory study of the conflict management styles of department heads in a research university setting. *Innovative Higher Education, 32*(1), 49–65. https://doi.org/10.1007/S10755-007-9035-Y

Stuart, G. R. (2009). *A benefit/cost analysis of three student enrollment behaviors at a community college: Dropout, transfer and completion of an associate's degree/certificate*

[Doctoral dissertation, Cleveland State University]. ETD Archive, 284. https://engagedscholarship.csuohio.edu/etdarchive/284/

Stuart, G. R., Rios-Aguilar, C., & Deil-Amen, R. (2014). "How much economic value does my credential have?" Reformulating Tinto's model to study students' persistence in community colleges. *Community College Review, 42*(4), 327–341. https://doi.org/10.1177/0091552114532519

Terenzini, P. T., & Reason, R. D. (2005, November). *Parsing the first year of college: Rethinking the effects of college on students* [Paper presentation]. Annual Conference of the Association for the Study of Higher Education, Philadelphia, PA, United States.

Thayer, P. B. (2000). *Retention of students from first generation and low income backgrounds.* Council for Opportunity in Education. https://files.eric.ed.gov/fulltext/ED446633.pdf

Thomas, J. M. (2018). Diversity regimes and racial inequality: A case study of diversity university. *Social Currents, 5*(2), 140–156. https://doi.org/10.1177/2329496517725335

Tinto, V. (1975). Dropout from higher education: A theoretical synthesis of recent research. *Review of Educational Research, 45*(1), 89–125. https://doi.org/10.3102/00346543045001089

Tinto, V. (1986). Theories of student departure revisited. In J. C. Smart (Ed.), *Higher education: Handbook of theory and research* (Vol. 2, pp. 359–384). Agathon.

Tinto, V. (1993). *Leaving college: Rethinking the causes and cures of student attrition* (2nd ed.). The University of Chicago Press.

Tinto, V. (2010). From theory to action: Exploring the institutional conditions for student retention. In J. Smart (Ed.), *Higher education: Handbook of theory and research* (Vol. 25, pp. 51–89). Springer. https://doi.org/10.1007/978-90-481-8598-6_2

Titus, M. A. (2006). Understanding college degree completion of students with low socioeconomic status: The influence of the institutional financial context. *Research in Higher Education, 47*(4), 371–398. https://doi.org/10.1007/S11162-005-9000-5

Titus, M. A. (2009). The production of bachelor's degrees and financial aspects of state higher education policy: A dynamic analysis. *Journal of Higher Education, 80*(4), 439–468. https://doi.org/10.1353/jhe.0.0055

Titus, M. A. (2020). Examining degree production and financial context at public master's colleges and universities in the United States: A distance function approach. *Tertiary Education and Management, 26*(2), 215–231. https://doi.org/10.1007/s11233-019-09049-6

Trowler, P., & Trowler, V. (2010). *Student engagement evidence summary.* The Higher Education Academy. https://eprints.lancs.ac.uk/id/eprint/61680/1/Deliverable_2._Evidence_Summary._Nov_2010.pdf

Van Dick, R., Christ, O., Stellmacher, J., Wagner, U., Ahlswede, O., Grubba, C., Hauptmeier, M., Höhfeld, C., Moltzen, K., & Tissington, P. A. (2004). Should I stay or should I go? Explaining turnover intentions with organizational identification and job satisfaction. *British Journal of Management, 15*(4), 351–360. https://doi.org/10.1111/J.1467-8551.2004.00424.X

Van Dick, R., & Wagner, U. (2002). Social identification among school teachers: Dimensions, foci, and correlates. *European Journal of Work and Organizational Psychology, 11*(2), 129–149. https://doi.org/10.1080/13594320143000889

Van Gennep, A. (1960). *The rites of passage.* The University of Chicago Press.

Van Knippenberg, D., & Sleebos, E. (2006). Organizational identification versus organizational commitment: Self-definition, social exchange, and job attitudes. *Journal of Organizational Behavior: The International Journal of Industrial, Occupational and Organizational Psychology and Behavior, 27*(5), 571–584. https://doi.org/10.1002/JOB.359

Van Knippenberg, D., & Van Schie, E. C. (2000). Foci and correlates of organizational identification. *Journal of Occupational and Organizational Psychology, 73*(2), 137–147. https://doi.org/10.1348/096317900166949

Villalpando, O. (2003). Self segregation or self preservation? A critical race theory and Latina/o critical theory analysis of a study of Chicana/o college students. *Qualitative Studies in Education, 16*(5), 619–646. https://doi.org/10.1080/0951839032000142922

Wagner, E. L., Sanchez, B., & Haley, K. (2019, February 18). Student perceptions of institutional care: Making sense of hardship funding as a retention tool. *Journal of College Student Retention: Research, Theory & Practice.* Advance online publication. https://doi.org/10.1177/1521025119830945

Webber, D. A., & Ehrenberg, R. G. (2010). Do expenditures other than instructional expenditures affect graduation and persistence rates in American higher education? *Economics of Education Review, 29*(6), 947–958. https://doi.org/10.1016/J.ECONEDUREV.2010.04.006

Wolniak, G. C., Mayhew, M. J., & Engberg, M. E. (2012). Learning's weak link to persistence. *Journal of Higher Education, 83*(6), 795–823. https://doi.org/10.1080/00221546.2012.11777270

Zell, M. C. (2010). Achieving a college education: The psychological experiences of Latina/o community college students. *Journal of Hispanic Higher Education, 9*(2), 167–186. https://doi.org/10.1177/1538192709343102

Zhang, L. (2006). *Does public funding for higher education matter?* Cornell Higher Education Research Institute.

Zhou, E., & Okahana, H. (2019). The role of department supports on doctoral completion and time-to-degree. *Journal of College Student Retention: Research, Theory & Practice, 20*(4), 511–529. https://doi.org/10.1177/1521025116682036

8

ARE YOU EXPERIENCED?

How College Environments, Programs, and Interactions Shape Student Retention, Persistence, and Graduation

KC Culver and Nicholas A. Bowman

There is little question that students' college experiences affect their retention, persistence, and degree attainment, and yet two aspects of this relationship reveal a complex reality. First, there is strong evidence that students' experiences vary more within institutions than between them (Mayhew et al., 2016; Pascarella & Terenzini, 2005). Some of this variation is the product of students' many choices, including where to live during college, which college major to pursue, and whether to be involved in clubs and organizations. At the same time, institutional agents shape students' choices directly through the opportunities that are made available and more indirectly through cultures and norms; moreover, student experiences are also a function of structural forces that extend well beyond the institution and that begin well before students enter college. Thus, recent theories of student departure have emphasized the joint responsibility of students and institutions in shaping students' engagement (see chapter 2). Second, students' experiences inform and are informed by their perceptions of themselves, their peers, institutional agents, and the institution. These perceptions then determine students' commitments and intentions. In other words, psychological processes explain the relationship between students' experiences and their attainment (Bowman et al., 2022; Braxton et al. 2004), such that the experiences themselves only influence persistence, retention, and attainment indirectly.

Additionally, as a result of institutional dynamics and structural forces, retention, persistence, and degree-attainment rates are often lower among students from social identity groups that have been minoritized and/or marginalized in higher education, including students with disabilities, LGBTQ students, racially minoritized students, first-generation students, students from low-income backgrounds, and students with lower levels of high school achievement (S. L. Pendakur et al., 2020). These gaps reveal that many institutions need to do more to effectively engage their students (V. Pendakur, 2016), especially using equity-minded approaches (Bensimon, 2007; Dowd et al., 2013). This chapter uses an antideficit perspective of students (S. L. Pendakur et al., 2020), presenting research that has predominantly been published in the last 10–12 years on the relationship of students' experiences with retention, persistence, and graduation. We focus on identifying the environments, opportunities, and resources that institutions can offer to promote the engagement and success of students from diverse backgrounds. And while student success is a broad concept, including students' persistence, learning, intellectual and personal development, and civic preparation (Braxton et al., 2014), we use the term to refer specifically to measures of students' academic progress, including their retention at a specific institution, their persistence within any institution, and their degree attainment.

We begin the chapter with a discussion of broad structural and cultural aspects of the overall institutional environment, along with residential environments. We then discuss comprehensive and student success programs that facilitate students' transition to college, followed by students' interactions and experiences with institutional agents, and programs and contexts that facilitate students' interactions and experiences with peers. The chapter concludes by presenting recommendations for future research.

In each section, we highlight scholarship that centers the increasingly diverse identities of today's college students to explore potential differences in students' experiences and related outcomes. We incorporate both quantitative and qualitative literature, drawing upon recent systematic reviews and meta-analyses to help provide an overview of this work. We also recognize that many studies on this topic do not use methods that lead to strong causal inferences about the extent to which college experiences actually affect students' retention and persistence, since students who decide to participate in these experiences may differ from students who do not participate. Therefore, whenever possible, we focus on quantitative studies with more rigorous experimental designs (in which students or groups of students are randomly assigned to conditions) or quasi-experimental designs (that seek to establish causality even when students are not randomly assigned). At the same time, we recognize that quantitative research can silence minoritized voices and that measures of engagement included in surveys often cannot capture the realities of students' experiences with their environments (Patton et al., 2015). Therefore, we also include qualitative studies that give voice to diverse students and that offer in-depth insights into the dynamics that occur within the environments, experiences, and programs that students encounter.

Academic Achievement as a Direct and Indirect Influence

Students' academic achievement and dispositions interact to have a powerful influence on retention. Two systematic reviews of recent scholarship have concluded that students' academic achievement in college has the most widespread influence on retention and persistence across different institutional contexts and student populations (Barbera et al., 2020; Mayhew et al., 2016). College grades can directly affect institutional retention through academic dismissal or losing financial aid as a result of a low GPA. More importantly, grades and other feedback on tests and assignments can influence students' academic self-efficacy, motivation, and sense of belonging, which then shape their intent to persist (e.g., Miller et al., 2020; Stinebrickner & Stinebrickner, 2012).

Given their direct influence on institutional attrition, grades comprise an equity issue requiring greater institutional attention. Academic achievement—and therefore the processes that result from it—is almost always measured via grades, which can (a) vary considerably across fields of study, (b) vary considerably across instructors within a field of study, (c) may or may not be based on a curve that places inherent limits upon success, and (d) can be subject to substantial explicit and/or implicit bias. Further, their indirect influence on persistence and degree attainment reflect long-standing inequities that privilege students from dominant identity groups. Indeed, in environments that are culturally relevant or that reduce social identity threat, students who hold marginalized identities fare notably better in terms of their belonging and academic achievement (Hurtado et al., 2015; Museus et al., 2017; Walton & Spencer, 2009).

College Environments

In the past 20 years, increasing attention has been paid to the role of environmental climates and cultures, and students' positionality within them, as evidenced in newer theories of retention discussed in this book (see chapter 2). Environmental climates and cultures are shaped by the composition, organization, and history of the institution as well as the attitudes, behaviors, norms, and expectations of its members (Hurtado et al., 2012; Jayakumar & Museus, 2012). In this section, we discuss how institutional and residential environments indirectly influence students' engagement and retention.

Institutional Climates and Cultures

Simply put, perceptions of a welcoming and friendly campus environment predict retention (Johnson et al., 2014). Yosso and Lopez (2010) identified several factors that contribute to a positive racial climate: compositional diversity, programs to support the retention and success of underrepresented students, and a mission that institutionalizes the campus commitment to plurality. In a recent study, Bowman and Denson (2022) examined institutional compositional diversity and equity gaps in degree attainment, finding smaller disparities in graduation rates between racially minoritized students and White students at institutions with a greater proportion of racially minoritized students. Further, graduation rates among Black, Latinx, and White students were nearly identical when students attended an institution where same-race peers comprised at least half of the undergraduate population. Thus, the authors posit that compositional diversity creates the conditions in which a positive climate for racially minoritized students is more likely to occur.

Compositional diversity by itself is not enough to create a positive racial climate, however; historically White institutions also must ensure that racially minoritized students have equal access and opportunities for engagement in inclusive spaces (Yosso & Lopez, 2010). At a historically White institution, Johnson et al. (2014) analyzed racially minoritized students and White students separately using structural equation modeling, finding that perceptions of the campus environment led to persistence among both groups, but different experiences predicted their perceptions. Among White students, opportunities for diversity interactions led to positive perceptions, whereas observed racism on campus led to negative perceptions among Students of Color. Similarly, a multi-institutional study found that the significantly lower likelihood of 4-year graduation among Black and Latinx students compared to their White peers was entirely explained by perceptions of campus racial climate, social identity threat, and college grades (Fischer, 2010).

Recent scholarship across a number of social identity characteristics also reveals adverse experiences for students from other marginalized groups. For instance, socioeconomic norms that privilege students from wealthier families often lead to feelings of invisibility among low-income and first-generation students (Buckley & Park, 2021; Stephens et al., 2014); cisgender norms silence queer and trans students (Catalano & Jourian, 2018); and students with disabilities often feel less welcomed, respected, and valued than their nondisabled peers (Nachman & Brown, 2020; Zehner, 2018). In an empirical examination of the culturally engaging campus environments model, Museus et al. (2017) identified several environmental qualities that were significantly related to students' sense of belonging, including cultural practices that validated students and provided holistic support, as well as an environmental ethos that valued cultural awareness, collectivist orientations, and proactive philosophies. And yet, across scholarship on institutional climates and culture, studies reveal that the dominant White, cisgendered, middle-class, and able-bodied culture still present in many institutional environments (S. L. Pendakur et al., 2020) does not foster the perceptions of a welcoming and friendly environment among many students that would ultimately promote retention.

Residential Environments

While many institutions are not residential, a good deal of research has examined the role of students' living environments on their persistence and retention. In some large-scale studies, living on campus appears to lead to higher retention and graduation rates (Oseguera & Rhee, 2009; Schudde, 2011). The benefits of living on campus likely accrue by providing students with opportunities for social and interpersonal engagement (Mayhew et al., 2016). Psychosocial attributes also matter; students who feel connected to others in their living environment are more likely to be retained. Matriculating students whose need to belong is unmet experience greater homesickness (Watt & Badger, 2009), and first-year students who report greater distress about missing family and friends back home are less likely to be retained (Sun et al., 2016). Given the importance of connection and belonging to the living environment, a few researchers have explored factors that may contribute to students' sense of safety and community, including the design of residence halls, the number of students who live together, and policies that promote peer interactions (Bronkema & Bowman, 2017; Brown et al., 2019; Hurtado et al., 2019; Samura, 2016).

At the same time, living on campus is not a panacea for retention. The price tag for living on campus is often prohibitive for low-income students, and two studies suggest that living on campus is not associated with second-year retention among this group (Schudde, 2011, 2016). Further, many first-generation students prioritize being able to live at home when deciding which institution to attend (Lohfink & Paulsen, 2005). Maintaining home and family connections may promote persistence among Indigenous students, especially by providing cultural sustainment (Lopez, 2018; Wright & Shotton, 2020). Further, students with marginalized identities often experience microaggressions and more overt forms of discrimination in residence halls (Harwood et al., 2012; Strayhorn & Mullins, 2012). Thus, the indirect link of living on campus with persistence and retention goes beyond social engagement to include financial and cultural considerations.

Transition-Focused Programs and Coursework

Colleges and universities have implemented a variety of programs that are intended to improve the transition to college in order to bolster a range of markers of student success, including learning, achievement, persistence, retention, and graduation; these efforts may be designed for all students or for certain student subgroups. This section reviews research on student success and support programs, first-year seminars, and developmental education, along with how the impact of these efforts may differ by student and institutional attributes. Experimental and quasi-experimental designs are far more common for examining these programs than for examining broader environments, climates, and cultures, so many of the citations in the following discussion refer to studies that use these rigorous methodological approaches.

Multifaceted Student Success Programs

Some institutional programs seek to integrate several elements into a coherent effort to foster students' success, with a focus on student retention and graduation. Such programs can consist of some combination of first-year seminars, learning communities, other program-specific coursework, mentoring, tutoring, academic advising or coaching, career services, events and workshops, shared housing or common space, financial aid, and more. The language to describe these programs may include "comprehensive support and retention programs" (Pascarella & Terenzini, 2005, p. 405), "comprehensive college transition programs" (Hallett et al., 2020, p. 230), and "multifaceted initiatives" to promote retention (Kramer et al., 2022, p. 18). Summer bridge programs often take the form of a multifaceted student success program that occurs before the start of the first academic year, and some honors programs and colleges also fit this description.

Several systematic reviews have concluded that comprehensive student success programs are more effective at promoting college retention and graduation than are single-component interventions (Mayhew et al., 2016; Page & Nurshatayeva, 2022; Tsui, 2007). Studies have frequently found positive and sizable results; most notably, the Accelerated Study in Associate Programs initiative nearly doubled 3-year graduation rates in New York and Ohio, along with providing sizable increases in students transferring from 2-year to 4-year institutions (Miller et al., 2020; Scrivener et al., 2015). Several comprehensive student success programs for lower-income students at 4-year colleges have also improved graduation rates (Angrist et al., 2020; Clotfelter et al., 2018; Page et al., 2019). Moreover, participating in a multi-faceted program that includes financial aid generally leads to more favorable retention and graduation outcomes than solely receiving the financial aid (Angrist et al., 2009; Evans et al., 2020).

Summer bridge programs serve to help incoming college students transition into higher education, and many of these are targeted toward students with marginalized identities. These programs often have a variety of components that may include first-year success seminars, learning communities, structured mentoring and/or advising, cocurricular and/or social programming, residential living, and more (see Ashley et al., 2017; Sablan, 2014). Consistent with research on comprehensive student success programs, summer bridge program participation often predicts greater college retention and graduation (e.g., Cabrera et al., 2013; Murphy et al., 2010; Summers & Hrabowski, 2006). Using a nationally representative sample, Douglas and Attewell (2014) found that summer bridge programs lead to a 10-percentage-point increase in 6-year graduation among students at 2-year and less selective 4-year institutions. STEM-focused programs also lead to positive effects on institutional retention (Windsor et al., 2015).

So why are multifaceted student success programs effective at fostering student success? Several factors may help individually or in combination. First, multifaceted programs position the use of one or more student services as normal and expected, and they facilitate easier access to these services (and sometimes require participation). This approach contrasts considerably with the usual structure of student services at many institutions, which requires notable student initiative to access resources, with offices scattered throughout campus and/or the internet; further, their use may be stigmatized as only for students who are struggling or are not prepared for college (e.g., Kinzie & Kuh, 2016). Second, the structure of multifaceted programs may help foster meaningful relationships with peers, staff, and instructors, which may be crucial for developing a sense of belonging (e.g., Felten & Lambert, 2020; Strayhorn, 2019). Third, in a related point, many of these programs send explicit and implicit messages to students that they have a place on campus and are capable of academic success, even when the program is targeted toward students from underrepresented and/or marginalized identities. The names of these programs themselves may send such signals: Meyerhoff

Scholars Program, Enhanced Academic Success Experience, Thompson Scholars Learning Community, and so on.

First-Year Seminars

First-year seminars constitute a diverse set of offerings that may take a variety of forms: (a) extended orientation (providing information about institutional resources and how to succeed in college), (b) academic seminar with uniform content (exploring a single topic in depth), (c) academic seminar on various topics, (d) preprofessional or discipline linked, (e) basic study skills, and (f) hybrid (a combination of two or more of the previous types; Tobolowsky & Associates, 2008). Despite the presence of several systematic reviews on first-year seminars and student retention (Mayhew et al., 2016; Permzadian & Credé, 2016; Robbins et al., 2009; Swaner & Brownell, 2010), the research is decidedly mixed between positive and nonsignificant findings. Even when focusing exclusively on experimental or quasi-experimental studies, some research yields positive effects (Clark & Cundiff, 2011; Tuckman & Kennedy, 2011), and other literature finds no impact (Culver & Bowman, 2020; Fitzpatrick et al., 2020; Rutschow et al., 2012).

Attempts to identify the characteristics of successful first-year seminars also lead to contradictory results. In terms of seminar type, the existing findings vary between academic-focused seminars having more positive results than extended orientation (Young, 2020), no difference based on type of seminar (Culver & Bowman, 2020), and differences that depend on the success outcome (Permzadian & Credé, 2016) or student characteristic (Weissman & Magill, 2008). Even reviews of this literature sometimes conflict with one another: Permzadian and Credé (2016) found that first-year seminars are less effective when they are part of a learning community, whereas Mayhew et al. (2016) found the exact opposite result, and Wurtz (2014) found that learning communities are more effective when they include an academic skills course (which is arguably a form of first-year seminar).

Given the indirect nature of the relationship between students' experiences and their persistence and retention, the divergent findings for first-year seminars may reflect differences among students and in program implementation. Students may experience practices that have been identified as "high impact," including first-year seminars, very differently depending on their identities, prior experiences, and other factors (Bowman et al., 2022; Stewart & Nicolazzo, 2019). However, educators can promote positive outcomes by designing and implementing programs that meet the following eight characteristics proposed by Kuh and O'Donnell (2013): (a) involve an investment of time and energy, (b) set high performance expectations,

(c) facilitate engagement with faculty and peers on substantive topics, (d) involve diversity, (e) have real-world relevance, (f) require reflection and integration of learning, (g) involve students' demonstration of competence, and (h) provide feedback in an effective manner. Although previous literature has supported these attributes, it is unclear whether they explain the divergent findings for first-year seminars and other practices.

Developmental Education

Developmental education coursework (also known as remedial education) is quite common at 2-year institutions and less selective 4-year institutions. While the intended purpose of developmental education is to promote student success, students who are placed into developmental education often suffer adverse outcomes according to strong causal evidence, including lower rates of course completion, upward transfer from a 2-year to 4-year institution, and degree attainment, as well as fewer credits earned (Jaggars & Bickerstaff, 2018; Valentine et al., 2017). A number of issues in the implementation of some developmental education may contribute to these adverse outcomes, including unreliable placement approaches, the time and money required for students to complete lengthy developmental sequences, and the prevalence of pedagogies in these courses that decontextualize skill building from intellectually engaging disciplinary content (Jaggars & Bickerstaff, 2018).

Institutions assess students' readiness for college-level courses in a variety of ways, including placement tests, standardized test scores (ACT/SAT), high school transcripts, and high school GPA. However, the prevalence of misalignment in placement decisions is clear. In a recent large-scale examination of community college students who received strong high school math grades, Ngo and Melguizo (2021) found that students who met multiple criteria for college readiness in math were frequently not placed in transfer-level math. In their study, misalignment occurred significantly more often for female students than for male students with the same level of high school preparation, and the degree of misalignment was higher among Black and Latinx students than among White and Asian/Pacific Islander students.

Reforming developmental education is thus an equity issue. Developmental coursework tends to lengthen time to degree (Bahr, 2012), with even greater delays occurring for students who are required to take more than one level of developmental coursework in a discipline or who are placed in developmental courses in multiple disciplines (Bahr, 2007). Further, many developmental courses are taught as "basic skills" courses, where course content is disconnected from skill building (N. Grubb, 2013). Innovative approaches to developmental education are thus being created, including accelerated courses in which students enroll for only part of the semester (Sheldon & Durdella, 2010). Another approach is to have students coenroll in the developmental course and the first credit-bearing course simulta-neously (Reeves, 2015). Institutions are also implementing other student supports in developmental courses, including intrusive advising approaches, to help students learn about and adopt effective behaviors for completing course assignments (Thomas, 2020).

Who Benefits the Most?

A critical question for practitioners involves tailoring programs and program participation to maximize student persistence. According to this research, the influence of programmatic interventions is often larger at institutions that are less selective (Angrist et al., 2020; Bowman & Culver, 2018b; Page et al., 2019; Permzadian & Credé, 2016). The apparent impact is also sometimes larger for racially marginalized students (Douglas & Attewell, 2014; Permzadian & Credé, 2016; Windsor et al., 2015) and for students with lower precollege academic achievement (Angrist et al., 2020; Douglas & Attewell, 2014; Oreopoulos & Petronijevic, 2018). All of these groups of students and institutions tend to have lower retention and graduation rates for a variety of reasons (some of which were discussed previously), so the larger increases may be partially driven by the greater room for improvement.

If programmatic interventions are targeted toward particular groups of students, practitioners must be very careful not to frame these in a way that suggests to students that they need help or they are "at risk," since this approach can backfire by contributing to concerns about their belonging and potential for success (Yeager & Walton, 2011). Perhaps providing an illus-tration of this problem, Permzadian and Credé (2016) found that first-year seminars targeted toward academically underprepared students were actually less effective at promoting retention than those designed for all students.

Interestingly, female students often benefit more from comprehensive student success programs (Angrist et al., 2009; Evans et al., 2020; Miller et al., 2020; Windsor et al., 2015), whereas male students benefit more from coaching (Bettinger & Baker, 2014; Oreopoulos & Petronijevic, 2018; van der Steeg et al., 2015). Coaching occurs primarily or exclusively in a one-on-one format, and male students appear to do well with this direct attention and advice. In contrast, the comprehensive programs that largely contributed to female students' success involved engagement either with a community of students, staff, and faculty or with several people who each provided specific services. Further attention is needed to explore the reasons for these conditional results.

Interactions and Experiences With Institutional Agents

Students interact with a number of institutional agents, such as administrative leaders, professionals in student affairs and academic affairs, and instructors (who may include tenure-track faculty, contingent and adjunct instructors, and graduate teaching assistants). Stanton-Salazar (2011) emphasized the potential for institutional agents to empower students by using their status and knowledge to provide support, connections, and advocacy to students who lack status or power. In addition to connecting students to opportunities and resources, institutional agents also play a critical role in socializing students to the culture of higher education (Museus & Quaye, 2009; Strayhorn, 2015). Felten and Lambert (2020) asserted that students' relationships with instructors and staff members are critical for fostering students' sense of belonging, learning, and achievement. Further, Dowd et al. (2013) discussed the importance of institutional agents for affirming and validating students, which can counteract the stereotype threat that marginalized students experience in higher education. Thus, the influence of students' interactions on their persistence is indirect, by communicating belonging and scholarly potential and empowering students to succeed. In this section, we discuss literature on interactions broadly, followed by advising, coaching, and mentoring programs; undergraduate research experiences; and instructor pedagogy.

Two separate reviews of literature conclude that it is the quality of interactions, rather than the frequency, that influences students' retention and success (Cole & Griffin, 2013; Mayhew et al., 2016). As with other experiences, the quality of interactions likely influences how connected to the institution students feel (Hurtado et al., 2015). For instance, Latinx alumni attributed their college persistence in large part to the support and mentoring they received from faculty and other student affairs professionals (Bordes-Edgar et al., 2011). Research on other marginalized groups similarly suggests the benefits of interactions with institutional agents that reflect care and support, along with promoting relationship-building (Cole et al., 2020; Wood & Harris, 2015).

At the same time, Kim and Sax's (2017) review illustrates that the impact of students' interactions with instructors is conditional on students' individual characteristics and the environment in which interactions occur. Further, the characteristics of institutional agents may also play a role. Among underrepresented students, interactions with institutional agents who share a marginalized identity can be very important; institutional agents here can function as same-identity models of success. For instance, studies of Black males attending historically White institutions underscore the importance of students' relationships with same-race faculty members and peers for persistence and success (Brooms & Davis, 2017; Harper, 2012; Strayhorn, 2017).

To help promote persistence, institutional agents must be available. As an illustration of this problem, Turner and Thompson (2014) found that 57% of first-year students reported not having an interactive relationship with any of their instructors. A number of challenges related to supporting students' interactions with instructors, especially in their first year, stem from the growing reliance on contingent instructors in higher education, who often face time constraints related to employment and lack the necessary resources (such as office space) to interact with students outside of class (Kezar et al., 2019). Further, as imposter syndrome and shame can make it difficult for marginalized students to seek help (Felten & Lambert, 2020), institutional agents need to be proactive in their efforts to connect with students.

Advising, Coaching, and Mentoring

Many colleges and universities facilitate a relationship with a staff member, faculty member, and/or an advanced student that will help guide students in their postsecondary decision-making, especially in relation to academics and planning for a future career. Academic advising is the most common approach at colleges and universities; many advising initiatives have positive effects on college grades, retention, and persistence (e.g., Bowman et al., 2020; Scrivener & Weiss, 2009). Perhaps not surprisingly, advising initiatives that do not substantially increase engagement with academic advisors tend to have mixed results (Angrist et al., 2009; Finnie et al., 2017; Schwebel et al., 2012).

Mentoring relationships may be developed through formal programs or informally; these are arguably broader in nature, but they can be difficult to define and are not well delineated in existing research (Crisp & Cruz, 2009; Lunsford et al., 2017). Nonetheless, a systematic review found consistently positive effects of student–faculty mentoring on college retention and graduation (Sneyers & De Witte, 2018). Student coaching is a structured approach that combines elements of academic advising and mentoring, and research also supports the effectiveness of coaching for bolstering college retention and graduation (Bettinger & Baker, 2014; Oreopoulos & Petronijevic, 2018; van der Steeg et al., 2015).

Undergraduate Research

A number of studies have linked students' participation in undergraduate research experiences with persistence and retention, with distinct benefits for students from minoritized identities (Chang et al., 2014; Cole & Espinosa,

2008; Jones et al., 2010; National Academies of Sciences, Engineering, and Medicine, 2017). Students may also have more favorable outcomes when they have early and sustained engagement with research experiences, so the intentional design of research experiences that offer multiyear engagement may be important (Jones et al., 2010). However, not all studies are consistent with this conclusion, as a multi-institutional, quasi-experimental study found that engagement in first-year research experiences was not significantly linked with retention or degree attainment (Bowman & Holmes, 2017). Equity-minded considerations for implementing undergraduate research include offering stipends for undergraduate researchers, providing support for instructors to be effective mentors, and promoting students' ownership and agency by making research socially relevant and offering opportunities for students to share their work with others (O'Donnell et al., 2015).

Pedagogy

Students' academic experiences are largely determined by the instructional pedagogies they experience in the classroom. In their review of literature on students' learning motivation and interest, Prenzel et al. (2002) differentiated six aspects of learning environments that support students' learning and success: high-quality instruction, relevant content, student agency and choice, social relatedness, feedback about competence, and caring about students. Kinzie and Kuh (2016) came to similar conclusions in their synthesis of work on student success, identifying instructors' high expectations, use of active and applied learning, diversity experiences, and student–instructor interactions as impactful for students' outcomes.

Recent scholarship provides further support for the benefits of these instructional practices among diverse students. Perceptions of teaching quality, especially clear and organized teaching, has been repeatedly associated with course and college persistence (e.g., Pascarella et al., 2011; Wolniak et al., 2012). Active learning experiences that include class discussions, concept mapping, and writing assignments, as well as collaborative learning experiences that engage students with diverse perspectives, appear to be especially beneficial for first-generation students, racially minoritized students, and students who are less academically prepared (Bowman & Culver, 2018a; Theobald et al., 2020). Students also benefit from practices that provide cognitive challenge (Culver et al., 2019, 2021) and from applied learning experiences like problem-based learning, service-learning, and internships (Jach & Trolian, 2019; Ovenden-Hope & Blandford, 2018; Youngerman & Culver, 2019). Further, there is increasing attention to connecting course content to students' lives to make learning relevant, especially by incorporating their lived experiences and valuing their funds of knowledge (Castillo-Montoya & Ives, 2020; Jehangir, 2010; see Braxton et al., 2014, for further discussion of pedagogies that indirectly influence persistence and graduation).

Facilitated Interactions and Experiences With Peers

Institutions have also designed a number of programs and experiences designed to facilitate students' interactions with their peers within and outside of coursework. As with other college experiences, these interactions indirectly affect persistence and retention. In this section, we discuss the mechanisms that likely support these outcomes among several forms of structured experiences: honors programs, learning communities, supplemental instruction, and affinity groups.

Honors Programs

In honors programs, students are often more likely to experience effective teaching practices and greater interactions with instructors. However, it is the role of taking courses with similar academically motivated peers that appears to drive their success (Bowman & Culver, 2018b). The National Collegiate Honors Council (n.d.) recommended that honors programs include not only a tailored curriculum, but also academic advising, physical space and resources, student leadership opportunities, and potentially a residential component. Honors participation has positive effects on the likelihood of college graduation (Bowman & Culver, 2018b; Keller & Lacy, 2013), as well as having a positive relationship with retention (e.g., Astin, 1993; Shushok, 2006; Slavin et al., 2008).

Learning Communities

Learning communities involve students taking two or more courses together, but they can differ in the number of linked courses, number of semesters, timing during students' attendance (e.g., during the first academic term), size of the classes, integration and coordination across courses, presence of a residential component, and other attributes. Overall, learning communities may primarily be effective at promoting student success when they take a more comprehensive or integrated approach. For instance, a meta-analysis found that learning communities in 2-year colleges are only associated with student success when they provide access to additional support services or counseling (Wurtz, 2014). A large-scale study of six community colleges found nonsignificant results overall, but learning communities led to more credits earned and a higher likelihood of graduation at the only institution that utilized a comprehensive approach, which included a greater integration of the curriculum, academic advising, tutoring, and a modest financial incentive (Visher et al., 2012). When synthesizing the literature on learning communities and educational attainment, Pascarella and Terenzini (2005) concluded that the mixed findings were the result of implementations that were often less intensive or comprehensive. In other words, learning communities primarily seem to promote retention and graduation when they look more like comprehensive student success programs rather than a standalone pairing of classes.

Supplemental Instruction

Supplemental instruction (SI) extends the classroom to provide additional support for course learning, while the embedded structure distinguishes it from other forms of tutoring. In SI, additional nonrequired class sessions provide peer learning opportunities to currently enrolled students; these sessions are led by advanced undergraduates who attend class lectures and who previously took the course and received a strong grade. A recent quasi-experimental study used doubly robust propensity score analysis to account for a number of potential differences among students who chose to participate in SI compared to those who did not participate, finding that participation was associated with academic achievement and retention, with greater benefits for racially minoritized students (Bowman et al., 2021). Nonexperimental studies suggest some of the mechanisms that likely contribute to retention over time, as participation in SI increases success in the corresponding course (Cheng & Walters, 2009), and SI engagement in first-year courses promotes persistence to the second year (Terrion & Daoust, 2011). In a review of research on SI conducted since 2000, Dawson et al. (2014) identified additional potential benefits of participation in SI that may also contribute to beneficial outcomes for students, including reduced anxiety and development of peer relationships.

Affinity Spaces

For students who have identities that are marginalized by dominant campus culture, affinity spaces such as cultural centers and student organizations can offer counter-spaces where these identities are affirmed and validated (Black & Bimper, 2020). These spaces are also particularly important for engaging students who attend primarily nonresidential institutions. Research suggests that students from nondominant groups often feel most welcome in organizations and spaces designed around specific social identities where they feel they can be authentic (Vaccaro & Newman, 2016). Lozano (2010) identified a number of ways that cultural centers increase retention among Latinx students, such as promoting racial/ethnic identity development and providing opportunities for students to engage in social justice activism, academic mentorship, leadership development, and networking. At the same time, centers also often fulfill an advocacy role; a recent study of LGBTQ center directors emphasizes their role in education and advocacy to create more welcoming environments on campus and in the local community (Mundy, 2018). Thus, affinity groups can also promote retention indirectly by shaping the larger environment.

Fraternities and sororities constitute another type of affinity space, which often includes a residential component. These organizations are generally segregated by sex, and the historical exclusion of racially minoritized students led to the development of separate fraternities and sororities for Asian, Black, Latinx, and Native students (Gillon et al., 2019). Overall, participating in a fraternity or sorority appears to increase college retention and graduation (Bowman & Holmes, 2017; Routon & Walker, 2014; Walker et al., 2015). These results seem to be driven by greater social engagement and satisfaction with the social experience of college. Although the results are not consistent, the link between fraternity/sorority engagement and student success is sometimes more favorable for female students (Bowman & Holmes, 2017; F. Grubb, 2006) and for Black students (Severtis & Christie-Mizell, 2007).

Conclusions and Implications for Future Research

Several directions for future research could be useful. We begin by discussing topics for which more attention is needed and then turn to methodological considerations for researchers. First, in his 2009 article on research on retention, Reason argued that more consideration was needed of the conditional effects of students' social identities and backgrounds on retention. Research has increasingly explored whether and how college impact differs by student subgroups based on a handful of precollege characteristics (typically race/ethnicity, sex, socioeconomic status, and/or precollege academic preparation). That said, more inquiry into conditional effects that explores the intersectionality of these characteristics is needed. Additional research should also examine how the relationships of college experiences and programs with student success may vary as a result of college environments and program attributes. For instance, under what conditions do student success programs achieve their intended outcomes? And how do students' perceptions of the institutional environment influence the effectiveness of college experiences and programs for promoting success and equity?

Second, mixed-methods research on college environments, experiences, and programs would provide insights into the processes and conditions under which any effects may occur, but this approach has been somewhat rarely used to date. Quantitative studies can be useful for determining the impact of environments, experiences, and programs, but they often do not examine how any effects may occur, which incorporating a qualitative element could provide. Mixed-methods approaches in higher education could take a variety of forms (e.g., see Griffin & Museus, 2011; Papadimitriou et al., 2014).

Finally, research on college retention and persistence frequently suffers from an underdiscussed form of selection bias: Many samples consist largely or entirely of students who are still retained at the institution or persisting in higher education. Qualitative studies of student success generally consist of students who are enrolled, even if they report not being pleased with their undergraduate experience, and quantitative studies that use surveys to explore environments, experiences, and programs will often miss students who have disengaged or disenrolled from the institution. Scholars clearly face substantial obstacles in recruiting former college students, but this group can provide critical insights into a phenomenon that they have personally experienced.

References

Angrist, J., Autor, D., & Pallais, A. (2020). *Evaluating college support: A study of the effects of targeted college aid offered by the Susan Thompson Buffett Foundation.* MIT. https://evaluatingcollegesupport.mit.edu/

Angrist, J. D., Lang, D., & Oreopoulos, P. (2009). Incentives and services for college achievement: Evidence from a randomized trial. *American Economic Journal: Applied Economics, 1*(1), 136–163. https://doi.org/10.1257/app.1.1.136

Ashley, M., Cooper, K. M., Cala, J. M., & Brownell, S. E. (2017). Building better bridges into STEM: A synthesis of 25 years of literature on STEM summer bridge programs. *CBE—Life Sciences Education, 16*(3), 1–18. https://doi.org/10.1187/cbe.17-05-0085

Astin, A. W. (1993). *What matters in college? Four critical years revisited.* Jossey-Bass.

Bahr, P. R. (2007). Double jeopardy: Testing the effects of multiple basic skill deficiencies on successful remediation. *Research in Higher Education, 48*(6), 695–725. https://doi.org/10.1007/s11162-006-9047-y

Bahr, P. R. (2012). Deconstructing remediation in community colleges: Exploring associations between course-taking patterns, course outcomes, and attrition from the remedial math and remedial writing sequences. *Research in Higher Education, 53*(6), 661–693. https://doi.org/10.1007/s11162-011-9243-2

Barbera, S. A., Berkshire, S. D., Boronat, C. B., & Kennedy, M. H. (2020). Review of undergraduate student retention and graduation since 2010: Patterns, predictions, and recommendations for 2020. *Journal of College Student Retention: Research, Theory & Practice, 22*(2), 227–250. https://doi.org/10.1177/1521025117738233

Bensimon, E. M. (2007). The underestimated significance of practitioner knowledge in the scholarship on student success. *Review of Higher Education, 30*(4), 441–469. https://doi.org/10.1353/rhe.2007.0032

Bettinger, E. P., & Baker, R. B. (2014). The effects of student coaching: An evaluation of a randomized experiment in student advising. *Educational Evaluation and Policy Analysis, 36*(1), 3–19. https://doi.org/10.3386/w16881

Black, R., & Bimper, A. Y., Jr. (2020). Successful undergraduate African American men's navigation and negotiation of academic and social counter-spaces as adaptation to racism at historically white institutions. *Journal of College Student Retention: Research, Theory & Practice, 22*(2), 326–350. https://doi.org/10.1177/1521025117747209

Bordes-Edgar, V., Arredondo, P., Kurpius, S. R., & Rund, J. (2011). A longitudinal analysis of Latina/o students' academic persistence. *Journal of Hispanic Higher Education, 10*(4), 358–368. https://doi.org/10.1177/1538192711423318

Bowman, N. A., & Culver, KC. (2018a). Promoting equity and student learning: Rigor in undergraduate academic experiences. In C. M. Campbell (Ed.), *Reframing Rigor: New Understandings for Equity and Student Success* (New Directions for Higher Education, no. 181, pp. 47–57). Wiley. https://doi.org/10.1002/he.20270

Bowman, N. A., & Culver, KC. (2018b). When do honors programs make the grade? Conditional effects on college satisfaction, achievement, retention, and graduation. *Research in Higher Education, 59*, 249–272. https://doi.org/10.1007/s11162-017-9466-y

Bowman, N. A., & Denson, N. (2022). Institutional racial representation and equity gaps in college graduation. *Journal of Higher Education, 93*(3), 399–423. https://doi.org/10.1080/00221546.2021.1971487

Bowman, N. A., & Holmes, J. M. (2017). A quasi-experimental analysis of fraternity or sorority membership and college student success. *Journal of College Student Development, 58*, 1018–1034. https://doi.org/10.1353/csd.2017.0081

Bowman, N. A., Jang, N., Kivlighan, D. M., III, Schneider, N., & Ye, X. (2020). The impact of a goal-setting intervention for engineering students on academic probation. *Research in Higher Education, 61*, 142–166. https://doi.org/10.1007/s11162-019-09555-x

Bowman, N. A., Mohebali, M., & Jarratt, L. (2022). An interdisciplinary theory of college student success. In N. A. Bowman (Ed.), *How college students succeed: Making meaning across disciplinary perspectives* (pp. 238–272). Stylus.

Bowman, N. A., Preschel, S., & Martinez, D. (2021). Does supplemental instruction improve grades and retention? A propensity score analysis approach. *Journal of Experimental Education*. Advance online publication. https://doi.org/10.1080/00220973.2021.1891010

Braxton, J. M., Doyle, W. R., Hartley, H. V., III, Hirschy, A. S., Jones, W. A., & McLendon, M. K. (2014). *Rethinking college student retention*. Wiley.

Braxton, J. M., Hirschy, A. S., & McClendon, S. A. (2004). *Understanding and reducing college student departure* (ASHE-ERIC Higher Education Report, Vol. 30, No. 3). Jossey-Bass.

Bronkema, R., & Bowman, N. A. (2017). A residential paradox?: Residence hall attributes and college student outcomes. *Journal of College Student Development*, 58(4), 624–630. https://doi.org/10.1353/csd.2017.0047

Brooms, D. R., & Davis, A. R. (2017). Staying focused on the goal: Peer bonding and faculty mentors supporting Black males' persistence in college. *Journal of Black Studies*, 48(3), 305–326. https://doi.org/10.1177/0021934717692520

Brown, J., Volk, F., & Spratto, E. M. (2019). The hidden structure: The influence of residence hall design on academic outcomes. *Journal of Student Affairs Research and Practice*, 56(3), 267–283. https://doi.org/10.1080/19496591.2019.1611590

Buckley, J. B., & Park, J. J. (2021). "Hard to tell": Students making assumptions about compositional socioeconomic diversity on campus. *Journal of Diversity in Higher Education*, 14(1), 110–122. https://doi.org/10.1037/dhe0000159

Cabrera, N. L., Miner, D. D., & Milem, J. F. (2013). Can a summer bridge program impact first-year persistence and performance? A case study of the new start summer program. *Research in Higher Education*, 54(5), 481–498. https://doi.org/10.1007/s11162-013-9286-7

Castillo-Montoya, M., & Ives, J. (2020). A *liberating* education: Integrating funds of knowledge and disciplinary knowledge to create tools for students' lives. In KC Culver & T. L. Trolian (Eds.), *Effective Instruction in College Classrooms: Research-Based Approaches to College and University Teaching* (New Directions for Teaching and Learning, no. 164, pp. 39–48). Wiley. https://doi.org/10.1002/tl.20422

Catalano, D. C. J., & Jourian, T. J. (2018). LGBTQ centers: A queering of gende-aware practice. In D. C. J. Catalano, R. Wagner, & T. Davis (Eds.), *Gender-Aware Practices: Intersectional Approaches to Applying Masculinities in Student Affairs* (New Directions for Student Services, no. 164, pp. 41–50). Wiley. https://doi.org/10.1002/ss.20282

Chang, M., Sharkness, J., Hurtado, S., & Newman, C. (2014). What matters in college for retaining aspiring scientists and engineers from underrepresented racial groups? *Journal of Research in Science Teaching*, 51(5), 555–580. https://doi.org/10.1002/tea.21146

Cheng, D., & Walters, M. (2009). Peer-assisted learning in mathematics: An observational study of student success. *Journal of Peer Learning*, 2(1), 23–39.

Clark, M. H., & Cundiff, N. L. (2011). Assessing the effectiveness of a college freshman seminar using propensity score adjustments. *Research in Higher Education*, 52(6), 616–639. https://doi.org/10.1007/s11162-010-9208-x

Clotfelter, C. T., Hemelt, S. W., & Ladd, H. F. (2018). Multifaceted aid for low-income students and college outcomes: Evidence from North Carolina. *Economic Inquiry*, 56(1), 278–303. https://doi.org/10.1111/ecin.12486

Cole, D., & Espinoza, A. (2008). Examining the academic success of Latino students in science technology engineering and mathematics (STEM) majors. *Journal of College Student Development, 49*(4), 285–300.

Cole, D., & Griffin, K. A. (2013). Advancing the study of student-faculty interaction: A focus on diverse students and faculty. In M. B. Paulsen (Ed.), *Higher education: Handbook of theory and research* (Vol. 28, pp. 561–611). Springer. https://doi.org/10.1007/978-94-007-5836-0_12

Cole, D., Newman, C. B., & Hypolite, L. I. (2020). Sense of belonging and mattering among two cohorts of first-year students participating in a comprehensive college transition program. *American Behavioral Scientist, 64*(3), 276–297. https://doi.org/10.1177/0002764219869417

Crisp, G., & Cruz, I. (2009). Mentoring college students: A critical review of the literature between 1990 and 2007. *Research in Higher Education, 50*(6), 525–545. https://doi.org/10.1007/s11162-009-9130-2

Culver, K., & Bowman, N. A. (2020). Is what glitters really gold? A quasi-experimental study of first-year seminars and college student success. *Research in Higher Education, 61*, 167–196. https://doi.org/10.1007/s11162-019-09558-8

Culver, K. C., Braxton, J., & Pascarella, E. (2019). Does teaching rigorously really enhance undergraduates' intellectual development? The relationship of academic rigor with critical thinking skills and lifelong learning motivations. *Higher Education, 78*(4), 611-627. https://doi.org/10.1007/s10734-019-00361-z

Culver, K. C., Braxton, J. M., & Pascarella, E. T. (2021). What we talk about when we talk about rigor: Examining conceptions of academic rigor. *The Journal of Higher Education, 92*(7), 1140–1163. https://doi.org/10.1080/00221546.2021.1920825

Dawson, P., van der Meer, J., Skalicky, J., & Cowley, K. (2014). On the effectiveness of supplemental instruction: A systematic review of supplemental instruction and peer-assisted study sessions literature between 2001 and 2010. *Review of Educational Research, 84*(4), 609–639. https://doi.org/10.3102/0034654314540007

Douglas, D., & Attewell, P. (2014). The bridge and the troll underneath: Summer bridge programs and degree completion. *American Journal of Education, 121*(1), 87–109. https://doi.org/10.1086/677959

Dowd, A. C., Pak, J. H., & Bensimon, E. M. (2013). The role of institutional agents in promoting transfer access. *Education Policy Analysis Archives/Archivos Analíticos de Políticas Educativas, 21*, 1–40. https://doi.org/10.14507/epaa.v21n15.2013

Evans, W. N., Kearney, M. S., Perry, B., & Sullivan, J. X. (2020). Increasing community college completion rates among low-income students: Evidence from a randomized controlled trial evaluation of a case-management intervention. *Journal of Policy Analysis and Management, 39*(4), 930–965. https://doi.org/10.3386/w24150

Felten, P., & Lambert, L. M. (2020). *Relationship-rich education: How human connections drive success in college.* Johns Hopkins University Press.

Finnie, R., Fricker, T., Bozkurt, E., Poirier, W., Pavlic, D., & Pratt, M. (2017). *Academic advising: Measuring the effects of "proactive" interventions on student outcomes.* Higher Education Quality Council of Ontario.

Fischer, M. J. (2010). A longitudinal examination of the role of stereotype threat and racial climate on college outcomes for minorities at elite institutions. *Social Psychology of Education, 13*(1), 19–40. https://doi.org/10.1007/s11218-009-9105-3

Fitzpatrick, D., Collier, D. A., Parnther, C., Du, Y., Brehm, C., Willson-Conrad, A., Beach, A., & Hearit, D. (2021). Experimental evidence for a first-year experience course plus mentoring on moderate-income university students' engagement, achievement, and persistence. *Higher Education Research & Development, 40*(3), 491–507. https://doi.org/10.1080/07294360.2020.1761303

Gillon, K. E., Beatty, C. C., & Salinas, C., Jr. (2019). Race and racism in fraternity and sorority life: A historical overview. In K. E. Gillon, C. C. Beatty, & C. Salinas, Jr. (Eds.), *Critical Considerations of Race, Ethnicity, and Culture in Fraternity and Sorority Life* (New Directions for Student Services, no. 165, pp. 9–16). Jossey-Bass. https://doi.org/10.1002/ss.20289

Griffin, K. A., & Museus, S. D. (2011). Application of mixed-methods approaches to higher education and intersectional analyses. In K. A. Griffin & S. D. Museus (Eds.), *Using Mixed-Methods Approaches to Study Intersectionality in Higher Education* (New Directions for Institutional Research, no. 151, pp. 15–26). Jossey-Bass. https://doi.org/10.1002/ir.396

Grubb, F. (2006). Does going Greek impair undergraduate academic performance? A case study. *American Journal of Economics and Sociology, 65*(5), 1085–1110. https://doi.org/10.1111/j.1536-7150.2006.00457.x

Grubb, N. (2013). *Basic skills education in community colleges: Inside and outside of classrooms.* Routledge. https://doi.org/10.4324/9780203094297

Hallett, R. E., Kezar, A., Perez, R. J., & Kitchen, J. A. (2020). A typology of college transition and support programs: Situating a 2-year comprehensive college transition program within college access. *American Behavioral Scientist, 64*(3), 230–252. https://doi.org/10.1177/0002764219869410

Harper, S. R. (2012). *Black male student success in higher education: A report from the National Black Male College Achievement Study.* University of Pennsylvania, Center for the Study of Race and Equity in Education.

Harwood, S. A., Huntt, M. B., Mendenhall, R., & Lewis, J. A. (2012). Racial microaggressions in the residence halls: Experiences of students of color at a predominantly White university. *Journal of Diversity in Higher Education, 5*(3), 159–173. https://doi.org/10.1037/a0028956

Hurtado, S., Alvarado, A. R., & Guillermo-Wann, C. (2015). Creating inclusive environments: The mediating effect of faculty and staff validation on the relationship of discrimination/bias to students' sense of belonging. *Journal Committed to Social Change on Race and Ethnicity, 1*(1), 59–81. https://doi.org/10.15763/issn.2642-2387.2015.1.1.59-81

Hurtado, S., Alvarez, C. L., Guillermo-Wann, C., Cuellar, M., & Arellano, L. (2012). A model for diverse learning environments. In M. B. Paulsen (Ed.), *Higher education: Handbook of theory and research* (Vol. 27, pp. 41–122). Springer. https://doi.org/10.1007/978-94-007-2950-6_2

Hurtado, S., Fassett, K., & BrckaLorenz, A. (2019). *Examining the relationship between living environments and sense of community: A multi-institution study* [Paper presentation]. Annual Meeting of the Association for the Study of Higher Education, Portland, OR, United States. https://scholarworks.iu.edu/dspace/bitstream/handle/2022/24672/ASHE19%20Belonging%20Paper.pdf?sequence=1

Jach, E. A., & Trolian, T. L. (2019). Defining applied learning and related student outcomes in higher education. In T. L. Trolian & E. A. Jach (Eds.), *Applied Learning in Higher Education: Curricular and Co-Curricular Experiences That Improve Student Learning* (New Directions for Higher Education, no. 188, pp. 7–11). Jossey-Bass. https://doi.org/10.1002/he.20340

Jaggars, S. S., & Bickerstaff, S. (2018). Developmental education: The evolution of research and reform. In M. B. Paulsen (Ed.), *Higher education: Handbook of theory and research* (Vol. 33, pp. 469–503). Springer. https://doi.org/10.1007/978-3-319-72490-4_10

Jayakumar, U. M., & Museus, S. D. (2012). Mapping the intersection of campus cultures and equitable outcomes among racially diverse student populations. In S. D. Museus & U. M. Jayakumar (Eds.), *Creating campus cultures: Fostering success among racially diverse student populations* (pp. 1–27). Routledge. https://doi.org/10.1353/csd.2013.0068

Jehangir, R. (2010). *Higher education and first-generation students: Cultivating community, voice, and place for the new majority.* Springer.

Johnson, D. R., Wasserman, T. H., Yildirim, N., & Yonai, B. A. (2014). Examining the effects of stress and campus climate on the persistence of students of color and White students: An application of Bean and Eaton's psychological model of retention. *Research in Higher Education, 55*(1), 75–100. https://doi.org/10.1007/s11162-013-9304-9

Jones, M. T., Barlow, A. E., & Villarejo, M. (2010). Importance of undergraduate research for minority persistence and achievement in biology. *Journal of Higher Education, 81*(1), 82–115. https://doi.org/10.1353/jhe.0.0082

Keller, R. R., & Lacy, M. G. (2013). Propensity score analysis of an honors program's contribution to students' retention and graduation outcomes. *Journal of the National Collegiate Honors Council, 14*(2), 73–84.

Kezar, A., DePaola, T., & Scott, D. T. (2019). *The gig academy: Mapping labor in the neoliberal university.* Johns Hopkins University Press. https://doi.org/10.1353/book.68032

Kim, Y. K., & Sax, L. J. (2017). The impact of college students' interactions with faculty: A review of general and conditional effects. In M. B. Paulsen (Ed.), *Higher education: Handbook of theory and research* (Vol. 32, pp. 85–139). Springer. https://doi.org/10.1007/978-3-319-48983-4_3

Kinzie, J., & Kuh, G. (2016, November). *Review of student success frameworks to mobilize higher education* (Report prepared for the Lumina Foundation). Indiana University, Center for Postsecondary Research.

Kramer, J. W., Rausch, S. K., & Braxton, J. M. (2022). Cataloguing institutional retention efforts and their empirical grounding. In N. A. Bowman (Ed.), *How college students succeed: Making meaning across disciplinary perspectives* (pp. 6–27). Stylus.

Kuh, G. D., & O'Donnell, K. (2013). *Ensuring quality and taking high-impact practices to scale.* Association of American Colleges & Universities.

Lohfink, M. M., & Paulsen, M. B. (2005). Comparing the determinants of persistence for first-generation and continuing-generation students. *Journal of College Student Development, 46*(4), 409–428. https://doi.org/10.1353/csd .2005.0040

Lopez, J. D. (2018). Factors influencing American Indian and Alaska Native post-secondary persistence: AI/AN Millennium Falcon persistence model. *Research in Higher Education, 59*(6), 792–811. https://doi.org/10.1007/s11162-017-9487-6

Lozano, A. (2010). Latina/o culture centers: Providing a sense of belonging and pro-moting student success. In L. D. Patton (Ed.), *Culture centers in higher education: Perspectives on identity, theory, and practice* (pp. 3–25). Stylus.

Lunsford, L. G., Crisp, G., Dolan, E. L., & Wuetherick, B. (2017). Mentoring in higher education. In D. A. Clutterbuck, F. K. Kochan, L. G. Lunsford, N. Dominguez, & J. Haddock-Millar (Eds.), *The SAGE handbook of mentoring* (pp. 316–332). SAGE. https://doi.org/10.4135/9781526402011.n20

Mayhew, M. J., Rockenbach, A. N., Bowman, N. A., Seifert, T. A., & Wolniak, G. C. (with Pascarella, E. T., & Terenzini, E. T.). (2016). *How college affects students: Vol. 3. 21st century evidence that higher education works.* Jossey-Bass.

Miller, C., Headlam, C., Manno, M. S., & Cullinan, D. (2020). *Increasing community college graduation rates with a proven model: Three-year results from the Accelerated Study in Associate Programs (ASAP) Ohio demonstration.* MDRC.

Mundy, D. (2018). Identity, visibility and measurement: How university LGBTQ centers engage and advocate for today's LGBTQ student. *Journal of Public Interest Communications, 2*(2), 239–239. https://doi.org/10.32473/jpic.v2.i2.p239

Murphy, T. E., Gaughan, M., Hume, R., & Moore, S. G., Jr. (2010). College graduation rates for minority students in a selective technical university: Will partic-ipation in a summer bridge program contribute to success? *Educational Evaluation and Policy Analysis, 32*(1), 70–83. https://doi.org/10.3102/0162373709360064

Museus, S. D., & Quaye, S. J. (2009). Toward an intercultural perspective of racial and ethnic minority college student persistence. *Review of Higher Education, 33*(1), 67–94. https://doi.org/10.1353/rhe.0.0107

Museus, S. D., Yi, V., & Saelua, N. (2017). The impact of culturally engaging campus environments on sense of belonging. *Review of Higher Education, 40*(2), 187–215. https://doi.org/10.1353/rhe.2017.0001

Nachman, B. R., & Brown, K. R. (2020). Omission and othering: Construct-ing autism on community college websites. *Community College Journal of Research and Practice, 44*(3), 211–223. https://doi.org/10.1080/10668926.2019 .1565845

National Academies of Sciences, Engineering, and Medicine. (2017). *Undergraduate research experiences for STEM students: Successes, challenges, and opportunities*. National Academies Press. https://doi.org/10.17226/24622

National Collegiate Honors Council. (2017). *About NCHC*. https://www.nchchonors.org/about-nchc

Ngo, F., & Melguizo, T. (2021). The equity cost of inter-sector math misalignment: Racial and gender disparities in community college student outcomes. *Journal of Higher Education, 92*(3), 410–434. https://doi.org/10.1080/00221546.2020.1811570

O'Donnell, K., Botelho, J., Brown, J., González, G. M., & Head, W. (2015). Undergraduate research and its impact on student success for underrepresented students. *New Directions for Higher Education, 2015*(169), 27–38. https://doi.org/10.1002/he.20120

Oreopoulos, P., & Petronijevic, U. (2018). Student coaching: How far can technology go? *Journal of Human Resources, 53*(2), 299–329. https://doi.org/10.3368/jhr.53.2.1216-8439r

Oseguera, L., & Rhee, B. S. (2009). The influence of institutional retention climates on student persistence to degree completion: A multilevel approach. *Research in Higher Education, 50*(6), 546–569. https://doi.org/10.1007/s11162-009-9134-y

Ovenden-Hope, T., & Blandford, S. (2018). *Understanding applied learning: Developing effective practice to support all learners*. Routledge. https://doi.org/10.4324/9781315692906

Page, L. C., Kehoe, S. S., Castleman, B. L., & Sahadewo, G. A. (2019). More than dollars for scholars: The impact of the Dell Scholars program on college access, persistence, and degree attainment. *Journal of Human Resources, 54*(3), 683–725. https://doi.org/10.2139/ssrn.2726320

Page, L. C., & Nurshatayeva, A. (2022). Behavioral economics of higher education: Theory, evidence, and implications for policy and practice. In N. A. Bowman (Ed.), *How college students succeed: Making meaning across disciplinary perspectives* (pp. 74–115). Stylus.

Papadimitriou, A., Ivankova, N., & Hurtado, S. (2014). Addressing challenges of conducting quality mixed methods studies in higher education. In J. Huisman & M. Tight (Eds.), *Theory and method in higher education research* (International Perspectives on Higher Education Research, Vol. 9, pp. 133–153). Emerald. https://doi.org/10.1108/s1479-3628(2013)0000009011

Pascarella, E. T., Salisbury, M. H., & Blaich, C. (2011). Exposure to effective instruction and college persistence: A multi-institutional replication and extension. *Journal of College Student Development, 52*(1), 4–19. https://doi.org/10.1353/csd.2011.0005

Pascarella, E. T., & Terenzini, P. T. (2005). *How college affects students: Vol. 2. A third decade of research*. Jossey-Bass.

Patton, L. D., Harper, S. R., & Harris, J. (2015). Using critical race theory to (re) interpret widely studied topics related to students in US higher education. In A. M. Martinez Alemán, E. M. Bensimon, & B. Pusser (Eds.), *Critical approaches to the study of higher education* (pp. 193–219). Johns Hopkins University Press.

Pendakur, S. L., Quaye, S. J., & Harper, S. R. (2020). The heart of our work: Equitable engagement for students in US higher education. In S. J. Quaye, S. R. Harper, & S. L. Pendakur (Eds.), *Student engagement in higher education: Theoretical perspectives and practical approaches for diverse populations* (pp. 1–16). Routledge.

Pendakur, V. (2016). Introduction. In V. Pendakur (Ed.), *Closing the opportunity gap: Identity-conscious strategies for retention and student success* (pp. 1–9). Stylus.

Permzadian, V., & Credé, M. (2016). Do first-year seminars improve college grades and retention: A quantitative review of their overall effectiveness and an examination of moderators of effectiveness. *Review of Educational Research, 86*(1), 277–316. https://doi.org/10.3102/0034654315584955

Prenzel, M., Kramer, K., & Drechsel, B. (2002). Self-determined and interested learning in vocational education. In K. Beck (Ed.), *Teaching and learning processes in vocational education* (pp. 43–68). Peter Lang.

Reeves, S. L. (2015). *Caught up in red tape: Bureaucratic hassles undermine sense of belonging in college among first generation students* [Unpublished master's thesis]. University of Texas.

Robbins, S. B., Oh, I.-S., Le, H., & Button, C. (2009). Intervention effects on college performance and retention as mediated by motivational, emotional, and social control factors: Integrated meta-analytic path analyses. *Journal of Applied Psychology, 94*(5), 1163–1184. https://doi.org/10.1037/a0015738

Routon, P. W., & Walker, J. K. (2014). The impact of Greek organization membership on collegiate outcomes: Evidence from a national survey. *Journal of Behavioral and Experimental Economics, 49*(1), 63–70. https://doi.org/10.1016/j.socec.2014.02.003

Rutschow, E. Z., Cullinan, D., & Welbeck, R. (2012). *Keeping students on course: An impact study of a student success course at Guilford Technical Community College.* MDRC. https://doi.org/10.2139/ssrn.2045924

Sablan, J. R. (2014). The challenge of summer bridge programs. *American Behavioral Scientist, 58*(8), 1035–1050. https://doi.org/10.1177/0002764213515234

Samura, M. (2016). How can residence hall spaces facilitate student belonging?: Examining students' experiences to inform campus planning and programs. *Planning for Higher Education, 44*(4), 90.

Schudde, L. (2016). The interplay of family income, campus residency, and student retention (what practitioners should know about cultural mismatch). *Journal of College and University Student Housing, 43*(1), 10–27.

Schudde, L. T. (2011). The causal effect of campus residency on college student retention. *Review of Higher Education, 34*(4), 581–610. https://doi.org/10.1353/rhe.2011.0023

Schwebel, D. C., Walburn, N. C., Klyce, K., & Jerrolds, K. L. (2012). Efficacy of advising outreach on student retention, academic progress and achievement, and frequency of advising contacts: A longitudinal randomized trial. *NACADA Journal, 32*(2), 36–43. https://doi.org/10.12930/0271-9517-32.2.36

Scrivener, S., & Weiss, M. J. (2009). *More guidance, better results? Three-year effects of an enhanced student services program at two community colleges.* MDRC.

Scrivener, S., Weiss, M. J., Ratledge, A., Rudd, T., Sommo, C., & Fresques, H. (2015). *Doubling graduation rates: Three-year effects of CUNY's Accelerated Study in Associate Programs (ASAP) for developmental education students*. MDRC.

Severtis, R. E., & Christie-Mizell, C. A. (2007). Greek-letter membership and college graduation: Does race matter? *Journal of Sociology and Social Welfare, 34*(3), 95–117.

Sheldon, C. Q., & Durdella, N. R. (2009). Success rates for students taking compressed and regular length developmental courses in the community college. *Community College Journal of Research and Practice, 34*(1–2), 39–54. https://doi .org/10.1080/10668920903385806

Shushok, F. J. (2006). Student outcomes and honors programs: A longitudinal study of 172 honors students 2000–2004. *Journal of the National Collegiate Honors Council, 7*(2), 85–96.

Slavin, C., Coladarci, T., & Pratt, P. A. (2008). Is student participation in an honors program related to retention and graduation rates? *Journal of the National Collegiate Honors Council, 9*(2), 59–69.

Sneyers, E., & De Witte, K. (2018). Interventions in higher education and their effect on student success: A meta-analysis. *Educational Review, 70*(2), 208–228. https://doi.org/10.1080/00131911.2017.1300874

Stanton-Salazar, R. D. (2011). A social capital framework for the study of institutional agents and their role in the empowerment of low-status students and youth. *Youth & Society, 43*(3), 1066–1109. https://doi.org/10.1177/0044118x10382877

Stephens, N. M., Hamedani, M. G., & Destin, M. (2014). Closing the social-class achievement gap: A difference-education intervention improves first-generation students' academic performance and all students' college transition. *Psychological Science, 25*(4), 943–953. https://doi.org/10.1177/0956797613518349

Stewart, D.-L., & Nicolazzo, Z. (2019). High impact of [whiteness] on trans* students in higher education. *Equity and Excellence in Education, 51*(2), 132–145. https://doi.org/10.1080/10665684.2018.1496046

Stinebrickner, R., & Stinebrickner, T. R. (2012). Learning about academic ability and the college dropout decision. *Journal of Labor Economics, 30*(4), 707–748. https://doi.org/10.1086/666525

Strayhorn, T. L. (2015). Reframing academic advising for student success: From advisor to cultural navigator. *Journal of the National Academic Advising Association, 35*(1), 56–63. https://doi.org/10.12930/nacada-14-199

Strayhorn, T. L. (2017). Factors that influence the persistence and success of Black men in urban public universities. *Urban Education, 52*(9), 1106–1128. https:// doi.org/10.1177/0042085915623347

Strayhorn, T. L. (2019). *College students' sense of belonging: A key to educational success for all students* (2nd ed.). Routledge.

Strayhorn, T. L., & Mullins, T. G. (2012). Investigating Black gay male undergraduates' experiences in campus residence halls. *Journal of College and University Student Housing, 39*(1), 140–161.

Summers, M. F., & Hrabowski, F. A. (2006). Preparing minority scientists and engineers. *Science, 311*(5769), 1870–1871. https://doi.org/10.1126/science.1125257

Sun, J., Hagedorn, L. S., & Zhang, Y. (2016). Homesickness at college: Its impact on academic performance and retention. *Journal of College Student Development, 57*(8), 943–957. https://doi.org/10.1353/csd.2016.0092

Swaner, L. E., & Brownell, J. E. (2010). *Outcomes of high impact practices for underserved students: A review of the literature.* Association of American Colleges & Universities.

Terrion, J. L., & Daoust, J. L. (2011). Assessing the impact of supplemental instruction on the retention of undergraduate students after controlling for motivation. *Journal of College Student Retention: Research, Theory & Practice, 13*(3), 311–327. https://doi.org/10.2190/cs.13.3.c

Theobald, E. J., Hill, M. J., Tran, E., Agrawal, S., Arroyo, E. N., Behling, S., Chambwe, N., Laboy Cintrón, D., Cooper, J. D., Dunster, G., Grummer, J. A., Hennessey, K., Hsiao, J., Iranon, N., Jones, L., II, Jordt, H., Keller, M., Lacey, M. E., Littlefield, C. E., . . . & Freeman, S. (2020). Active learning narrows achievement gaps for underrepresented students in undergraduate science, technology, engineering, and math. *Proceedings of the National Academy of Sciences, 117*(12), 6476–6483. https://doi.org/10.1073/pnas.1916903117

Thomas, N. G. (2020). Using intrusive advising to improve student outcomes in developmental college courses. *Journal of College Student Retention: Research, Theory & Practice, 22*(2), 251–272. https://doi.org/10.1177/1521025117736740

Tobolowsky, B. F., & Associates. (2008). *2006 National Survey of First-Year Seminars: Continuing innovations in the collegiate curriculum* (Monograph No. 51). National Resource Center for The First-Year Experience and Students in Transition, University of South Carolina.

Tsui, L. (2007). Effective strategies to increase diversity in STEM fields: A review of the research literature. *Journal of Negro Education, 76*(4), 555–581.

Tuckman, B. W., & Kennedy, G. J. (2011). Teaching learning strategies to increase success of first-term college students. *Journal of Experimental Education, 79*, 478–504. https://doi.org/10.1080/00220973.2010.512318

Turner, P., & Thompson, E. (2014). College retention initiatives meeting the needs of millennial freshman students. *College Student Journal, 48*(1), 94–104.

Vaccaro, A., & Newman, B. M. (2016). Development of a sense of belonging for privileged and minoritized students: An emergent model. *Journal of College Student Development, 57*(8), 925–942. https://doi.org/10.1353/csd.2016.0091

Valentine, J. C., Konstantopoulos, S., & Goldrick-Rab, S. (2017). What happens to students placed into developmental education: A meta-analysis of regression discontinuity studies. *Review of Educational Research, 87*(4), 806–833. https://doi.org/10.3102/0034654317709237

van der Steeg, M., van Elk, R., & Webbink, D. (2015). Does intensive coaching reduce school dropout? Evidence from a randomized experiment. *Economics of Education Review, 48*, 184–197. https://doi.org/10.1016/j.econedurev.2015.07.006

Visher, M. G., Weiss, M. J., Weissman, E., Rudd, T., & Wathington, H. D. (2012). *The effects of learning communities for students in developmental education: A synthesis of findings from six community colleges.* MDRC.

Walker, J. K., Martin, N. D., & Hussey, A. (2015). Greek organization membership and collegiate outcomes at an elite, private university. *Research in Higher Education, 56,* 203–227. https://doi.org/10.1007/s11162-014-9345-8

Walton, G. M., & Spencer, S. J. (2009). Latent ability: Grades and test scores systematically underestimate the intellectual ability of negatively stereotyped students. *Psychological Science, 20*(9), 1132–1139. https://doi.org/10.1111/j.1467-9280.2009.02417.x

Watt, S. E., & Badger, A. J. (2009). Effects of social belonging on homesickness: An application of the belongingness hypothesis. *Personality and Social Psychology Bulletin, 35*(4), 516–530. https://doi.org/10.1177/0146167208329695

Weissman, J., & Magill, B. A. (2008). Developing a student typology to examine the effectiveness of first-year seminars. *Journal of the First-Year Experience and Students in Transition, 20*(2), 65–90.

Windsor, A., Bargagliotti, A., Best, R., Franceschetti, D., Haddock, J., Ivey, S., & Russomanno, D. (2015). Increasing retention in STEM: Results from a STEM talent expansion program at the University of Memphis. *Journal of STEM Education, 16*(2), 11–19.

Wolniak, G. C., Mayhew, M. J., & Engberg, M. E. (2012). Learning's weak link to persistence. *Journal of Higher Education, 83*(6), 795–823. https://doi.org/10.1080/00221546.2012.11777270

Wood, J. L., & Harris, F., III. (2015). The effect of academic engagement on sense of belonging: A hierarchical, multilevel analysis of black men in community colleges. *Spectrum: A Journal on Black Men, 4*(1), 21–47. https://doi.org/10.2979/spectrum.4.1.03

Wright, E. K., & Shotton, H. J. (2020). Engaging indigenous students. In S. J. Quaye, S. R. Harper, & S. L. Pendakur (Eds.), *Student engagement in higher education: Theoretical perspectives and practical approaches for diverse populations* (3rd ed., pp. 69–88). Routledge.

Wurtz, K. A. (2014). *Effects of learning communities on community college students' success: A meta-analysis* [Unpublished doctoral dissertation]. Walden University.

Yeager, D. S., & Walton, G. M. (2011). Social-psychological interventions in education: They're not magic. *Review of Educational Research, 81,* 267–301. https://doi.org/10.3102/0034654311405999

Yosso, T., & Lopez, C. B. (2010). Counterspaces in a hostile place. In L. D. Patton (Ed.), *Culture centers in higher education: Perspectives on identity, theory, and practice* (pp. 83–104). Stylus.

Young, D. G. (2020). Is first-year seminar type predictive of institutional retention rates? *Journal of College Student Development, 61*(3), 379–390. https://doi.org/10.1353/csd.2020.0035

Youngerman, E., & Culver, KC. (2019). Problem-based learning (PBL): Real-world applications to foster (inter) disciplinary learning and integration. In T. L. Trolian & E. A. Jach (Eds.), *Applied Learning in Higher Education: Curricular and Co-Curricular Experiences That Improve Student Learning* (New Directions for Higher Education, no. 188, pp. 23–32). Jossey-Bass. https://doi.org/10.1002/he.20342

Zehner, A. L. (2018). Campus climate for students with disabilities. In K. M. Soria (Ed.), *Evaluating campus climate at US research universities* (pp. 125–149). Palgrave Macmillan. https://doi.org/10.1007/978-3-319-94836-2_6

9

STUDYING STUDENTS AS THEY SWIRL

Methodological Challenges of Studying Student
Retention in the Age of Student Mobility

Jungmin Lee

ollege retention has gained a significant amount of attention from both researchers and practitioners. In higher education research, student retention has long been studied both theoretically and empirically. Among a few theoretical frameworks proposed, Tinto's interactionalist theory has gained a near-paradigmatic status in the higher education literature, despite criticisms regarding its focus on traditional college students in residential colleges (Braxton, 2000). Using empirical data, researchers also find predictors of student retention including student demographics, academic preparation, a sense of belonging, and financial aid, to name a few (Goldrick-Rab et al., 2007; Nguyen et al., 2019; Pascarella & Terenzini, 2005). Retention is a critical issue for practitioners and policymakers as well. Colleges and universities have implemented various programs designed to promote student engagement, such as high-impact practices to keep their students within the institutions (Kuh et al., 2008). Retention has policy implications as many states have adopted performance funding that ties state appropriations to institutional outcomes including student retention and degree attainment (Education Commission of the States [ECS], 2014).

Despite these continued efforts, a vast majority of retention studies focus on first-to-second fall retention of first-time college students attending 4-year institutions (Goldrick-Rab et al., 2007; Pascarella & Terenzini, 2005). Although first-time college students are a majority of college freshmen, especially in 4-year institutions, it leaves another important piece of the student retention puzzle unanswered—the retention of "swirling" students (students who move from one institution to another institution; Allen et al., 2008). These students are not negligible in number; one in four college students across the United States attended two or more higher education institutions during the first 3 years of their college education (Ifill et al., 2016). In addition, some types of swirling (e.g., stop-out and reverse transfer) are related to socioeconomic status (SES)—low-SES students are less likely to reenroll in college than high-SES students (Goldrick-Rab, 2006; Goldrick-Rab & Pfeffer, 2009; Kim et al., 2012). Attending multiple institutions without formal transfer is also negatively related to degree attainment (Adelman, 2006). In other words, swirling students may be at a higher risk of dropping out, but little is known about these students and their retention.

To fill the gap in the literature, this chapter reviews previous studies on the retention and degree attainment of swirling students as well as the methodological challenges of studying student retention in the age of student mobility. First, I define the concept of *swirling* and explore its prevalence using the Beginning Postsecondary Students (BPS) 12:17 data, which ran through 2017 and is the latest available data for a nationally representative sample of first-time college students. The second section of this chapter briefly reviews previous studies on the retention or degree attainment of swirling students. Based on the literature review, I provide recommendations for future research. Then I discuss methodological challenges in studying retention of swirling students with quantitative data. This chapter concludes with a brief concluding thoughts section.

Swirling

College students are mobile. These days, it has become less common for students to attend one institution until they graduate. Instead, students take semesters off, transfer to another college, enroll in two different institutions simultaneously, or return to their first institution. Acknowledging these complex enrollment patterns, McCormick (2003) used the terms "swirling (enrolling back-and-forth among two or more institutions)" and "double-dipping (attending two institutions simultaneously)" as examples of complex attendance patterns (p. 14). Transfer, which is a traditional measure of student mobility, is not enough to describe various enrollment patterns of today's college students.

To describe the prevalence of student mobility, I used the BPS 12:17 data, administered by the National Center for Education Statistics (NCES)

(Brian et al., 2019). Students in the data constituted a nationally representative sample of first-time college students in the 2011–2012 academic year. These students were tracked for 6 years after they started college. Table 9.1 shows the prevalence of stop-out, transfer, simultaneous enrollment, and the number of institutions that students attended, broken down by the institutional sector of their first institution. In the BPS data, *transfer* is defined as a student leaving their original institution and enrolling at another institution for 4 or more months consecutively (Pretlow et al., 2020). Thus, this definition of *transfer* does not include students who take dual enrollment courses in high school, take courses at another college while still being enrolled in their original institution (simultaneous enrollment), or transfer credits without attending the destination institution as observed in reverse credit transfer (Taylor & Bragg, 2015).

Overall, more than a third of first-time college students stopped out or transferred to another institution at least once in college. The stop-out rates are much higher for students who started at 2-year institutions or for-profit institutions than those who started at public or not-for-profit, private

TABLE 9.1
Prevalence of Stop-Out, Coenrollment, and Transfer

	Ever Stopped Out	*Ever Transferred*	*Ever Coenrolled*	*Number of Institutions*
Public 4-year	28%	31%	27%	1.72 (0.89)
Private 4-year (nonprofit)	24%	28%	26%	1.71 (0.95)
Public 2-year and less	45%	40%	23%	1.75 (0.94)
Private 2-year and less (nonprofit)	55%	34%	25%	1.76 (0.82)
For-profit 4-year	51%	30%	41%	1.91 (1.13)
For-profit 2-year and less	72%	26%	47%	1.82 (0.94)
Total	38%	34%	27%	1.75 (0.94)

Note. Following the NCES rules about using a restricted dataset, I rounded the number of students in each group into the nearest 10 and rounded percentages to whole numbers.

Source. Brian, M., Cooney, C., Elliott, B., & Richards, D. (2019, October). *2012/17 Beginning Postsecondary Students Longitudinal Study (BPS 12:17)*. National Center for Education Statistics.

4-year institutions. Transfer rates are relatively consistent across different sectors except for public 2-year and less-than-2-year institutions. Simultaneous enrollment is quite prevalent as well. In public or private nonprofit institutions, about one in four students attended two or more institutions at the same time. The rates are much higher for students who started at for-profit institutions. About 41–47% of college students at for-profit schools took courses at two or more institutions simultaneously.

When it comes to multi-institution attendance, students attended an average of 1.75 institutions during 6 years in college, which is quite consistent regardless of the institutional sector where they first attended. In percentages, about half of first-time college students (50%) attended only one institution, while 33% and 12% of students attended two and three institutions, respectively. In other words, only half of first-time college students stayed in their first institution for 6 years after their initial enrollment, and another half either took courses at other institutions or transferred to another institution. Coenrollment, transfer, and multi-institution attendance have been more prevalent for this cohort of first-time college students than those who entered college in 1996 (Peter & Cataldi, 2005).

In Table 9.2, I explore degree attainment outcomes for students depending on their transfer type. The transfer type in this table is based on students' first transfer because a majority of transfer students made only one transfer. Of all students, about 42% never earned a college degree by the sixth year after their initial enrollment. Please note that this does not necessarily mean that they would never earn a college degree. It may take more than 6 years for some students to earn a college degree, especially if they had stopped out or transferred before. Due to data availability, I could only track them up to 6 years after they started college. Of all students regardless of their transfer status, 38% earned a bachelor's degree, 11% earned an associate degree, and 9% earned a certificate. The degree-attainment outcomes for students who never transferred were similar to those for all students.

There are different types of college transfer, and degree outcomes vary depending on students' first transfer type (see Taylor, 2016, for a review of transfer type). Vertical transfer refers to transferring from a 2-year college (or less-than-2-year college) to a 4-year college, and this is the most common type of transfer. In the BPS 12:17 data, students who transferred from 2-year to 4-year colleges earned a degree, especially a bachelor's degree, at higher rates than students who transferred to a 2-year institution or a less-than-2-year institution. Lateral transfer means moving within the same sector of institutions such as transferring between 4-year institutions or transferring between 2-year institutions. Degree outcomes are starkly different for lateral transfer students. Students who transferred from a 4-year college to another

TABLE 9.2
Degree Attainment Outcomes After Transfer

	No Degree	*Certificate*	*Associate*	*Bachelor's*
Total (N = 22,530)	42%	9%	11%	38%
Never transferred (N = 14,630)	44%	8%	9%	39%
Vertical transfer (N = 1,880)	29%	6%	22%	43%
4-year lateral transfer (N = 2,710)	32%	3%	8%	57%
2-year lateral transfer (N = 1,280)	55%	19%	21%	5%
Reverse transfer (4-year to 2-year or less) (N = 1,410)	49%	11%	14%	26%
Reverse transfer (2-year to less-than-2-year) (N = 130)	35%	62%	3%	N/A
Ever stopped out (N = 8,240)	58%	16%	13%	14%
Ever coenrolled (N = 6,890)	33%	13%	13%	41%
Multi-institution enrollment (N = 10,780)	38%	12%	13%	38%

Note. Following NCES rules about using a restricted dataset, I rounded the number of students in each group into the nearest 10 and rounded percentages to whole numbers. N/A means that the percentage is suppressed following NCES's rules.

Source. Brian, M., Cooney, C., Elliott, B., & Richards, D. (2019, October). *2012/17 Beginning Postsecondary Students Longitudinal Study (BPS 12:17)*. National Center for Education Statistics.

4-year college had the highest rates of bachelor's degree attainment (57%), while more than half of students who transferred between 2-year colleges never earned a certificate or a degree within 6 years of their initial enrollment. This does not necessarily mean that lateral transfer itself caused them not to earn a degree. Instead, it may be the case that students who were not interested in earning a college degree transferred to a 2-year institution or a less-than-2-year institution, or it may take them extra years to meet the degree requirement in their destination institutions. Lastly, more than 6% of students transferred from a 4-year college to a 2-year college or a less-than-2-year college. Only one in four students who made the reverse transfer earned a bachelor's degree, while slightly less than half of these reverse transfer students have not earned a certificate or a degree. For those who transferred from a 2-year institution to a less-than-2-year institution, approximately 62% of students earned a certificate, while very few students received an associate degree.

The three bottom rows in Table 9.2 present degree-attainment outcomes for stop-out students, coenrolled students, or students who attended more than one institution, respectively. More than half the stop-out students did not earn a certificate or a diploma by the sixth year after their initial enrollment. Some of these students never came back after they left, while others transferred to another institution. Simultaneous enrollment or attending multiple institutions did not necessarily harm their degree attainment, given that more than half of them earned an associate or a bachelor's degree.

These descriptive statistics suggest that more than one third of first-time college students have not earned a college certificate or degree within 6 years, and their degree outcomes are widely varied depending on their enrollment pathways. In particular, students who transferred to 2-year colleges or those who took time off had relatively lower attainment rates compared to those who transferred to 4-year institutions or those who never transferred. However, it is noteworthy that student characteristics are related to enrollment pathways, which then influence their degree-attainment outcomes. I will review the relationship among student characteristics, transfer types, and degree outcomes in the next section to better understand the retention and degree-attainment outcomes for swirling students.

Relationship Among Swirling, Retention, and Degree Attainment

Despite the prevalence of complex enrollment patterns, most retention studies, especially those that focus on retention in a single institution, have not paid much attention to these various pathways. Adelman's (1999, 2006) reports are exceptions: Using data for national representatives of high school students, he found that swirling was negatively associated with bachelor's degree attainment. In particular, he warns that stop-out or attending multiple institutions without formal transfer significantly decreased one's probability of degree attainment. Focusing on a single public research university, Johnson and Muse (2012) showed that coenrollment negatively influences retention. Students who simultaneously attended other institutions were more likely to leave and not return after leaving the original institution.

Except for these studies, very few studies simultaneously consider the role of stop-out, coenrollment, and transfer on persistence and degree attainment. Most of the existing studies in the literature focus on transfer, especially vertical transfer, and there is very limited literature on other types of transfer, stop-out, or coenrollment. Keeping in mind this general lack of previous research, I will review empirical studies that examine persistence and degree attainment for swirling students.

Stop-Out, Persistence, and Degree Attainment

Taking time off is negatively associated with college persistence and degree attainment. Unfortunately, it is often disadvantaged or academically under-prepared students who take time off in the first place. Looking at a public research university, Johnson (2006) found that racial minority students, students who delayed college entry, and academically underprepared students were more likely to stop out and less likely to return to their first institution. Part-time students, low-income students, students with a low college GPA, students who received any type of financial aid (grants, loans, or work-study), and students who attended an orientation were less likely to stop out.

Johnson and Muse (2012) explored how simultaneous enrollment affects stop-out and return decisions. In their study university, stop-out students were less likely to come back to their first institution if they attended another institution after the stop-out. Return rates were almost zero if students had not returned within three semesters after they stopped out. State residency and cumulative GPA significantly predicted one's stop-out behavior as well. Out-of-state students or students with a cumulative GPA below 2.0 were more likely to leave the institution and not come back. In contrast, students who spent more years at their first institution were less likely to stop out and more likely to return even after stop-out. These results suggest that it is those who are not well integrated into their first institution who decide to take time off and not come back.

Losing stop-out students can be a negative outcome for higher education institutions, but it may be a good choice for students if they move to another institution that is a better fit and persist in the destination institution until graduation. Unfortunately, this is not the case even when researchers track students across institutions. In Adelman's (1999, 2006) reports, stop-out behaviors significantly decreased one's chance to earn a bachelor's degree among 4-year college students across the country. This negative relation-ship holds even after controlling for student demographics and precollege characteristics. Previous studies consistently report that stop-out negatively influences student persistence and degree attainment.

Coenrollment, Persistence, and Degree Attainment

Even fewer empirical studies explore the role of simultaneous enrollment on students' persistence and degree attainment. Most existing studies find that students who simultaneously enrolled in more than one institution had higher persistence rates, vertical transfer rates, academic performance, and graduation rates than those who never coenrolled (Crisp, 2017; Peter & Cataldi, 2005; Wang & Wickersham, 2014). Using the BPS 04:09 data, which tracked first-time first-year students who entered college in the academic year 2003–2004 until 2009, Wang and McCready (2013) concluded that coenrollment is positively associated with persistence and degree attainment. This positive effect is consistent for both community college students and 4-year college students. Interestingly, they found that coenrolled students were not very different from those who never coenrolled to begin with, in terms of demographics (i.e., gender, race and ethnicity, first-generation status, family income, and home language) and academic performance. This lack of difference suggests that students attend multiple institutions not because they do not fare well in their first institutions but because taking courses from multiple institutions provides a more convenient and fast way to complete courses necessary to graduate. In this regard, Wang and McCready (2013) argued that coenrollment should not be considered as swirling, given that most swirling behaviors often involve disruptive enrollment patterns, which are related to negative persistence and degree-attainment outcomes (Adelman, 1999, 2006).

Vertical Transfer, Persistence, and Degree Attainment

Vertical transfer is regarded as a traditional pathway for community college students (Baldwin, 2017). However, only a small percentage of community college students who initially aspire to transfer to a 4-year college and earn a bachelor's degree do so within 6 years of their initial enrollment (LaViolet et al., 2018). Students who transfer from a 2-year college to a 4-year college are usually the most motivated and organized ones among 2-year college students (Jenkins & Fink, 2016). Transfer processes are often complex and not clearly articulated, but many community college students must navigate the process on their own, as academic advisors in community colleges are already overwhelmed with their high caseloads. As a result, it is usually a few well-organized, highly motivated, and better prepared community college students who successfully transfer to 4-year institutions and continue their study toward a bachelor's degree (Jenkins & Fink, 2016). Empirical studies show that vertical transfer students resemble those who start at 4-year colleges more than their peers at community colleges who do not transfer to 4-year colleges in terms of demographics, family backgrounds, and high school performances (Lee & Frank, 1990). Vertical transfer students are also academically better prepared in community college. Community college students who took math and/or science courses were more likely to transfer to another institution within 3 years (Cohen & Kelly, 2019).

Even though vertical transfer students are comparable to 4-year college students, there are mixed results regarding whether there is a penalty for starting at community colleges as opposed to 4-year colleges. Traditionally, community colleges are deemed to "cool out" students' aspirations of bachelor's degree attainment even though they initially plan to transfer to a 4-year college and earn a bachelor's degree upon college entry (Brint & Karabel, 1989). In addition, Hills (1965) pointed out that community college students who successfully transfer to a 4-year college experience "transfer shock," which is a sudden drop in GPA immediately after their transfer, as they try to adjust to the new institutions. Although empirical evidence demonstrates that this drop in GPA is temporary (e.g., Laanan, 2007), there has been a long-held belief that vertical transfer students are less likely to earn a bachelor's degree than native 4-year college students.

Two empirical studies that use rigorous quasi-experimental methods substantiate the penalty hypothesis. According to Long and Kurlaender (2009), starting at community colleges significantly decreased the probability of one's bachelor's degree attainment within 9 years after initial enrollment. This negative result was consistent for different model specifications (e.g., probit models, propensity score matching, and instrumental variables) as well as for the sample excluding students who started at highly selective 4-year institutions. Alfonso (2006) also found a negative relationship between starting at community colleges and bachelor's degree attainment among National Education Longitudinal Study of 88 (NELS 88) students, even after controlling for students' educational expectations measured in the 12th grade and college enrollment pathways (e.g., delayed enrollment, enrollment intensity, continuous enrollment).

In contrast, other studies conclude that vertical transfer students are as likely to graduate as native 4-year college students. Using the High School and Beyond 1992 (HS&B) data, Lee et al. (1993) found that there was no significant difference in bachelor's degree attainment and graduate school enrollment between vertical transfer students and native 4-year college students. Similarly, Melguizo et al. (2011) also found no significant difference in the number of nonremedial course credits earned and bachelor's degree attainment between the two groups in the NELS 88 data. Both results are surprising given that vertical transfer students came from relatively lower-SES backgrounds, had lower college GPAs, and were less satisfied with academic and social aspects of college than students who started at 4-year colleges. Using propensity score matching, Xu et al. (2018) demonstrated that vertical transfer students in the state of Virginia are as likely to earn a bachelor's degree as native 4-year college students if these two groups are comparable in terms of credits and GPAs earned at the time of transfer (or junior year for native 4-year college students).

It is noteworthy that all three studies that find no significant difference limit their samples to those who were already enrolled in 4-year colleges (either by starting at a 4-year college or transferring to a 4-year college). In contrast, studies that demonstrate a significant penalty for starting at community colleges included all community college students who aspire to earn a bachelor's degree, regardless of their actual transfer behavior. These contrasting results depending on the sample selection suggest that there would be no penalty for starting at community colleges *if* students successfully transferred to a 4-year college. However, many community college students who initially plan to transfer to 4-year institutions fail to do so (LaViolet et al., 2020).

Lastly, not all vertical transfer students succeed in their destination institutions. Wang (2009) showed that being female, taking rigorous coursework in high school, aspiring to earn a bachelor's degree, engaging in college, taking remedial courses, and community college GPAs were related to one's bachelor's degree attainment among vertical transfer students. However, only two variables, internal locus of control and community college GPAs, were significantly related to their persistence in 4-year institutions. Using descriptive statistics, Doyle (2006) demonstrated that credit transferability can make a huge difference: Students whose college credits were fully accepted at the destination institutions were much more likely to earn a bachelor's degree than those whose credits were partially or not at all accepted. However, there are very few empirical studies that explore the role of state transfer policies, and results from these studies are not conclusive (Taylor & Jain, 2017).

Lateral or Reverse Transfer Students From 4-year College

Relatively little is known about transfer of students who start at 4-year colleges. In contrast to vertical transfer students, transfer students who start at 4-year colleges leave their institution because they face challenges or do not fare well (Soares & Watson, 2016). According to Ishitani and Flood

(2018), among those who started at 4-year colleges, male students, White students, low-income students, and students with low test scores or college grades were more likely to transfer to another institution. In particular, one's social integration was negatively associated with one's transfer decisions consistently through the college years (Ishitani & Flood, 2018). Focusing on public 4-year college students in Indiana, Gross and Berry (2016) found that receiving federal or institutional grants significantly decreased one's transfer-out behaviors, while state grants did not have a significant relationship. Other than financial aid, having lower test scores, high school GPA, and college GPA significantly predicted transfer-out. Although these studies shed light on the predictors of transfer-out behaviors among 4-year college students, they did not make a distinction between reverse transfer and lateral transfer.

In fact, scholars argue that there are different correlates of reverse transfer and lateral transfer, respectively. Kim et al. (2012) showed that lower-SES students were more likely to make reverse transfer and stop-out, but student SES was not related to lateral transfer. In addition, working more hours in college led to reverse transfer as well as stop-out behaviors, while getting less financial aid or starting at an out-of-state college increased odds of lateral transfer. Goldrick-Rab (2006) and Goldrick-Rab and Pfeffer (2009) also found that students with lower college grades or with less educated parents tended to transfer from 4-year colleges to 2-year colleges, while middle-income students transferred between 4-year colleges. When students transferred, low-SES students experienced interruption in their enrollment, while middle-income students managed to move across different institutions seamlessly. These studies suggest that students' social class, financial difficulty, or academic challenge predict reverse transfer, while lateral transfer is more related to social or adjustment issues.

When it comes to the relationship between reverse transfer, lateral transfer, and degree attainment, there are mixed results. A few studies find that there is not a significant negative impact for reverse or lateral transfer on degree attainment. Using statewide data, Liu (2016) examined the impact of reverse transfer among 4-year college students whose first semester GPA was less than a 3.0. Surprisingly, these students were as likely as nontransfer students to earn a college degree, to attend college in the fourth year or later, and to get paid jobs postgraduation. Based on these similar outcomes, Liu concluded that reverse transfer can be a good alternative for academically struggling students in 4-year colleges. 2-year colleges provide a more nurturing classroom culture based on lower student–faculty ratio (Townsend & Wilson, 2006) and charge lower tuition rates than 4-year colleges (Snyder et al., 2018), which may improve chances of success for struggling students.

In Texas, Andrews et al. (2014) examined the effect of various transfer paths on bachelor's degree attainment within 8 years. They did not directly look at reverse transfer but explored what happened if students transferred from more selective to less selective 4-year institutions, or vice versa. Overall, students who transferred from flagship institutions (e.g., The University of Texas at Austin and Texas A&M University) to nonflagship 4-year institutions were more likely to graduate than students who stayed in the initial institution. However, if they transferred in their third year or later, they were less likely to graduate than peers who remained in the initial institution in the third year. This study therefore indicated that transfer itself does not decrease degree attainment, but that the timing of transfer matters.

In contrast, Li (2010) showed that 4-year college students who stopped out or transferred to another 4-year college were significantly less likely to earn a bachelor's degree than 4-year college students who never left their first institutions. The negative relationship was less pronounced for students who transferred without an interruption. Two single institutional studies found that transfer students are more likely to leave their destination institutions again than native students who start at the institutions. Comparing transfer students to native students at a public 4-year college, Ishitani (2008) found that transfer students who transferred in as first-year students were more likely to leave the institution than native students. However, the departure rate was not significantly different for both groups if students transferred as a sophomore or later. Among transfer students, adult students were more likely to leave the institution, while GPA earned at the institution was negatively associated with departure. Blekic et al. (2020) found that the second-to-third fall retention rates were lower for transfer students than native students and called for increased advising and student services specifically designed for transfer students.

Lateral Transfer Between 2-year Colleges

Transferring between 2-year institutions is understudied but quite prevalent in practice. For example, more than one fourth of first-time community college students in California transferred to another 2-year institution (Bahr, 2009). According to Bahr (2009, 2012), Black and Asian students, male students, and younger community college students were more likely to make a lateral transfer and have a greater number of lateral transfers than White students, female students, and older community college students. Students who completed more semesters or earned more credits at their first institution tended not to transfer to another community college (Bahr, 2012). To my knowledge, there is no empirical study that has explored persistence and degree attainment for lateral transfer students between 2-year colleges. Given the prevalence of this type of transfer, it is critical to learn whether and how lateral transfer affects student persistence and degree outcomes.

Summary of Findings

- Overall, swirling students are heterogeneous in their demographics, academic preparation, and college experience. Their persistence and degree attainment outcomes are also varied by the type of swirling.
- Attending multiple institutions (coenrollment) is positively associated with persistence, degree attainment, and vertical transfer. There is no significant difference between students who attend multiple institutions and students who do not. Coenrollment is a fast and convenient way to complete courses necessary to graduate.
- Stop-out is negatively associated with persistence and degree attainment. Racial minority students, students who delay college enrollment, out-of-state students, and academically underperforming students are more likely to stop out.
- Vertical transfer students come from more advantaged backgrounds and are academically better prepared than their community college peers who do not transfer to a 4-year college.
- Evidence is not yet conclusive as to whether starting at a community college lowers the probability of earning a bachelor's degree. One of the key milestones is to transfer to a 4-year college. Community college students who successfully transferred to a 4-year college are as likely to earn a bachelor's degree as those who started at a 4-year college.
- Many students who start at a 4-year college transfer to a 2-year college (reverse transfer) or a 4-year college (lateral transfer). Low-SES students, students who work more hours in college, and students with lower college grades are more likely to stop out and reverse transfer. Middle-income students and out-of-state students tend to transfer from a 4-year college to another 4-year college.
- Only a few studies are available for persistence and degree attainment of reverse transfer students and lateral transfer students. Reverse transfer students are as likely to earn any college degree as those who stay in their first institutions. Lateral transfer students are more likely to leave their destination institutions and less likely to earn a bachelor's degree than native students. Note that the relationship is not yet conclusive given the small number of empirical studies.
- Despite the prevalence of lateral transfer between 2-year colleges, little is known about these students and their persistence and degree attainment.

In California, racial minority students, male students, and younger community college students tend to transfer to another community college at higher rates than White students, female students, and adult students.

Recommendations for Future Research

College pathways are very complex for today's college students. They attend more than one institution, take time off, and move across different institutions back and forth until they earn a college degree. Swirling has been a norm rather than an exception, but empirical research on this topic is extremely scarce, except for those on vertical transfer students. Many studies on swirling students are descriptive in nature and focus on who and how many students show these complex enrollment patterns. Although we know that there are a great number of swirling students, very little is known about their persistence and degree attainment. In this chapter, I explored the prevalence of different types of swirling and reviewed previous studies that examined the relationship among swirling, persistence, and degree attainment. Based on the literature review, I provide several recommendations for future research in this section.

Overall, I found that swirling is increasingly common among a nationally representative cohort of beginning college students, but most empirical studies still focus on vertical transfer students and their bachelor's degree attainment. Although these studies employ rigorous quantitative methods that take into account precollege differences between vertical transfer students and native 4-year college students, their results are mixed depending on their sample selection. Other studies that compare transfer-in students to native 4-year college students often do not take into account from which sector of transfer students come, although there are stark differences between vertical transfer students and lateral transfer students. Previous studies on reverse transfer report no significant penalty for transferring from a 4-year college to a 2-year college, but we need more empirical studies to reach a consensus.

In addition, very few studies address retention or degree attainment of students who simultaneously enroll in more than one institution or lateral transfer students between 2-year institutions. This lack of studies is surprising given the prevalence of these enrollment paths among today's college students. Lastly, retention studies often include stop-out in analytical models that predict college persistence or degree attainment and find that it is negatively associated with the outcomes. However, except for a few studies (e.g., Johnson, 2006), most retention studies focus only on the first stop-out and do not consider when and how many times it happened. Since the timing of stop-out can lead to different degree-attainment outcomes (e.g., stop-out in the first couple of semesters may lead to dropout, while stop-out in later semesters may result in transfer or return to the original institution after the time off), it is important to consider the timing of stop-out in addition to stop-out behavior itself. Based on the review of previous studies, I provide several recommendations for future research.

First, I strongly recommend researchers track students for a period longer than the 150% of normal duration of degree attainment and acknowledge that a great number of students are still enrolled in college by the end of 150% of the normal duration. As students take time off, move across institutions, and switch between full time and part time, it would take longer than 3 years (or 6 years) for students who start at community colleges (or 4-year colleges) to earn a degree (Peter & Cataldi, 2005). If data availability prevents researchers from tracking students longer than the 150% of normal duration, I suggest that researchers use college attendance at the third (or sixth) year along with degree attainment outcomes to see whether students who have not yet earned a degree are on track. Surprisingly few studies that examine degree outcomes for swirling students explore the attendance outcome, which would underestimate these students' academic progress. Extending the duration of study or including college attendance at the end of the data collection period would provide more accurate estimates of persistence and degree outcomes for swirling students.

Second, more studies should explore college pathways than merely focusing on retention at a specific time point (usually first-to-second fall retention). Although there is a recent increase in the number of empirical studies on student pathways (e.g., Marti, 2008), they are still few in number, and most of them are descriptive in nature without looking at their relationship with persistence and degree outcomes (Haas & Hadjar, 2020). As I illustrated previously, a great number of students return to their first institution after taking time off. Excluding these students from the sample altogether would lose many students who have the potential to persist and earn a degree. Considering that students from disadvantaged backgrounds are more likely to experience interruption (Goldrick-Rab & Pfeffer, 2009), it is even more important to pay attention to these students' pathways and find ways to help them succeed in college.

Third, I call for more empirical studies that focus on retention and degree attainment for those who start at less selective 4-year institutions or those who move across 2-year institutions. Far fewer studies focus on retention and degree attainment for these students while they tend to experience transfer, stop-out, and simultaneous enrollment at higher rates than students who start at highly selective 4-year colleges (Bahr, 2012; Crisp, 2017).

Lastly, I suggest researchers explore the role of state transfer policies on the prevalence of student transfer and their degree-attainment outcomes. It is well known that many transfer students take extra years to earn a college degree because they often experience credit loss after transfer (Baldwin, 2017). To promote seamless transfer, at least 30 states have a policy on transfer articulation and common course numbering (ECS, 2020). As a response to the criticism that traditional transfer policies only target vertical transfer students, 22 states have recently adopted statewide reverse transfer policies that retroactively grant an associate degree to vertical transfer students who had not met the degree requirement before transfer (ECS, 2020). However, very few studies empirically examine whether statewide transfer policy promotes degree attainment of transfer students, and evidence from these studies is not conclusive (Taylor & Jain, 2017). Given that credit transferability can make a big difference in transfer students' degree attainment and time to degree (e.g., Doyle, 2006), more studies should explore whether a statewide transfer policy leads to better degree-attainment outcomes and provide suggestions regarding how to provide a seamless and efficient pathway for swirling students.

Methodological Challenges

This section reviews methodological challenges in conducting quantitative research that examines retention and degree attainment of swirling students. I focus on quantitative research in this chapter because an overwhelming majority of existing studies on this topic are quantitative except for a few interview studies on transfer students (e.g., Jabbar et al., 2021; Miller & Goldrick-Rab, 2015). Moreover, these few qualitative studies focus on the transfer decision itself rather than examining these students' persistence through degree attainment. For these reasons, this chapter only discusses methodological challenges found in quantitative studies that explore persistence of swirling students, but I call for more qualitative studies on this topic that can shed light on nuanced experiences of swirling students as they pursue their college degrees.

One of the most critical issues in conducting research on the topic is to track students across different institutions. Traditional retention research focuses on a single institution and excludes students once they stop enrolling for any reason (stop-out, dropout, transfer, etc.; Johnson, 2006; Porter, 2003). This may be an appropriate decision if the focus of the study is enrollment management for individual institutions. It is inherently difficult for individual institutions to differentiate stop-out students from dropout students because stop-out students may have the potential to come back anytime (Johnson & Muse, 2012). However, given that three in five students who attended multiple institutions come back to their first institution (McCormick, 2003), excluding all students who stop enrolling may significantly underestimate their persistence and degree-attainment outcomes. Moreover, it is important to differentiate between transfer-out students and true dropout students (who leave higher education altogether), because these two groups have different needs and challenges, which require different institutional practices and policies (Porter, 2003).

To complement this limitation with institutional data, recent studies use statewide or national data that allow researchers to track students who enroll in other institutions across the country. Researchers using statewide data (or system-wide data within a state) can often track students as long as they remain in the state's public higher education system, excluding students who transfer to private institutions or out-of-state institutions (e.g., Bahr, 2009, 2012; Long & Kurlaender, 2009). One way to track students who are enrolled in private or out-of-state institutions is to link state data with National Student Clearinghouse (NSC, 2020) data, which covers more than 98% of students enrolled in higher education institutions across the country. As of this writing, the combination of statewide data with the NSC data is the best way to track swirling students. However, it is also noteworthy that for-profit institutions are not very well represented in the NSC data (Cowan & Goldhaber, 2015), and it can be costly for individual researchers and states to link state data with the NSC data.

Lastly, a majority of empirical studies use data from the NCES, which track nationally representative cohorts of high school students (e.g., HS&B or NELS 88) or first-time college students (e.g., BPS) for 6 to 12 years. Because these data follow individual students, they can track swirling students regardless of the sector and location of their higher education institutions as long as students do not drop out of the survey. These NCES data also collect transcripts from all institutions that students have attended and provide more accurate and objective enrollment information than solely relying on student self-report data. One of the critical issues with the NCES data is duration; BPS data follow students up to 6 years after their initial enrollment, which would not be long enough for swirling students to earn a degree. Other NCES data that track high school students (e.g., NELS 88, Educational Longitudinal Survey 2002) follow students 8 to 10 years after a majority of them entered college for the first time. However, these data represent a cohort of high school students, not college students, and include a high proportion of students who did not go to college at all. Lastly, NCES data were collected from a sample of college students across the country, which resulted in including only a few students from each higher education institution. Therefore, using NCES data may not be appropriate to explore the role of institutional culture, practice, and policy on swirling students. Table 9.3 provides examples of data used by previous researchers, broken down by types of swirling behaviors.

When choosing data, researchers should consider the trade-off between coverage and amount of information available (Porter, 2003). Institutional or national survey data can provide rich information about students, including course-level performances, financial aid information, and psychological and social variables (e.g., the level of social integration). In particular, research using institutional data may provide more nuanced results that consider institutional culture and practice related to swirling students. Statewide data (with or without NSC data) cover all students within its public higher education system, but it has limited information about students. State data usually include demographics, academic performances (standardized test scores, high school GPA, college GPA, etc.), and enrollment outcomes, but they do not provide detailed information such as students' educational aspirations or finances.

Another critical issue in studying retention of swirling students is accounting for precollege characteristics. To control for preexisting characteristics, researchers should carefully choose statistical methods and comparison groups to which they will compare swirling students. As reviewed in the previous section, transfer students or stop-out students are starkly different from students who never leave their first institution in terms of demographics, precollege academic achievement, and enrollment patterns. For example, researchers studying the relationship between vertical transfer and degree attainment should consider students' educational aspirations in their sample selection given that not every community college student is interested in earning a bachelor's degree (Alfonso, 2006). This is why researchers often limit their sample to community college students who aspire to earn a bachelor's degree before college or upon college entry (e.g., Alfonso, 2006; Xu et al., 2018). In addition, it is also important to find comparison groups that are nearly identical to transfer students. Li (2010) argued that researchers should compare transfer-in students to juniors or seniors who start at 4-year colleges instead of all native 4-year college students. Because transfer-in students typically have a couple of years college experience before transfer, it is not appropriate to compare them to freshman students who just start at 4-year colleges. Similarly, it would be more appropriate to compare vertical transfer students to native 4-year college students at less selective 4-year institutions, given that these two groups have more comparable demographics and academic preparedness compared to students who start at highly selective 4-year colleges (Long & Kurlaender, 2009).

TABLE 9.3
Examples of Data Used

National Data	State Data	Institutional Data
Any Transfer, Stop-Out, Coenrollment HS&B 1992 (Adelman, 1999) NELS 88 (Adelman, 2006) BPS 04 (Crisp, 2017; Ishitani & Flood, 2018; Wang & McCready, 2013; Wang & Wickersham, 2014)	*Any Transfer, Stop-Out, Coenrollment* Indiana, public 4-year (Gross & Berry, 2016)	*Any Transfer, Stop-Out, Coenrollment* Public research university (Blekic et al., 2020; Ishitani, 2008; Johnson, 2006; Johnson & Muse, 2012) NLSF (Soares & Watson, 2016) A community college in New York (Cohen & Kelly, 2019)
Vertical Transfer HS&B 1992 (Lee et al., 1993) NELS 88 (Alfonso, 2006; Melguizo et al., 2011; Wang, 2009)	*Vertical Transfer* Ohio, public 4-year (Long & Kurlaender, 2009) Virginia, public 4-year with NSC (Xu et al., 2018)	*Vertical Transfer*
Lateral Transfer BPS 96 (Li, 2010)	*Lateral Transfer* California, community college with NSC (Bahr, 2009, 2012)	*Lateral Transfer*
Reverse Transfer ELS 02 (Kim et al., 2012) NELS 88 (Goldrick-Rab & Pfeffer, 2009)	*Reverse Transfer* Texas public 4-year and community college (Andrews et al., 2014) Public higher education in a small (anonymous) state (Liu, 2016)	*Reverse Transfer*

Note. BPS (Beginning Postsecondary Students), ELS (Education Longitudinal Survey), HS&B (High School and Beyond), NELS (National Education Longitudinal Study of 1988), NLSF (National Longitudinal Survey of Freshmen), NSC (National Student Clearinghouse).

When it comes to choosing statistical methods, researchers may need to consider the trade-off between causal inference and temporal aspects of swirling. A majority of studies regarding retention and degree attainment of swirling students use logistic regression, propensity score matching, or instrumental variables methods to control for preexisting differences between swirling students and nonswirling students (e.g., Andrews et al., 2014; Liu, 2016). These studies typically focus on the first transfer or stop-out that students make and explore whether transferring to another institution (or taking time off in college) influences their persistence and degree outcomes later. Although these studies, especially those using propensity score matching or instrumental variables, are strong in terms of addressing selection bias, they rarely reflect the time-varying nature of swirling behaviors. Scholars who focus on the temporal aspect of swirling often employ the event history model and include time-varying predictors of student persistence (e.g., Johnson, 2006; Ishitani, 2008; Ishitani & Flood, 2018). This would provide a more accurate relationship between swirling and persistence because students' persistence decisions would change each semester depending on their college experiences (e.g., GPAs) and personal factors (e.g., finances or family responsibility), which may vary over time as well. As the model allows time-varying predictors, researchers can explore the influence of multiple stop-outs or transfers as opposed to logistic regression or quasi-experimental models that typically look at the first swirling behavior. However, the event history model is less appropriate to find a causal relationship compared to quasi-experimental models, and its estimates should be interpreted as a correlation rather than a causation.

Lastly, it is also important to provide a clear definition of *transfer* and determine a primary institution for students who attend more than one institution. A traditional form of transfer is that students leave one institution for another institution permanently. According to Pretlow et al. (2020), *transfer* in the BPS 2012:17 data is defined as

> leaving one institution, before and after attaining a credential, and enrolling in another for 4 or more consecutive months. This definition does not take into account whether transfer credits were requested by the student or granted by the subsequent institution. (p. 1)

This definition excludes high school students who take dual-enrollment courses in college as well as students who take courses at another institution only for a summer semester. However, it would still be difficult to determine students' transfer status if they attended multiple institutions simultaneously or took a few courses at another institution for a regular semester and came back to the original institution later. For the former, researchers often determine "the primary institution" in which students enrolled in the most credits in a given semester (e.g., Bahr, 2012) and consider whether students' primary institutions have changed over time to identify transfer students.

Concluding Thoughts

This chapter examined the prevalence of swirling, reviewed previous studies on swirling students and their persistence and degree attainment outcomes, provided recommendations for future research, and discussed methodological challenges in conducting quantitative research on this topic. I find that swirling students are heterogeneous in their demographics, academic preparation, and college experience, and their outcomes should be explored separately by the type of swirling. However, most existing studies focus on vertical transfer students and their degree-attainment outcomes. Clearly, there should be more empirical studies on various types of swirling, including stop-out, coenrollment, reverse transfer, and lateral transfer. When addressing persistence and degree attainment of swirling students, researchers should consider potential trade-offs in choosing their data and analytical methods. As of this writing, there are no existing data that track all undergraduate students across the country *and* provide rich data on students' academic, social, and psychological experiences. Similarly, researchers need to decide if they estimate a causal relationship or reflect temporal aspects of swirling based on their choice of analytic methods. Researchers should carefully define *transfer* and *stop-out* as well, because there is no standard definition of these terms with the ever-increasing complexity of students' enrollment pathways.

Despite these methodological challenges, there are many promising opportunities for researchers interested in this topic. While the number of swirling students continues to increase, we know very little about them and their outcomes. What are predictors of lateral transfer between 2-year colleges? What are persistence and degree-attainment outcomes for reverse transfer students and lateral transfer students? What predicts the return of stop-out students to their first institutions? Are there typical enrollment pathways for today's college students? All these questions are awaiting answers based on research, which will then help institutional practitioners and policymakers better serve our growing population of swirling students.

References

Adelman, C. (1999). *Answers in the tool box. Academic intensity, attendance patterns, and bachelor's degree attainment.* U.S. Department of Education, Office of Educational Research and Improvement. https://files.eric.ed.gov/fulltext/ED431363.pdf

Adelman, C. (2006). *The toolbox revisited: Paths to degree completion from high school through college*. U.S. Department of Education. https://files.eric.ed.gov/fulltext/ED490195.pdf.

Alfonso, M. (2006). The impact of community college attendance on baccalaureate attainment. *Research in Higher Education, 47*(8), 873–903. http://www.jstor.org/stable/40197515.

Allen, J., Robbins, S. B., Casillas, A., & Oh, I.-S. (2008). Third-year college retention and transfer: Effects of academic performance, motivation, and social connectedness. *Research in Higher Education, 49*(7), 647–664. https://doi.org/10.1007/s11162-008-9098-3

Andrews, R., Li, J., & Lovenheim, M. F. (2014). Heterogeneous paths through college: Detailed patterns and relationships with graduation and earnings. *Economics of Education Review, 42*, 93–108. https://doi.org/10.1016/j.econedurev.2014.07.002

Bahr, P. R. (2009). College hopping: Exploring the occurrence, frequency, and consequences of lateral transfer. *Community College Review, 36*(4), 271–298. https://doi.org/10.1177/00915521083309

Bahr, P. R. (2012). Student flow between community colleges: Investigating lateral transfer. *Research in Higher Education, 53*(1), 94–121. http://www.jstor.org/stable/41348999

Baldwin, C. A. (2017). The evolving transfer mission and student mobility. In K. B. Wilson & R. L. Garza Mitchell (Eds.), *Forces Shaping Community College Missions* (New Directions for Community Colleges, no. 180, pp. 37–45). Jossey-Bass. https://doi.org/10.1002/cc.20279

Blekic, M., Carpenter, R., & Cao, Y. (2020). Continuing and transfer students: Exploring retention and second-year success. *Journal of College Student Retention: Research, Theory & Practice, 22*(1), 71–98. https://doi.org/10.1177/1521025117726048

Braxton, J. M. (2000). *Reworking the student departure puzzle*. Vanderbilt University Press.

Brian, M., Cooney, C., Elliott, B., & Richards, D. (2019, October). *2012/17 Beginning Postsecondary Students Longitudinal Study (BPS 12:17)*. National Center for Education Statistics.

Brint, S. G., & Karabel, J. (1989). *The diverted dream: Community colleges and the promise of educational opportunity in America, 1900–1985*. Oxford University Press.

Cohen, R., & Kelly, A. M. (2019). Community college chemistry coursetaking and STEM academic persistence. *Journal of Chemical Education, 96*(1), 3–11. https://doi.org/10.1021/acs.jchemed.8b00586

Cowan, J., & Goldhaber, D. (2015). How much of a "running start" do dual enrollment programs provide students? *Review of Higher Education, 38*(3), 425–460. https://doi.org/10.1353/rhe.2015.0018

Crisp, G. (2017). Student flow and success at 2- and 4-year broadly accessible institutions. In X. Wang (Ed.), *Studying Transfer in Higher Education: New Approaches to Enduring and Emerging Topics* (New Directions for Institutional Research, no. 170, pp. 103–113). Wiley. https://doi.org/10.1002/ir.20188

Doyle, W. R. (2006). Community college transfers and college graduation: Whose choices matter most? *Change: The Magazine of Higher Learning, 38*(3), 56–58. https://doi.org/10.3200/CHNG.38.3.56-58

Education Commission of the States. (2014). *Performance-funding model.* https://www.ecs.org/bpcr/html/educationissues/blueprint/bphemain8c.html#Report50

Education Commission of the States. (2020). *Transfer and articulation policies.* https://doi.org/https://www.ecs.org/transfer-and-articulation-policies-db/

Goldrick-Rab, S. (2006). Following their every move: An investigation of social-class differences in college pathways. *Sociology of Education, 79*(1), 67–79. https://www.jstor.org/stable/25054302

Goldrick-Rab, S., Carter, D. F., & Wagner, R. W. (2007). What higher education has to say about the transition to college. *Teachers College Record, 109*(10), 2444–2481. https://doi.org/10.1177/016146810710901007

Goldrick-Rab, S., & Pfeffer, F. T. (2009). Beyond access: Explaining socioeconomic differences in college transfer. *Sociology of Education, 82*(2), 101–125. https://doi.org/10.1177/003804070908200201

Gross, J. P., & Berry, M. S. (2016). The relationship between state policy levers and student mobility. *Research in Higher Education, 57*(1), 1–27. https://www.jstor.org/stable/43920028.

Haas, C., & Hadjar, A. (2020). Students' trajectories through higher education: A review of quantitative research. *Higher Education, 79*(6), 1099–1118. https://doi.org/10.1007/s10734-019-00458-5

Hills, J. R. (1965). Transfer shock: The academic performance of the junior college transfer. *Journal of Experimental Education, 33*(3), 201–215. https://www.jstor.org/stable/20156766

Ifill, N., Radford, A. W., Wu, J., Cataldi, E. F., Wilson, D., & Hill, J. (2016). *Persistence and attainment of 2011–12 first-time postsecondary students after 3 years: First look* (NCES 2016-401). National Center for Education Statistics. https://nces.ed.gov/pubs2019/2019401.pdf

Ishitani, T. T. (2008). How do transfers survive after "transfer shock"? A longitudinal study of transfer student departure at a 4-year institution. *Research in Higher Education, 49*(5), 403–419. https://www.jstor.org/stable/25704572

Ishitani, T. T., & Flood, L. D. (2018). Student transfer-out behavior at 4-year institutions. *Research in Higher Education, 59*(7), 825–846. https://doi.org/10.1007/s11162-017-9489-4

Jabbar, H., Epstein, E., Sánchez, J., & Hartman, C. (2021). Thinking through transfer: Examining how community college students make transfer decisions. *Community College Review, 49*(1), 3-29. https://doi.org/10.1177/0091552120964876

Jenkins, P. D., & Fink, J. (2016). *Tracking transfer: New measures of institutional and state effectiveness in helping community college students attain bachelor's degrees.* Community College Research Center.

Johnson, I. Y. (2006). Analysis of stopout behavior at a public research university: The multi-spell discrete-time approach. *Research in Higher Education, 47*(8), 905–934. https://doi.org/10.1007/s11162-006-9020-9

Johnson, I. Y., & Muse, W. B. (2012). Student swirl at a single institution: The role of timing and student characteristics. *Research in Higher Education, 53*(2), 152–181. https://doi.org/10.1007/s11162-011-9253-0

Kim, D., Saatcioglu, A., & Neufeld, A. (2012). College departure: Exploring student aid effects on multiple mobility patterns from 4-year institutions. *Journal of Student Financial Aid, 42*(3), 1. https://doi.org/10.55504/0884-9153.1006.

Kuh, G. D., Cruce, T. M., Shoup, R., Kinzie, J., & Gonyea, R. M. (2008). Unmasking the effects of student engagement on first-year college grades and persistence. *Journal of Higher Education, 79*(5), 540–563. https://doi.org/10.1080/00221546.2008.11772116

Laanan, S. F. (2007). Studying transfer students: Part II: Dimensions of transfer students' adjustment. *Community College Journal of Research and Practice, 31*(1), 37–59. https://doi.org/10.1080/10668920600859947

LaViolet, T., Fresquez, B., Maxson, M., & Wyner, J. (2018). *The talent blind spot: The practical guide to increasing community college transfer to high graduation rate institutions.* https://eric.ed.gov/?id=ED585516

Lee, V. E., & Frank, K. A. (1990). Students' characteristics that facilitate the transfer from 2-year to 4-year colleges. *Sociology of Education, 63*(3), 178–193. https://doi.org/10.2307/2112836

Lee, V. E., Mackie-Lewis, C., & Marks, H. M. (1993). Persistence to the baccalaureate degree for students who transfer from community college. *American Journal of Education, 102*(1), 80–114. https://www.jstor.org/stable/1085696

Li, D. (2010). They need help: Transfer students from 4-year to 4-year institutions. *Review of Higher Education, 33*(2), 207–238. 10.1353/rhe.0.0131.

Liu, V. Y. T. (2016). *Do students benefit from going backward? The academic and labor market consequences of four-to 2-year college transfer.* Community College Research Center. https://ccrc.tc.columbia.edu/media/k2/attachments/capsee-do-students-benefit-from-going-backward.pdf.

Long, B. T., & Kurlaender, M. (2009). Do community colleges provide a viable pathway to a baccalaureate degree? *Educational Evaluation and Policy Analysis, 31*(1), 30–53. https://doi.org/10.3102/016237370832775

Marti, C. N. (2008). Latent postsecondary persistence pathways: Educational pathways in American 2-year colleges. *Research in Higher Education, 49*(4), 317–336. https://doi.org/10.1007/s11162-007-9083-2

McCormick, A. C. (2003). Swirling and double-dipping: New patterns of student attendance and their implications for higher education. In J. E. King, E. L. Anderson, & M. E. Corrigan (Eds.), *Changing Student Attendance Patterns: Challenges for Policy and Practice* (New Directions for Higher Education, no. 121, pp. 13–24). Wiley. https://doi.org/10.1002/he.98

Melguizo, T., Kienzl, G. S., & Alfonso, M. (2011). Comparing the educational attainment of community college transfer students and 4-year college rising juniors using propensity score matching methods. *Journal of Higher Education, 82*(3), 265–291. https://doi.org/10.1080/00221546.2011.11777202

Miller, H., & Goldrick-Rab, S. (2015, June). *Making sense of transitions: An examination of transfer among economically disadvantaged undergraduates.* AERA.

National Student Clearinghouse. (2020). *StudentTracker for educational organizations.* https://www.studentclearinghouse.org/educational-organizations/student-tracker-for-educational-organizations/

Nguyen, T. D., Kramer, J. W., & Evans, B. J. (2019). The effects of grant aid on student persistence and degree attainment: A systematic review and meta-analysis of the causal evidence. *Review of Educational Research, 89*(6), 831–874. https://doi.org/10.3102/0034654319877156

Pascarella, E. T., & Terenzini, P. T. (2005). *How college affects students: A third decade of research* (Vol. 2). ERIC.

Peter, K., & Cataldi, E. F. (2005). The road less traveled? Students who enroll in multiple institutions. *Education Statistics Quarterly, 2*(7), 161–166. https://nces.ed.gov/pubs2005/2005157.pdf

Porter, S. R. (2003). Understanding retention outcomes: Using multiple data sources to distinguish between dropouts, stopouts, and transfer-outs. *Journal of College Student Retention: Research, Theory & Practice, 5*(1), 53–70. https://doi.org/10.2190/NV6H-55NG-8EYW-EKGP

Pretlow, J., Jackson, D., & Bryan, M. (2020). *A 2017 follow-up: Six-year withdrawal, stopout, and transfer rates for 2011–12 first-time postsecondary students* (web tables; NCES 2020-239). National Center for Education Statistics. https://nces.ed.gov/pubs2020/2020239rev.pdf

Snyder, T. D., De Brey, C., & Dillow, S. A. (2018). *Digest of education statistics 2016* (NCES 2017-094). National Center for Education Statistics. https://nces.ed.gov/pubs2017/2017094.pdf

Soares, J. A., & Watson, K. (2016). Transfer students and the mismatch hypothesis. *International Journal of Educational Studies, 3*(1), 19–27. https://esciencepress.net/journals/index.php/IJES/article/view/1415

Taylor, J. L. (2016). Reverse credit transfer policies and programs: Policy rationales, implementation, and implications. *Community College Journal of Research and Practice, 40*(12), 1074–1090. https://doi.org/10.1080/10668926.2016.1213673

Taylor, J. L., & Bragg, D. D. (2015). *Optimizing reverse transfer policies and processes: Lessons from twelve CWID states.* Office of Community College Research and Leadership, University of Illinois at Urbana-Champaign. https://www.lumina-foundation.org/files/resources/optimizing-reverse-transfer.pdf

Taylor, J. L., & Jain, D. (2017). The multiple dimensions of transfer: Examining the transfer function in American higher education. *Community College Review, 45*(4), 273–293. https://doi.org/10.1177/0091552117725177

Townsend, B. K., & Wilson, K. (2006). "A hand hold for a little bit": Factors facilitating the success of community college transfer students to a large research university. *Journal of College Student Development, 47*(4), 439–456. https://doi.org/10.1353/csd.2006.0052

Wang, X. (2009). Baccalaureate attainment and college persistence of community college transfer students at 4-year institutions. *Research in Higher Education, 50*(6), 570–588. https://doi.org/10.1007/s11162-009-9133-z

Wang, X., & McCready, B. (2013). The effect of postsecondary coenrollment on college success: Initial evidence and implications for policy and future research. *Educational Researcher, 42*(7), 392–402. https://doi.org/10.3102/0013189X13505683

Wang, X., & Wickersham, K. (2014). Postsecondary co-enrollment and baccalaureate completion: A look at both beginning 4-year college students and baccalaureate aspirants beginning at community colleges. *Research in Higher Education, 55*(2), 166–195. https://doi.org/10.1007/s11162-013-9317-4

Xu, D., Jaggars, S. S., Fletcher, J., & Fink, J. E. (2018). Are community college transfer students "a good bet" for 4-year admissions? Comparing academic and labor-market outcomes between transfer and native 4-year college students. *Journal of Higher Education, 89*(4), 478–502. https://doi.org/10.1080/00221546.2018.1434280

PART THREE

PRACTICE

10

CREATING AND SUSTAINING ORGANIZATIONAL CHANGE TO PROMOTE COLLEGE STUDENT PERSISTENCE IN NATURAL AND OPEN SYSTEMS

Kristen A. Renn and Brandon R. G. Smith

A s is clear in previous chapters in this book, decades of research on student retention have identified a number of proven or promising institutional strategies to promote student success. There are successful strategies that connect research, theory, and practice that can benefit an institution's goal of supporting persistence and retaining students. There are also, however, organizational features that interfere with efforts to implement potential solutions to enduring challenges with student attrition, and there are factors in the overall postsecondary ecosystem that work against institutional and systemic improvement. Drawing from experiences with data-based decision-making, strategic enrollment management, and networked innovation efforts such as the University Innovation Alliance, we focus in this chapter on what keeps institutions from implementing research findings that might increase student persistence and how to overcome these challenges.

Good intentions on the part of institutional actors and policymakers do not always lead to good implementation of strategies to improve student outcomes including persistence. So what goes wrong? Here are three common scenarios we have observed. In the first, high-level leaders in a position to make decisions about curriculum, programs, and resource allocation pay more attention to external factors like college rankings than to the data they have in front of them about student needs. In the second, student-facing and midlevel practitioners attend a conference or webinar and learn about a program that works somewhere else, try to replicate it on their home campus without considering key differences in context, and ultimately fail. In the third example, faculty operate independently to ignore or bypass institutional efforts to engage them in student retention activities such as real-time course progress alerts or making course materials available in open educational resource (OER) formats. We could go on. Indeed when one considers all of the factors that must align for effective implementation of strategies to promote student persistence, it may seem surprising that any of them ever succeed. Misalignment of organizational factors and disregard for data also explain why so many "I heard about it at a conference" ideas for improving student persistence fail to take root at other institutions.

In the first example, leaders prioritize external factors over internal data that identify opportunities to address student needs through curriculum, programs, and resource allocation. In the 4-year institution sector, external factors might include gaining prestige, achieving higher rankings, joining particular athletic conferences, and moving into what they perceive as higher Carnegie Classification categories.[1] The phenomenon of institutional striving is well established in the literature (Doran, 2015; Gonzales, 2013; Gonzales et al., 2014; McClure & Titus, 2018; O'Meara, 2007), with the common motivations of chasing rankings and aspiring to move "up" the Carnegie Classifications (O'Meara, 2007).

Rankings (e.g., *U.S. News and World Report* [*USNWR*] and *Times Higher Education* World University Rankings) are based on a number of inputs. For the *USNWR* rankings, many of these inputs relate to decisions about student admissions/selectivity and resource allocation such as student–instructor ratios, research dollars per faculty member, and fundraising (endowment dollars per student, percentage of graduates who donate to the institution). The rankings reflect some assumptions about what makes better undergraduate education—for example, smaller class sizes and more endowment resources available per student—and what marks the reputation of the institution, such as admissions selectivity and donations (Morse & Brooks, 2020). Although evidence for positive effects of smaller class size on college

---

[1] We note that the Carnegie Classification system is not a ranking or rating system. It is "a framework for recognizing and describing institutional diversity." Nevertheless, many institutions with graduate programs of any size strive to move "up" the categories to reach the "R1" classification, which is "Doctoral Universities—Very High Research Activity" (see O'Meara, 2007, pp. 121–122).

student learning is limited (see Ake-Little et al., 2020; Shi, 2019), it is hard to argue that a lower student–instructor ratio detracts from student success. Shifting resources to hire more instructors and improve a rankings factor might also serve student retention goals. It is difficult, however, to believe that rejecting a higher proportion of applicants in and of itself contributes to persistence of the students who do enroll. Investing in recruiting more students and then admitting from the top of the pool might increase the institutional retention rate by bringing in students with higher ACT or SAT scores (one *USNWR* measure of incoming student quality), but it represents a sleight of hand by shifting priorities to increase the size of the applicant pool and change the student population rather than changing the organization to better serve students.

The Carnegie Classifications are descriptive and based on degrees awarded, yet the allure of striving toward the next category can influence institutional priorities away from undergraduate students. McClure and Titus (2018) identified shifts in resource allocation toward administrative spending at public institutions that had recently gained research university status. They found that this surge in administrative funding dissipated over time, indicating that it may have been related to strategies for achieving reclassification.

In the second example we offered, professionals who provide direct services to students learn about a promising practice at another institution. Conferences about student persistence and success have become commonplace, drawing thousands of educators every year. Plenaries feature good news about how a campus is increasing completion, decreasing time to degree, and/or closing opportunity gaps. Breakout sessions may dig into specifics of programs on predictive analytics, proactive academic advising, cohort and peer mentor programs, and other approaches to increasing persistence. Reenergized in their commitment to improving outcomes on their home campus, professionals bring these ideas back to their institution. They gather a group of similarly committed colleagues and start developing a plan to implement a new program. They may spend a lot of time on the plan only to have it denied funding; if they are fortunate enough to get this idea in front of someone "up the line" in administration who can provide resources for implementation, they may be able to launch it. But within a few years, enthusiasm fades, the champions of the effort are involved in other work, and there are no lasting results to show for the investment of time, energy, and resources. We do not paint this picture cynically or to cast blame on the good work and ideas of student success professionals, but to point out a situation we have seen repeatedly across our combined 40-plus years of higher education practice. What went wrong?

We identify a number of factors in this common scenario. The enthusiastic professionals may not have done thorough background research to identify the organizational context and challenges that had to be overcome at the model institution, or fully understand the context and challenges at their own institution. Scholarship on innovation through networks in higher education shows that ideas may not transfer well to new settings without some adaptations (Hill et al., 2019; Kezar, 2014; Kezar et al., 2019). Specific student persistence challenges may differ in ways that doom the idea from the start, or organizational dynamics at the home institution may not bode well for an idea bubbling up from a group of frontline student service providers. We have observed that access to institutional data—knowing what data exist, knowing how to obtain the information, knowing what to do with it—is another potential hurdle for practitioners on some campuses, preventing them from adapting good ideas from other campuses to work effectively at home. Or perhaps they did not engage enough of the political actors on campus who could provide access to resources necessary for continued implementation of the initiative. Maybe their networks did not extend enough into the level of decision-makers and their ideas ended up in competition with other good ideas related to other institutional priorities, losing out when the time came to allocate resources.

In our final example, faculty and other instructors derail attempted interventions by not participating in activities necessary for their success. Certainly instructors have many responsibilities to their students and to the institution, and we leave space for the possibility that some of them remain unaware of efforts to include them in persistence efforts. Here we are addressing intentional disregard for participating in, for example, voluntary adoption of OER course materials, which have been suggested to improve outcomes for low-income students (Jenkins et al., 2020). Or instructors ignore nonmandatory requests to report real-time course progress in campus early alert systems, another intervention with proven results (Dwyer et al., 2019; Villano et al., 2018). Learning management systems can be used in ways that allow for analysis of student engagement (e.g., signing on to access readings, completing homework assignments) and performance (graded assignments) without involving instructors. But other forms of getting real-time information about students in courses may rely on instructor participation, and faculty have offered a number of reasons for not participating, including student privacy, added workload, and pedagogical philosophy (see Johnson, 2018; McKenzie, 2018). Because so much of student academic success relies on instructor behavior (Braxton, 2008; Mayhew et al., 2016; Renn & Reason, 2021), nonparticipation by faculty can derail well-intentioned institutional efforts.

In this introduction we have highlighted a number of factors that can interfere with institutional efforts to improve student outcomes such as student persistence. They are features of organizational aspirations, culture, capacity, and citizenship, none of which are known in higher education to be particularly susceptible to quick fixes. The student success landscape that has emerged in postsecondary education is littered with false starts and the detritus of "shiny object-ism," when the latest predictive analytics software platform, student-facing app, or underresourced support program is abandoned. In this chapter we attempt to explain how student persistence reform efforts might stand a better chance of surviving long enough to make a difference for the students they are meant to serve.

For some readers of this chapter, the scenarios we present in our introduction are likely familiar, possibly cyclical, or perhaps even occurring in this moment. More readers may agree that higher and postsecondary education is seemingly in a constant state of change and responsiveness—internally, involving various divisions and departments likely trying to accomplish similar things in different ways, and externally, responding to stakeholders in government, industry, and the public. Yet most institutional missions continue to maintain commitment to the undergraduate student experience. While the institution keeps the interests of students in mind—albeit, at times for competing factors such as enrollment, rankings, and revenue—*change* is a constant, challenging, but necessary experience for faculty, staff, and administration. We have observed that change occurs but argue its sustainability and success can be restrained by a number of factors even while lasting and productive change *is* possible. In this chapter we consider selected theories to describe organizational features that influence how change occurs. Next, we discuss examples of initiatives that are tested, scaled, and diffused to identify facilitators of and obstacles to adoption. Finally, we offer strategies for engaging organizational change to promote student persistence.

Systems Perspectives on Postsecondary Education

A quote widely attributed to W. Edwards Deming is "Every system is perfectly designed to get the results it gets."[2] By this principle, postsecondary institutions are perfectly designed to continue to fail substantial proportions of their students who leave college without having met their educational goals (transfer, a degree, or other educational credential). Viewing colleges

---

[2] The source of this quote is not clear. See https://deming.org/quotes/10141/ for a discussion.

and universities as complex organizations and systems helps understand how and why they embrace or resist the changes necessary to increase student persistence. In this section we describe the complexity of understanding postsecondary education institutions as organizations and discuss two common models that we apply to postsecondary institutions: natural systems and open systems.

As organizations, postsecondary institutions have been described as "collectivities whose participants are pursuing multiple interests, both disparate and common, but who recognize the value of perpetuating the organization as an important resource" (Scott & Davis, 2016, p. 28). Thinking about colleges as collective organizations is a way to understand interactions among systems, environments, and people. There are a number of classical perspectives on organizations in general and higher education organizations in particular: scientific management (Taylor, 1919), organizational behavior (Maslow, 1943; Mayo, 1933), the structural lens of Mintzberg's (1980) organizational design model and the loose coupling of colleges as organizations by Weick (1976), modern studies of organizational culture and institutional theory (Bolman & Deal, 1984, 2017), and the influence of politics (Mintzberg, 1980) and change (Schein, 2004) on and within the organization. Taken together they make clear that organizational change is complex, does not happen in isolation, and requires guidance and leadership. These perspectives help explain change in the context of institutions, their leadership, and environmental influences on them and their resources (Katz & Kahn, 1966; Pfeffer & Salancik, 2003).

For decades, higher education scholars have employed these theories, without fully considering the ways that the models themselves may pattern and constrain thinking about what it is about higher education organizations that perpetuates unacceptably inequitable student outcomes. Recently, critical organizational scholars have pointed to the ways that these models fall short in understanding the conditions necessary for implementing changes that can improve and sustain goals such as increasing retention and completion, reducing student debt, and closing opportunity gaps. For example, in considering Bolman and Deal's (1984, 2017) classic four-frame model of organizational thinking, critics question whether or not an organization can be so organized, specifically voicing "concern over whether the route from a leader's thoughts to actions is as simple as the model presumes" (Vuori, 2018, p. 174). In addition, this traditional approach excludes diverse perspectives, coming across as a heteropatriarchal way to view the functioning of organizations (Acker, 1992; Vuori, 2018).

The historical absence of diverse perspectives in organizational theory is also not directly addressed, nor are further considerations regarding the decolonization of postsecondary education, broadly, and specifically the organization as the institution (Gonzales et al., 2018). However, a *systems* perspective (Scott & Davis, 2016) of organizations provides a more inclusive understanding of organizations, their location within inequitable power structures, and how colleges as organizations continuously respond and adapt to these conditions. Understanding postsecondary institutions as systems provides a way to observe and understand these inherent internal and external complexities. Ultimately, a systems perspective helps to make sense of organizations and how change occurs.

Postsecondary Education as Natural and Open Systems

Thinking of universities and colleges as organizations that are natural and open systems (Scott & Davis, 2016) are just two of many perspectives that can be used to understand how change occurs in postsecondary education— and what keeps institutions from acting. In foundational research on organizational theory, *systems* are positioned to function by "tracing the pattern of energy exchange or activity of people as it results in some output" and "ascertaining how the output is translated into energy which reactivates the pattern" (Katz & Kahn, 1978, p. 61). In short, when considering organizations, one can see systems as interconnections within a greater body, working together to achieve certain goals. Various systems theories in higher education help explain the complexity of postsecondary organizations, the multiple actors within them, and the success or failure of attempts to change practices, culture, policies, or values. In this section, we briefly introduce two models—natural and open systems in higher education—and then discuss how change occurs (or is resisted) in each.

Natural Systems

Developed in the 1930s, natural systems theory emerged in response to the rational systems[3] perspective of organizations, which focused exclusively on the formal aspects of organizations. From the natural system perspective, organizations are described as "collectivities whose participants are pursuing multiple interests, both disparate and common, but who recognize the value of perpetuating the organization as an important resource" (Scott & Davis,

---

[3] Rational systems contrast natural systems, as they are "instruments designed to attain goals" (Scott & Davis, 2016, p. 35), illustrated as a machine exclusively focusing on the formality of organizing within the organization. Accordingly, rational systems reject all social aspects about and within the organization, preferring technicality, productivity, and efficiency.

2016, p. 28). Participants engage within this informal structure, and their relationships have influence on each other and on the organization. Natural systems constitute "a machine for accomplishing goals, or as a small society with a social structure and culture" (p. 27).

Natural systems are rooted in social context and the behavior of participants, which influence how the system's informal structures assist in achieving common goals through a shared sense of purpose (Jackson, 2003; Scott & Davis, 2016). In a college or university setting, there are protocols and operational procedures, but actors prioritize interpersonal connections and informalities over goal attainment per se, as relationships themselves are what lead to action that ultimately achieves shared objectives. Consequently, these informal and relational aspects of organizations are more influential than formal systems and structures, as seen by how people engage to share knowledge, work together, cooperate, and respond to organizational values and norms in order to achieve specific goals and objectives (Jackson, 2003; Mohajan, 2019).

Because natural systems operate within social interests of organizational members, they are complex settings. Whether through consensus, conflict, or engagement, natural systems endeavor to achieve "real goals" that are socially constructed over the stated, operational goals of the organization—all of which are governed and decided by the social aspects of the institution. Therefore, natural systems typically do not respond to the environment around them, but will adapt to surroundings after focusing within, and attend to informal structures and behavioral elements of the organization itself (Scott & Davis, 2016). Our second scenario at the opening of the chapter might offer one example, as student-facing staff often operate within campus networks of colleagues who share perspectives on student persistence, demonstrating the value of relationships in sharing ideas that might help meet mutual goals. While the staff who attended the webinar were excited to implement a program and able to recruit colleagues who shared this enthusiasm, they were not in campus networks and relationships that could enable sustainable change, demonstrating a downside to trying to implement change in a natural system. Meanwhile, from the third scenario, faculty were engaged in their own networks, separate from conversations about student persistence that might have motivated them to participate in the early alert or OER initiatives, or at least to join others on campus in working on ideas to improve this student outcome.

Open Systems

While natural systems focus on growing and evolving internally to meet the organization's needs, open systems take a different approach. Open systems interact with formal and informal processes and characteristics by responding to and interacting with multiple environments with the intention to attain goals. Open systems focus strongly on how environments influence organizations (Bastedo, 2004; Scott & Davis, 2016), and specifically the political and social contexts. This approach frames organizational survival and goal achievement as functions of constant adaptations of formal systems and behavior. Consequently, the framework relies on "non-uniformity that preserves the differential structure of an open system" (Scott & Davis, 2016, p. 95) in organizations that are not isolated from their surroundings. Internal and external environments interact, resulting in complexity and change within the institution as it depends on maintenance afforded by external resources that in turn allow the organization the opportunity to sustain change. In essence, due to everything happening outside and making its way into the organization, open systems seek stability. As a result, the organization—from the highest level of administration—will endeavor to engage change to balance organizational needs in response to and while responding to the environment.

To be sure, there are a number of features of postsecondary institutions that we believe need to be changed to achieve equitable student outcomes, and if external forces are the motivator, then that is for the good. Like the leaders in our first hypothetical example, senior leaders in contemporary higher education are acutely aware of their environment—one in which, for a number of often unhappy reasons, "the motto adapt or die has been embraced as a rallying cry that promotes transformative change through innovation" (Tierney & Lanford, 2016, p. 3). A challenge for improving student persistence, however, lies in part in what leaders decide is the goal of that transformative change and what other outcomes they are willing to alter or disregard to achieve it.

Natural Systems, Open Systems, and Change

As we have emphasized, understanding system dynamics helps explain how change happens (or is resisted), and consequently how "the academy will often fail to engage the very people who must bring about the change" (Kezar, 2001, p. 8). Natural and open systems share some characteristics: Both view organizational behavior as being more than a top-down, linear approach to decision-making and change, and both embrace the human and social component of organizations that inherently influences systems, functionality, and change. Furthermore, both natural and open systems depend in some way on environmental factors for growth, which opens opportunities to influence the organization's structure and behavior. There are, however, nuances between natural and open systems, particularly with regard to how environments engage with or within the organization. Integrating both perspectives allows greater meaning-making of implications for creating change, and the actors and stakeholders who are involved.

When considering postsecondary institutions as natural and open systems, campus stakeholders can understand change, where and how it occurs, and why implementing it can be challenging, yet also sometimes successful. For example, feedback loops within these systems help identify expectations and parameters within independent units—such as committees, boards, faculty, staff, alumni, and the external community—which in turn help define change as a process. Considering change within postsecondary institutions and viewing postsecondary education organizations as natural and open systems allows for engagement among all stakeholders, while also permitting external environments to influence, not disrupt, change processes. Change is thus interdependent with goals and their attainment, performance outcomes of the organization, and resources that are provided to the organization for maintenance, which are described in the following section.

Goal Attainment, Performance Outcomes, and Resource Dependency

Goals for postsecondary institutions require specificity, are generally complex, and are often used as measures of performance. As publicly funded institutions—and nearly all postsecondary institutions in the United States are publicly funded either directly (e.g., state appropriations, federal grants) or indirectly (e.g., student tuition paid through federal loans)—colleges and universities are open systems that are dependent on external resources for maintenance and thus accountable to those external forces. Accountability comes with expectations for meeting goals that increasingly include measures of student success (e.g., transfer rate, retention, graduation rate). Yet even when these goals are shared by internal actors, organizations that focus entirely on external performance, process, and outcome goal attainment can lose focus on the human aspect of the organization (McClure & Titus, 2018).

Resource dependency theory argues that organizations operating in open systems tend to act in ways to respond to environmental pressures that may impede their organizational autonomy (Barnhardt et al., 2017). This theory holds that organizations need to maximize and draw resources from the environment, therefore making the organization more dependent on stakeholders and the external environment than on internal structures and resources (Scott & Davis, 2016). The relationships and values that turn the gears of natural systems take a backseat to the resource dependence of the open system. Furthermore, resource dependency can assert power from the private over the public sector, particularly education, forcing organizations to "outperform one's competitors [which is] all-important" and fields like postsecondary education "may find once secure niches completely eroded by more nimble service-oriented firms in the private sector" (Morgan, 2006, p. 61). Consequently, the organization's need to survive becomes the primary objective, a phenomenon particularly experienced during challenging economic times (Powell & Rey, 2015) and magnified during the disruption of the COVID-19 pandemic.

Depending on the context (i.e., institutional type, other funding sources), colleges as open systems face a constant need to respond to change because they depend on external resources, often forfeiting opportunities to intentionally plan and navigate toward originally internal goals. A natural systems perspective highlights the opportunity for postsecondary institutions to be the site of multiple and conflicting objectives of internal interest groups who may share some but not all goals and priorities. Resource dependence may force compromises by interest groups, thus blending open and natural systems. If the leaders in our first hypothetical example were at a public university in a state with a performance-based funding system that included progressive student completion targets, one would expect their decisions to align with this external force; faculty might capitulate to participating in student success initiatives if they were convinced that the programs would support the student completion goals and therefore protect institutional funding.

Applying Systems Perspectives to the Case of Student Success

As described, systems perspectives are a way to understand postsecondary institutions as organizations and how change occurs within them. Systems also help identify how intentionality and informed change as a process are possible when trying to achieve student success goals, whether internal or external, tied to specific resources. We have observed that deliberate and organized change is not always the case in practice, and deliberate attempts to create change do not always succeed. There are, however, examples of purposeful change in the direction of increased student persistence *and* equity. We present an example to illustrate the potential of using organizational systems theories to understand how postsecondary institutions have made changes that led to improved student persistence. Georgia State University has emerged as a leader in this work (see Fausset, 2018; McMurtrie, 2018). We highlight it here along with the influence it has had on other institutions in part through the University Innovation Alliance (Burns et al., 2015).

Georgia State University

In 2003, only 32% of entering students graduated from Georgia State University (GSU) in 6 years, with 22% of Latinx students and 29% of Black students reaching that goal (Complete College Georgia, 2016). For the class that entered 9 years later (fall 2013), the graduation rate had increased to 55% overall, with Black, Latinx, Native American, and Asian American students slightly outpacing White students; Pell Grant recipients and their peers who did not receive Pell Grants graduated at virtually the same rate (National Center for Education Statistics [NCES], Integrated Postsecondary Education Data System, 2019). A 55% 6-year graduation rate is closing in on the national public university average of 62.4% and nearly meets the 56.2% average of institutions in GSU's admissions selectivity range (NCES, 2020), but remains below GSU's goal to continue to improve outcomes for all students. They achieved these results *without* altering admissions requirements to change the academic profile of the incoming class, while doubling the number of students of color and Pell-eligible students. How did they do it?

Beginning in 1999, GSU implemented a set of initiatives that addressed a host of student success challenges including persistence (Gumbel, 2020b; Kurzweil & Wu, 2015; Renick, 2020). Building from first-year student learning communities (1999), GSU accelerated the pace of initiatives after adding the Supplemental Instruction program (2005), redesigning introductory math courses (2006) to add financial interventions in 2008 and 2011, initiating predictive analytics and proactive advising (2012), and beginning a summer success academy (2012). An experimental chatbot program for summer melt introduced in 2016 (Page & Gehlbach, 2017) has expanded into other uses and proved helpful during the COVID-19 disruption in 2020 (Gumbel, 2020a). An enumeration of interventions may be interesting, particularly for understanding the scope of organizational transformation including curriculum, pedagogy, admissions, financial aid, and academic advising. But just knowing that GSU started using an approach does not help other institutions know how to begin or which approach(es) to adopt; indeed, just reading about GSU's innovations and success risks adding to the "shiny object-ism" that happens when one goes to a conference, hears about a new approach, and returns home to attempt to implement it without understanding the backstory or critical elements of one's own campus context vis-à-vis the innovation. Another risk lies in higher education's version of exceptionalism: Because we at Fill-in-the-Blank University are unique, and therefore not like GSU in such-and-such way, those ideas will never work here.

Knowing a bit more about the organizational ecosystem and approach to change at GSU can help explain how they decided to undertake this transformation and how they have been so successful to date. Martin Kurzweil and D. Derek Wu (2015) conducted a case study of GSU's process and concluded,

> Indeed, no single initiative is responsible for the dramatic gains at GSU; the university's improvement represents the accumulated impact of a dozen or more relatively modest programs. As it turns out, the recipe for GSU's success is not a particular solution, but rather *a particular approach to problem-solving*. (p. 3, emphasis added)

They identified an overarching approach of "using [GSU's] student-data warehouse to identify soluble barriers to student progression and graduation, and attacking them systematically" (Kurzweil & Wu, 2015, p. 3) and three key interactive contributors: (a) administrative reorganization to combine "critical functions (financial aid, academic support and advising, student accounts, admissions, and the registrar) under one vice provost"; (b) "full backing of both senior administrators and the university senate"; and (c) "a deliberate cycle of piloting innovative responses to identified barriers, testing their efficacy, and rapidly scaling them up if there is evidence of effectiveness" (p. 3).

GSU leadership engaged organizational structure, culture, and strategy in service of a systemic and systematic data-centric approach. By putting staff in critical functional areas together to solve problems, they created new networks within the natural system and directed those networks toward shared goals of improving the student experience. Engaging senior leaders and faculty through shared governance created additional locations for natural systems to work through innovation and compromise (as needed). GSU leaders understood that they needed a foundation of "clean, reliable data" (Renick, 2020, p. 183) to identify and address institutional challenges to persistence. Then strategic engagement of external stakeholders, including a critical "ask" to the state legislature when GSU decided to place all of its budgetary eggs in one basket and request over $1 million to increase its academic advising capacity, demonstrates how open systems and resource dependence can be turned to the advantage of an institution with a very focused student success agenda.

Diffusing Innovations From GSU to the University Innovation Alliance

GSU is a founding member of the University Innovation Alliance (UIA; www.theuia.org). The group began in 2014 with 11 large public research universities committed to increasing the number of low-income students who earn college degrees. Our home institution, Michigan State University (MSU), is a founding member, and each of us has been involved in UIA projects. One of us (Renn) has served as institutional liaison to the UIA from its initiation, and one of us (Smith) received a UIA doctoral research fellowship to study the impact of completion grants.

The general approach of the UIA is to identify, scale, and diffuse proven practices that promote retention and degree attainment for low-income students (Burns et al., 2015); the UIA is now expanding to add a few more public institutions and rearticulating a focus on racially minoritized, as well as low-income and first-generation students in its priorities. Mirroring the GSU approach to identifying obstacles, then testing and scaling strategies on campus, UIA institutions come together to address specific issues for student persistence and success (e.g., unclear pathways to graduating in 4 years, misalignment between employer expectations and graduates' preparation). The UIA was specifically designed to work as a "collaborative innovation model for higher education" (Burns et al., 2015, p. 13) that could overcome four obstacles to interinstitutional learning in the postsecondary ecosystem: competition among institutions (e.g., that which drives rankings systems), structures that encourage exclusivity (e.g., denying admission to some students for the purpose of appearing selective), dearth of effective ways to share ideas in small networks of trust, and lack of useful models for scaling innovation in higher education.

The UIA enacts a scale project each year, and four projects to date (predictive analytics, proactive advising, completion grants, chatbots) have roots largely or completely in the work at GSU. Institutions that have effective models serve as leads, with other campuses engaging in exploration and/or implementation. What makes the UIA more than just a network of institutions that share ideas about interventions is the focus across the UIA on learning how the processes of scaling and diffusion work in postsecondary education. Similar to lessons learned from the Center for the Integration of Research, Teaching, and Learning and Association of American Universities STEM networks aimed at improving STEM education (Hill et al., 2019; Kezar et al., 2019), lessons learned from UIA focus on how student success innovations can spread and improve the conditions necessary for effective scaling and diffusion.

One key lesson is that, as illustrated in the opening examples, what works there may not work here. We use the completion grants initiative as an example of a student persistence innovation that worked well at GSU and MSU, but not as well at all UIA institutions. The differential success of the innovation across the UIA illustrates our points about implementing new initiatives learned from peer institutions. A scale project on completion grants, inspired by GSU's Panther Retention Grant initiative, serves as an example. Panther Retention Grants (GSU, 2020) are microgrants to students who are about to be dropped from enrollment for nonpayment of a balance to the university. According to the website (GSU, 2020),

> Staff examine the drop lists for students who are on track for graduation using our academic analytics, and have unmet need and modest balances for tuition and fees. Students are offered micro grants on the condition they agree to certain activities, including meeting with a financial counselor to map out plans to finance the rest of their education. (para. 4)

With funding from the Bill & Melinda Gates Foundation and the Ascendium Education Group (formerly the Great Lakes Higher Education Corporation), the UIA took up a national diffusion experiment of completion grants. Per agreement with the funder, grants were to be given to students within 1 year of graduating, with an expected family contribution (EFC) up to $7,000, owing up to $1,000 at the time they would face institutional consequences (e.g., being dropped from enrollment for the present or upcoming semester). At first consideration, these criteria would seem to work at most large public universities like those in the UIA, and adoption of a student persistence idea that has been successful at GSU should go smoothly at the other 10 UIA institutions. At MSU, we were able to identify enough students meeting the criteria each semester to run the implementation as a randomized control trial (RCT), using the grant funds to pay off balances the day before students faced enrollment consequences, with a control group whose balances were not paid off. Students were not aware of the possibility of receiving the grant, as it was not announced, nor could they apply for it. After several semesters, the RCT demonstrated positive outcomes for students who received the grant; they were more likely to graduate and had higher semester GPAs than the comparison group after the intervention. But at some other institutions, the completion grant program was either impossible to implement or showed little effect. What happened?

First, context mattered at the institutions that tried to implement the intervention. At MSU and a few other UIA members, the solution aligned with a student persistence challenge we could identify in our data: Low-income students who were within range of graduation but owed modest amounts of money were being dropped from enrollment and did not always come back to finish. But at one UIA institution that tried to implement the grants, institutional policy did not require dropping students before or on the first day of class if they owed a balance; indeed they had students who might complete all degree requirements while owing a balance who could then not graduate until the balance was paid. The UIA completion grants project as defined with the funders' criteria was not a good fit, although one could imagine a different solution to this completion obstacle, such as forgiving the outstanding balances and awarding degrees. Knowing one's data and institutional policy context is a key to successfully adapting a promising student persistence initiative. Understanding what policies related to enrollment, fee paying, registration holds, or other critical student persistence functions are within control of the institution is essential, as is identifying potential solutions to obstacles created by these policies.

Another key is understanding the state policy context, such as constraints and affordances of public system-level guidelines for financial aid. One institution was unable to give the completion grants under the UIA-set criteria, because they had few or no students eligible. Students in the stated EFC range automatically had all tuition and fees covered by a state scholarship program. The institution could design a similar program that would pay off balances for higher income students, but that approach would not address goals to increase lower income student completion. Another possibility would be to go back to the fundamentals of the Panther Retention Grant program, which is not restricted to the last part of a student's process but can occur any semester. Without the constraints of the funders' criteria it might be possible to create a microgrants program that would benefit students at this institution, but the example illustrates the complexity of implementing "one-size-fits-all" solutions that circulate in conversations about student success.

GSU led another scale project, an ambitious randomized control trial of over 10,000 students across UIA campuses. Funded by an $8.9 million grant from the U.S. Department of Education, the project was designed to scale a program of predictive analytics, degree mapping, and proactive advising that had been found to be effective at GSU. Results varied across UIA institutions, and project leadership and evaluators determined that fidelity of implementation was one factor. MSU, for example, did not see expected gains for treatment group students. We attributed this result to several differences in organizational structure and culture (e.g., MSU does not have the kind of centralized academic advising that GSU has) and challenges implementing the intervention at full fidelity from the outset (e.g., it took us months to get 4-year degree plans, which were central to the intervention, from every major on campus). Although MSU was able to leverage the scale project to effect substantial positive change on campus, we did not see that change reflected in the outcome variables of direct interest in the project (i.e., student progression toward completing in 4 years). Other UIA institutions also varied in implementation fidelity, and outcomes varied. At least as important as what the project taught us about degree maps and advising was what we learned about challenges to scaling and diffusion in natural and open systems.

Throughout the completion grants and degree mapping scale projects, among other UIA scaling and diffusion efforts, lessons emerged that conform to ideas from natural and open systems theories. Observations from the UIA work include the following:

1. Context matters, both internal and external.
2. Local adaptation—and freedom to adapt—is essential to successful diffusion.
3. Natural systems and networks within each institution are the engines that make scale projects work, or that interfere with their adoption and implementation as intended.
4. Iteration in the original attempt at innovation and in the attempted diffusion of change are likely to lead to more positive outcomes.
5. Having models in other institutions is valuable, both for understanding an innovation and in making the case for it to internal skeptics.
6. There is no replacement for senior leadership making undergraduate student success the highest priority, but equally critical is buy-in for innovation from faculty and from midlevel and student-facing staff who make it work.

Engaging across all levels and functions of the institution is a key to distributing the commitment to student persistence according to roles and shared leadership for common goals.

Recommendations for Practice

Taking these lessons learned using systems theory to understand the examples from GSU and the UIA scale projects, alongside the three hypothetical-but-plausible scenarios with which we started the chapter, we present some ideas for how institutions might improve student outcomes. It starts by adopting what we call a *student success mindset* (Renn, 2020) focused on student persistence and diffusing it in the organization through natural systems. Such a mindset entails the belief-in-action that all students admitted to an institution have "the capacity to learn, thrive, and graduate" (Largent, 2020, para. 8), and that it is the institution's responsibility to ensure conditions that make this outcome possible. From this mindset flow a number of institution-specific strategies. The strategies we note here are designed to facilitate the implementation of a student persistence mindset across the institution:

- *Senior institutional leaders.* It is critical that senior leaders clearly articulate expectations for student persistence and closing opportunity gaps and understand how other goals such as climbing in rankings or changing Carnegie categories may present conflicting priorities. Rewards structures (e.g., resource allocation, promotion) and thoughtful human resource management should be aligned with student persistence values in ways that influence organizational culture and provide incentives for acting in ways that prioritize student success outcomes. If institutional goals create competing internal priorities, senior leaders need to rearticulate the value of student persistence and demonstrate that they understand that compromises in other areas may be necessary at times to reach these goals. Senior leaders should have access to good data and the capacity to use the information effectively. In order to do so, depending on the size and resources of the institution, they may need to invest in data infrastructure and staff capable of understanding how to aggregate, disaggregate, and interpret data relevant to student success for cohorts and subpopulations. Ideally, data professionals, whether in information technology, institutional research, or another unit, will be able to serve senior leaders as well as midlevel and frontline staff. A culture of data transparency in service of decision-making for student success is essential to support a natural or open systems approach to data-informed organizational change.
- *Institutional leaders.* Understanding how to tell a story about their organization is essential for internal and external audiences. Translating a student persistence mindset into stories may help trustees and other stakeholders understand how the organization is transforming to improve outcomes. Good—and honest—storytelling also helps internal actors understand their role in the transformation in ways that support continued buy-in when hard decisions are made or outcomes do not shift as quickly as they might wish.
- *Midlevel administrators and student-facing professionals.* Midlevel administrators and direct-service professionals should understand how their work fits into the overall student persistence transformation of the institution and how they may be able to influence or introduce practices and processes related to student persistence. They should have input into what initiatives are undertaken, especially those that will affect their work with students; we are not saying that they should have veto power over new ideas but

should have the opportunity to contribute what they know as decisions are being made. Staff should have tools to identify student persistence challenges using evidence. Engaging in iterative improvement cycles through process mapping (see Burns & Aljets, 2018) is one technique to identify and remove or ameliorate sticking points for student progress. Facility with data access, analysis, and interpretation (e.g., constructing and reading dashboards, working with trend data) is another asset that can be developed in this group.

- *Faculty and instructional staff.* Faculty are key purveyors of institutional culture and with other instructional staff are central to the educational processes that ultimately affect student success. Adopting a student persistence mindset compared to, for example, an academic gatekeeping philosophy that aims to "weed out" less well-prepared students, sets a foundation for transforming the institution in the direction of student success. Faculty engagement in learning analytics, early alert systems, curricular reform, and pedagogical innovation can contribute to productive change. Instructor engagement with campus systems in place to support students is another critical element to changing the culture away from one that sections off students' academic work from the rest of their lives and that connects support across the range of institutional resources.

Conclusion

If indeed higher education is a system designed to get the unsatisfactory results that it currently gets, then it can be redesigned to get better results for more students. Postsecondary institutions are not usually quick to change (the sudden shift to remote teaching at the onset of the COVID-19 pandemic being the most striking counterexample in our careers), but certainly have the ability to do so. Engaging organizational change in the direction of a student persistence mindset from senior leadership, midlevel management, student-facing staff, and faculty and instructional staff is one way to move toward necessary adaptation. Further, *student persistence* as a stated goal is key; however, how this message is communicated and prioritized operationally is crucial, particularly in connection with environments and stakeholders outside of the institution. Assessing the context and modeling initiatives on successful efforts at other institutions, as GSU and the UIA have demonstrated, is a promising strategy. We are realistic but also optimistic about the potential for change in the area of student persistence, but there are networks that show how it can be done and institutions—and their leaders, staff, and faculty—ready to undertake the challenge.

References

Acker, J. (1992). Gendering organizational theory. *Classics of Organizational Theory, 6*, 450–459. https://doi.org/10.1007/0-387-36218-5_9

Ake-Little, E., von der Embse, N., & Dawson, D. (2020). Does class size matter in the university setting? *Educational Researcher, 49*(8), 595–605. https://doi.org/10.3102/0013189X20933836

Barnhardt, C. L., Young, R. L., Sheets, J. K., Phillips, C. W., Parker III, E. T., & Reyes, K. (2017). Campus strategic action in the fisher case: Organizational stakeholder advocacy across the field of higher education. *Research in Higher Education, 58*(3), 313–339. https://doi.org/10.1007/s11162-016-9428-9

Bastedo, M. N. (2004). Open systems theory. In F. W. English (Ed.), *The encyclopedia of educational leadership and administration* (pp. 711–712). SAGE.

Bolman, L. G., & Deal, T. E. (1984). *Modern approaches to understanding and managing organizations.* Jossey-Bass.

Bolman, L. G., & Deal, T. E. (2017). *Reframing organizations: Artistry, choice, and leadership.* Wiley.

Braxton, J. M. (2008). Toward a theory of faculty professional choices in teaching that foster college student success. In J. C. Smart (Ed.), *Higher education: Handbook of theory and research* (Vol. 23, pp. 181–207). Springer. https://doi.org/10.1007/978-1-4020-6959-8_6

Burns, B., & Aljets, A. (2018, March 26). Using process mapping to redesign the student experience. *EDUCAUSE Review.* https://er.educause.edu/articles/2018/3/using-process-mapping-to-redesign-the-student-experience

Burns, B., Crow, M., & Becker, M. (2015). Innovating together: Collaboration as a driving force to improve student success. *EDUCAUSE Review, 50*(2), 10–20. https://er.educause.edu/articles/2015/3/innovating-together-collaboration-as-a-driving-force-to-improve-student-success

Complete College Georgia. (2016). *Georgia State University campus plan: Update 2016.* Georgia State University. https://completegeorgia.org/georgia-state-university-campus-plan-update-2016

Doran, E. E. (2015). Negotiating access and tier one aspirations: The historical evolution of a striving Hispanic-serving institution. *Journal of Hispanic Higher Education, 14*(4), 343–354. https://doi.org/10.1177/1538192715570638

Dwyer, L. J., Williams, M. R., & Pribesh, S. (2019). Impact of early alert on community college student persistence in Virginia. *Community College Journal of Research and Practice, 43*(3), 228–231. https://doi.org/10.1080/10668926.2018.1449034

Fausset, R. (2018, May 15). Georgia State, leading U.S. in Black graduates, is engine of social mobility. *The New York Times.* https://www.nytimes.com/2018/05/15/us/georgia-state-african-americans.html

Georgia State University. (2020). *Student success programs: Panther Retention Grants.* https://success.gsu.edu/initiatives/panther-retention-grants/

Gonzales, L. D. (2013). Faculty sensemaking and mission creep: Interrogating institutional ways of knowing and doing legitimacy. *Review of Higher Education, 36,* 179–209. https://doi.org/10.1353/rhe.2013.0000

Gonzales, L. D., Kanhai, D., & Hall, K. (2018). Reimagining organizational theory for the critical study of higher education. In M. B. Paulsen (Ed.), *Higher education: Handbook of theory and research* (Vol. 33, pp. 505–559). Springer.

Gonzales, L. D., Martinez, E., & Ordu, C. (2014). Exploring faculty experiences in a striving university through the lens of academic capitalism. *Studies in Higher Education, 39*(7), 1097–1115. https://doi.org/10.1080/03075079.2013.777401

Gumbel, A. (2020a, September 1). This public US university has seen grades soar despite Covid. What's it doing right? *The Guardian.* https://www.theguardian.com/us-news/2020/sep/01/georgia-state-university-covid-19-low-income-students

Gumbel, A. (2020b). *Won't lose this dream: How an upstart urban university rewrote the rules of a broken system.* The New Press.

Hill, L. B., Savoy, J. N., Austin, A. E., & Bantawa, B. (2019). The impact of multi-institutional STEM reform networks on member institutions: A case study of CIRTL. *Innovative Higher Education, 44,* 187–202. https://doi.org/10.1007/s10755-019-9461-7

Jackson, M. (2003). *Systems thinking: Creative holism for managers.* Wiley.

Jenkins, J. J., Sánchez, L. A., Schraedley, M. A., Hannans, J., Navick, N., & Young, J. (2020). Textbook broke: Textbook affordability as a social justice issue. *Journal of Interactive Media in Education, 1*(3), 1–13. http://dx.doi.org/10.5334/jime.549

Johnson, S. (2018, March 1). *"Faculty told me they hated it." When an academic-alert system backfires—twice.* EdSurge. https://www.edsurge.com/news/2018-03-01-faculty-told-me-they-hated-it-when-an-academic-alert-system-backfires-twice

Katz, D., & Kahn, R. L. (1966). *The social psychology of organizations.* Wiley.

Katz, D., & Kahn, R. L. (1978). *The social psychology of organizations* (2nd ed.). Wiley.

Kezar, A. (2001). *Understanding and facilitating organizational change in the 21st century: Recent research and conceptualizations* (ASHE-ERIC Higher Education Reports, Vol. 28, No. 4). Jossey-Bass.

Kezar, A. (2014). Higher education change and social networks: A review of research. *Journal of Higher Education, 85*(1), 91–125. https://doi.org/10.1080/00221546.2014.11777320

Kezar, A., Miller, E., Bernstein-Serra, S., & Holcombe, E. (2019). The promise of a "network of networks" strategy to scale change: Lessons from the AAU STEM Initiative. *Change: The Magazine of Higher Learning, 51*(2), 47–54. https://doi.org/10.1080/00091383.2019.1569973

Kurzweil, M., & Wu, D. D. (2015). *Building a pathway to student success at Georgia State University* (GHPC Article 142). Georgia State University. https://scholarworks.gsu.edu/ghpc_articles/142

Largent, M. A. (2020, January 30). Good signs. *Michigan State University APUE Blog*. https://undergrad.msu.edu/news/view/id/255

Maslow, A. H. (1943). A theory of human motivation. *Psychological Review, 50*(4), 370–396. https://doi.org/10.1037/h0054346

Mayhew, M. J., Rockenbach, A. N., Bowman, N. A., Seifert, T. A., Wolniak, G. C. (with Pascarella, E. T., & Terenzini, P. T.). (2016). *How college affects students: Vol. 3. 21st century evidence that higher education works*. Jossey-Bass.

Mayo, E. (1933). The human problems of an industrial civilization. *The ANNALS of the American Academy of Political and Social Science, 172*(1), 171. https://doi.org/10.1177/000271623417200135

McClure, K. R., & Titus, M. A. (2018). Spending up the ranks? The relationship between striving for prestige and administrative expenditures at US public research universities. *Journal of Higher Education, 89*(6), 961–987. https://doi.org/10.1080/00221546.2018.1449079

McKenzie, L. (2018, September 11). Early alert systems seen as mixed bag. *Inside Higher Ed*. https://www.insidehighered.com/news/2018/09/11/academics-question-system-measuring-academic-performance-flagging-potential-problems

McMurtrie, B. (2018, May 25). Georgia State U made its graduation rate jump. How? *Chronicle of Higher Education*. https://www.chronicle.com/article/georgia-state-u-made-its-graduation-rate-jump-how

Mintzberg, H. (1980). Structure in 5's: A synthesis of the research on organization design. *Management Science, 26*(3), 322–341. http://www.jstor.org/stable/2630506

Mohajan, H. K. (2019). Knowledge sharing among employees in organizations. *Journal of Economic Development, Environment and People, 8*(1), 52–61.

Morgan, G. (2006). *Images of an organization*. SAGE.

Morse, R., & Brooks, E. (2020, September 13). How *U.S. News* calculated the 2021 Best Colleges rankings. *U.S. News*. https://www.usnews.com/education/best-colleges/articles/how-us-news-calculated-the-rankings

National Center for Education Statistics. (2020). *Condition of education, 2020* (Table 326.10). U.S. Department of Education. https://nces.ed.gov/programs/digest/d19/tables/dt19_326.10.asp

National Center for Education Statistics, Integrated Postsecondary Education Data System. (2019). *Georgia State University retention and graduation rates*. U.S. Department of Education. https://nces.ed.gov/collegenavigator/?q=georgia+state+university&s=all&id=139940#retgrad

O'Meara K. (2007) Striving for what? Exploring the pursuit of prestige. In J. C. Smart (Ed.), *Higher education: Handbook of theory and research* (Vol. 22, pp. 121–179). Springer. https://doi.org/10.1007/978-1-4020-5666-6_3

Page, L. C., & Gehlbach, H. (2017). How an artificially intelligent virtual assistant helps students navigate the road to college. *AERA Open, 3*(4). https://doi.org/10.1177/2332858417749220

Pfeffer, J., & Salancik, G. R. (2003). *The external control of organizations: A resource dependence perspective*. Stanford Business Books.

Powell, K. K., & Rey, M. P. (2015). Exploring a resource dependency perspective as an organizational strategy for building resource capacity: Implications for public higher education universities. *Management in Education, 29*(3), 94–99. https://doi.org/10.1177/0892020615586805

Renick, T. M. (2020). Predictive analytics, academic advising, early alerts, and student success. In K. L. Webber & H. Zheng (Eds.), *Big data on campus: Data analytics and decision making in higher education.* Johns Hopkins University Press.

Renn, K. A. (2020). Student success mindset: How residential peer staff understand and enact their role in student success. *Journal of College and University Student Housing, 46*(2), 10–27. https://www.nxtbook.com/nxtbooks/acuho/journal_vol46no2/index.php#/10

Renn, K. A., & Reason, R. D. (2021). *College students in the United States: Characteristics, experiences, and outcomes* (2nd ed.). Stylus.

Schein, E. (2004). *Organizational culture and leadership* (3rd ed.). Jossey-Bass.

Scott, W. R., & Davis, G. F. (2016). *Organizations and organizing: Rational, natural and open systems perspectives.* Routledge.

Shi, M. (2019). The effects of class size and instructional technology on student learning performance. *International Journal of Management Education, 17*(1), 130–138. https://doi.org/10.1016/j.ijme.2019.01.004

Taylor, F. W. (1919). *The principles of scientific management.* Harper & Brothers.

Tierney, W. G., & Lanford, M. (2016). *Cultivating strategic innovation in higher education.* TIAA Institute. https://www.tiaa.org/public/pdf/cultivating_strategic_innovation_in_higher_ed.pdf

Villano, R., Harrison, S., Lynch, G., & Chen, G. (2018). Linking early alert systems and student retention: A survival analysis approach. *Higher Education, 76*(5), 903–920. https://doi.org/10.1007/s10734-018-0249-y

Vuori J. (2018). Understanding academic leadership using the four-frame model. In E. Pekkola (Ed.), *Theoretical and methodological perspectives on higher education management and transformation—An advanced reader for PhD students* (pp. 167–178). Tampere University Press. https://www.theseus.fi/handle/10024/267655

Weick, K. (1976). Educational organizations as loosely coupled systems. *Administrative Science Quarterly, 21*(1), 1–19. https://doi.org/10.2307/2391875

II

A TRANSLATION OF RESEARCH INTO ACTION?

Toward a Pragmatic Conceptualization of Social
Mechanisms in Retention Research and Practice

Ezekiel Kimball and Garrett Gowen

One editor of this volume, John M. Braxton (2000), has characterized student departure as a puzzle and noted that higher education
administrators and researchers have been trying to answer fundamental questions about student retention for now more than 90 years.
Questions such as "Why do so many students depart voluntarily from their
institutions? What accounts for student departure?" (Braxton, 2000, p. 1).
Reframing these questions from the perspective of colleges and universities,
this volume's second editor, Robert D. Reason (2009), has suggested that
retention "has been the primary goal for higher education institutions for
several decades" (p. 659). However research describes the phenomenon—
whether departure or retention, persistence or attrition, student success or
degree completion—it is clear that nearly a century of relevant empirical
inquiry culminating in a series of recent works synthesizing key empirical
findings (e.g., Mayhew et al., 2016; Pascarella & Terenzini, 2005; Renn &
Reason, 2012) has done little to provide the answers that higher education
administrators, student affairs professionals, instructors, and policymakers
seek. Likewise, despite a robust body of supporting literature intended to
distill insight from this research to support effective practice (e.g., Blimling,
2014; Greenfield et al., 2013; Grites et al., 2016), colleges and universities
of all types and institutional controls still report suboptimal retention rates
(National Center for Education Statistics [NCES], 2019).

As noted by Vincent Tinto (2012), the lingering retention problem in
higher education stems both from the "nature of the research on student

attrition" and "the character of most efforts to improve retention" (pp. 4–5). Simply put, research on retention prioritizes work that addresses theoretical problems (e.g., academic engagement, social integration) and the description of discrete outcomes (e.g., departure, completion) rather than long-running student processes rooted in complex learning environments. Tinto (2012) went on to note that this difference in orientations toward research renders "our knowledge of effective action . . . fragmented and poorly organized" (p. 5)—complicating the pursuit of goal-directed, evidence-based institutional action. Despite Tinto's (2012) call for a more coherent synthesis of research and practice, serious challenges remain. Notably, retention rates display marked disparities between students with minoritized and majoritarian identities (e.g., DeAngelo & Franke, 2016; Toutkoushian et al., 2019; Xu & Webber, 2018). Moreover, as noted by Tinto (2012), the key roles of faculty and staff in the student experience have often been ignored in prior explorations of how retention research can inform practice. Consequently, it appears that solving the retention problem requires a flexible framework wherein disparate research can be synthesized to develop strategies for practice for individual faculty and staff within a given institutional context while also responding with sensitivity to variations in student identities and experiences.

Simply put, retention or attrition arises from the sum total of the interactions that students have with campus leaders, faculty, staff, and fellow students. An effective model for translating retention research into retention practice requires a sensitivity to the multivalent factors that give rise to departure or retention. Higher education researchers have labeled student departure an "ill-structured problem" (Braxton et al., 2004, p. 1); attempting to address the problem makes clear that efforts to encourage retention meet the social science definition for a *wicked problem* (Ackoff, 1974; Head & Alford, 2015). By definition, a wicked problem is one that defies easy solution because the actors involved are limited by imperfect information and subject to limited, shifting, confusing, and even paradoxical guidelines for that solution (Conklin, 2006). Moreover, many wicked problems may be or appear to be fundamentally unsolvable because introducing one solution can lead to unintended consequences that prompt the reappearance of the problem elsewhere within the organization in a slightly new way (Alford & Head, 2017). According to Ackoff (1974), the challenge in solving wicked problems is that they are not really unitary problems at all but rather a complex, interrelated series of problems that are part of the same system. Rather than a unitary problem with a singular solution, wicked problems are really a series of problems that must be solved individually but simultaneously such that all the solutions to the problem set align. That is, social messes are problems of coordinated action. They require the integration and coordination of multiple divergent viewpoints, the alignment of multiple contradictory solutions, careful attention to foreseeable and unforeseeable externalities of decision-making, and the capacity to tolerate ambiguous or even changing data (Conklin, 2006).

Consistent with this conceptualization of retention as a wicked problem, we argue in this chapter that the primary problem for retention researchers and practitioners is not the production of better data but rather the more effective utilization of that evidence as the basis for shared understanding and action in the midst of uncertainty. Given that prior work has emphasized both how the behaviors of individual faculty and staff contribute to retention and the inadequacy of monolithic institutional responses (e.g., Braxton et al., 2004; Tinto, 2012), an effective model for the use of retention research to inform practice must function as both a guide for individual action and a framework for constructing shared understanding. Higher education researchers have typically addressed this problem through the lens of theory-to-practice models and discussions (summarized in Kimball & Friedensen, 2019; Reason & Kimball, 2012). In the remainder of this chapter, we describe recent work on theory-to-practice conversations in student affairs specifically and higher education more generally. We then turn to pragmatism to help identify challenges that a theory-to-practice model should address. Specifically, pragmatism treats both truth and action as social products. In so doing, it offers a probabilistic interpretation of outcomes and a consequentialist understanding of practice. Doing so helps to reconcile the potentially incommensurable orientations to truth and utility held by practitioners and researchers by offering a flexible framework for shared understanding driven by mutual attention to results. Finally, we propose a heuristic model for incorporating these insights into institutional decision-making and individual practice related to retention.

Research, Theory, and Practice in Social Science

Discontinuity between research and practice is a classic problem of education research. Indeed, both social scientists broadly (e.g., Badgett, 2016; Lindblom & Cohen, 1979) and higher education researchers specifically (e.g., Love, 2012; Reason & Kimball, 2012) have highlighted the gaps in the production of knowledge and its productive application. Within the applied sphere of education work, research can be an obstacle rather than a useful mechanism for change and success; without aligning research with practice, education practitioners are likely to operate based upon implicit theories and assumptions that may not adequately capture the problem in question (Bensimon, 2007). In understanding retention, despite decades of research on increasingly diverse samples of students and institutional types, marked disparities remain.

To scaffold our understanding of how research can be more intentionally related to the practical challenges of retention, we will first turn to the processes that organize higher education research. Although historically informed by an array of disciplines, higher education research is traditionally considered a field, united around an agreed set of problems but with low consensus as to training, systems of methods, epistemologies or frameworks, and prioritization of topics (Eisenmann, 2004; Shulman, 1997). Moreover, the lack of consensus within the field means there is often little agreement between researchers and practitioners over what is important, let alone what works in practice (Kezar, 2000). Therefore, we will examine what constitutes legitimate knowledge within the low-consensus realm of higher education research, and indeed social science more broadly. We will then turn to the tradition of philosophical pragmatism as a way of reframing how we think about "research," "practice," and "application."

Constructing and Legitimating Knowledge

In this section, we show that higher education research constructs and legitimates knowledge discursively. We argue that, since it already regards truth as a social product, higher education research has a latent pragmatic orientation; by exploring this epistemological stance further, higher education researchers can produce more practice-relevant work. Like all academic fields, the study of higher education is nested within the constellation of tradition, history, philosophy, and modes of thinking that organize the construction of knowledge. The delineation of higher education as a "field" rather than a "discipline" is important—disciplines are "bounds of formal knowledge, or rationalized conceptions of the world, established through the empirical study of the world's phenomena," whereas fields refer to "the practical application of knowledge from many disciplines to address current social needs and problems" (Friesen, 2020, p. 7). Accordingly, researchers within fields rely upon methods, frameworks, epistemologies, and other ways of constructing and interpreting knowledge from a patchwork of disciplinary sources. Higher education historically has drawn primarily from psychology, sociology, political science, economics, history, and philosophy—each with its own "cultural frame that defines a great part of one's life" (Geertz, 1982, p. 24). Thus, the disciplines that inform the work of a field each contain tacit assumptions that shape perspectives on the objects of scholarship, such as "what counts as a relevant contribution, what counts as answering a question, what counts as having a good argument for that answer or a good criticism of it" (Rorty, 1979, p. 320), and, ultimately, truth.

As a result, higher education's position as a field presents several unique challenges for researchers and practitioners. First, although the field is relatively united around the types of problems to investigate (e.g., applied problems), there is little to no agreement on the appropriate strategies or ways of thinking that might characterize a higher consensus discipline. This lack of agreement translates into a variety of approaches to educating higher education graduate students (and, ultimately, professionals and academics) spread among disparate institutional programs (Altbach, 2014). Consequently, higher education scholars are not consistently socialized into one or more disciplines as part of their graduate study (Altbach, 2014), which further compounds the fragmentation of the field and allows researchers to be unreflective on their epistemologies and methodologies (Bensimon, 2007). The mechanisms that promote uniformity within disciplines, such as professional organizations and disciplinary standards, do not function in the same way within the field of higher education; student affairs organizations (i.e., NASPA and ACPA) promote professional "competencies," which do not necessarily align well with the skills needed to socialize researchers with disciplinary techniques.

Second, despite a general agreement on applied problems, higher education exists within a competitive ecosystem of other fields and disciplines wherein the disciplines populate the most prestigious echelon (Friedland & Alford, 1991). With prestige comes relevance and widespread recognition—as other disciplines produce work on the subjects of higher education, higher education scholars continually (and probably rightfully) gripe that their long history of research is ignored due to the prominence of other disciplines, the silos that prevent cross-disciplinary knowledge, and the assumptions that higher education, as a field, produces low-quality work (Mayhew et al., 2016). In response, higher education researchers are turning evermore toward more complex quantitative, quasi-experimental analyses, which are more likely to focus on institutions or systems rather than individuals, to shore up the scholarly legitimacy of the field (Tight, 2007; Wells et al., 2015). The focus on prestige reorients the goal and reward structures within the field, creating incentives to use particular methods or answer particular questions to secure positions or advance the field rather than to provide solutions for practitioners.

Finally, a fragmented, unreflective field that is focused on pursuit of prestige elides the central object of scholarly work: truth. It is a touchy and oblique subject, especially in a chapter that seeks to more readily connect research and practice. Yet assumptions about what is true and what can be known are embedded within all scholarship, and, in the case of higher education, there is little agreement as to what constitutes either. The legacy of the positivists, who spent the last century translating the objectivity, rigor, and method of "normal science" as ways to discover "Nature's Own Language," permeates the prestige-driven turn toward paradigmatic norms (Rorty, 1981, p. 571). In other words, the idea of truth as something inherent to reality, that can be grasped by humans using the scientific method, papers over a less intrinsic, more perspectival way of knowing. To reiterate a point we have now made several times: Truth frequently functions as a social product, and adopting this pragmatic orientation to truth can be enormously helpful in reconciling different people's truths.

These challenges are not distinct; rather, they intersect in multiple ways that compound their effects on the translation from theory-to-practice. Taken together, the tensions felt by everyone within the field of higher education provide a serious disincentive to either address problems articulated by practitioners and professionals or to produce knowledge that is easy to understand and apply by those who are not steeped in the jargon and complex methods of prestigious academia. A preference for particular methods, for instance, leads the researcher to ask questions that can be analyzed using the preferred methods as opposed to choosing the method that best addresses the question. Moreover, a lack of consistency in method or way of thinking further increases the barrier to understanding by practitioners—if no two researchers act alike over time, then practitioners, already limited by time, context, and circumstance, lose the shortcuts necessary to process knowledge easily. If higher education researchers seek to produce knowledge that is useful and can be applied by others, they could be well served by turning to the work of pragmatism.

Pragmatism and Action

Although commonly confused with the colloquial usage of the word *pragmatic*, philosophical pragmatism does not simply equate with utilitarianism, but rather seeks to describe how and why humans "act." The American pragmatists, notably including George Herbert Mead, William James, Charles Peirce, and John Dewey, argued that humans are problem-solvers, meaning "thought is to guide action in the service of solving practical problems that arise in life" (Gross, 2009, p. 366). Pragmatist descriptions of action capture the human reliance on "habit," which refers to techniques of practice or problem-solving that are formed through experience and are deployed in response to familiar (or unfamiliar) situations (Gross, 2009; Joas, 1996).

These responses are not rote or mechanistic; rather, pragmatic accounts of action maintain contingency and some indeterminacy as characteristic of human behavior: The ability of individuals to define and interpret their situation, much less knowing how to react appropriately, reflects the array of habits that are available (Joas, 1996). Mead (1913, 1922) elaborated the cognitive elements of pragmatism through his concept of the self, wherein individuals can interpret themselves in addition to the social environment. This capability enables perspective-taking and other aspects of social interaction, wherein individuals interpret the meaning of one another's behaviors and act accordingly (Becker, 1986; Blumer, 1969).

This understanding of human behavior contrasts heavily with the positivistic elements of the scientific method, which emphasizes replicability and predictability, and where causal questions are often asked before understanding the utility of knowledge. Pragmatism takes an element of social constructionism as an assumption behind the social world: Social constructionism emphasizes the human capacity for language as a way to assign meanings to the world and to transmit those meanings from person to person. Thus, objects that may physically exist within an objective world are given social reality through the human process of "world-building":

> Man, as we know him empirically, cannot be conceived of apart from the continuous outpouring of himself into the world in which he finds himself. Human being cannot be understood as somehow resting within itself, in some closed sphere of interiority, and *then* setting out to express itself in the surrounding world. Human being is externalizing in its essence from the beginning. (Berger, 1967, p. 4)

The externalization, objectivation, and subsequent internalization of social meanings form the foundation for the forces of society—they frame how individual human beings interpret their interactions within their environment and how those experiences are integrated into future action.

As a way of structuring inquiry, pragmatism rejects dualistic accounts of knowledge construction, focusing instead upon the "intersubjectivity" that makes social reality possible (Biesta & Barbules, 2003, p. 108). Knowledge itself emerges from the process of engaging in action in response to the environment and developing habits or techniques of practice for future reference. The processes of interpreting those experiences and the ability to transmit resultant meanings across individuals and groups are a consequence of the socially constructed frames that we apply to new and familiar situations. People are thus capable of "doing things together," sharing meanings, purposes, intents, and, ultimately, strategies of action (Becker, 1986; Swidler, 1986). In short, pragmatism can help us understand the social elements of how researchers and practitioners approach their work and how they might be reconciled, which we believe to be a reasonable starting point in efforts to utilize retention research to inform research practice.

Applying Pragmatism to Higher Education Research

With a general understanding of pragmatism in tow, we return to the challenges outlined previously—the disagreement over ways of thinking, the privileging of positivistic method, the allure of prestige within the organizational field, and how these challenges intersect. We apply pragmatic thinking to identify the issues that our proposed theory-to-practice framework must address, which will serve as a flexible framework for use by researchers and practitioners alike.

Reflection and Awareness

A fragmented field is both blessing and curse. A field replete with multiple, transdisciplinary ideas and ways of thinking is ripe for creative and integrative research that high consensus scholarship can find challenging or unacceptable. Yet the inconsistencies in training and socialization that contribute to such fragmentation can also encourage researchers to double down on their epistemological and methodological training with little reflection on how their training ultimately structures their research (Bensimon, 2007; Johnson & Onwuegbuzie, 2004). All practitioners and researchers whether positivist, constructivist, or some other epistemological orientation benefit from critically reflecting on what they believe and how that belief gets infused into action consciously or unconsciously. Pragmatism encourages this reflexivity and reflection: By rejecting dualistic accounts of knowledge and research (i.e., quantitative vs. qualitative), a pragmatic approach encourages (a) an understanding of your own ways of thinking and interpretation, (b) an appreciation of other methods and how they might supplement or complement your original conceptualizations, (c) a critical appraisal of what approaches best serve a research question, and (d) whether answering the question will have important practical consequences. Ultimately, disagreements will still exist and the implicit assumptions undergirding some theories or epistemologies likely will not be compatible (Bacharach, 1989). What is important, however, is the act of consideration and the awareness required to assess your own beliefs and how they connect to other ways of thinking.

Pragmatic awareness is not only useful in constructing research and knowledge but in analyzing and translating existing research as well. As researchers and practitioners, we constantly make decisions about what research to read, what research to trust, which findings are relevant, and what is worth pursuing, whether in application or future research. These decisions are meaningfully and, largely, unconsciously tied to our positionalities, including our identities, our method specialties, our epistemologies, and our context (Ray, 2019). Moreover, we make decisions with an implicit under-standing of "gold standards" within the field regardless of their applicability (Wells et al., 2015). A framework for mapping theory into practice requires active consideration of our choices and how they relate to both knowledge production and actual practice.

Experience and Habit

The pragmatist account of action understands humans as problem-solvers, unconsciously drawing upon social experience, creativity, and previous effort to navigate present situations (Joas, 1996). This conceptualization is evident in descriptions of student affairs practice, where professionals deploy infor-mal theories to more efficiently apply formal knowledge and past experience to a situation (Love, 2012). Informal theorizing is, in many ways, similar to pragmatist conceptions of habit—routine techniques of practice that are informed by social experience. However, as Bensimon (2007) warned, there is a danger that informal theorizing could actually be implicit theorizing, in which actions are based upon stereotyping rather than experience or theory. Practitioners should be able to turn to research as a corrective for implicit thinking and a guide for new situations.

This corrective presents two challenges. First, the factors shaping our experience as researchers (habits) are likely to influence how we interpret and respond to investigating a topic or question. When the experiences of the researcher and practitioner do not align and the guiding pressures of the field do not encourage practice-oriented questions, then practitioners will likely find little in the way of relevant formal theorizing to guide future action. Second, like researchers, practitioners are socialized as part of their graduate education and professional memberships (Perez, 2016). As discussed previously, socializa-tion can guide how professionals decide what research to read, which research is or is not applicable, and what older research to draw upon. A framework needs to consider both the informal ways that theory is applied and the poten-tial disconnect between research choices and professional demands.

A Conceptual Model of Research and Theory Use in Retention Practice

Building on our earlier discussion of pragmatic mechanisms, we now describe a framework for the use of empirical research and theory in retention practice based on Reason and Kimball's (2012) model for theory-to-practice translations in student affairs. This framework can serve as a structured tool for the identification and application of knowledge generated in a variety of ways, with goal-directed strategies for practice. Notably, our proposed model does not offer specific strategies for action but rather a systematic way for individual scholars, individual practitioners, research communities, and higher education institutions to think about retention by targeting the underlying social mechanisms producing observed equity gaps in retention. That is, our model addresses the need for researchers and practitioners to think carefully about the relationships between strategies for practice and the student populations they are intended to serve in order to address lingering retention problems and to produce consistent, socially just learning environments.

Rather than simply observing discrepancies in retention rates, our model highlights the need for researchers to ask: Why does this gap exist? And rather than simply creating interventions for student populations with disproportionately low retention rates, our model highlights the need for practitioners to create theories of action that address the question: How will this intervention lead to meaningful change?

The Reason and Kimball (2012) model consists of five elements: formal theory, institutional context, informal theory, practice, and feedback loops for ongoing adjustments in theory-to-practice work. Each of these elements will be subsequently described in this chapter. Additional information about each of these steps is provided in the following discussion as we describe our model in greater detail. Reason and Kimball's (2012) model focuses on theory-to-practice translations in student development, but it can serve as a useful cognitive heuristic for understanding effective theory-to-practice translations in retention work as well, since its primary intention is to provide a guiding structure for thought and action. However, in applying the Reason and Kimball (2012) model to retention, it is important to note that retention work is supported by a much broader theoretical tradition and empirical evidence drawn from a wider variety of subfields in higher education research (and beyond). As a result, some expansion of Reason and Kimball's (2012) thinking is required when applying the model to retention. This expansion also accounts for complexity of retention; arising from the confluence of multiple campus learning environments and also from the multiple institutional and social positionalities of learners, retention research attempts to explain a voluntary, socially constructed, and interdependent process, whereas student development attempts to describe the near inevitability that students will change in college in some discernible way.

Specifically, our reconfiguration of Reason and Kimball's (2012) model reframes (a) formal theory as expert knowledge of student population(s) of interest, (b) institutional context as institutional data about campus learning environments, (c) informal theory as the cognitive schema of faculty and staff, and (d) practice as retention strategy (see Figure 11.1). We follow

Figure 11.1. Conceptual model of theory-to-practice translation for retention.

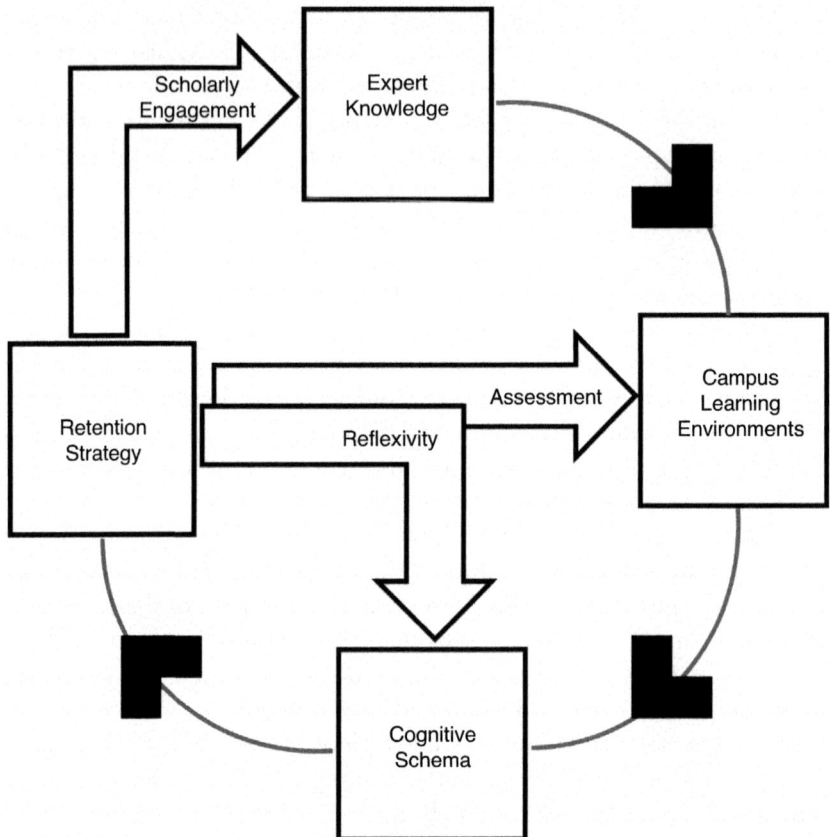

Reason and Kimball (2012) in including feedback loops for reflexivity and assessment, but we also add an additional feedback loop from retention strategy to expert knowledge of student population(s) of interest, which we call scholarly engagement, to highlight that practice should be a vital supply of information for scholars about what topics warrant inquiry and should also help inform retention practitioners about their learning edges. In the section that follows, we describe each of these stages in the retention theory-to-practice translation.

Formal Theory → Expert Knowledge

For Reason and Kimball (2012), *formal theory* encapsulates both student development theories and empirical research on student change during college. They followed Evans and Guido (2012) in arguing that the utilization of formal theory can serve as a constraint on baseless assumptions about student experiences. Consequently, they argued that formal theory therefore serves as a reasonable starting point for understanding what students might be experiencing in a given campus environment. However, Reason and Kimball (2012) also noted higher education and student affairs administrators typically only access formal theory in response to a pressing problem of *practice*. That is, theory-to-practice translations are cyclical; they typically begin and end (and begin and end again) with practice. However, it is precisely this deep connection to practice that makes modifying Reason and Kimball's (2012) model necessary in order for it to be used to support the development of effective retention strategy. Whereas student development represents a relatively well-codified body of literature and is framed largely in terms of student affairs work, the literature on retention is both voluminous and ill-defined. As summarized in this volume, robust empirical literature suggests that student preentry characteristics, institutional policies, built environments, campus climate, peer cultures, microclimates, instructional practices, advising practices, student affairs practices, the decisions of individual students, and many more multivalent factors all contribute to student persistence. Moreover, this same literature base makes it clear that college campuses both replicate and actively reproduce broader systems of oppression used to reify existing structures of power and privilege such as racism, colorism, shadism, classism, cisheteropatriarchy, trans erasure, heterosexism, cisgenderism, disableism, and ableism (Hurtado et al., 2012). Understanding the pervasive, insidious effects of oppression in the lives of college students with both majoritarian and minoritized identities often benefits from access to literature bases beyond those produced by higher education researchers.

As a result, we suggest that researchers and practitioners doing retention work should adopt an expansive definition of *expert knowledge* as they consider what information is available to them in relevant literature to support their response to a pressing retention problem. Quantitative work can indeed help us to understand population-level trends in student experience and to pinpoint causal effects. However, as higher education researchers specifically and social scientists more generally have often noted (cf. Kezar, 2000; Lindblom & Cohen, 1979; Porter, 1996), the primary limitation of quantitative work is its struggle to address the experiences of statistical outliers and the erasure of variability in experiences through aggregation. Qualitative work is essential in connecting broad institution-level patterns to the varied, nuanced experiences of individuals. It can help to sensitize both researchers and practitioners to potential ways that the scholarly record has elided the experiences of some groups of students while centering others.

Good historical scholarship, although rarer than it should be in higher education, can do the same (cf. Hevel, 2016; Kimball & Ryder, 2014). Works of scholarship that are sometimes dismissed by social scientists for their lack of empirical foundation (e.g., works of philosophy and social theory) can do the same while both providing a population-level account of student experience and connecting those experiences to broader societal narratives. Finally, and most importantly, we suggest that existing definitions of *expert knowledge* have often failed to take into account students' individual and collective capacities to create, curate, and disseminate information about their own experiences.

Our main suggestion at the level of expert knowledge is that researchers begin the theory-to-practice translation process by reading and thinking broadly. Scholarly methods such as the counter-narrative, the testimonio, participatory action research, and life history interviews all provide a mechanism for translating the expert knowledge of students about their own experiences into a format more consistent with scholarly norms while also pushing the boundaries of that form. That work is vitally important and its capacity to help deconstruct and then reconstruct academic discourse is critical. However, researchers and practitioners can also learn from the expert knowledge of students outside of formal academic structures; for example, recent scholarship has highlighted the key role that student advocacy on social media has played in changing institutional and societal response (Dache, 2019; Griffin et al., 2019; Wheatle & Commodore, 2019), and many campuses have rich traditions of informal student advising documents that suggest how students can navigate inhospitable campus learning environments (e.g., the University of Pennsylvania's Penn Course Reviews and Middlebury College's MiddCourses).

In an academic world of our creation, we would encourage everyone to begin an exploration of what is known about student experience by accessing existing knowledge produced by students. Key sources of this information would include venues such as social media, student-run blogs, student newspapers, and works of student advocacy. Although we lack an empirical citation for this claim, our general observation as both student affairs practitioners and historians of higher education is that students generally know what the problems are on campus long before administrators, faculty, and staff "discover" them. Thereafter, we would suggest that time spent connecting the knowledge produced by students with works of social theory would be well spent. Social theory can help researchers and practitioners alike to think about the deep interconnectedness of issues of social justice and problems of retention. Before even getting to considerations of campus learning environments or the cognitive schema of faculty and staff, social theory can help sensitize researchers and practitioners to the near certainty that those campus learning environments will be constructed in ways that advantage some students while disadvantaging others and that the cognitive schema of faculty and staff will embed both known and unknown biases about who students are and how they experience the world. Thereafter, we suggest that qualitative work (and works of institutional history if they are available) can help to connect student accounts, which tend to be the focus of most qualitative research in higher education, with the works of social theory that undergird many qualitative research agendas. Then and only then would we suggest looking at quantitative evidence for patterns in persistence outcomes. Reviewing expert knowledge in this way will help to provide context for both what this evidence says and what it does not as well as provide a mechanism for thinking about why the data might reflect the trends it does.

Institutional Context → Campus Learning Environments

Reason and Kimball (2012) also suggested that good theory-to-practice translations need to take into account the *institutional context* within which student experience takes place. This institutional context consists of both what is known about students within a given campus environment based on institutional data as well as how the institution's faculty, staff, and administrators collectively think about student experience. In this regard, they follow a long-running tradition in higher education research that regards *campus learning environments* as an essential feature of the student success outcomes—ranging from enrollment to retention to learning to completion—realized by individual students therein (e.g., Hurtado et al., 2012; Reason, 2009; Strange & Banning, 2015). We adopt the term *campus learning environments* both in recognition of the growing importance of this body of literature and also because it draws explicit attention to the multiplicity of contexts within which the retention practices that shape the experience of a single student at a single institution are enacted—ranging from classrooms to laboratories to student organizations to residence halls to on-campus employment. That is, while Reason and Kimball's (2012) model sought to explore how student affairs professionals ought to think about the varied developmentally instigative features of a given institutional context as they refined viable strategies for practice, the readers of this chapter have a more complicated task: thinking about the systemic interplay of every possible contributor and inhibitor of retention at the institutions where they work.

To do so, we suggest that readers begin by embracing an expansive understanding of campus learning environments that includes attention to both intentionally designed and unintentionally chaordic components of an institution with which students must interact. That is to say, higher education institutions often exist in their present form as a series of historical accidents and may display bureaucratic, organizational, or policy logics that do not center student experience—privileging instead administrative or financial expediency or the convenience of those faculty, staff, and administrators who tend to be longer-term inhabitants of institutions than the students whom they serve. In recent years, conceptual models of the interactions between higher education institutions and students have proliferated (e.g., Hurtado et al., 2012; Reason, 2009; Vaccaro & Newman, 2016). These models provide both a useful heuristic tool for and an example of how to parse campus learning environments to find the rough edges on which students might otherwise find themselves caught on their student success journeys through an institution. This sort of conceptual review can also be greatly enhanced by empirical review—either formalized as in the assessment feedback loop described in a following section or as a catalyst for reflective practice. Although there are a variety of ways that one can think about an empirical review of campus learning environments from the standpoint of retention (e.g., Kuh et al., 2005; Ostrom et al., 2011), they all share in common the goal of making a familiar campus strange by exploring it from a new perspective.

In addition to these conceptual and empirical reviews of campus learning environments from a systemic, holistic perspective, those concerned about retention also benefit greatly from a deep acquaintance with campus assessment data and conversation with colleagues. As Ryder and Kimball (2015) suggested, assessment data not only provides higher education professionals with actionable insights about their students but can also help to provide a catalyst for reflection about the informal and implicit theories operant within the institution. Most importantly, when considering campus learning environments, conversations with colleagues—whether about assessment data or their professional experiences more generally—can help to surface potentially problem areas in one's own practice as well as potentially incommensurate ways that those with the same retention goals engage in retention practice. These minor discontinuities in practice can help to produce a form of institutional ambiguity that students—particularly those who might already be organizationally vulnerable—struggle to navigate. This level of careful consideration of campus learning environments as well as the way that our thinking about them accords with that of our colleagues can help to produce better retention practice.

Informal Theory → Cognitive Schema

As noted in the discussion of campus learning environments, people develop theories or frameworks with which they can understand the world, and in the context of higher education, these theories become part and parcel of the way that teaching, administration, and student affairs practice get enacted. Reason and Kimball (2012) followed Love (2012) in labeling these kinds of theories "informal theory" and in suggesting that they were the fundamental building blocks for student affairs practice rather than the formal theory that prior models of theory-to-practice had centered. However, unlike Love (2012), Reason and Kimball (2012) argued that the key distinction between informal theory, which they described as the carefully considered knowledge, beliefs, and assumptions of an experienced student affairs practitioner, and implicit theory, which they followed Bensimon (2007) in describing as a form of stereotype adopted without careful thought, necessitated the use of formal theory as a form of corrective. We employ the term *cognitive schema* to capture the aggregate understanding produced by the combination of formal theory, informal theory, implicit theory, and experiential knowledge. Simply put, cognitive schema for retention are the latent dispositions of a given higher education professional as they pursue retention practice, and further, these same cognitive schema serve as the filter through which judgments about campus learning environments and formal theory are constantly being made.

As Perez (2016) has noted, graduate students in higher education and student affairs programs receive socialization to the overt and hidden assumptions of the profession as part of their graduate training. Similar forms of socialization take place across fields of study (e.g., Egan, 1989; Helm et al., 2012; Sulé, 2014) and provide foundational elements of the cognitive schema that higher education professionals—including faculty, student affairs staff, and higher education administrators alike—will eventually utilize as the foundation for their practices. For example, as some of our prior work has shown, both faculty members in STEM disciplines and student affairs professionals utilize their professional socialization as the primary means by which to understand the experiences of disabled college students when confronted with the limits of their own knowledge and training (cf. Bettencourt et al., 2018; Kimball et al., 2016). These cognitive schema change over time as the result of exposure to new knowledge claims or on the basis of discrepant experiences—that is, the mental models that higher education professionals use change when those models cannot account for new information (Kimball, 2016). In the context of theory-to-practice translations, this framing is critical as it both surfaces the idea that people's individual understandings of retention might condition their response to specific strategies and also that theory-to-practice translations must afford an opportunity to adjust the cognitive schema.

Practice → Retention Strategy

In their model, Reason and Kimball (2012) describe *practice* as the outcome of a carefully considered theory-to-practice translation. They describe practice as planned behavior intended to produce desirable student development outcomes. In this regard, they follow Harper (2011) in suggesting the importance of intentionality to practice. That is, higher education professionals benefit from differentiating those actions that they perform because they carefully planned to do so from those actions that they performed unthinkingly. As conceptualized in this chapter, we think of these intentional and unintentional practices as *retention strategy*.

This distinction can also help to untangle the intended and unintended outcomes of a deliberate practice from the hidden outcomes of an unintentional practice. Manning et al. (2013) make this case clearly in *One Size Does Not Fit All* when they noted that navigating a complex bureaucratic structure in a large, famously complicated research university might over time become viewed as a rite of passage for students—although still posing challenges to minoritized students with less access to navigational capital—whereas the same structure would not be workable at a liberal arts college given the smaller, more human-scale environment. In the case of the research university, bureaucracy-as-rite-of-passage is likely an unintended outcome of a more intentional practice (e.g., organizing for supervisory expediency), whereas the negative outcomes for minoritized students are a hidden outcome of unintentional practices that result (e.g., lack of communication between disparate offices, poor wayfinding). Meanwhile, in the case of the liberal arts college, the decision to limit bureaucracy represents an intentional choice about institutional culture. Higher education institutions and the people within them make innumerable decisions of every scope and scale that contribute to the overall way that students will experience the institution. Whether apparent or not, these decisions ultimately represent a form of retention strategy, which exists at both the level of the individual higher education professional and the institution.

As should be clear from the previous example, better practice results from intentional retention strategy than from unintentional retention strategy. From a pragmatic standpoint, it is easier for institutions to align campus learning environments and the cognitive schema of higher education professionals when goals for practice, plans for practice, and communication mechanisms for aligning practice are all clearly specified. However, we also recognize that the entirety of institutional retention strategy is beyond the remit of most readers of this chapter. In that case, we believe that there is still considerable benefit to thinking holistically and systematically—that is, about how one's own intentional practice might contribute to the broader institution's retention efforts—but at minimum we argue that all faculty and staff charged with developing policies and programs to increase student persistence must be mindful of the retention strategy they pursue and its likely effect on students. The feedback loops we describe subsequently can be of great help in this regard.

Feedback Loops: Reflexivity, Assessment, and Scholarly Engagement

Following Reason and Kimball (2012), we argue that reflexivity and assessment represent important *feedback loops* that can help to produce better theory-to-practice translations by making ongoing corrections in the way that each stage in the model is applied. Specifically, Reason and Kimball (2012) suggested that reflexivity can help to better align practice and informal theory by allowing the refinement of informal theory based on new information derived from practice. In our revised model, the reflexivity feedback loop does precisely the same thing by connecting retention strategy to cognitive schema. Simply put, the knowledge that human beings have about themselves and the world around them is always limited and perspectival; by recognizing that fact and committing to an ongoing cycle of inquiry intended to improve their understanding of the world, higher education professionals can produce better cognitive schema with which to support retention. Reason and Kimball (2012) had the same goal in suggesting a feedback loop between practice and institutional context. In their model, they suggested that student affairs professionals benefit from assessment both because it produces data with which to calibrate practice—that is, to ask, "Did I do what I thought I was doing?"—and also because it can help to calibrate knowledge of institutional context—that is, to ask, "Was what I thought I knew about the institution and its students actually true?"

Although Kimball (2016) has suggested a third feedback loop to the Reason and Kimball (2012) model previously, we reframe this feedback loop here. Instead of thinking about this feedback loop primarily as a mechanism for higher education professionals to produce empirical knowledge about the field as Kimball (2016) did, we argue that scholarly engagement must be a two-directional relationship. As is quite clear from the entirely of this volume, the field needs both new ways of thinking about retention and also new ways of talking about it. Based on our reading of retention literature, we are thoroughly convinced that the problem is not that we need more empirical literature nor that the empirical literature that exists is fundamentally inconsistent with the needs of the field. Instead, it appears to us that higher education researchers too often frame their work in ways that are inconsistent with the perceived needs of higher education professionals (summarized in Kezar, 2000; Kimball & Friedensen, 2019). Having a scholarly engagement feedback loop in theory-to-practice translations would encourage more active conversation between those engaged in retention research and those engaged in retention practice. This connection would assist higher education researchers in better understanding how to communicate their findings in an actionable way, which is a frequent but not insurmountable struggle for many natural and social scientists (Badgett, 2016). Additionally, the scholarly engagement feedback loop also implies the importance of ongoing acquaintance with emerging literature for higher education professionals: If a key outcome of retention strategy is data about the success or failure of the associated practices, then a reasonable next step for higher education professionals is a deep dive into available expert knowledge to consider what is next.

(In)Concluding Thoughts

Higher education professionals confronting inadequate retention outcomes face a complicated, long-running, and multifaceted wicked, or ill-structured, problem. As noted previously, wicked problems defy easy understanding because they require both coordinated, goal-directed action and a common set of assumptions about what that goal-direction action should be, driven by a shared understanding of the underlying problems. As the long history of efforts to improve retention have shown, it is entirely possible but remarkably difficult to meaningfully improve retention outcomes. In this chapter, we have noted what we believe to be the primary reason why: All of social science suffers from the pragmatic action problem, and although a great deal of effort has been expended to try to solve it—and even more in ignoring its existence—meaningful solutions remain elusive. We argue that practitioners do not need full agreement about the nature of a problem, or even the means by which to solve that problem, before pursuing meaningful change. That is, simply beginning the process of developing the shared strategies and understandings necessary to meaningfully improve retention will in fact improve retention. As such, we propose a structured way of thinking about and integrating various forms of knowledge that can apply across multiple contexts and student populations. By adopting a theory-to-practice model, practitioners can synthesize relevant knowledge with institutional and individual practices into a more coherent overall retention strategy. We also propose three feedback loops that would make this model self-correcting. That is, rather than viewing retention strategy in "all-or-nothing" terms, we suggest that adopting an iterative approach allows for the calibration of expert knowledge, campus learning environments, the cognitive schema of individual higher education professionals, and retention strategy.

The stakes for getting retention "wrong" are high and getting higher. For individual students, the cost of college-going continues to rise, and the opportunity costs for stopping out, dropping out, or never attending in the first place—sometimes based on the departure stories of friends and family—have never been higher. Simply put, although far from a guarantee, higher education can provide a mechanism for accessing forms of economic, healthcare, and quality-of-life security not often granted to those without a postsecondary degree. For institutions, retention problems can compromise the integrity of academic programs and the viability of budgets. They can derail people's careers and carefully made institutional plans. They can reinforce rather than resist existing societal inequities. Finally, for society, the stakes are even higher; as Hurtado et al. (2012) have noted, higher education can be a catalyst for a more democratic, more socially just society. But that promise can only be realized if higher education enrollments mirror society's diversity while institutions themselves exist as more socially just environments than the society of which they are a part. In short, our inability to get retention "right" comes with great costs, but when we do, the benefits can be enormous for individuals, institutions, and society.

References

Ackoff, R. (1974). *Redesigning the future: A systems approach to societal problems.* Wiley.

Alford, J., & Head, B. (2017). Wicked and less wicked problems: A typology and a contingency framework. *Policy and Society, 36*(3), 397–413. https://doi.org/10.1080/14494035.2017.1361634

Altbach, P. (2014). The emergence of a field: Research and training in higher education. *Studies in Higher Education, 39*(8), 1306–1320. https://doi.org/10.1080/03075079.2014.949541

Bacharach, S. B. (1989). Organizational theories: Some criteria for evaluation. *Academy of management review, 14*(4), 496-515. https://doi.org/10.5465/amr.1989.4308374

Badgett, M. L. (2016). *The public professor: How to use your research to change the world.* New York University Press.

Becker, H. (1986). *Doing things together.* Northwestern University Press.

Bensimon, E. (2007). The underestimated significance of practitioner knowledge in the scholarship on student success. *Review of Higher Education, 30*(4), 441–469. https://doi.org/10.1353/rhe.2007.0032

Berger, P. (1967). *The sacred canopy: Elements of a sociological theory of religion.* Anchor.

Bettencourt, G., Kimball, E., & Wells, R. (2018). Disability in postsecondary STEM learning environments: What faculty focus groups reveal about definitions and obstacles to effective support. *Journal of Postsecondary Education and Disability, 31*(4), 383–396.

Biesta, G. J. J., & Burbules, N. C. (2003). *Pragmatism and educational research.* Rowman & Littlefield.

Blimling, G. (2014). *Student learning in college residence halls: What works, what doesn't, and why.* Jossey-Bass.

Blumer, H. (1969). *Symbolic interactionism: Perspective and method.* University of California Press.

Braxton, J. M. (2000). Introduction: Reworking the student departure puzzle. In J. M. Braxton (Ed.), *Reworking the student departure puzzle* (pp. 1–8). Vanderbilt University Press.

Braxton, J. M., Hirschy, A. S., & McClendon, S. A. (2004). *Understanding and reducing college student departure* (ASHE-ERIC Higher Education Report, Vol. 30, No. 3). Jossey-Bass.

Conklin, J. (2006). *Dialogue mapping: Building shared understanding of wicked problems.* Wiley.

Dache, A. (2019). Ferguson's Black radical imagination and the scyborgs of community-student resistance. *Review of Higher Education, 42*(5), 63–84. https://doi.org/10.1353/rhe.2019.0045

DeAngelo, L., & Franke, R. (2016). Social mobility and reproduction for whom? College readiness and first-year retention. *American Educational Research Journal, 53*(6), 1588–1625. https://doi.org/10.3102/0002831216674805

Egan, J. (1989). Graduate school and the self: A theoretical view of some negative effects of professional socialization. *Teaching Sociology, 17*(2), 200–207. https://doi.org/10.2307/1317462

Eisenmann, L. (2004). Integrating disciplinary perspectives into higher education research: The example of history. *Journal of Higher Education, 75*(1), 7–22. https://doi.org/10.1080/00221546.2004.11778893

Evans, N. J., & Guido, F. M. (2012). Response to Patrick Love's "informal theory": A rejoinder. *Journal of College Student Development, 53*(2), 192–200. https://doi.org/10.1353/csd.2012.0022

Friedland, R., & Alford, R. (1991). Bringing society back in: Symbols, practices, and institutional contradictions. In W. W. Powell & P. J. DiMaggio (Eds.), *The new institutionalism in organizational analysis* (pp. 232–263). The University of Chicago Press.

Friesen, K. (2020). *Exploring the organizational emergence of academic leadership programs* [Unpublished doctoral dissertation]. Iowa State University.

Geertz, C. (1982). The way we think now: Toward an ethnography of modern thought. *Bulletin of the American Academy of Arts and Sciences, 35*(5), 14–34. https://doi.org/10.2307/3823993

Greenfield, G., Keup, J., & Gardner, J. (2013). *Developing and sustaining successful first-year programs: A guide for practitioners.* Jossey-Bass.

Griffin, K., Hart, J., Worthington, R., Belay, K., & Yeung, J. (2019). Race-related activism: How do higher education diversity professionals respond? *Review of Higher Education, 43*(2), 667–696. https://doi.org/10.1353/rhe.2019.0114

Grites, T., Miller, M., & Voler, J. G. (Eds.). (2016). *Beyond foundations: Developing as a master academic advisor.* Jossey-Bass.

Gross, N. (2009). A pragmatist theory of social mechanisms. *American Sociological Review, 74*, 358–379. https://doi.org/10.1177/000312240907400302

Harper, S. (2011). Strategy and intentionality in practice. In J. Schuh, S. Jones, & S. Harper (Eds.), *Student services: A handbook for the profession* (5th ed., pp. 287–302). Jossey-Bass.

Head, B. W., & Alford, J. (2015). Wicked problems: Implications for public policy and management. *Administration and Society, 47*(6), 711–739. https://doi.org/10.1177/0095399713481601

Helm, M., Campa, H., III, & Moretto, K. (2012). Professional socialization for the Ph.D.: An exploration of career and professional development preparedness and readiness for Ph.D. candidates. *Journal of Faculty Development, 26*(2), 5–23.

Hevel, M. (2016). Toward a history of student affairs: A synthesis of research, 1996–2015. *Journal of College Student Development, 57*(7), 844–862. https://doi.org/10.1353/csd.2016.0082

Hurtado, S., Alvarez, C. L., Guillermo-Wann, C., Cuellar, M., & Arellano, L. (2012). A model for diverse learning environments. In M. Paulsen (Ed.), *Higher education: Handbook of theory and research* (Vol. 27, pp. 41–122). Springer.

Joas, H. (1996). *The creativity of action.* The University of Chicago Press.

Johnson, R. B. & Onwuegbuzie, A. J. (2004). Mixed methods research: A research paradigm whose time has come. *Educational Researcher, 33*, 14-26. https://doi.org/10.3102/0013189X033007014

Kezar, A. (2000). Higher education research at the millennium: Still trees without fruit? *Review of Higher Education, 23*(4), 443–468. https://doi.org/10.1353/rhe.2000.0018

Kimball, E. (2016). Reconciling the knowledge of scholars and practitioners: An extended case analysis of the role of theory in student affairs. *Critical Questions in Education, 7*(3), 269–288.

Kimball, E., & Friedensen, R. E. (2019). The search for meaning in higher education research: A discourse analysis of ASHE presidential addresses. *Review of Higher Education, 42*(4), 1549–1574. https://doi.org/10.1353/rhe.2019.0075

Kimball, E., & Ryder, A. (2014). Using history to promote reflection: A model for reframing student affairs practice. *Journal of Student Affairs Research and Practice, 51*(3), 298–310. https://doi.org/10.1515/jsarp-2014-0030

Kimball, E., Vaccaro, A., & Vargas, N. (2016). Student affairs professionals supporting students with disabilities: A grounded theory model. *Journal of Student Affairs Research and Practice, 53*(2), 175–189. https://doi.org/10.1080/19496591.2016.1118697

Kuh, G. D., Kinzie, J., Schuh, J. H., & Whitt, E. J. (2005). *Assessing conditions to enhance educational effectiveness: The inventory for student engagement and success.* Jossey-Bass.

Lindblom, C. E., & Cohen, D. K. (1979). *Usable knowledge: Social science and social problem solving* (Yale Fastback Series, Vol. 21). Yale University Press.

Love, P. (2012). Informal theory: The ignored link in theory-to-practice. *Journal of College Student Development, 53*(2), 177–191. https://doi.org/10.1353/csd.2012.0018

Manning, K., Kinzie, J., & Schuh, J. H. (2013). *One size does not fit all: Traditional and innovative models of student affairs practice.* Routledge.

Mayhew, M. J., Rockenbach, A. N., Bowman, N. A., Seifert, T. A., & Wolniak, G. C. (2016). *How college affects students: 21st century evidence that higher education works.* Jossey-Bass.

Mead, G. H. (1913). The social self. *Journal of Philosophy, Psychology and Scientific Methods, 10*(14), 374–380. https://doi.org/10.2307/2012910

Mead, G. H. (1922). A behavioristic account of the significant symbol. *Journal of Philosophy, 19*(6), 157–163. https://doi.org/10.2307/2939827

National Center for Education Statistics. (2019). *Digest of education statistics, 2018* (NCES 2020-009). U.S. Department of Education.

Ostrom, A. L., Bitner, M. J., & Burkhard, K. A. (2011). *Leveraging service blueprinting to rethink higher education: When students become "valued customers," everybody wins.* Center for American Progress.

Pascarella, E. T., & Terenzini, P. T. (2005). *How college affects students: A third decade of research.* Jossey-Bass.

Perez, R. J. (2016). A conceptual model of professional socialization within student affairs graduate preparation programs. *Journal for the Study of Postsecondary and Tertiary Education, 1*, 35–52. http://www.jspte.org/Volume1/JSPTEv1p035-052Perez2057.pdf

Porter, T. M. (1996). *Trust in numbers: The pursuit of objectivity in science and public life.* Princeton University Press.

Ray, V. (2019). A theory of racialized organizations. *American Sociological Review, 84*(1), 26–53. https://doi.org/10.1177/0003122418822335

Reason, R. D. (2009). An examination of persistence research through the lens of a comprehensive conceptual framework. *Journal of College Student Development, 50*(6), 659–682. https://doi.org/10.1353/csd.0.0098

Reason, R. D., & Kimball, E. W. (2012). A new theory-to-practice model for student affairs: Integrating scholarship, context, and reflection. *Journal of Student Affairs Research and Practice, 49*(4), 359–376. https://doi.org/10.1515/jsarp-2012-6436

Renn, K. A., & Reason, R. D. (2012). *College students in the United States: Characteristics, experiences, and outcomes.* Jossey-Bass.

Rorty, R. (1979). *Philosophy and the mirror of nature.* Princeton University Press.

Rorty, R. (1981). Method social science, and social hope. *Canadian Journal of Philosophy, 11*(4), 569–588. https://doi.org/10.1080/00455091.1981.10716323

Ryder, A. J., & Kimball, E. W. (2015). Assessment as reflexive practice: A grounded model for making evidence-based decisions in student affairs. *Research & Practice in Assessment, 10*, 30–45.

Shulman, L. S. (1997). Disciplines of inquiry in educational research: A new overview. In R. M. Jaeger (Ed.), *Complementary methods for research in education* (2nd ed., pp. 3–31). American Educational Research Association.

Strange, C. C., & Banning, J. H. (2015). *Designing for learning: Creating campus environments for student success.* Jossey-Bass.

Sulé, V. T. (2014). Enact, discard, and transform: A critical race feminist perspective on professional socialization among tenured Black female faculty. *International Journal of Qualitative Studies in Education, 27*(4), 432–453. https://doi.org/10.1080/09518398.2013.780315

Swidler, A. (1986). Culture in action: Symbols and strategies. *American Sociological Review, 51*(2), 273–286. https://doi.org/10.2307/2095521

Tight, M. (2007). Bridging the divide: A comparative analysis of articles in higher education journals published inside and outside North America. *Higher Education, 53*(2), 235–253. https://doi.org/10.1007/s10734-005-2429-9

Tinto, V. (2012). *Completing college: Rethinking institutional action.* The University of Chicago Press.

Toutkoushian, R. K., May-Trifiletti, J. A., & Clayton, A. B. (2019, January 21). From "first in family" to "first to finish": Does college graduation vary by how first-generation college status is defined? *Educational Policy.* Advance online publication. https://doi.org/0895904818823753

Vaccaro, A., & Newman, B. M. (2016). Development of a sense of belonging for privileged and minoritized students: An emergent model. *Journal of College Student Development, 57*(8), 925–942. https://doi.org/10.1353/csd.2015.0072

Wells, R., Kolek, E. A., Williams, E., & Saunders, D. B. (2015). "How we know what we know": A systematic comparison of research methods employed in higher education journals, 1996–2000 v. 2006–2010. *Journal of Higher Education, 86*(2), 171–198. https://doi.org/10.1080/00221546.2015.11777361

Wheatle, K. I., & Commodore, F. (2019). Reaching back to move forward: The historic and contemporary role of student activism in the development and implementation of higher education policy. *Review of Higher Education, 42*(5), 5–35. https://doi.org/10.1353/rhe.2019.0043

Xu, Y. J., & Webber, K. L. (2018). College student retention on a racially diverse campus: A theoretically guided reality check. *Journal of College Student Retention: Research, Theory & Practice, 20*(1), 2–28. https://doi.org/10.1177/1521025116643325

12

SHIFTING ENVIRONMENTS, EMERGING NORMS

How Changes in Policy, Technology, Data, and Market Competition Affect Enrollment Management Processes

P. Jesse Rine and Joshua T. Brown

College choice and student persistence have remained priority concerns among various higher education stakeholders, such as scholars, policymakers, and administrators—and rightfully so. The extent to which we understand the conditions supporting student access and success will ultimately determine our ability to craft equitable and effective institutions of higher education. Given the stakes, it is little surprise that voluminous research has been conducted on these topics using a wide range of student populations, institutional contexts, and theoretical lenses (Hirschy, 2015). The resulting literature is remarkably comprehensive in its scope, yet it has not adequately accounted for a series of interrelated shifts in the organizational environment occurring during the first 2 decades of the 21st century (Brown, 2017, 2018), shifts that have resulted in new norms that hold significant implications for the study of college student retention.

As socially constructed phenomena, norms are complex, and their trajectories are neither uniform nor necessarily linear, often resisting tidy "before and after" analyses. At times, however, environmental shifts can be so pronounced that they produce clear-cut changes in organizational behavior that fundamentally alter the ways in which individuals interact with institutions and each other. Such is the case with a group of policy, technology, data, and market competition drivers that together have shifted the environment toward more disconnected, impersonal, commodified, and hypercompetitive norms for college student recruitment and retention. The extent to which our field understands and integrates these shifts into the dominant conceptual models for college student retention will ultimately determine their effectiveness in empowering institutions to support student success.

Our goal in this chapter, then, is threefold. First, we briefly survey the college student recruitment and retention literature to highlight a relatively stable set of preexisting institutional norms, or expectations for behavior (Hodum & James, 2010) that previously governed college recruitment and retention processes. Next, we describe in greater detail how various environmental drivers have considerably shifted these norms over the past 2 decades. Finally, we outline the implications of these shifts for future research into four previously identified factors that influence college student persistence: (a) student perceptions of institutional integrity, (b) entering characteristics of students, (c) student social and academic integration, and (d) institutional concern for student welfare.

Previous Norms in Student Recruitment and Retention

We begin by providing a summative overview of the norms operating across four dimensions of student recruitment—professionalism, process, outreach, and pricing—and four dimensions of student retention—funding, stakeholders, information, and departure. It is important to note that while these norms were widely held and relatively stable prior to the turn of the 21st century, their expression undoubtedly varied to some degree within and across institutions, as did the timing of their evolution within the field. What follows, therefore, is a brief outline of how student recruitment and retention norms typically operated across each dimension as a form of "best practice" prior to the introduction of various drivers of change.

Student Recruitment

Previous norms in student recruitment were informed largely by characteristics such as institutional mission, setting, and type. Those characteristics directed outreach to prospective students, defined the parameters for assessing person-institution fit, provided a backdrop for engagement, and determined the institution's pricing model. Postsecondary approaches to student recruitment coalesced around the following four norms.

Professional Norm: Advising Approach to Admissions
Throughout the history of American higher education, colleges and universities have faced what Henderson (1998) has termed the "twin prongs of the admissions dilemma: the quantity and quality of students" (p. 25). Simply put, the admissions office is tasked with recruiting enough students

to meet the financial needs of the institutional budget while at the same time maximizing the academic profile of the incoming class. In spite of these institutional needs, the fundamental identity of the admissions officer has always been that of trusted advisor, particularly given the ethical dimensions inherent in representing the institution to prospective students. Swan (1998) noted that "counseling" and "customer service" have traditionally been used as descriptors for admissions officers, terms that emphasize the primary goal of assessing the match between student and institution rather than "selling" the college to prospective students (p. 31). Fundamental to this ethical stance are notions of honest representation of institutional character, transparent disclosure of policies and requirements, and the primacy of student interests.

Professional associations in higher education have codified these values in various ways. Underscoring the professional norm of assessing student fit through an advising approach to admissions are codes of ethics formulated by various national associations, such as the American Association of Collegiate Registrars and Admissions Officers (AACRAO, 2020), the National Association for Collegiate Admissions Counseling (NACAC, 2019), and the Council for the Advancement of Standards in Higher Education (CAS, 2012). For example, the *CAS Professional Standards for Higher Education* (2012) defines the mission of Undergraduate Admissions Programs and Services (UAPS) as enrolling applicants "whose academic and personal credentials are consistent with the overall priorities and mission of the institution" (p. 482) and emphasizes the responsibility of UAPS professionals to accurately represent the policies and procedures of the institution. Research suggests that admissions practitioners have adopted these espoused principles to serve as a normative guide for professional behavior (Hodum & James, 2010).

Process Norm: Substantial Personal Engagement

Outreach efforts that foster substantial personal engagement with prospective students have remained bedrock strategies for college admissions offices. The goal of these strategies has been to make an in-person connection between an admissions officer and prospective student, whether extending outward to various venues where students are located or drawing students onto campus. Smith (1998) identified three in-person strategies for student engagement typically used by college admissions offices, each with an increasing level of prospective student interest. In the first, travel to high schools enables the admissions officer to visit with school counselors, meet with groups of prospective students, and assess the character of the likely applicant pool. Second, college fairs present an opportunity for the admissions officer to raise the visibility of the institution among prospective students currently in the market for a college and engage in one-on-one conversations. Finally, campus visits allow the admissions officer to showcase the college campus during an itinerary of events customized to the prospective student's interest. At all three levels of student interest, the process norm is substantial personal engagement to facilitate and deepen the relationship between the prospective student and the institution.

Outreach Norm: Prospect Pool Defined by Institutional Decisions

For decades, student outreach has largely been conducted in a "push" manner, with institutions primarily defining their prospect pools and pushing their messaging out to potential students. Colleges and universities have historically delineated the academic and geographic parameters of their desired prospect pools, then purchased student contact information from sources such as ACT's Educational Opportunity Service or the College Board's Student Search Service (Smith, 1998). This contact information allowed the institution to engage prospective students in direct mail campaigns consisting of print and physical materials such as letters, brochures, announcements, invitations, and videocassettes (Smith, 1998). Early digital outreach practices supplemented traditional mail campaigns by leveraging customer relationship management (CRM) software to contact prospective students via email (Kahler, 2008). Regardless of whether the form of communication was material or digital, the norm directing outreach remained institutional definition of the prospect pool.

Pricing Norm: Different Pricing Models for Different Sectors

Because ability to pay is a major factor in the college search process (Cabrera & La Nasa, 2000; Hu & Hossler, 2000; Perna, 2008), tuition pricing has been a key consideration in prospective student recruitment, one historically managed differently by public and private institutions. On the one hand, public universities have typically charged students differential tuition prices based on their residence. Students from the state in which the institution is located have paid a lower in-state tuition rate, while students from other states have paid a higher out-of-state tuition rate. On the other hand, private colleges have typically posted the same tuition "sticker price" for all students, regardless of residence, then used a differential pricing model designed to maximize net tuition revenue while meeting enrollment goals (Breneman, 1994). This differential pricing model raises the tuition sticker price above the actual cost of education to signal institutional quality and then discounts the tuition rate for individual students according to varying levels of demand (Rine, 2016). For decades the norms governing institutional pricing varied according to institutional control; private colleges priced tuition according to student demand, while public institutions priced tuition according to student residency.

Student Retention

Previous norms in student retention were defined by well-established and internally conducted institutional approaches. Once enrolled, students were presumed to be under the care of one particular institution until they themselves initiated departure, and state funding was determined by enrollment headcount with the presumption of student persistence. The following four norms directed institutional behavior in the area of student retention.

Funding Norm: State Support Determined by Enrollment

In the latter half of the 20th century, many state legislatures tended to allocate financial resources to all institutions within the state, both public and private, based on student enrollments. In other words, a specific dollar amount was allocated per student (i.e., indirect funding). Thus, larger institutions such as state research universities often received more money than smaller regional comprehensive institutions. Lawmakers and institutional leaders relied on "front end" admissions metrics to regulate the flow of resources across a diverse set of institutions in the state (McLendon et al., 2006). As direct state appropriations began their continual decline in the 1970s, legislators granted increased autonomy to institutions to set their own tuition levels in order to compensate for the lost state revenues (McLendon & Mokher, 2009). However, even as direct state allocations diminished, indirect funding was still available to public and private institutions, determined by the total number of students enrolled at the institution.

Stakeholder Norm: Retention Function Housed Internally

Many colleges and universities have specific departments established to oversee and coordinate retention efforts for the broader institution. The placement of the office within the organization has varied considerably, as some institutions included the office as part of enrollment management, others within academic affairs, and still others embedded in student affairs (Dolence, 1998). While the specific placement of the retention function varied from one institution to the next, the common thread was that retention efforts were limited to stakeholders operating within the institution itself. Institutional actors commonly connected to the retention function have typically included faculty, residence life staff, campus counselors, and academic advisors (Hossler, 1986; Hossler et al., 1990).

Information Norm: Data Collected According to Predetermined Best
Practice Model
College and university retention offices focus their efforts on the central-
ized collection of information across multiple departments and divisions
(Heverly, 1999; Murtaugh et al., 1999; Tinto, 2010). These offices have
served as a hub for the acquisition, analysis, and reporting of retention information. Historically, the information collected by these retention offices has
been limited to elements found in predetermined "best practice" models
(Bean, 2005). In this approach, the retention office focuses its attention on
factors previously identified by a trusted model as most likely to affect student persistence. This confirmatory approach provides a clear direction for
information gathering and interpretation.

Departure Norm: Students Initiate Transfer Conversation
Colleges and universities have long operated in a competitive environment
governed by a larger professional obligation to the educational best interests of students—namely, the successful completion of a selected academic
program (Henderson, 2008). For this reason, the NACAC (2017) *Code
of Ethics and Professional Practices* has historically prohibited institutions
from soliciting transfer applications from prospective students who have
enrolled elsewhere unless the students have themselves initiated a transfer
inquiry. In addition, the CAS *Professional Standards for Higher Education*
(2012) has prohibited UAPS staff from distributing "biased, unflattering,
and/or potentially inaccurate information about other secondary or postsecondary institutions, their admission criteria, their curricular offerings,
or other related information" (p. 486). Thus, the operational norm guiding student departure has been an understanding that once a student has
chosen to enroll in a particular program of study, other institutions do not
make unsolicited attempts to lure that student away via transfer prior to
program completion.

Environmental Shifts and New Norms

We now turn attention to the ways in which the aforementioned enrollment
management norms have been altered by a series of environmental shifts
in society at large. In particular, we identify four types of environmental
drivers—policy, technology, data, and market competition—and consider
their influence within both the student recruitment and retention domains
(see Figure 12.1). We then describe the striking alterations of professional
norms that have occurred in response to these drivers, whether by their
revision or outright replacement.

Figure 12.1. Components of environmental shift and resulting norms for institutional enrollment management processes.

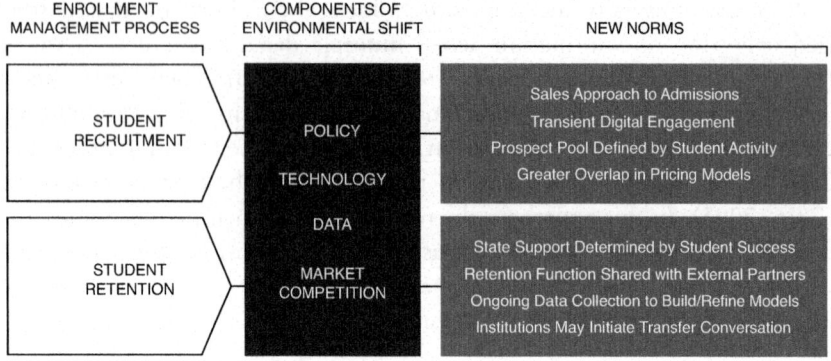

Student Recruitment

Student recruitment behavior has become both more aggressive and more reactive in response to environmental drivers. Because the college search process increasingly takes place in the digital realm, institutions now attempt to capture organic interest signaled online by prospective students, often outsourcing their outreach to third parties. Tuition discounting has been widely adopted across institutional types to encourage matriculation, and nonmonetary incentives are gaining acceptance within the admissions profession.

Policy Drives New Professional Norm: Sales Approach to Admissions
The first major shift in student recruitment norms resulted from changes to the NACAC *Code of Ethics and Professional Practices*. Under pressure from the U.S. Department of Justice (USDOJ), the national association voted to eliminate three long-standing provisions of its code of ethics. One such eliminated provision prevented colleges from offering special incentives for early decision applicants, while others established a national decision day and required that colleges cease recruitment of students once they have made an official commitment to another institution. While the USDOJ understood these provisions as inappropriately limiting competition among colleges, their inclusion in the code of ethics was designed to ensure that a student's college choice was "informed, well-considered, and free from coercion" (NACAC, 2017, p. 6), and thus upheld the historic advising norms of the admissions profession.

These revisions of membership expectations by the largest and most influential national association of college admissions officers signaled a shift in professional norms away from the historic advising approach to student recruitment and toward an emphasis on sales. Although institutional marketing has always been a component of any college's recruitment efforts, the NACAC stipulations provided important ethical guiderails that served to balance student needs in the college search process with institutional interests. Removal of these guiderails shifted the balance toward a sales approach to student recruitment, in which new incentives—such as preferred campus parking, early housing confirmation, and bookstore discounts or credits—direct prospective student focus away from assessing institutional fit, and a now-endless recruitment cycle distracts prospective students from deep commitment and full integration after an enrollment decision has been made. While it is unlikely that the field has witnessed the full impact of this relatively recent redefinition of membership expectations, early evidence suggests a shift in professional norms is indeed underway. One well-known annual national survey of admissions officers found that nearly a quarter of colleges are already offering new incentives for prospective students that had been prohibited only a year before (Jaschik, 2020).

Technology Drives New Process Norm: Transient Digital Engagement
The second major shift in recruitment norms is the increasing role digital engagement now plays in college choice as a result of advances in technology. The advent and near-universal adoption of smartphones, combined with the development of associated mobile websites, has changed the way high school students engage with colleges and universities (Ruffalo Noel Levitz & OmniUpdate, 2019). A prospective student now experiences the postsecondary environment in digital as well as physical ways, through interactive online tools such as virtual tours and live chat. In addition, these tools enable prospective students to access institutional information more quickly and easily than ever before. Although certainly more efficient, the character of this digital engagement is also more transient than that of the substantial in-person contact required by an earlier era. Many prospective students may end their association with the institution after obtaining information digitally, while others may decide to visit campus as a result of their digital engagement. However, the potential digitization of all elements of the student recruitment process—from electronic applications to admissions interview via videoconference—means that students can move through the admissions funnel with little—if any—in-person contact with the physical campus and face-to-face interaction with institutional representatives prior to matriculation.

The increasing role of online program management (OPM) companies in recruitment processes underscores the widening acceptance of more transient forms of student engagement within the field. OPMs are third-party organizations that provide support for developing and delivering online programs (EDUCAUSE, 2020), and their ranks have swelled over the past decade from just a handful of major players to dozens of firms serving a few hundred colleges and universities (McKenzie, 2018). Eduventures (2018) has grouped the levels of service offered by OPMs into three categories: comprehensive, selective, and specialized. Of particular note is the comprehensive level of service, which involves third-party assumption of the recruiting function for particular academic programs, a move made possible by the wider shift away from in-person, on-campus engagement and toward more fleeting digital interactions, especially during the early stages of the college search process. In sum, whether managed by third-party partners or by the institutions themselves, this technological shift in the process norms for student recruitment has resulted in engagement of a more temporary and shallow nature, requiring colleges and universities to take greater care in orienting and integrating newly enrolled students into the campus community upon their matriculation.

Data Drives New Outreach Norm: Prospect Pool Defined by Student Activity

A third shift in recruitment norms has resulted from the expansion of data generation and tracking capabilities made possible by new technologies. Previously, colleges and universities defined their prospect pools according to academic and geographic considerations, then "pushed" information out to institutionally identified students using largely print materials. Adoption of email and creation of websites digitized communication and opened up new avenues for college outreach at the close of the 20th century. In the following decades, the rise of search engine optimization (WebFX, 2020) combined with the development of sophisticated CRM tracking capabilities (A. McClure, 2012), fostered a mechanism for identifying and measuring student interest in particular institutions. Thus, prospect pools are now defined in greater measure by organic student activity, which effectively "pulls" institutional information toward signaled interest.

The technological architecture supporting the new outreach norm is threefold. First, a college optimizes its website by seeding keywords holding currency among prospective students throughout its various program pages (Ruffalo Noel Levitz, 2015). Second, prospective students use internet search engines such as Google, Bing, or Yahoo to look for colleges that match their interests and preferences. Well-optimized websites matching student queries appear higher in the results returned by the search engine and are more likely to be visited (OmniUpdate, 2020). Once on the college's webpage, the prospective student encounters enough information to pique interest, but often discovers inbound marketing techniques (Hope, 2014; Royo-Vela & Hünermund, 2016) that require submission of personal information in order to receive additional details about particular programs. Third, colleges can input student personal information into CRM software programs such as Technolutions SLATE, which enable customized communication flows and real-time tracking of student engagement with the institution's messaging (e.g., email successfully delivered, email opened, link embedded in email clicked, etc.) and website (e.g., when, how often, and in what order particular webpages are visited). In sum, the existence of more detailed data regarding student activity, combined with the technological tools to effectively mine said data, has rendered the definition of prospect pools a function of student activity more so than institutional projection.

Market Competition Drives New Pricing Norm:
Greater Overlap in Pricing Models
A final shift in recruiting norms involves the acceleration of tuition discounting as a pricing strategy. The financial consequences of divestment in public higher education following the Great Recession have been significant, with per-student state appropriations to higher education having recovered only halfway a decade later (State Higher Education Executive Officers Association [SHEEO], 2018). Consequently, state universities have been forced to cover budget shortfalls by finding new revenue streams or expanding existing ones, such as student tuition. To better compete for prospective students, public universities have more fully embraced tuition discounting as a pricing strategy in the years following the Great Recession. While Baum and Lapovsky (2006) found evidence of tuition discounting among public 4-year universities as early as 1994–1995, discount rates were modest and relatively stable, ranging from only 11.7% that year to just 14.7% in 2004–2005. However, discount rates have steadily climbed among public institutions in recent years, with one study finding an average tuition discount of 24.6% among public flagship universities in 2016 (Davis & Kirshtein, 2019). Thus, students applying to public institutions can now expect not only to see a lower sticker price than their private counterparts, but also to receive a larger average discount than was available prior to the Great Recession.

During the same period, discount rates continued to dramatically climb among private colleges. As tuition-dependent institutions, private colleges sought to navigate the choppy financial waters following the Great Recession by attracting prospective students via ever-increasing tuition discounts, even as yield rates steadily declined during this period (Rine et al., 2021). According to Baum and Lapovsky (2006), the discount rate at private 4-year colleges was only 23.8% in 1994–1995; by 2019–2020, the average tuition discount for first-time, full-time, first-year students climbed to 52.6% (NACUBO, 2020). For years, economists of education have warned that tuition discounting is susceptible to unsustainable escalation, as heightened consumer awareness combined with the strategic competitive response of postsecondary competitors could lead to a so-called "race to the bottom" (Breneman et al., 2001). The results of NACUBO's (2020) latest Tuition Discount Study suggests that the market may have indeed moved into unsustainable territory, as first-year enrollment declined at a plurality of institutions (47%) and net tuition revenue dropped by 1.3% after adjusting for inflation, even though discount rates continued to increase year-over-year. In addition to the increased competition from public universities seeking to backfill the losses of state appropriations through increased tuition dollars, private colleges in the Northeast and Midwest have also had to contend with population declines and demographic shifts (Bransberger & Michelau, 2016), forcing them to expand their recruiting footprint and compete for students from other parts of the country, which in turn has increased the downward pressure on price and fueled further increases in the tuition discount rate.

Student Retention

In response to environmental drivers, student retention efforts have become more complex and involved more external partners. Performance-based state funding formulas and the removal of historic prohibitions against recruiting enrolled students have placed heightened emphasis on student retention. In turn, institutions have increased data collection to support building and refining models for student success and sought third-party support to enhance and even perform elements of the retention function.

Policy Drives New Funding Norm: State Support Determined by Student Success

The Great Recession brought about notable changes in how American colleges and universities were funded by state governments. The emphasis in funding norms shifted from a "front end" focus on enrollment-based funding formulas to a "back end" focus on using measures of student success to determine state support. The shift in norms was driven by policy changes governing the statewide distribution of limited financial resources that support all state public services (Archibald & Feldman, 2014). As part of a "new accountability" movement, legislators established higher education policies known as "performance-based funding" grounded in a philosophy that institutions would operate more efficiently and effectively if guided by financial incentives (K. R. McClure et al., 2020).

The diffusion of performance-based funding in higher education came in two distinct waves. In the first wave, during the latter decades of the

20th century a handful of states adopted a policy approach that emphasized allocating a portion of an institution's budget based on specific outcomes such as credit attainment, course completion, graduation rates, diversity, job placement, and pass rates, among many others (McLendon et al., 2006). The second wave of performance-based funding, also referred to as "PBF 2.0," further expanded the implementation of PBF policies in the years immediately following the Great Recession when legislators were confronted with even further reductions in state budgets (Kelchen, 2018). In addition to government, many philanthropic organizations also implemented performance-based funding strategies to incentivize colleges and universities to focus on degree completion. Kelchen noted that nearly 70% of all states had implemented some form of PBF 2.0 by 2015, which made a notable impact in institutional retention strategies.

To account for institutional diversity, state legislators established unique algorithms and performance metrics to allocate financial resources according to institutional type. For example, the Ohio legislature created three unique formulas, one for flagship universities, another for regional universities, and another for community colleges (Miao, 2012). The formulas awarded some institutions for achieving course completion and degree-completion targets, while it awarded others for completing developmental education courses and successful transfers. Consequently, the particular facet of retention an institution pursued was, by design, a function of the policy-driven algorithm.

Within the literature on the efficacy of performance-based funding, a further divide exists, as some scholars assert the strategy undermines the social issues it attempts to ameliorate. It would seem that the allocation of key financial resources to institutions based on improved student retention metrics might be a widely celebrated policy advancement. However, there is a growing body of work that suggests PBF may contribute to social and organizational inequality. Two essential questions have been levied against the strategy: (a) Does it work? (b) Does it disadvantage students? Based on longitudinal analyses, one group of researchers has contended that institutional actions tied to retention metrics are not associated with improved retention rates (Sanford & Hunter, 2011). Another group of researchers asserted that PBF metrics yielded unintended consequences, specifically higher admissions standards for access-oriented institutions and the disproportionate enrollment of minorities in less selective institutions (Li, 2019). In short, although the literature has not yet established a conclusive connection between PBF policies and educational outcomes (Hillman, 2016), the willingness of multiple state legislatures to move away from allocations based solely on enrollment has resulted in a new funding norm for many public institutions.

Technology Drives New Stakeholder Norm: Retention
Function Shared With External Partners

In the past decade, advancements in technology prompted a shift in stakeholder norms from retention functions that were predominantly housed internally to retention functions predominantly shared with external partners in varying capacities. As explained further in this section, colleges and universities increasingly turned to outside companies (i.e., "external partners") to either provide or augment services and products that would improve their institutional retention efforts. This change commenced as colleges and universities strengthened their technological infrastructure, making strategic improvements to their software and data management systems. A focal component of the technological infrastructure was the student information system (SIS), which focused on centralizing all student records information from across the institution. An equally vital component was the complementary collection of software products for the various university divisions that integrated with the SIS to improve service and efficiency. For example, institutions acquired learning management systems (LMSs) for academic departments, including modules for divisions of student housing, and student success management systems (SSMSs) for areas with oversight of student support.

While many software products were acquired to support broad divisions of colleges and universities, the SSMS software provided a unique focus that sought to improve retention by considering multiple aspects of the student experience, such as course enrollment, participation, financial aid, student engagement, physical/mental health, and more. The early warning SSRM systems are designed to identify students who may be less likely to persist. Flagging specific students allows administrators, faculty, and staff to proactively encourage a student to take action and get back on track. This approach relies on technology to assess multiple types of student data to successfully and expeditiously identify students in need.

In pursuing technology-based retention strategies, institutions often selected one of four viable options: (a) purchase the various software products from external partners, (b) internally develop the software themselves, (c) outsource the service to a third-party vendor, or (d) adopt a hybrid approach. Many institutions purchased SSMSs from external partners, such as Starfish, CampusLabs, CampusNexus Succeed, or SignalVine. These retention software products integrated with the institution's SIS to enable tracking and monitoring of student performance on essential retention topics such as academics, finances, and engagement. Rather than purchase software from an external partner, some institutions opted for an alternate retention strategy and developed their own student success software "in-house" to help students more effectively navigate curricular structures. For example, Austin Peay State University developed the software program Degree Compass, which was later expanded and offered to other institutions. This, in turn, made Austin Peay an external partner supporting peer institutions in retention efforts across the state (Denley, 2014).

Institutions with limited financial means often implemented a third strategy, one that relied on outsourcing retention services to third-party vendors who could offer the service at a reduced cost. In this model, organizations such as Ruffalo Noel Levitz could analyze the institution's SIS records over time and provide strategies to improve student retention based on historical trends. Outsourcing these institutional functions enabled third-party vendors to provide immediate technological and human resources to colleges and universities that desperately wanted to improve retention and completion rates in the face of a rapidly shrinking applicant pool. Finally, some institutions opted to pursue a fourth technology-based retention strategy that blended internal and external approaches. For example, a diverse set of three institutions partnered with Civitas Learning to design an SSMS that aggregated data from across their LMS, SIS, and enterprise resource platforms to establish an early alert mechanism to improve course completion and student retention (Milliron et al., 2014).

In the past decade, advancements in technology prompted a shift in stakeholder norms from retention functions that were housed internally to retention functions shared with external partners. At one end of the spectrum, some institutions now rely on external partners to simply secure necessary software. At the other end of the spectrum, some institutions depend on outsourcing all retention functions to external partners. While there is certainly not a uniform approach to retention across institutions, the use of external partners has become an observable and consistent emergent norm within the field.

Data Drives New Information Norm: Ongoing Data Collection
to Build/Refine Models
The continued advancement of technology also brought about a transformation in the way most organizations processed information, including colleges and universities. This new type of information that emerged was termed "big data" because its volume, variety, and velocity were significantly larger than in prior eras (Macfadyen et al., 2014; Thille et al., 2014). The phenomenon brought about a change in information norms in student retention; whereas retention efforts had previously focused on collecting data according to predefined rules and best practice models (Bean, 2005), the emergent

information norms emphasized ongoing data collection to both build and refine new models (Milliron et al., 2014).

Over time, advancements in technology enabled the various components of an institution's digital infrastructure to rapidly generate large volumes of student data at granular levels. Thus, these data were simultaneously "broad and deep" (Thille et al., 2014). For example, LMS software generated granular *learning data* for each student, such as course log-ins, time spent on a given assignment, and individual test questions. The LMS system also generated large volumes of *social data* between persons, such as peer discourse and faculty engagement in both asynchronous and synchronous classroom formats. With seemingly limitless amounts of new types of data at their disposal, administrators and researchers sought to identify the specific interactions and experiences that most supported student retention.

As these tools grew in sophistication, the new field of information analytics provided university leaders with guidance concerning how best to examine and deploy the expansive data available to them. Both information analytics broadly and its particular manifestations in higher education developed in three phases. Initial efforts in analytics were used for decision support and relied heavily on descriptive analyses to explain what had happened in the past (Davenport & Harris, 2017). For example, demographics from the SIS could be integrated with social and learning data from the LMS and used to inform decision-making about the academic components of courses that were contributing to low retention rates in specific student populations. The aim was to integrate large amounts of data from different sources across the institution to generate models of student progression and completion (Macfadyen et al., 2014).

The second development in analytics emphasized "predictive analytics," whereby data were analyzed to inform the future. The analyses examined data across multiple platforms to specifically shape decisions and educational products. A notable example was the Degree Compass software used by many colleges and universities in Tennessee to "level the playing field" for underprepared students (Denley, 2014). Information on the prior patterns of student behavior were used to generate academic retention models to guide students with a "choice architecture" regarding degree programs and course sequencing. The aim in this second phase of analytics was to "produce deep predictive flow models of student progression and completion coupled with applications that take these data and bring them to advisors, students, faculty, and administrators in highly consumable/useable ways" (Milliron et al., 2014, p. 70).

In the third and most recent phase, the use of "autonomous analytics" has been emphasized. Autonomous analytics refer to those data that are analyzed using artificial intelligence techniques (i.e., machine learning) in addition to their integration in processes and systems (Davenport & Harris, 2017). For example, some institutions have used the machine learning approach to generate a predictive model of student success based on student attendance (Gray & Perkins, 2019), while others have leveraged it to identify at-risk students and corresponding models of intervention (Delen, 2010). This phase embeds analytics into processes to offer real-time assessment and feedback systems to improve learning and student success (Gašević et al., 2016), and does so with the assistance of artificial intelligence.

The preceding discussion demonstrates how advances in technology have altered the way colleges and universities use data and analytics to support student retention. A function that had once focused on collecting data according to predefined models now operates according to information norms that direct data collection efforts toward the building and refining of new models. The rapidly evolving nature of the information analytics field has required scholars, researchers, and practitioners to remain alert to frequent developments that hold implications for institutional retention efforts.

Market Competition Drives New Departure Norm: Institutions May Initiate Transfer Conversation

A final driver of change in retention norms stems from the recent removal of key guidance regarding transfer student recruitment from the NACAC (2019) *Code of Ethics and Professional Practices.* As referenced previously, under legal pressure from the USDOJ for codifying industry standards viewed as limiting competition between institutions, the association's membership chose to eliminate various provisions from its professional code of ethics, one of which prohibited solicitation of transfer applications from students enrolled in other institutions. The guideline reflected a widely held sense within the field that once a student had made a college choice and matriculated, competitors should place the student's long-term educational interests—namely, college completion—ahead of their own short-term financial interests—namely, increased tuition from transfer students. This norm placed the profession at odds with the USDOJ, which equated "poaching" of students with employee recruitment practices and launched a federal antitrust investigation (Jaschik, 2019). One media outlet recorded the reaction of a member that reflected well the prevailing mood: "Many of us are sad and somewhat angry, because we are committed to doing what's right for kids and families, and we think this goes backwards" (Jaschik, 2019, para. 13). In spite of this widely held sentiment, the NACAC membership ultimately voted to remove the disputed provisions from the code of ethics in order to avoid a costly legal battle that would threaten the financial viability of the association (Jaschik, 2019).

Poaching of enrolled students has thus become a sanctioned practice within college admissions. Although many admissions professionals undoubtedly frown upon poaching, recent changes to the resource environment are likely to encourage adoption of this practice. Total college enrollment has declined since its peak in the years immediately following the Great Recession, providing fewer prospective students to fill existing institutional capacity and provide tuition dollars to support current financial obligations (Schmidt, 2018). Tuition-dependent private colleges and public regional universities located in states experiencing demographic declines are particularly at risk, as campus leaders search for new revenue streams to ensure financial survival. Compounding these difficulties is the COVID-19 pandemic, which has resulted in a 4% decline in undergraduate enrollment from the previous year (Sedmak, 2020). In this context of resource scarcity, it is perhaps unsurprising that early research into the competitive response of institutions has found that 35% of enrollment officers had already considered offering transfer incentives to students enrolled at other institutions just weeks after the NACAC guidelines were changed (Burke, 2020), suggesting that the new norm of student poaching has already taken root.

Implications for Research on College Student Retention

It is admittedly difficult to capture all of the nuances inherent in each of the aforementioned domains, yet the preceding overview of recent shifts in enrollment management processes begins to trace the contours of an emergent landscape for college student recruitment and retention. Moreover, the shifts previously outlined reveal a complex terrain in which some changes enhance—while others undermine—existing institutional recruitment and retention efforts. It is important for researchers to be mindful of the rapidly changing resource environment as institutions increasingly turn to innovative methods of recruitment and retention to maintain their student enrollments. The broad contextual changes illumined in this chapter should be given consideration in both the content and design of future research into college student persistence. In particular, special attention should be given to the implications of these changes for four factors identified by previous research as consequential to student retention: (a) student perceptions of institutional integrity, (b) entering characteristics of students, (c) social and academic integration, and (d) institutional concern for student welfare. We conclude by tracing a few implications of the aforementioned emergent norms for future research into each of these factors.

Student Perceptions of Institutional Integrity

Research has demonstrated a connection between students' persistence and their sense of institutional integrity, or "the degree to which students perceive the institution's actions to be aligned with its vision and mission" (Reason, 2009, pp. 668–669). According to Braxton et al. (2014), institutional integrity manifests in two practical ways: (a) fair administration of policies and rules, and (b) fulfillment of student expectations. In particular, student perceptions of institutional integrity were positively influenced when their expectations were fulfilled (Braxton et al., 2014). As institutional norms change to accommodate shifts in the resource environment, one might expect disruption of established persistence patterns should students take a negative view of new institutional policies or feel as if their expectations have not been reasonably met.

Two dimensions of the emergent norms merit special attention. First, researchers should examine to what extent the adoption of a sales approach to recruitment shapes the expectations of students. As emphasis shifts away from helping students find the right institutional fit and toward securing enough paying students to meet budget goals, attention should turn to how institutional signals and incentives are transformed, and in turn, how they affect student behavior. Does more aggressive marketing messaging change the ways in which students envision their college experience? Do sales tactics such as early decision incentives affect the length and character of the typical student's college search process? Taken together, do these shifts result in short-circuited decision-making processes and distorted student perceptions that engender disappointment upon matriculation, ultimately depressing student satisfaction and lowering persistence?

Second, researchers should examine how emergent norms surrounding tuition discounting practices affect student perceptions of institutional integrity. As unfunded aid becomes a more commonly used recruitment strategy among public universities, so too does the practice of marking up the institutional "sticker price" above the actual cost of education in order to maximize tuition revenue through differential pricing. The disparity in pricing between students is largely obscured during the recruitment process, as each prospective student sees only an individual, personalized financial aid offer. However, once students enroll and begin taking classes with one another, differences in both academic ability and financial obligation become apparent. What happens to student perceptions when it becomes clear that students who applied to multiple competitors or waited to decide until later in the recruitment cycle received larger "scholarships" than their equally—or perhaps more—academically capable peers? Are students who perform well academically during their first year but feel disappointed with their tuition rate more likely to be "poached" by competitor institutions?

Entering Characteristics of Students

Demographic shifts in the American population highlight two notable trends for the coming decade in student recruitment: a steep decline in the traditional-age college population and an increase in students of color (Grawe, 2018). According to Tinto (2006–2007), the field has long recognized both "how a broader array of forces, cultural, economic, social, and institutional shape student retention" (p. 3) and "how the process of student retention differs in different institutional settings" (p. 4). As institutions located in areas experiencing population decline and/or demographic shifts adapt to the emergent environment, the influence of these two factors will likely become less stable and perhaps more pronounced, particularly as admission offices employ sales tactics in tandem with more aggressive tuition discounting to meet their recruitment goals and the college search process takes on a more transient digital character. Future recruitment and retention research must give attention to how these institutional responses to population changes intersect with and even magnify the specific social, cultural, and educational needs that may differ across various institutional types and settings.

Additionally, we recommend that future research on student recruitment and retention should give immediate attention to the central role that external partners now play in recruitment and retention processes. For instance, as more institutions turn to OPMs to assist with achieving student enrollment goals, how might these external for-profit organizations support or alter the educational goals of the institution, particularly when they are servicing multiple competing institutions (Carey, 2019)? Likewise, many institutions are turning away from the traditional approach of buying lists from the College Board for mailing purposes and toward companies like Google who provide institutions with custom analytics for targeted admissions and recruitment. In what ways does the targeted admissions approach impact students, student groups, and the institution more broadly? Moreover, will differences in retention emerge as these methods of recruitment change over time? Most importantly, in what ways do these third-party vendors impact student access and degree attainment?

Social and Academic Integration

Broader environmental shifts and new norms not only influence institutions; they also have a direct impact on individual students whose social and academic integration is vital for success (Braxton et al., 2014; Tinto, 1993).

The advancement of technology and analytics and their application to student retention hold great potential for supporting this social and academic integration, and the increased use of behavioral economics has highlighted how information is "pushed" to students in proactive ways in an attempt to ameliorate socioeconomic disparities that influence student success (Denley, 2014). "Nudges" were a proposed solution to address widespread "undermatching" in student recruitment, a phenomenon wherein well-qualified individuals from lower SES backgrounds ultimately enroll in less competitive institutions (Hoxby & Turner, 2015). Researchers have relied on technological nudges such as text messages to provide important information to students regarding admissions, financial aid, enrollment, and course registration (Castleman & Page, 2016) and Web 2.0 communication technologies to promote social integration among first-generation students (Rowan-Kenyon et al., 2018). However, emerging research on this topic has underscored that the impact of "nudges" on student recruitment may either be ineffectively scaled or possibly waning (Gurantz et al., 2020). As institutions conduct ongoing data collection to build and refine their student retention models, often in partnership with third-party providers, it is critical that investigation into the nature of "nudges" become more granular and systematic to unlock their full potential for supporting student social and academic integration. What types of "nudges" are most effective across multiple contexts and student populations, and which ones are best deployed in more targeted ways? In the context of rapidly changing technology and data information, how long can specific interventions realistically maintain their efficacy? Finally, in what ways can technological and social "nudges" be coupled to maximize social and academic integration?

Institutional Concern for Student Welfare

A final pertinent factor related to student persistence is the institution's level of commitment to student welfare, which can be defined as an "abiding concern for the growth and development of its students" that is expressed through the "high value the institution places on its students, treating each student with respect as an individual, and the equitable treatment of students" (Braxton et al., 2014, p. 86). Recruitment technologies such as real-time CRM databases and retention software with large-scale analytics provide efficient ways to pay greater attention to students from their first engagement with the institution. Researchers should examine the extent to which these personalized, if not personal, mechanisms effectively represent and convey institutional concern for student welfare at various stages of their engagement with the institution. Does the more transient nature of these communications lessen their impact on student persistence? Can they be deployed as stand-alone measures, or does their efficacy depend upon their use in tandem with other tactics? How do their effects vary, if at all, across program modalities—are they more effective with online populations accustomed to virtual interaction and less effective with residential students? Finally, as more institutions turn over elements of student advising and retention to OPMs, researchers should explore the ways in which those expressions of institutional concern qualitatively differ from ones handled directly by the host university. With regard to student retention, does the messenger matter if the message is the same? Or is something "lost in translation"?

Conclusion

The series of interrelated shifts and resulting norms reviewed in this chapter hold significant implications for the study of college student retention. Indeed, the emergent landscape presents new challenges to and opportunities for supporting student success, even as changes to policy, technology, data, and market competition remake the ways in which postsecondary institutions interact with individuals. Higher education researchers have a critical role to play not only in assessing the impact of these changes on the student experience, but also in articulating how the long-standing values of the academy can best be expressed in our present context. Finally, the extent to which institutional leaders—and student affairs professionals in particular—understand these emergent norms and their implications for the student experience will determine their ability to effectively embody institutional integrity, extend concern for student welfare, and engender the social and academic integration necessary to ensure student success.

References

American Association of Collegiate Registrars and Admissions Officers. (2020). *Ethics and practice.* https://www.aacrao.org/who-we-are/mission-vision-values/ethics-practice

Archibald, R. B., & Feldman, D. H. (2014). *Drivers of the rising price of a college education.* Midwestern Higher Education Compact. https://www.mhec.org/sites/default/files/resources/mhec_affordability_series7_20180730.pdf

Baum, S., & Lapovsky, L. (2006). *Tuition discounting: Not just a private college practice.* The College Board.

Bean, J. P. (2005). Nine themes of college student retention. In A. Seidman (Ed.), *College student retention: Formula for student success* (pp. 215–244). Praeger.

Bransberger, P., & Michelau, D. K. (2016). *Knocking at the college door: Projections of high school graduates.* WICHE.

Braxton, J. M., Doyle, W. R., Hartley, H. V., Hirschy, A. S., Jones, W. A., & McLendon, M. K. (2014). *Rethinking college student retention.* Jossey-Bass.

Breneman, D. W. (1994). *Liberal arts colleges: Thriving, surviving, or endangered?* Brookings.

Breneman, D. W., Doti, J. L., & Lapovsky, L. (2001). Financing private colleges and universities: The role of tuition discounting. In M. B. Paulsen & J. C. Smart (Eds.), *The finance of higher education: Theory, research, policy & practice* (pp. 461–479). Agathon.

Brown, J. T. (2017). The seven silos of accountability in higher education: Systematizing multiple logics and fields. *Research and Practice in Assessment, 11,* 41–58. https://www.rpajournal.com/dev/wp-content/uploads/2017/03/A3.pdf

Brown, J. T. (2018). Leading colleges and universities in a new policy era: How to understand the complex landscape of higher education accountability. *Change: The Magazine of Higher Learning, 50*(2), 30–39. https://doi.org/10.1080/0009 1383.2018.1483175

Burke, L. (2020, February 10). Preparing to poach. *Inside Higher Ed.* https://www .insidehighered.com/admissions/article/2020/02/10/some-enrollment-officers-now-considering-poaching-students

Cabrera, A. F., & La Nasa, S. M. (2000). Understanding the college-choice process. In A. F. Cabrera & S. M. La Nasa (Eds.), *Institutional Research's Role in Student Success* (New Directions for Institutional Research, no. 107, pp. 5–22). Jossey-Bass. https://doi.org/10.1002/ir.10701

Carey, K. (2019, April 1). The creeping capitalist takeover of higher education. *HuffPost Highline.* https://www.huffpost.com/highline/article/capitalist-takeover-college/

Castleman, B. L., & Page, L. C. (2016). Freshman year financial aid nudges: An experiment to increase FAFSA renewal and college persistence. *Journal of Human Resources, 51*(2), 389–415. https://doi.org/10.3368/jhr.51.2.0614-6458R

Council for the Advancement of Standards in Higher Education. (2012). *CAS professional standards for higher education* (8th ed.).

Davenport, T., & Harris, J. (2017). *Competing on analytics: The new science of winning.* Harvard Business Press.

Davis, L. M., & Kirshtein, R. J. (2019, March 22). *It's not just the privates: Tuition discounting and enrollments in public flagship universities* [Paper presentation]. 44th Annual Conference of the Association for Education Finance and Policy, Kansas City, MO, United States.

Delen, D. (2010). A comparative analysis of machine learning techniques for student retention management. *Decision Support Systems, 49*(4), 498–506. https://doi .org/10.1016/j.dss.2010.06.003

Denley, T. (2014). How predictive analytics and choice architecture can improve student success. *Research and Practice in Assessment, 9,* 61–69. https://www .rpajournal.com/dev/wp-content/uploads/2014/10/A6.pdf

Dolence, M. G. (1998). Strategic enrollment management. In C. C. Swan & S. E. Henderson (Eds.), *Handbook for the college admissions profession* (pp. 71–91). Greenwood Press.

EDUCAUSE. (2020). *7 things you should know about online program management.* https://library.educause.edu/-/media/files/library/2020/2/eli7171.pdf

Eduventures. (2018). *Expanding the OPM definition.* Eduventures Research.

Gašević, D., Dawson, S., Rogers, T., & Gasevic, D. (2016). Learning analytics should not promote one size fits all: The effects of instructional conditions in predicting academic success. *The Internet and Higher Education, 28,* 68–84. https://doi.org/10.1016/j.iheduc.2015.10.002

Grawe, N. D. (2018). *Demographics and the demand for higher education.* JHU Press.

Gray, C. C., & Perkins, D. (2019). Utilizing early engagement and machine learning to predict student outcomes. *Computers & Education, 131,* 22–32. https://doi.org/10.1016/j.compedu.2018.12.006

Gurantz, O., Howell, J., Hurwitz, M., Larson, C., Pender, M., & White, B. (2020). *Realizing your college potential? Impacts of College Board's RYCP campaign on postsecondary enrollment.* Ed Working Papers, Annenberg Institute for School Reform at Brown University. https://doi.org/10.26300/nqn3-sp29

Henderson, S. E. (1998). A historical view of an admissions dilemma: Seeking quantity or quality in the student body. In C. C. Swan & S. E. Henderson (Eds.), *Handbook for the college admissions profession* (pp. 11–26). Greenwood Press.

Henderson, S. E. (2008). Admissions' evolving role: From gatekeeper to strategic partner. In B. Lauren (Ed.), *The college admissions officer's guide* (pp. 1–22). American Association of Collegiate Registrars and Admissions Officers.

Heverly, M. A. (1999). Predicting retention from students' experiences with college processes. *Journal of College Student Retention: Research, Theory & Practice, 1*(1), 3–11. https://doi.org/10.2190/C1MB-YP0J-UHJ0-MGMB

Hillman, N. (2016). *Why performance-based college funding doesn't work.* The Century Foundation. https://tcf.org/content/report/why-performance-based-college-funding-doesnt-work/

Hirschy, A. S. (2015). Models of student retention and persistence. In D. Hossler & B. Bontrager (Eds.), *Handbook of strategic enrollment management* (pp. 268–288). Jossey-Bass.

Hodum, R. L., & James, G. W. (2010). An observation of normative structure for college admission and recruitment officers. *Journal of Higher Education, 81*(3), 317–338. https://www.jstor.org/stable/40606859

Hope, J. (2014). Add inbound marketing to your mix for greater impact. *Enrollment Management Report, 18*(5), 9.

Hossler, D. (1986). *Creating effective enrollment management systems.* College Entrance Examination Board.

Hossler, D., Bean, J. P., & Associates. (1990). *The strategic management of college enrollments.* Jossey-Bass.

Hoxby, C. M., & Turner, S. (2015). What high-achieving low-income students know about college. *American Economic Review, 105*(5), 514–517. https://doi.org/10.1257/aer.p20151027

Hu, S., & Hossler, D. (2000). Willingness to pay and preference for private institutions. *Research in Higher Education, 41*(6), 685–701. https://www.jstor.org/stable/40196411

Jaschik, S. (2019, September 30). NACAC agrees to change its code of ethics. *Inside Higher Ed.* https://www.insidehighered.com/admissions/article/2019/09/30/nacac-agrees-change-its-code-ethics

Jaschik, S. (2020, September 21). 2020 survey of admissions leaders: A mess of a year. *Inside Higher Ed.* https://www.insidehighered.com/admissions/article/2020/02/10/some-enrollment-officers-now-considering-poaching-students

Kahler, D. (2008). Technology-enhanced recruitment communications. In B. Lauren (Ed.), *The college admissions officer's guide* (pp. 145–163). AACRAO.

Kelchen, R. (2018). Do performance-based funding policies affect underrepresented student enrollment? *Journal of Higher Education, 89*(5), 702–727. https://doi.org/10.1080/00221546.2018.1434282

Li, A. Y. (2019). The weight of the metric: Performance funding and the retention of historically underserved students. *Journal of Higher Education, 90*(6), 965–991. https://doi.org/10.1080/00221546.2019.1602391

Macfadyen, L. P., Dawson, S., Pardo, A., & Gaševic, D. (2014). Embracing big data in complex educational systems: The learning analytics imperative and the policy challenge. *Research and Practice in Assessment, 9*, 17–28. https://www.rpajournal.com/dev/wp-content/uploads/2014/10/A2.pdf

McClure, A. (2012, October). CRM grows up: Reaching beyond admissions to cover the entire lifecycle. *University Business, 43*–47.

McClure, K. R., Barringer, S. N., & Brown, J. T. (2020). Privatization as the new normal in higher education: Synthesizing literature and reinvigorating research through a multilevel framework. In L. W. Perna (Ed.), *Higher education: Handbook of theory and research* (Vol. 35, pp. 589–666). Springer. https://doi.org/10.1007/978-3-030-31365-4_13

McKenzie, L. (2018, June 4). A tipping point for OPM? *Inside Higher Ed.* https://www.insidehighered.com/digital-learning/article/2018/06/04/shakeout-coming-online-program-management-companies

McLendon, M. K., Hearn, J. C., & Deaton, R. (2006). Called to account: Analyzing the origins and spread of state performance-accountability policies for higher education. *Educational Evaluation and Policy Analysis, 28*(1), 1–24. https://doi.org/10.3102/01623737028001001

McLendon, M. K., & Mokher, C. G. (2009). The origins and growth of state policies that privatize public higher education. In C. Morphew and P. Eckel (Eds.), *Privatizing the public university: Perspectives from across the academy* (pp. 7–32). Johns Hopkins University Press.

Miao, K. (2012). *Performance-based funding of higher education: A detailed look at best practices in 6 states.* Center for American Progress. https://cdn.americanprogress.org/wp-content/uploads/issues/2012/08/pdf/performance_funding.pdf

Milliron, M. D., Malcolm, L., & Kil, D. (2014). Insight and action analytics: Three case studies to consider. *Research and Practice in Assessment, 9*, 70–89. https://www.rpajournal.com/dev/wp-content/uploads/2014/10/A7.pdf

Murtaugh, P. A., Burns, L. D., & Schuster, J. (1999). Predicting the retention of university students. *Research in Higher Education, 40*(3), 355–371. http://dx.doi.org/10.1023/A:1018755201899

National Association for College Admissions Counseling. (2017). *Code of ethics and professional practices.*

National Association for College Admissions Counseling. (2019). *Code of ethics and professional practices.*

National Association of College and University Business Officers. (2020, May 20). *Before COVID-19, private college tuition discount rates reached record highs.* https://www.nacubo.org/Press-Releases/2020/Before-COVID-19-Private-College-Tuition-Discount-Rates-Reached-Record-Highs

OmniUpdate. (2020). *Increase enrollment with SEO: An action guide for higher ed.* https://omniupdate.com/resources-gated/seo-white-paper.html

Perna, L. W. (2008). Understanding high school students' willingness to borrow to pay college prices. *Research in Higher Education, 49*(7), 589–606. https://doi.org/10.1007/s11162-008-9095-6

Reason, R. D. (2009). An examination of persistence research through the lens of a comprehensive conceptual framework. *Journal of College Student Development, 50*(6), 659–682. https://doi.org/10.1353/csd.0.0098

Rine, P. J. (2016). *A shell game by any other name: The economics and rationale behind tuition discounting.* Center for Innovative Higher Education. https://www.cehd.umn.edu/OLPD/PCLN/Rine-WhitePaper.pdf

Rine, P. J., Brown, J. T., & Hunter, J. M. (2021). How institutional identity shapes student recruitment: The relationship between religious distinctiveness and market demand. *American Journal of Economics and Sociology, 80*(1), 133–159. https://doi.org/10.1111/ajes.12375

Rowan-Kenyon, H. T., Martinez Aleman, A. M., & Savitz-Romer, M. (2018). *Technology and engagement: Making technology work for first-generation college students.* Rutgers University Press.

Royo-Vela, M., & Hünermund, U. (2016). Effects of inbound marketing communications on HEIs' brand equity: The mediating role of the student's decision-making process. *Journal of Marketing for Higher Education, 26*(2), 143–167. https://doi.org/10.1080/08841241.2016.1233165

Ruffalo Noel Levitz. (2015). *Search engine optimization 101 for higher education* [White paper]. RNL. https://learn.ruffalonl.com/WEB2015_SEO101_HigherEd_WP_LandingPage.html

Ruffalo Noel Levitz & OmniUpdate. (2019). *2019 E-expectations trend report.* RNL. https://learn.ruffalonl.com/rs/395-EOG-977/images/2019_E_Expectations_Report__EM-011.pdf

Sanford, T., & Hunter, J. M. (2011). Impact of performance funding on retention and graduation rates. *Education Policy Analysis Archives, 19*, 33.

Schmidt, E. P. (2018). *Postsecondary enrollment before, during, and since the Great Recession* (P20-580). U.S. Census Bureau. https://www.census.gov/content/dam/Census/library/publications/2018/demo/P20-580.pdf

Sedmak, T. (2020, October 15). *Fall 2020 undergraduate enrollment down 4% compared to same time last year* [Press release]. National Student Clearing House. https://www.studentclearinghouse.org/blog/fall-2020-undergraduate-enrollment-down-4-compared-to-same-time-last-year/

Smith, J. E. (1998). Recruitment: Student outreach strategies. In C. C. Swan & S. E. Henderson (Eds.), *Handbook for the college admissions profession* (pp. 127–139). Greenwood Press.

State Higher Education Executive Officers Association. (2018). *State higher education finance: FY 2018—Executive summary.* https://sheeo.org/wp-content/uploads/2019/04/SHEEO_SHEF_FY18_Report.pdf

Swan, C. C. (1998). Admissions officer: A profession and a career. In C. C. Swan & S. E. Henderson (Eds.), *Handbook for the college admissions profession* (pp. 29–35). Greenwood Press.

Thille, C., Schneider, E., Kizilcec, R. F., Piech, C., Halawa, S. A., & Greene, D. K. (2014). The future of data-enriched assessment. *Research and Practice in Assessment, 9,* 5–16. https://www.rpajournal.com/dev/wp-content/uploads/2014/10/A1.pdf

Tinto, V. (1993). *Leaving college: Rethinking the causes and cures of student attrition.* The University of Chicago Press.

Tinto, V. (2006–2007). Research and practice of student retention: What's next? *Journal of College Student Retention, 8*(1), 1–19. https://doi.org/10.2190/4YNU-4TMB-22DJ-AN4W

Tinto, V. (2010). From theory to action: Exploring the institutional conditions for student retention. In J. C. Smart (Ed.), *Higher education: Handbook of theory and research* (Vol. 25, pp. 51–89). Springer. https://doi.org/10.1007/978-90-481-8598-6

WebFX. (2020). *How to increase higher education enrollment with SEO.* https://www.webfx.com/industries/education/higher-education/seo/

13

FORGING THE TWO-WAY PRACTITIONER–RESEARCHER LOOP FOR ENROLLMENT MANAGEMENT

An Examination of the Research and Communication Needs of Enrollment Managers

Alexandra Cannell Wendt, John M. Braxton,
Don Hossler, Wendy Kilgore, and Heather Zimar

Enrollment management is both an organizational concept as well as a systematic set of activities designed to enable educational institutions to exert more influence over their student enrollments and total net tuition revenue derived from enrolled students (Hossler, 2014). Organized by strategic planning and supported by institutional research, enrollment management activities concern student college choice, transition to college, student attrition and retention, and student outcomes. These processes are studied to guide institutional practices in the areas of new student recruitment and financial aid, student support services, curriculum development and other academic areas that affect enrollments, student persistence, and student outcomes from college (Hossler, 2014).

Over the last 4 decades, enrollment management (EM) has made the transition from being a new administrative function in colleges and universities to becoming, arguably, one of the most important organizational functions on most campuses. Initially, EM units were started in private colleges and universities. Jack Maguire (1976), who is credited with coining the term *enrollment management*, was quite possibly the first enrollment manager—he served in this role at Boston College. The first professional conferences for enrollment managers were sponsored by the College Board and Loyola University of Chicago and took place in the 1980s (Hossler, 2014). The American Association for Collegiate Registrars and Admissions Officers (AACRAO) held the first annual Strategic Enrollment Management Conference in 1990. Now, EM functions can be found in most 4-year colleges and universities in the United States, as well as in Canada and several countries in Europe (Hossler, 2014). In 2019, this annual conference drew nearly 800 registrants. Each year this conference attracts representatives from around the globe.

The growing importance of tuition and fees to both public and private universities spurred the expansion of EM. Senior university officers with EM titles and responsibilities are now commonplace. The term *enrollment management* quickly became replaced with *strategic enrollment management* (SEM) and has become an area of publication for both peer-reviewed academic research journals and for professional publications in the field of higher education. Studies on topics related to enrollment such as research on college choice, college knowledge, marketing in higher education, the influence of financial aid on student enrollment decisions, continued studies of student attrition, and so forth grew exponentially starting in the 1990s. Graduate courses and degrees in EM are found in higher education curricula.

These developments have also raised questions about the extent to which EM is a profession (Henderson, 2001; Ward & Hossler, 2016). One of the attributes of professions is that they have an identifiable body of knowledge. This body of knowledge then becomes part of the formal education and training of individuals in the field of EM. Indeed, in applied fields of research (e.g., higher education) there needs to be an ongoing dialogue between EM professionals and the higher education research community. Braxton and Hossler (2019) framed this issue as a two-way practitioner–researcher loop for EM research. The practitioner-to-researcher loop entails the delineation of topics for research needed by enrollment managers. Enrollment managers identify such topics to form a practitioner-defined research agenda (Braxton & Hossler, 2019). In contrast, the researcher-to-practitioner loop involves two types of action by the community of researchers who study topics relevant to EM. The first of these actions involves conducting research on topics of the practitioner-defined research agenda for EM (Braxton & Hossler, 2019). The second action entails communicating the findings of such research to enrollment practitioners. As part of our discussion, we offer thoughts on issues associated with communication between busy enrollment managers and researchers.

Braxton and Hossler (2019) also stated that successful enrollment managers need to stay abreast of useful research so that they can use the findings of such research to guide their professional practice. Moreover, the most useful type of empirical research would address topics of a practitioner-defined research agenda. In addition, the use of the findings of such empirical research by enrollment managers to guide their professional practice prevents commonsensical "shooting from the hip" or "trial-and-error" forms of action (Braxton & Ream, 2017).

Nevertheless, there has been slow and steady movement to link practitioners and researchers. AACRAO-sponsored "60-Second Surveys" constituted such an effort. These web-based studies collected data on the following topics: data analytics to improve student outcomes and close attainment gaps (AACRAO, n.d.-b), student retention and success (AACRAO, n.d.-a), and the use of EM strategies and plans (AACRAO, n.d.-c).

To help advance both relevant research and practice, we outline in this chapter a practitioner-defined research agenda critical to the formation of the practitioner-to-researcher loop. We also contribute to the shaping of the researcher-to-practitioner loop by identifying channels of communication for researchers to report to practitioners the findings of their studies on topics of the practitioner-defined research agenda for EM. We use data collection through a 60-Second Survey conducted by AACRAO to contribute to these two important steps in the formation of the two-way practitioner–researcher loop for EM. In addition to reporting relevant findings derived from the survey data, we also present the implications of our research for both enrollment managers and higher education researchers.

The 60-Second Survey

In January 2020, the 60-Second Survey was successfully emailed to 11,119 members of AACRAO using the Qualtrics survey platform. A total of 1,184 individuals responded to this survey, which consisted of 16 items. Of these 16 items, three pertained directly to the delineation of the practitioner-defined research agenda for EM and the channels of communication from researchers to EM practitioners.

The Practitioner-Defined Research Agenda

As previously indicated, the practitioner-defined research agenda stands as a significant aspect of the practitioner-to-researcher loop for a scholarship of practice. We fully recognize that the development of such an agenda takes place on a reoccurring basis because new, pressing topics or issues emerge due to circumstances external and internal to colleges and universities. With this caveat in place, the January survey of enrollment managers is an initial step toward the development of a practitioner-defined research agenda for EM. We start with responses to the survey question: As you consider the types of decisions and actions you encounter in your practice of EM, what are the most pressing topics/issues that you think would benefit from a study conducted by researchers? In total, 550 responses were collected, and they ranged from one-word answers to responses several sentences in length.

An analysis of these 550 responses was conducted in three separate stages employing an iterative qualitative coding process in Excel (Miles & Huberman, 1994). The first stage of analysis included an initial line-by-line reading of the data and coding any responses according to the topics/issues represented by the checkbox options of the survey. Few of the responses fit into these checkbox categories. The second stage of analysis encompassed an iterative, initial coding process to identify emergent themes by analyzing the responses through line-by-line analysis (Miles & Huberman, 1994; Strauss, 1987). This inductive analytical approach aligns to grounded theory coding developed by Glaser and Strauss (1967), although the aim of this approach was not to construct a theory but, instead, to identify research topics of interest by EM practitioners (Strauss & Corbin, 1990). The third and final stage of analysis included a third line-by-line reading of the data and their initial codes in order to identify focused codes (Charmaz, 2014). The focused codes identified in this study represent the most salient initial codes. Finally, the saliency of each focused code was tracked and documented so researchers could understand which research topics/issues practitioners were most interested in (Charmaz, 2014).

The three-stage iterative qualitative coding process used to outline a practitioner-defined research agenda for EM resulted in the formation of 46 categories of the most pressing issues or topics that enrollment managers think would benefit from a research study. Of these 46 categories, 27 of them had fewer than 10 respondents that specified a topic for research. However, we focused upon 19 topics that were identified by 10 or more respondents. As stated previously, the number of individuals listing a topic germane to a category offers an indication of the saliency of the topic/issues to EM practitioners. Accordingly, 19 categories of topics and issues hold a high degree of salience for EM practitioners.

In descending order of their salience (saturation), the 19 categories were delineated to form a practitioner-defined research agenda for EM. For each of these 19 categories, we also indicate the institutional affiliation of those respondents who suggested a pressing issue or topic subsumed under each of the categories. We present this information for only those types of colleges and universities that garner the largest percentage of respondents suggesting a pressing issue or topic for research germane to the focal category. Members of the research community of EM who elect to conduct a study that addresses a topic delineated in one of the 19 topical areas can use this information to select the institutional setting for their study. We elaborate further on the importance of the selection of the institutional setting for studies in a subsequent section of this chapter titled "Necessary Elements of Articles." Table 13.1 provides an overview of the 19 categories in descending order of their salience in a practitioner-defined research agenda. Following the table are descriptions of each of the 19 categories.

Efficacy of Various Retention Strategies (90)

This category captures responses from respondents requesting more research on a wide array of retention strategies and their effectiveness in the context of

TABLE 13.1
Categories of Interest in Enrollment Management

Category	Salience
Efficacy of Various Retention Strategies	90
Enrollment Management Trends	57
Strategic Enrollment Management Planning	46
Changing Enrollment Landscape	41
Enrollment Management Best Practices	35
Shifting Demographics	32
Cost of Higher Education	32
Curriculum	32
Recruitment Markets	19
Diversity	17
Financial Aid	17
Projection Modeling	17
Attrition	15
Transfer	15
Data in Enrollment Management	14
Technology in Enrollment Management	14
Access	11
Graduation	11
Trends in Changing and Evolving Roles in Admissions	10

Note. EM—enrollment management; SEM—strategic enrollment management.

varying institution types and for students of varying backgrounds. Responses ranged from an interest in strategies to retain "students of color," "African American males," "adult learners," "part-time students," "first-generation students," "low-income students," "graduate students," and "nontraditional students." Also requested was a need for more research on retention interventions, specifically for undergraduate students and the efficacy of those interventions.

Bolstering the importance of retention strategies, in the open-ended section of the survey respondents indicated a desire to know more about the effects of financial aid on retention, research on graduation strategies, and more insights into research on college completion. Respondents also expressed a desire to understand the relationships between majors and student persistence and if rates of retention vary by major.

Public universities, private universities, and public 2-year colleges constitute the institutional affiliation of the largest percentage of respondents, suggesting a needed study of this category. Of the 90 individuals suggesting a study pertinent to this category, 37% were employed by a public university, 29% at a private university, and 16% at a public 2-year college.

EM Trends (57)

This category represents the concerns of respondents who communicated a desire for research on current and emerging EM trends at colleges and universities in the United States. Responses ranged from an interest in general trends to more specific trend interests relating to international students, community colleges, the types of institutions different groups of students seem to seek out and enroll in, and graduate students and adult learners. Several respondents requested that trends be analyzed in spaces beyond admissions to include offices of student success, career centers, and student life centers, among others.

In addition, several respondents expressed an interest in topics that fall under the general rubric of EM trends, including research on decision points in the admissions process and/or decisions related to EM in institutions. The open-ended comments revealed an interest in knowing what the critical decision points are for students, what factors influence decisions for parents and students, why students choose to attend or not to attend an institution, and who "matters most" in the decision-making process.

The largest percentage of respondents suggesting a needed study of this category were affiliated with public universities, public baccalaureate-granting institutions, and private universities. Of the 57 individuals suggesting a study pertinent to this category, 46% were employed at a public university, 21% at a public baccalaureate-granting institution, and 14% at a private university.

SEM Planning (46)

The SEM planning category represents the concerns of respondents who would like to see more research on SEM planning. Many communicated a desire to know more about SEM planning that is comprehensively integrated into college/university campuses and SEM planning processes that engage multiple stakeholders on college and university campuses. Other respondents expressed a need for SEM planning research that addresses how colleges and universities are integrating strategies to reduce equity gaps and support minority students. Additionally, other respondents communicated a need for research on SEM planning that is specific to community colleges. Finally, many respondents expressed an interest in how different stakeholders are engaged in and/or influence the SEM planning processes on their campuses. The open-ended questions reflected an interest to see research on enrollment goals at institutions, including how institutions determine and meet enrollment goals as well as how they set and meet revenue goals.

The largest percentage of respondents suggesting a needed study of this category were employed by public universities, public baccalaureate-granting institutions, and private universities. More specifically, of the 46 individuals suggesting a study of this category, 40% were employed at a public university, 24% at a public baccalaureate-granting institution, and 17% at a private university.

Changing Enrollment Landscape (41)

This category depicts an interest from respondents in the many factors that are influencing the enrollment landscape. Respondents demonstrated an interest in how recruitment markets have changed in recent years. Specific recruitment markets that were listed by respondents included international recruitment markets, graduate recruitment markets, undergraduate recruitment markets, and online education recruitment markets.

Most salient in the responses was an interest in research that might address how to navigate a changing enrollment landscape as competition among institutions continues to increase. Specifically, respondents indicated interest in how to increase enrollment in the midst of a changing and increasingly competitive enrollment landscape. Some respondents communicated a curiosity regarding how this changing enrollment landscape will impact the varying types of institutions. The code also encompasses an interest in how political factors such as *U.S. v. the National Association for College Admission Counseling* (U.S. Department of Justice, 2019) lawsuit may impact the changing enrollment landscape. Finally, an additional dimension of this code includes an interest in research addressing the pressures institutions are facing in this changing enrollment landscape and how institutions are planning to respond to such pressures during change and declining enrollments.

Public and private universities represent the institutional affiliations of the largest percentage of respondents suggesting a needed study of this category. Of the 41 respondents who listed a study pertinent to this category, 42% were employed at a public university and 40% at a private university. Another 7% of respondents were employed by a public 2-year college.

EM Best Practices (35)

This category encompasses an interest in research on best practices in EM. Responses ranged from interest in best practices in general to specific best practices relating to particular areas of EM. The following list highlights the variety of specific topics respondents were interested in regarding best practices:

- educational experiences
- housing
- class sizes
- ease of navigation for students
- communication with stakeholders
- best practices for community colleges
- increasing enrollment
- launching and supporting student success initiatives
- marketing and recruitment

EM best practices hold salience for respondents employed at public 2-year colleges, as 46% of the 35 individuals designating a topic pertinent to this area were employed by this type of higher education institution. In addition, 29% of the 35 respondents were at a public university, followed by 11% at a private university.

Shifting Demographics (32)

The shifting demographics category reflects respondents who were mostly concerned about how student demographics have shifted in the United States, though some were interested in research that would explore demographic shifts on a global scale. Nearly all respondents who expressed an interest in shifting demographics also expressed the desire to understand how these shifts might impact institutions of higher education. Some respondents also expressed an interest in understanding how best to support students from different demographic groups.

This topic area holds significance for respondents at public and private universities, as 47% of the 32 individuals designating a needed study for this topical area were employed by a public university, followed by 20% at a private university. In addition, public and private 2-year colleges constitute the employing type of institution for an additional 9% of respondents at each of these two types of higher education, for a total of 18%.

Cost of Higher Education (32)

This category captures a wide array of interests in the cost of higher education for students, families, and institutions of higher education. Additionally, this code captures an interest in more research on how free tuition may impact institutions of higher education. Some respondents communicated an interest in more research on student debt and debt reduction efforts.

Costs of higher education constitute a topical area of significance to respondents at private universities given that 41% of the 32 individuals suggesting a study regarding this topic were working at this type of higher education institution. Moreover, public universities stand as the institutional setting for 34% of the 32 respondents who registered a need for studies regarding the costs of higher education. An additional 13% of these 32 individuals were affiliated with a private baccalaureate-granting institution.

Curriculum (32)

This category covers respondent interest in matters related to curriculum, from aspects of scheduling to research on aligning majors and degree programs with demand in industries. The following list outlines topics covered under this code:

- majors in demand by students
- majors in demand by employers
- scheduling

Also included are majors/degree programs for which employer need is decreasing and whether colleges and universities should scale these programs down to save costs and reallocate resources to support degree programs in demand by employers.

Of the 32 respondents who suggested a research study concerning the curriculum, an equal percentage of these individuals worked at private universities (38%) and at public universities (38%). In addition, 9% of the 32 individuals expressing an interest in a study concerning curriculum work were at private baccalaureate-granting institutions of higher education.

Recruitment Markets (19)

This category represents an interest from respondents wanting to see research addressing how recruitment markets have changed in recent years. These responses varied from general interest in how recruitment markets have changed to how specific recruitment markets have changed. The following specific recruitment markets were listed by respondents:

- international recruitment markets
- graduate recruitment markets
- undergraduate recruitment markets
- online education

Public universities, private universities, and public 2-year colleges represented the institutional affiliations of the largest percentage of respondents suggesting a needed study of this category. Of the 19 respondents who recorded a study regarding recruitment markets, an equal percentage of them worked at public 2-year colleges (32%) and at public universities (32%), whereas another 26% of these 19 individuals worked at private universities.

Diversity (17)

This topical area covers the need for research on EM practices for increasing and supporting diversity in student bodies at varying institution types. It also captures an interest in knowing more about what factors might impact diversity at colleges and universities.

This topical area occupies the interest of individuals employed at public universities, with 52% of the 17 respondents delineating the need for research on diversity work in this type of institution. This topic also attracts the attention of respondents who work at public 2-year colleges, as 24% of the 17 respondents suggested a needed study related to this topical area. In addition, another 18% of these 17 individuals worked at private universities.

Financial Aid (17)

This category captures interest in more research on financial aid and/or financial aid trends. Dimensions of this code include the following:

- correlations between financial aid and retention
- correlations between financial aid and student success in general
- managing financial aid discounts in varying types of institutions
- Free Application for Federal Student Aid
- financial aid for first generation and Pell-eligible students

Needed research on financial aid constituted a concern of individuals at public universities, since 53% of the 17 respondents who suggested studies needed on this topical area worked at such universities. In addition, 23% of these individuals worked at a private university.

Projection Modeling (17)

Projection modeling covers an interest in research on enrollment projection modeling, which ties to SEM plans and goals of institutions as well as enrollment projection modeling for undergraduates, graduates, international students, and transfers.

This topical area concerns respondents who work at private universities given that 41% of these 17 individuals worked at an institution of this type. Respondents from public universities also share an interest in studies of this topical area, as 29% of the 17 were employed at a university of this type. An additional 12% of these 17 individuals were working at public 2-year colleges, and an additional 12% were working at public baccalaureate-granting institutions.

Attrition (15)

In general, this category denotes an interest in more research on attrition issues at varying types of institutions and how institutions are addressing such issues. Some responses reflected an interest to further understand reasons students leave institutions and whether those reasons could be categorized as academic, financial, or some combination of the two.

Individuals working at public universities expressed the greatest interest in this topical area, as 53% of the 15 respondents designating a study pertaining to attrition worked in this type of university. This topical area also holds significance for respondents at public 2-year colleges given that 27% of the 15 respondents of this topical area listed a needed attrition study. An additional 20% of these respondents worked at a private university.

Transfer (15)

This category reflects topics and issues related to transfer students. Respondents listed the need for more research on the increased competition for transfer students, trends relating to transfer students, student success measures for transfer students, and general EM practices related to transfer students. In the open-ended questions, four respondents wanted to know more about transfer articulation agreements and their relationship with transfer student enrollments.

All 15 of the respondents who listed a study concerning transfer worked at either a public or private university. Specifically, 60% worked at a public university, whereas 40% of them were at a private university.

Data in EM (14)

This category includes responses related to an interest in more research on the use and management of data in EM. Several responses revealed an interest to learn more about how institutions engage in data-driven decision-making. A few responses communicated the need to learn more about how institutions are managing data since data collection is decentralized within many institutions of higher education.

Respondents in four types of colleges and universities listed a study focused on this topical area. Individuals at public universities expressed the greatest interest as indexed by 30% of the 14 individuals who listed a study of this category. Equal percentages (21%) of the 14 respondents worked at private universities, public baccalaureate-granting institutions, and public 2-year colleges.

Technology in EM (14)

This category captures an interest in more research on the varying technologies used in EM as well as the impact of technology in EM. Specificities include the following:

- using social media to communicate with prospective and current students and its effectiveness
- appropriate practices in using technology to text prospective and current students
- technology supporting the work of EM (i.e., electronic information exchange, electronic transcripts, etc.)
- impacts of artificial intelligence on enrollment

Individuals who work at public universities espoused the greatest interest in studies about technology and EM given that 44% of the 14 respondents listed a needed study germane to this topical area. This topical area also concerned individuals working in private universities, as 21% of the 14 individuals worked in this type of university. This topical area also garnered the attention of respondents at public 2-year colleges, as 14% of the individuals who registered a study needed for this topic were employed at this type of college.

Access (11)

This category reflects an interest in research related to increasing access to higher education for students of all backgrounds, understanding what barriers currently exist for graduating high school students, closing equity gaps within institutions, and the effectiveness of strategies being used to increase access.

The majority of respondents (55% of 11 individuals) who suggested a study related to access worked at public universities, whereas 9% of these 11 individuals worked at private universities. Another 9% of these respondents worked at private baccalaureate-granting institutions.

Graduation (11)

This topical area indexes a general interest in graduation trends at varying institution types. It also reflects an interest in whether or not there are correlations between major selections and graduation rates, how to increase graduation rates, and how to increase graduation rates for underrepresented students (in terms of socioeconomic and ethnic diversity).

Studies about graduation concerned respondents employed by public (37% of 11 respondents) and by private universities (27% of 11). Equal percentages (9% of 11) of those individuals delineating a study focused on graduation worked at public baccalaureate-level institutions, public 2-year colleges, and private 2-year colleges.

Trends in Changing and Evolving Roles in Admissions (10)

Most responses under this category reflect an interest in research on the role of faculty in admissions as well as an interest to see research on the role current students play in the admissions process (i.e., involving students in recruitment). A few respondents communicated an interest in research on the role of the registrar in admissions processes.

A significant majority (60% of 10 respondents) of the individuals who espoused a needed study on this topical area worked at a public university. In addition, private universities and private 2-year colleges employed equal percentages (20% of 10) of these individuals for a total of 40%.

Further Considerations

Although 19 categories of topics or issues needing research were suggested by 10 or more survey respondents, eight categories were suggested by 30 or more EM practitioners. Consequently, the efficacy of various retention strategies (90), EM trends (58), SEM planning (46), changing enrollment landscape (41), EM best practices (35), shifting demographics (33), cost of higher education (32), and curriculum issues (32) constitute the most pressing topics or issues to EM practitioners.

This practitioner-defined research agenda offers members of the EM research community a wide range of topics to investigate. The research community of EM stands as a loose collection of individuals who study various topics germane to EM. These individuals include faculty members affiliated with graduate programs in higher education as a field of study, doctoral students engaged in dissertation research, institutional research officers, and researchers associated with organizations such as the American College Testing Program, the College Board, Educational Testing Service, and the National Student Clearing House Research Center (Braxton & Hossler, 2019). Other members of this research community include EM officers who conduct research on EM, as well as a variety of enrollment consulting organizations (Braxton & Hossler, 2019).

Although all 19 of the categories of this practitioner-defined research agenda merit attention by members of this research community, the eight highly salient categories of practitioner-defined research afford researchers opportunities to conduct studies with a high potential for usefulness to EM practitioners. In addition to individual studies that address these categories, we recommend that scholars of EM conduct literature reviews of research conducted on these eight categories, as research might already exist on these topics. Such reviews of literature could identify further research needed on the focal topic and posit recommendations to EM practitioners for policy and practice.

In summary, the research topics delineated in a practitioner-defined research agenda will likely be pursued by individual researchers who comprise the previously described research community of EM. Completion of the loop from the research community to practitioners depends on such individual researchers to select topics, design studies to address these topics, carry out the studies, and disseminate their findings to EM practitioners.

The selection of topics and the execution of studies of the practitioner-defined research agenda by members of the research community of EM falls outside the scope of this article, as it depends on the choices of individual researchers. Nevertheless, we offer members of the research community information on the types of colleges and universities that employ respondents who suggested a needed study for each of the 19 topical areas. We provide this information to assist researchers in their selection of an institutional setting for their research on a topical area of the practitioner-defined research agenda. We elaborate further on this information in a subsequent section of this chapter.

A delineation of possible channels of communication of research findings and recommendations for policy and practice to practitioners, however, falls within the scope of this section. Accordingly, we describe possible channels of communication in the next section.

Channels of Communication to Enrollment Management

The communication of findings of studies conducted on the topics or issues of the practitioner-defined research agenda to EM practitioners stands as a critical juncture in the completion of the loop from the research community of EM to the community of EM practitioners. Members of the research community who choose to conduct research on topics or issues of the practitioner-defined research agenda can place the findings of their research in multiple outlets (Braxton & Hossler, 2019).

Because EM practitioners deem the topics and issues of the practitioner-defined research agenda as the most pressing, the usefulness of the findings of such studies and their accompanying recommendations depend on their timely communication to EM practitioners (Love & Braxton, 2020). The various sources of information that are discussed in the next section of this chapter identify possible outlets for the timely communication of research findings to practitioners of EM.

Channels for Timely Communication

We used responses to the following 60-Second Survey question to identify sources of information: "Which of the following possible sources of information do you use in your role as an EM professional (check all that apply): *AACRAO Connect, Chronicle of Higher Education, ETS Education Research Update, Diverse Issues in Higher Education, Inside Higher Ed, Inside Higher Ed Admissions Insider, NACAC Connect, University Business Daily Newsletter,* or the AACRAO Strategic Enrollment Management Conference?"

Chronicle of Higher Education (73% of respondents) and *Inside Higher Ed* (71% of respondents) stand as the two sources of information most frequently used by EM practitioners, according to the respondents to the 60-Second Survey. However, their use as mediums for the communication of research findings to practitioners is uncertain because of predilections of these two publications. However, the *Inside Higher Ed Admissions Insider* might be a possible outlet used by one third of the respondents to the 60-Second Survey for findings of studies conducted on topics or issues of the practitioner-defined research agenda such as recruitment markets, trends in changing and evolving roles in admissions, decision points, yields, and summer melt. Moreover, *NACAC Connect* might serve as another medium for such studies despite the relatively low percentage (13%) of EM practitioners designating it as a source of information they used.

More likely outlets include *AACRAO SEM Quarterly* (50%), *AACRAO Research Reports* (46%), *AACRAO College and University* (44%), and *AACRAO Connect* (40%), given that a sizeable percentage of respondents designated them as sources of information used by EM practitioners. In particular, *SEM Quarterly* merits attention given that 50% of survey respondents identified this as a source of information. In addition to these four outlets, the presentation of findings at an AACRAO Strategic Enrollment Management Conference warrants serious attention by researchers, as 31% of 60-Second Survey respondents delineated it as a useful source of information.

Although we urge individual researchers to submit brief articles to these various sources, we also fully recognize that some members of the research community of EM will need to submit manuscripts reporting the results of their research and recommendations for policy and practice for publication consideration by other academic and professional publications. In particular, faculty members affiliated with graduate programs in higher education as a field of study in research and doctoral-granting universities might need to submit manuscripts to academic and professional journals. There are prevailing reward structures at such universities that place an emphasis on publication in academic and professional journals for various faculty personnel decisions such as annual salary increases, reappointment, tenure, and promotion. Doctoral students engaged in dissertation research on topics of the practitioner-defined research agenda may also elect to submit manuscripts to academic and professional journals to enhance their *curriculum vitae* or résumés.

Nevertheless, the choice of academic and professional journals matters as researchers should choose those journals frequently read by EM practitioners. In the next section, we indicate such academic and professional journals.

Academic and Professional Journals as Channels of Communication

We used responses to the following question on the 60-Second Survey to identify those academic and professional journals used as a resource by EM practitioners: "Select the other higher education academic or professional publications that you use as a resource (check all that apply): *Journal of College Admissions, Journal of Student Financial Aid, Innovative Higher Education, Journal of Hispanic Higher Education, Journal of Diversity in Higher Education, Journal of College Student Development, Journal of Student Affairs Research and Practice, Journal of Higher Education, Journal of Higher Education Management, Journal of Marketing in Higher Education, Research in Higher Education*, and the *Review of Higher Education*." None of the previously mentioned academic and professional journals stand out as a clear choice as a resource used by EM professionals. However, the *Journal of Higher Education* (46%) and *Research in Higher Education* (41%) serve as a resource for more than two fifths of management professionals. Consequently, these two journals stand as suitable publication outlets for members of the EM research community to submit manuscripts reporting research results and recommendations for policy and practice pursuant to one of the topics or issues identified on the practitioner-defined research agenda for EM. Because these two journals constitute core journals in the field of higher education (Bray & Major, 2011), articles published in them accrue value in the academic reward structure of doctoral-granting and research universities.

Depending on the topic or issue addressed in a manuscript, other journals that merit consideration as publication outlets for researchers who study a topic or issue of the practitioner-defined research agenda include the *Journal of College Admissions* (34%), *Journal of College Student Development* (29%), *Journal of Student Affairs Research and Practice* (27%), *Journal of Higher Education Management* (27%), and *Journal of Marketing in Higher Education* (25%). Because only 18% of EM professionals indicated the *Journal of Student Financial Aid* as a resource, only researchers who conduct research focused on the financial aid category of the practitioner-defined research agenda should consider this journal as a publication destination.

Necessary Elements of Articles

The notion that enrollment managers should use the findings of research to guide their professional practice constitutes the underlying rationale for formation of the two-way practitioner-to-research loop for EM. As previously stated, the use of the findings of empirical research by enrollment managers to guide their professional practice prevents commonsensical "shooting from the hip" or "trial-and-error" forms of action (Braxton & Ream, 2017).

Accordingly, articles written by researchers to communicate study findings to enrollment managers should emphasize the most important findings pertinent to the topic derived from the practitioner-defined research agenda (Love & Braxton, 2020). Such articles should also describe in some detail the institutional setting for the study because practitioners will more likely view the findings and recommendations of a study as useful to their professional practice if they perceive similarities between the characteristics of their college or university and the institution for the study (Morphew & Braxton, 2017). As a consequence, members of the research community who focus upon topics relevant to EM need some indication of the importance practitioners at different types of colleges and universities ascribe to each of the 19 topical areas of the practitioner-defined research agenda. Members of the research community need such indications to guide their selection of institutional settings for studies designed to address one of the areas of the practitioner-defined research agenda for EM. We provided such information for each of the topical areas of this research agenda.

In addition to these necessary elements, articles should also include recommendations for policy and practice that emanate from their research findings. The reactions of presidents and chief academic affairs officers of independent colleges to the recommendations for implementation offered by higher education scholars on topics relevant to their institutions offer two guidelines for the presentation of recommendations for policy and practice (Morphew & Braxton, 2017).

First, only realistic recommendations should be offered. Recommendations involving large investments of resources or long timelines should not be offered. Moreover, recommendations involving changes in institutional mission or the type of students served should not be advanced (Morphew & Braxton, 2017). The second guideline for the presentation of recommendations for institutional action by enrollment managers is that researchers should assign a priority for the implementation of the recommendations they advance. They should also offer a rationale for the assignment of priorities (Morphew & Braxton, 2017).

Questions for Consideration by Practitioners and Researchers

Our results provide important guidance for both practitioners and researchers who focus on student enrollment policies and practices in postsecondary education. However, we would be remiss if we did not also raise critical questions for both practitioners and researchers to advance the field of EM. Several scholars have raised questions about the extent to which managers (practitioners) use research to inform their practice. Renn and Jessup-Anger (2008) reported that the results in a study of graduates of student affairs preparation programs revealed that most respondents did not use their coursework to inform their practice. Studies in nursing, human relations, and public health have critiqued the extent to which professionals use evidence-based research to guide their practice (Barends et al., 2015; Brown et al., 2009; Smith & Wilkins, 2018). These studies also report that professionals do not make time to keep abreast of research that could improve their practice.

Moreover, some topics of the practitioner-defined research agenda suggest that EM practitioners may not draw sufficiently upon established research. The respondents in this survey indicated that research related to student retention to guide practice was their highest priority. We assert that the literature related to student retention consists of hundreds of studies, literature reviews, books, and monographs. Many of these are focused upon enhancing practice in the area of student retention. It is possible that a significant barrier for practitioners is their own professional behaviors. Many respondents to the AACRAO 60-Second Survey reported that they looked to the following sources to improve their practice: *AACRAO Connect, Chronicle of Higher Education, ETS Education Research Update, Diverse Issues in Higher Education, Inside Higher Ed, Inside Higher Ed Admissions Insider, NACAC*

Connect, University Business Daily Newsletter, and the AACRAO Strategic Enrollment Management Conference, none of which are likely to provide sufficient detail and insights to improve EM practice.

Critiques of the practices of researchers can also be offered. In the analyses of presidential addresses of the Association for the Study of Higher Education, Kimball and Friedensen (2019) found that the need to make higher education research relevant for institutional and public policymakers has been a recurring theme. For example, Laura Perna in her 2016 presidential address titled "Throwing Down the Gauntlet: Ten Ways to Ensure That Higher Education Research Continues to Matter" called for greater efforts to make higher education more relevant for campus-based and public policymakers. Perhaps the most often cited critique of higher education research came from George Keller (1985) in an essay in *Change Magazine,* "Trees Without Fruit: The Problem With Research About Higher Education." Like many professional fields that have spawned undergraduate and graduate programs at research universities, more status accrues for faculty members who publish in high-status journals than those attempting to have a demonstrable impact on the professional fields that they study.

Closing Thoughts

Toward the forging of a two-way practitioner-to-researcher loop for EM, this chapter presents a practitioner-defined research agenda comprising topics that EM professionals consider important to their practice of EM. This practitioner-defined research agenda, in turn, provides useful information for researchers seeking to conduct investigations on topics relevant to EM. We also present ways for researchers to communicate to practitioners the findings of their studies on topics of the practitioner-defined research agenda. However, we close with some concerns for EM practitioners and higher education scholars. Higher education is an applied field of study. For those scholars who concentrate on topics relevant to EM, the apparent lack of interest in influencing practice is surprising. What is the purpose of research in an applied field if not to improve the world of practice? For practitioners, many fail to keep in mind that faculty members—and many administrators who have come from faculty ranks—are socialized to look for research to guide their decisions. In this context, senior enrollment professionals may reduce their effectiveness when working with academics if they do not use research to guide their actions and to make the case for new initiatives and for more funding. This may be the result of their respective habits of mind that we outlined in the previous section. The failure to overcome these habits of mind undercuts the fundamental purpose of the two-way practitioner-to-researcher loop of providing research findings relevant to the practice of enrollment managers. Clearly, these habits of mind necessitate change by both practitioners and researchers of EM.

References

American Association for Collegiate Registrars and Admissions Officers. (n.d.-a). *Student success: March 2019 | 60-Second Survey*. https://www.aacrao.org/research-publications/research/special-topics-reports/student-success-60-second-survey-march-2019

American Association for Collegiate Registrars and Admissions Officers. (n.d.-b). *Use of and access to data: Opinions on institutional data practices: Results of the AACRAO-ACE November 2017 60-Second Survey*. https://www.aacrao.org/research-publications/research/special-topics-reports/use-of-and-access-to-data-opinions-on-institutional-data-practices---november-60-second-survey-2017

American Association for Collegiate Registrars and Admissions Officers. (n.d-c). *Use of, and interest in, enrollment management: January 2020 | 60-Second Survey*. https://www.aacrao.org/research-publications/research/special-topics-reports/use-of-and-interest-in-enrollment-management---60-second-survey-january-2020

Barends, E., Villenueva, J., Briner, R. B., & ten Have, S. (2015). Managers' attitudes and perceived barriers to evidence-based management: An international survey. *PLoS One 12*(10), 143e179. https://doi.org/10.1371/journal.pone.0184594

Bray, N. J., & Major, C. H. (2011). Status of journals in the field of higher education. *Journal of Higher Education, 82*(4), 479–503. https://eric.ed.gov/?id=EJ936379

Braxton, J. M. (2017). Editor's notes. In J. M. Braxton (Ed.), *Toward a Scholarship of Practice* (New Directions for Higher Education, no. 178, pp. 5–8). Jossey-Bass.

Braxton, J. M., & Hossler, D. (2019). Developing the two-way practitioner-researcher loop for enrollment management. *Strategic Enrollment Management Quarterly, 7*(2), 7–12. https://eric.ed.gov/?id=EJ1241063

Braxton, J. M., & Ream, T. C. (2017). The scholarship of practice and stewardship of higher education. In J. M. Braxton (Ed.), *Toward a Scholarship of Practice* (New Directions for Higher Education, no. 178, pp. 95–102). Jossey-Bass.

Brown, C. E., Wickline, M. A., Ecoff, L., & Glaser, D. (2009). Nursing practice, knowledge, attitudes, and perceived barriers to evidence-based practice at an academic medical center. *Journal of Advanced Nursing, 65*(2), 371–381. https://doi.org/10.1111/j.1365-2648.2008.04878.x

Charmaz, K. (2014). *Constructing grounded theory*. SAGE.

Glaser, B. G., & Strauss, A. L. (1967). *The discovery of grounded theory: Strategies for qualitative research*. Aldine.

Henderson, S. E. (2001). On the brink of a profession: A history of enrollment management in higher education. In J. Black (Ed.), *The strategic enrollment management revolution* (pp. 3–36). American Association of Collegiate Registrars and Admissions Officers.

Hossler, D. (2014). The origins of strategic enrollment management. In D. Hossler, R. Bontrager, and Associates (Eds.), *The handbook of strategic enrollment management* (pp. 3–17). Jossey-Bass.

Keller, G. (1985). Trees without fruit: The problem with research about higher education. *Change: The Magazine of Higher Learning, 17*(1), 7–10. https://doi.org/10.1080/00091383.1985.9940513

Kimball, E., & Friedensen, R. E. (2019). The search for meaning in higher education research: A discourse analysis of ASHE presidential addresses. *Review of Higher Education, 42*(4), 1549–1574. https://doi.org/10.1353/RHE.2019.0075

Love, P. G., & Braxton, J. M. (2020). Invigorating a scholarship of practice for the profession of student affairs. *Developments, 17*(2). https://developments.myacpa.org/invigorating-a-scholarship-of-practice-for-the-profession-of-student-affairs-written-by-patrick-g-love-and-john-m-braxton/

Maguire, J. (1976). To the organized go the students. *Bridge Magazine, 39*(1), 16–20. https://cdn2.hubspot.net/hubfs/1940013/To%20the%20Organized%20Go%20the%20Students%20-%20Boston%20College.pdf

Miles, M. B., & Huberman, A. M. (1994). *Qualitative data analysis: An expanded sourcebook* (2nd ed.). SAGE.

Morphew, C. C., & Braxton, J. M. (2017). Trusses and gaps in the bridge from research to practice. In C. C. Morphew & J. M. Braxton (Eds.), *The challenge of independent colleges: Moving research to practice* (pp. 231–242). Johns Hopkins University Press.

Perna, L. W. (2016). Throwing down the gauntlet: Ten ways to ensure that higher education research continues to matter. *Review of Higher Education, 39*(3), 319–338. https://eric.ed.gov/?id=EJ1093053

Renn, K. A., & Jessup-Anger, E. R. (2008). Preparing new professionals: Lessons for graduate preparation programs from the national study of new professionals in student affairs. *Journal of College Student Development, 49*(4), 319–335. https://doi.org/10.1353/CSD.0.0022

Smith, L. S., & Wilkins, N. (2018). Mind the gap: Approaches to addressing the research-to-practice, practice-to-research chasm. *Journal of Public Health Management and Practice, 24*(Suppl. 1), S6–S11. https://doi.org/10.1097/PHH.0000000000000667

Strauss, A. L. (1987). *Qualitative analysis for social scientists.* Cambridge University Press. https://doi.org/10.1017/CBO9780511557842

Strauss, A., & Corbin, J. M. (1990). *Basics of qualitative research: Grounded theory procedures and techniques.* SAGE.

U.S. Department of Justice. (2019, December 12). *Justice Department files antitrust case and simultaneous settlement requiring elimination of anticompetitive college recruiting restraints* [Press release]. https://www.justice.gov/opa/pr/justice-department-files-antitrust-case-and-simultaneous-settlement-requiring-elimination

Ward, M., & Hossler, D. (2016). From admissions to enrollment management. In N. Zhang (Ed.), *Rentz's student affairs practice in higher education* (3rd ed.). Charles Thomas.

14

IMPROVING COLLEGE COMPLETION

What Have We Learned About "Policy Levers"?

William R. Doyle

State-level policymakers and institutional leaders have placed an unprecedented focus on college retention and completion in the past decade (Rubin & Hearn, 2018). Previously, most state policies have been designed to improve student access to higher education (Trow, 2007). In the period 2010–2020, a widespread change occurred, with foundations, policymakers, and thought leaders all emphasizing a new focus on ensuring that students complete once enrolled (Gándara & Hearn, 2019). The most prominent of these efforts was the one undertaken by Complete College America, which in 2010 unveiled a set of "essential steps" to college completion, including setting statewide goals for completion, performance funding, eliminating developmental education, and restructuring delivery (Complete College America, 2010). In addition, many reformers touted online instruction and various text- and email-based reminder systems as keys to improving student success (Castleman, 2015; Waldrop, 2013).

Essentially none of the reforms pushed by Complete College America and others—with the possible exception of changes in developmental education—had any measurable impact on college retention and completion (Bell et al., 2018; Wang, 2017). Instead, other, more intensive reforms that had been in existence previously continued to be the most important policy levers for improving student success (Ehrenberg & Zhang, 2005).

In this chapter I will review the evidence on both well-known state policy reforms for improving retention and completion. These include the "game changers" that Complete College America assured policymakers would increase college completion and two low-cost initiatives that reformers also suggested could dramatically increase student success. Throughout I empha-size the importance of theoretical frameworks, or "theories of action," in designing and implementing state policy in this arena. One key reason that so many of these policies failed is that they had poorly thought-out or inap-plicable theories of action for the policy problem of retention and completion (Dougherty et al., 2016). The chapter will conclude with recommendations for moving forward with well-grounded policies in the future.

Goals for Completion

The late 2000s were the time for ambitious goals for college completion. In 2008, Lumina Foundation set its "Big Goal"—stating that 60% of Americans should have a postsecondary credential by the year 2025 (Lumina Foundation, 2020). The Obama administration stated that America should regain its lead in college attainment by the year 2020 (Obama, 2009). The Gates Foundation set a goal of doubling the number of low-income young people who complete a degree (Bill & Melinda Gates Foundation, 2008). Complete College America (2011) pushed states across the nation to adopt aggressive goals for college completion (Gandara et al., 2017). These led to initiatives such as Tennessee's "Drive to 55" goal, which looked for 55% of the state's population to have a postsecondary credential by 2025, or Oregon's ambitious goal to have 80% of its population attain some form of postsecondary completion by 2025 (Fulton, 2017).

Complete College America (2010) included setting a completion goal as one of its "game changers," stating that states must take the "essential step" of setting "a state commitment to a specific number of graduates by a cer-tain date"(p. 1). Other organizations agreed, including Lumina, which noted that states must set goals and delineate priorities in order to come up with a meaningful plan for completion (Lumina Foundation, 2020).

Theory of Action for Goal Setting

As with other "game changers" the theory of action for goal setting is rarely completely articulated by its proponents. As will become clear through-out the chapter, many times policymakers and intermediary organizations express their theory of action in use and lack an espoused theory of action for a given policy intervention (Argyris et al., 1996). In essence, it appears that proponents suggest that a clear goal communicated widely will help to focus efforts at every level on that goal. Decisions about the allocation of resources, personnel, and time will all become clearer to decision-makers when they know which goal they are pursuing. In the absence of such a clear goal, decision-makers will either not know which goals to pursue or will pursue their own goals at the expense of state priorities. A second possible explanation of goal setting is that by publicly committing themselves to such a goal, policymakers and institutional leaders will have no choice but to commit the necessary resources in order to accomplish it; otherwise, they risk facing the disappointment of their constituents or stakeholders when they fall short. These two articulations of goal setting follow two different theoretical traditions—the first, which posits that goal setting can constitute an individual and institutional guide to action, is Locke and Latham's (2006) goal-setting theory. The second, which posits that public statements for a given goal will act as a "precommitment" follows behavioral economics and its emphasis on the notions of time-inconsistent preferences and precommitment (Ariely & Wertenbroch, 2002).

Locke and Latham (2006) defined *goal-setting theory* as follows:

> Specific, high (hard) goals lead to a higher level of task performance than do easy goals or vague, abstract goals such as the exhortation to "do one's best." So long as a person is committed to the goal, has the requisite ability to attain it, and does not have conflicting goals, there is a positive, linear relationship between goal difficulty and task performance. Because goals refer to future valued outcomes, the setting of goals is first and foremost a discrepancy-creating process. It implies discontent with one's present condition and the desire to attain an object or outcome. (p. 265)

As Locke and Latham discussed, goal setting is focused on actual task performance—in this case, the broad array of tasks required from administrators, faculty, and staff to ensure that more students remain in higher education and complete their educational goals. Following this theory, state policymakers who set out ambitious goals for their systems of higher education will find higher levels of task performance among those charged with accomplishing this goal. This includes institutional leaders, college and university staff, and faculty. I examine the extent to which the conditions set out by Locke and Latham apply to each of these groups.

For institutional leaders, the adoption of goal setting may indeed by within their requisite ability. But many times the link between seeking out higher attainment rates and specific institutional actions are less than clear. In addition, institutional leaders must manage a variety of constituencies, each of which has a distinct set of interests and goals for higher education (Cohen & March, 1974). As Clark Kerr famously said, "The three major administrative problems on a campus are sex for the students, athletics for the alumni and parking for the faculty" (View from the Bridge, p. 96). Added to this for the recent decade might be "completion for state policymakers." Goal setting for administrators must be constrained by the constant reality of conflicting goals. Institutional presidents may be aware of the statewide goal, but it will not be the single "North Star" for their campus administration.

For campus staff such as student affairs professionals, goal conflict is likely less of an issue. Campus staff in general would likely be happy to commit to a singular goal of ensuring that students complete their educational objectives (Dougherty & Natow, 2015). What's lacking for this group is the requisite ability to attain the goal. In particular, most staff lack either the requisite training that would allow them to successfully implement an improved system for student success or, if they have the requisite training and knowledge, they may not have the financial resources. As with performance funding (discussed in a following section) goal setting assumes that either an actor knows what to do but will not do it without proper motivation or that an actor does not know what to do but will learn what to do with proper motivation. The second assumption has proven to be the condition that is least likely to be met in studies of goal setting. Individuals who do not know how to accomplish a goal will not learn how simply by setting the goal for them (Phillips & Gully, 1997). Instead, organizational leaders also need to provide the requisite learning, once it is clear what individuals should learn.

For faculty, goal commitment has not proven to be a useful guide in terms of setting priorities. Faculty in institutions of higher education are beset by goal ambiguity, in that they typically are trying to respond to incentives provided from multiple stakeholders. These include institutional priorities, disciplinary priorities, and student demands (Olsen & Near, 1994). These rarely align. Even given a clearly communicated goal of a certain number of graduates from a given institution, it's not clear how state goals for completion would not simply become yet another conflicting goal for individual faculty members.

The other possible rationale for goal setting comes from behavioral economics and involves the concept of precommitment. Behavioral economists point out that many times individuals do not behave in the short term in ways that will benefit them in the long term. Classic examples include retirement saving—while many people say that they would like to save more for retirement at some point, most individuals underinvest in their retirement. Another example is diet and exercise—many individuals have a long-term desire for better diet and more exercise, yet do not diet or exercise (Thaler & Sunstein, 2009). One solution to this problem is precommitment. Precommitment involves committing oneself to short-term activities that will benefit long-term goals (Ariely & Wertenbroch, 2002).

In the area of college completion, many institutional leaders and policymakers might want to eventually have higher attainment, but are focused in the short term on other goals. A precommitment to a goal might force decision-makers to emphasize completion in the short term. Typically a precommitment device involves substantial penalties for not engaging in short-term activities that benefit a long-term goal. These penalites might be self-imposed or imposed by a third party. For instance, a person might precommit to sending money to a political cause they oppose if they do not exercise every day for a month. The precommitment forces the individual to make short-term decisions that match long-term goals (Ariely & Wertenbroch, 2002). For colleges and universities, these goals rarely include specific precommitment devices beyond simply stating that this is the goal for the state. Of course it might be embarrassing for all involved if the goal is not met, but it's not clear that this is a sufficient precommitment device.

Evidence of the Effectiveness of Goal Setting

To the best of my knowledge, there is little or no research on the effectiveness of goal setting as a strategy for improving completion. Instead, journalists and policy analysts have tracked progress toward these goals over time. The results are not heartening. None of the states that set a completion goal are on track to meet it. The Obama administration's goal to regain the international lead in degree completion was not met, and neither the Lumina goal nor the Gates Foundation goal is within reach. As quoted in Kelderman (2020),

> "Every state has a goal, but how many states have a robust plan to get there?" asked Kim Hunter Reed, Louisiana's commissioner of higher educa-tion. "We have incremental excellence, but we don't have scaling of things we know that work." (p. 1)

Goal setting alone is not enough to increase educational attainment—the underlying theory of action for goal setting was never well matched to the strategic situation faced by policymakers, college leaders, and faculty. Goal setting works best when individuals are committed to a goal, know how to accomplish the goal, and do not face conficting goals. These conditions have rarely been met for administrators, faculty, or staff.

Performance Funding

The next key game change promoted by Complete College America was per-formance funding. Performance funding for higher education in the United States has had two distinct phases. In the first phase, institutions were offered bonuses for reaching certain clearly defined goals. These bonuses were in addition to existing base funding, and generally most institutions received almost all of the money for which they were eligible in a given year. In the second phase of performance funding—which began with Tennessee's creation of an outcomes-based funding formula—all or most of the state funding for institutions became contingent on the institution's fulfillment of certain goals, set out in some kind of formula (Dougherty et al., 2014).

Theory of Action for Performance Funding

Performance funding was touted by many advocates as one of the most promising interventions available to improve student retention. While rarely articulated directly, the logic of performance funding initiatives borrowed heavily from the new institutional analysis of bureaucracies within political science. New institutionalists began by observing that bureaucracy as an organizational form had begun to spread not because it was efficacious in a given context but largely because of institutional isomorphism (DiMaggio & Powell, 1983). New institutionalists, within political science, built on DiMaggio and Powell's work observing that bureaucracies are an extended version of the principal–agent game, in which the principal (state policymakers) must entrust the agent (bureaucrats) to accomplish some important goal. State policymakers provide bureaucrats with money and other resources to accomplish this goal, and bureaucrats undertake activities that are purported to accomplish the outcome (Moe, 1984).

According to new institutionalists, bureaucrats have little incentive to be particularly effective in accomplishing these goals and have every incentive to work to make their own lives better and more pleasant (Moe, 1984). This does not mean out-and-out theft; it simply involves bureaucrats being more focused on their own comfort and security in their work environment than they are with any goal that the state might have. The term of art for this is *feathering* as in "feathering the nest" (Heath, 2009). This could include redirecting resources that state policymakers would prefer be spent directly on some goal back to the bureaucrats in order to improve their working environment.

In the case of higher education, colleges and universities are given funding in order to create a more highly educated population for the state. Policymakers may suspect that college leaders and faculty may not be using this funding for its intended purpose. Instead, college leaders may spend this money on pursuing personal or institutional prestige, while faculty members may choose to deemphasize the goal of educating students and instead use the available funding for either making their own working conditions better or pursuing activities that don't result in more state citizens with higher levels of educational attainment. However, studies of the efficiency of colleges and universities find little evidence of this kind of activity. Instead, most studies of institutions of higher education find that colleges are operating quite close to their efficiency frontier, using existing knowledge and technology in the most effective way possible to ensure positive student outcomes (Doyle, 2014; Titus et al., 2017).

Performance funding is intended to push back against any "feathering" by providing college and university leaders with incentives to perform well on goals set for the institution by the state. A typical funding formula for a college or university will include a series of specific indicators in different areas that campuses are required to meet. For instance, a campus may be required to have a certain number of students completing 24 and 48 credit hours as a measure of persistence. Other measures include the number of degrees completed and the number of students placed in the workforce (Hillman et al., 2018). Given these kinds of specific goals, the theory is that institutional leaders and faculty will align their activities toward these concrete goals and will avoid "feathering."

Evidence on the Effectiveness of Performance Funding

One of the more remarkable aspects of the championing of performance funding as a game changer is that it occurred in the absence of any systematic evidence. Ten years later, researchers have developed a more substantial base of knowledge regarding performance funding (Bell et al., 2018; Hillman et al., 2014, 2018). Essentially, the results are not as bad as detractors feared, but they are nowhere near as good as proponents hoped. In most states, for most institutions, performance funding has not done much.

Tennessee and Ohio stand out from other states in having more comprehensive performance funding systems than other states. In Tennessee, all funding is based on outcomes, while in Ohio a majority of funding is awarded based on outcomes. In a study comparing public 2- and 4-year colleges and universities in Tennessee and Ohio with public colleges in other states, Hillman et al. (2018) found that there were no observable effects of performance funding on the number of associate or bachelor's degrees produced in either state. The authors did find a substantial increase in the number of short-term certificates awarded by community colleges in Tennessee. They concluded that performance funding in these two states was only able to increase degree production in certificates (Hillman et al., 2018).

In a longer term study of performance funding, Rutherford and Rabovsky (2014) investigated whether having any kind of performance funding is associated with differential outcomes. The authors looked at degree and retention outcomes for all public 4-year institutions in the United States covering the time period 1993–2010. They included both performance funding 1.0 and performance funding 2.0 policies. Performance funding 1.0 is defined as a system that allocates bonus funding, while performance funding 2.0 is defined as a system that allocates base funding.

Rutherford and Rabovsky (2014) found little to no evidence that institutions in states with either type of policy have better outcomes than institutions in states without performance funding. The authors summarized their results as follows:

> This finding implies that either performance funding policies do not change institutional strategies for retaining students or institutional actions that occur in response to performance funding are not associated with the retention of more students (and thus improved performance). In fact, responses to performance funding policies may have negative implications for student retention, as indicated by the negative and significant trend over time. (p. 201)

Other studies have found remarkably similar results, with very little variation in any study that includes some form of counterfactual group; results in performance funding states are not terribly different than in states without performance funding (Bell et al., 2018).

In their remarkable article "Merchants of Optimism," G. N. S. Miller and Morphew (2017) summarized the role of agenda-setting organizations (ASOs) in higher education policy such as Complete College America. These organizations do more than simply advocate for programs such as performance funding. Instead, the authors argue, the organizations attempt to control the terms of the debate about such programs:

> Our work suggests that ASOs engage in political tactics that set the terms of policy debate, certify actors and information, and discredit the work of others who produce different findings. ASOs advance a diagnostic frame arguing that low degree attainment is linked to traditional funding formulae that do not promote accountability at public postsecondary institutions. ASOs offer PBF as a solution (prognostic framing) and argue that appropriate financial incentives will eliminate public higher education's shortcomings and create more effective and efficient systems. (G. N. S. Miller & Morphew, 2017, p. 777)

Performance funding, like goal setting, appears to be a policy direction based more on hope than actual empirical evidence. As the limited impacts of performance funding have become clearer, it's obvious that optimism is not enough—the theory of action behind performance funding does not appear to be supported by the actual observed behavior of institutional leaders or faculty. I next turn to developmental education, an area in which a more fully developed theory of action has resulted in a much more effective set of interventions.

Developmental Education

In one of its most famous reports, Complete College America stated that developmental education is higher education's "bridge to nowhere."[1] Relying on descriptive statistics, it stated that students who begin in developmental education rarely complete the sequence of development education courses, and that the only solution for state policymakers is to eliminate developmental education altogether. The functions of developmental education could then be taken up either by corequisite classes, in which students receive extra assistance for the class they're taking, or by receiving additional out-of-class assistance.

Theory of Action Behind Developmental Education Reform

The essential logic of developmental education reform as proposed by Complete College America relies on the idea that students should sink or swim on their own in regular credit-bearing courses. If students are truly unprepared to take any college-level courses, then pressure should be placed on the K–12 system in order to ensure that students are prepared to take postsecondary-level courses. As Logue et al. (2019) stated, developmental education is typically structured "based on the theory that students need to pass the remedial courses to have the knowledge and skills needed to pass the college level courses" (p. 294). Advocates of corequisite education instead posited that students who are not ready for college-level work need only "extra academic support covering just the remedial mathematics needed for the college level course" (p. 296).

Evidence of Effectiveness of Developmental Education Reform

Alone among the programs touted as "game changers" by Complete College America, corequisite education has turned out to be an effective means by

---

[1] Complete College America actually used the term *remediation*, which is a pejorative term favored by activists who oppose developmental education. I use *developmental education* as it is consistent with the terminology used by practitioners in the field.

which to increase college completion. Multiple studies have found students in corequisite courses are more likely to complete college-level courses than students who are in developmental courses. In a well-designed experimental study at the City University of New York, Logue et al. (2019) found that students enrolled in corequisite courses were just as likely as others to pass entry-level college credit mathematics courses and were more likely to pass subsequent math courses than students who had been enrolled in developmental education.

While there are certainly specific lessons to be learned from the effectiveness of corequisite courses, there is also a broader lesson for policymakers. Unlike goal setting and performance funding, there was both a compelling theoretical framing and a considerable body of evidence regarding the effectiveness of corequisite education, going back to the models of corequisite education developed by Uri Treisman (1992) in the late 1980s and 1990s. In particular, proponents of developmental education reform understood that the key issue for students was the inability to tie the intervention of developmental education to the students' goals of degree completion. Making specific links between what students are learning in their developmental education courses and their ability to complete credit-bearing courses that would lead to a degree has resulted in better outcomes (Bailey et al., 2016). Unlike the "merchants of optimism" pushing performance funding, advocates of corequisite education had a breadth of research and practitioner knowledge from which to operate.

Restructuring Delivery

Restructuring delivery was the least clear of the "game-changing" strategies, but was summarized as "meeting students where they are." The key elements of restructuring delivery are guided pathways, block scheduling, encouraging students to enroll in cohorts, and using hybrid models of delivery. All of these modes of delivery are predicated on the reasonable idea that standard approaches to delivering courses, such as scheduling courses during 9–5 operating hours on a semester-by-semester basis will not work for many students who have significant responsibilities, including childcare and work.

Theory of Action for Restructuring Delivery

The theory of action behind restructuring delivery focuses on the idea that the informational complexity of college-going should be lowered as much as possible. Instead of burdening students with multiple decision points, policymakers and institutional leaders should provide well-designed student experiences that allow students to experience the educational, advisory, and support functions of a given institution in a seamless fashion. In the following, I focus on two of the most prominent of these types of policies: guided pathways and the Accelerated Study in Associate Programs (ASAP) model from the City University of New York.

Evidence of Effectiveness: Guided Pathways

Guided pathways are a reform designed to reduce the burden of choice for college students. Initially a narrower intervention primarily for community college students, guided pathways have been reconceptualized as a "whole college reform" that could apply to either community colleges or 4-year colleges. A guided pathways approach moves the responsibility for navigating toward an academic goal away from the student and to the institution. The guided pathways concept was derived from previous work by Kuh et al., where they emphasized the crucial importance of charting pathways for students and giving students clear markers for success (Kuh et al., 2011).

Among the key aspects of guided pathways are "meta majors" and program maps, career exploration and planning, redesigned advising, better transfer and career information, and improved progress monitoring (Bailey et al., 2015, Jenkins et al., 2019). The theory of action for guided pathways revolves around reducing the complexity of choice for students. While neoclassical economic theory suggests that having more choices increases a person's utility and therefore their happiness, consumer research actually suggests that too much choice can discourage a consumer, leading them to be less likely to pursue their goals (Iyengar & Lepper, 2000). By usefully limiting choices for students, guided pathways can actually improve their likelihood of success by making it clear what needs to be done to succeed.

The evidence for guided pathways is unclear at this point. In part because of the whole-college nature of this reform, identifying the particular impact of guided pathways as an educational reform has been difficult. Interrupted time series evidence from the institutions that have implemented guided pathways appears promising, but it is still too early to tell if this approach will be successful in the long run in improving student outcomes (Jenkins et al., 2019).

Evidence of Effectiveness: Accelerated Study in Associate Programs Model

The most successful version of restructuring delivery was the ASAP model, which incorporated several of the previously described reforms, including block scheduling and cohorts, but also "wraparound" services, including advising, tutoring, a student success seminar, a tuition waiver, transportation vouchers, monthly incentives, and strong encouragement to enroll full time and graduate within 3 years. This program, now demonstrated in both New York City and in public institutions in Ohio, has proven to be remarkably effective in increasing graduation rates (C. Miller et al., 2020). Left unexplored in the literature is the extent to which these wraparound services might also increase students' perceptions of the institutions' commitment to their well-being, a factor that has been found to be tied to persistence and completion (Braxton et al., 2014).

Other Reforms: "Nudges" and Massive Open Online Courses

Behavioral nudges and massive open online courses are the two other prominent reforms that were promoted during the 2010s. Although these were not touted by Complete College America as "game changers," many reformers thought that these two technologically mediated interventions could, in different ways, dramatically increase college completion.

The first reform—"nudges"—involved sending current and prospective students information about key actions that they needed to take, at exactly the time that students needed to take these actions. In his book *The 160 Character Solution* Benjamin Castleman (2015) laid out the logic of this approach, which drew inspiration from behavioral economists Richard Thaler and Cass Sunstein's (2009) book *Nudge*. Nudges, as espoused by Castleman et al. (2012), were actually distinct from the theory of "nudging" put forth by Thaler and Sunstein. Thaler and Sunstein described nudging as setting default choice opportunities in a way that would maximally benefit the individual, instead of relying on individual preferences to accomplish a given goal. For instance, providing someone with a healthier meal alternative as the "default" choice could improve people's diets, even if they still have the option to choose less healthy alternatives. In their canonical example, Thaler and Sunstein discussed how researchers have shown that setting different default choices for retirement plans can improve people's outcomes, even though people should be choosing the ideal retirement plan on their own (Benartzi & Thaler, 2002).

The nudges suggested by Castleman were frequent but brief informational interventions, designed to provide students with key information at exactly the right time. For instance, students could be reminded to fill out the Free Application for Federal Student Aid (FAFSA) shortly before the deadline for filing. These informational interventions usually took the form of text messages. The idea was that at the exact moment a student needed to do something—register for classes, file paperwork, make a payment—the student would receive information about how and when to complete this task. Initial results from these kinds of interventions were promising, particularly in solving the problem of what's called "summer melt"—students failing to show up for fall classes after having registered in the spring (Castleman, 2015; Castleman et al., 2012).

This concept was taken to scale by Castleman and his colleagues in an impressive research project in which 800,000 students were texted via various means in order to improve rates of completion of the FAFSA (Bird et al., 2019). Completing the FAFSA does constitute a burden for some students, but most students are able to complete it within about 90 minutes. Many states have led efforts that have increased FAFSA completion substantially. The "nudge" intervention to increase FAFSA completion rates did not have any effect at all on students:

> We consistently find no effect of these messages on student enrollment or financial aid outcomes. This null finding is consistent across samples, content, timing, visual presentation, and offers of personalized help. Large sample sizes allow us to rule out very small effects of these 4 interventions. (Bird et al., 2019, pp. 3–4)

Stated another way, in the largest intervention of this type, with a well-designed, well-powered experiment, there was absolutely no observable effect of any type of nudge intervention. Similarly disappointing results have been found using other types of nudge interventions (Gurantz et al., 2019). It appears that the initial promising results may simply have been the result of random chance or the novelty of the original intervention.

The other major higher education reform touted during this time period were massive open online courses (MOOCs). This highly descriptive name pretty much covers how these classes were supposed to work. By adopting sophisticated techniques used by social media and content providers, it was thought that courses taught by world-renowned faculty at the most prestigious institutions could be made widely available for little or no cost. Because students could attend any course they wanted, at any time they wanted, essentially for free, it was thought that many of the issues that prevented students from completing college could be overcome through technology (Carey, 2016). Evangelists of MOOCs predicted the demise of the majority of institutions of higher education, and that these new types of course design and delivery would dramatically increase college completion (Waldrop, 2013). Ten years later, neither has happened.

Course completion for MOOCs has remained abysmally low. Typical course completion rates are between 5% and 10%. Even the most successful interventions designed to improve course completion for MOOCs have not raised success rates above 20%, a rate that would merit administrative intervention in any standard class offered face to face (Li & Baker, 2018; Weinhardt & Sitzmann, 2019; Williams et al., 2018). MOOCs, along with nudges, failed to become technological fixes to the problem of low college completion rates.

Lessons Learned From the Completion Agenda

In chapter 2 of *Rethinking College Student Retention* we examined the set of policy levers available circa 2010 that had been shown to improve college student success (Braxton et al., 2014). Several of the interventions addressed in this chapter were addressed previously, including developmental education and performance funding. A key intervention identified in that chapter was not identified as a "game changer" by Complete College America and other groups that pushed the completion agenda. More full-time faculty, particularly tenure-line faculty, are strongly associated with student success. More recent evidence has only bolstered this finding. Full-time faculty are uniquely situated to address student needs and to provide the academic setting for student support. Even in states with ambitious completion goals, the trend has been not toward hiring more full-time faculty but instead toward increasing reliance on adjuncts (McNaughtan et al., 2017; Morphew et al., 2017). The budgetary reasons for this are clear; facing an increasingly uncertain funding environment, institutions and state policymakers are reluctant to make long-term investments in more full-time faculty (Doyle & Zumeta, 2014). However, if state policymakers are serious about their completion goals, one key finding cannot be overlooked: Colleges with a higher proportion of full-time faculty—particularly tenure-line faculty—have much better student success rates (Ehrenberg & Zhang, 2005).

The work of college completion as undertaken by faculty is an example of what Murnane and Nelson (1984) termed a *tacit production process.* Murnane and Nelson contrast the standard theory of production with a theory of production in sectors such as higher education that have poorly articulated techniques. In a standard theory of production, Murnane and Nelson stated that the following conditions hold: The inputs and technology used by a firm are rationally chosen from a set of widely known possibilities, observations of inputs and outputs occur in the absence of any experimentation, the inputs required are widely available, and any experimentation with technology happens at a remove from production (Murnane & Nelson, 1984). By contrast, in education settings, Murnane and Nelson suggested that a much wider set of possible techniques are available, with low levels of shared knowledge and, crucially, with experimentation happening in production almost constantly.

The implication of this for improvements in retention and completion is first that we would benefit enormously from ceasing to think of the internal operations of institutions of higher education in standard production metaphor terms. Instead, it may be better to adopt Murnane and Nelson's (1984) approach of thinking of education as a process of constant experimentation, during which successful techniques "can only be discovered through a process of trial and error and adaptations" (p. 369). This would mean instead of four "game changers" we may need 400. The goal would not be so much to dictate to institutional leaders, staff, and faculty the one way to do things but instead to enable the process of learning and experimentation that will create the conditions for student success. Instead of looking for the small set of solutions to the issue of completion, we should most likely be expanding the scope and scale of our investigations to include a much broader set of possible actions for policymakers and practitioners. This echoes the policy implications in Braxton et al. (2004): "The ill-structured nature of the problem of college student departure . . . suggests the use of multiple policy levers" (p. 231). The other chapters in this volume contain a wealth of research that could help to begin this longer, more difficult, but in the end more successful effort to ensure student retention.

References

Argyris, C., Schon, D. A., Schön, D. A., & Schon, D. (1996). *Organizational learning II: Theory, method, and practice.* Addison-Wesley.

Ariely, D., & Wertenbroch, K. (2002). Procrastination, deadlines, and performance: Self-control by precommitment. *Psychological Science, 13*(3), 219–224. https://doi.org/10.1111/1467-9280.00441

Bailey, T., Bashford, J., Boatman, A., Squires, J., Weiss, M., Doyle, W., Valentine, J. C., LaSota, R., Polanin, J. R., Spinney, E., Wilson, W., Yelde, M., & Young, S. H. (2016). *Strategies for postsecondary students in developmental education: A practice guide for college and university administrators, advisors, and faculty* (NCEE 2017-4011). What Works Clearinghouse. http://eric.ed.gov/?id=ED570881

Bailey, T., Jaggars, S. S., & Jenkins, D. (2015). *What we know about guided pathways: Helping students to complete programs faster.* Community College Research Center, Columbia University. http://eric.ed.gov/?id=ED562052

Bell, E., Fryar, A. H., & Hillman, N. (2018). When intuition misfires: A meta-analysis of research on performance-based funding in higher education. In E. Hazelkorn, H. Coates, & A. C. McCormick (Eds.), *Research handbook on quality, performance and accountability in higher education* (pp. 108–124). Edward Elgar. http://www .elgaronline.com/view/edcoll/9781785369742/9781785369742.00017.xml

Benartzi, S., & Thaler, R. H. (2002). How much is investor autonomy worth? *The Journal of Finance, 57*(4), 1593–1616. https://doi.org/10.1111/1540-6261 .00472

Bill & Melinda Gates Foundation. (2008). *New initiative to double the number of low-income students in the U.S. who earn a postsecondary degree.* https://tinyurl .com/y68sr5c2

Bird, K. A., Castleman, B. L., Denning, J. T., Goodman, J., Lamberton, C., & Rosinger, K. O. (2019). *Nudging at scale: Experimental evidence from FAFSA completion campaigns* (No. w26158). National Bureau of Economic Research. https://doi.org/10.3386/w26158

Braxton, J. M., Doyle, W. R., Hartley, H. V., III, Hirschy, A. S., Jones, W. A., & McLendon, M. K. (2014). *Rethinking college student retention.* Wiley.

Braxton, J. M., Hirschy, A. S., & McClendon, S. A. (2004). *Understanding and reducing college student departure* (ASHE-ERIC Higher Education Report, Vol. 30, no. 3). Wiley.

Carey, K. (2016). *The end of college: Creating the future of learning and the university of everywhere.* Penguin.

Castleman, B. L. (2015). *The 160-character solution: How text messaging and other behavioral strategies can improve education.* Johns Hopkins University Press.

Castleman, B. L., Arnold, K., & Wartman, K. L. (2012). Stemming the tide of summer melt: An experimental study of the effects of post-high school summer intervention on low-income students' college enrollment. *Journal of Research on Educational Effectiveness, 5*(1), 1–17. https://doi.org/10.1080/19345747.2011 .618214

Cohen, M. D., & March, J. G. (1974). *Leadership and ambiguity: The American college president.* McGraw-Hill.

Complete College America. (2010). *Essential steps for states.*

Complete College America. (2011). *Time is the enemy: The surprising truth about why today's college students aren't graduating . . . and what needs to change.* http:// eric.ed.gov/?q=complete+college+america&id=ED536827

DiMaggio, P. J., & Powell, W. W. (1983). The iron cage revisited: Institutional isomorphism and collective rationality in organizational fields. *American Sociological Review, 48*(2), 147–160. https://doi.org/10.2307/2095101

Dougherty, K. J., Jones, S. M., Lahr, H., Natow, R. S., Pheatt, L., & Reddy, V. (2014). Performance funding for higher education: Forms, origins, impacts, and futures. *ANNALS of the American Academy of Political and Social Science, 655*(1), 163–184. https://doi.org/10.1177/0002716214541042

Dougherty, K. J., Jones, S. M., Lahr, H., Natow, R. S., Pheatt, L., & Reddy, V. (2016). Looking inside the black box of performance funding for higher education: Policy instruments, organizational obstacles, and intended and unintended impacts. *RSF: The Russell Sage Foundation Journal of the Social Sciences*, *2*(1), 147–173. https://doi.org/10.7758/RSF.2016.2.1.07

Dougherty, K. J., & Natow, R. S. (2015). *The politics of performance funding for higher education: Origins, discontinuations, and transformations.* Johns Hopkins University Press.

Doyle, W. (2014). Efficiency in degree completion among public comprehensive universities. In M. Schneider & K. C. Deane (Eds.), *The university next door: What is a comprehensive university, who does it educate, and can it survive?* (pp. 93–119). Teachers College Press.

Doyle, W., & Zumeta, W. (2014). State-level responses to the access and completion challenge in the new era of austerity. *ANNALS of the American Academy of Political and Social Science*, *655*(1), 79–98. https://doi.org/10.1177/0002716214534606

Ehrenberg, R. G., & Zhang, L. (2005). Do tenured and tenure-track faculty matter? *Journal of Human Resources*, *40*(3), 647–659. https://doi.org/10.3368/jhr.XL.3.647

Fulton, M. (2017). *Attainment plans and goals.* Education Commission of the States.

Gándara, D., & Hearn, J. C. (2019). College completion, the Texas way: An examination of the development of college completion policy in a distinctive political culture. *Teachers College Record*, *121*(1), 1–40.

Gandara, D., Rippner, J. A., & Ness, E. C. (2017). Exploring the "how" in policy diffusion: National intermediary organizations' roles in facilitating the spread of performance-based funding policies in the states. *Journal of Higher Education*, *88*(5), 701–725. https://doi.org/10.1080/00221546.2016.1272089

Gurantz, O., Howell, J., Hurwitz, M., Larson, C., Pender, M., & White, B. (2019). *Realizing your college potential? Impacts of College Board's RYCP campaign on postsecondary enrollment* [EdWorkingPaper]. Annenberg Institute at Brown University. https://www.edworkingpapers.com/ai19-40

Heath, J. (2009). The uses and abuses of agency theory. *Business Ethics Quarterly*, *19*(4), 497–528.

Hillman, N. W., Hicklin Fryar, A., & Crespín-Trujillo, V. (2018). Evaluating the impact of performance funding in Ohio and Tennessee. *American Educational Research Journal*, *55*(1), 144–170. https://doi.org/10.3102/0002831217732951

Hillman, N. W., Tandberg, D. A., & Gross, J. P. K. (2014). Performance funding in higher education: Do financial incentives impact college completions? *Journal of Higher Education*, *85*(6), 826–857. https://doi.org/10.1080/00221546.2014.11777349

Iyengar, S. S., & Lepper, M. R. (2000). When choice is demotivating: Can one desire too much of a good thing? *Journal of Personality and Social Psychology*, *79*(6), 995–1006. https://doi.org/10.1037/0022-3514.79.6.995

Jenkins, D., Lahr, H., Brown, A. E., & Mazzariello, A. (2019). *Redesigning your college through guided pathways: Lessons on managing whole-college reform from the AACC Pathways Project.* Community College Research Center, Teachers College, Columbia University. http://eric.ed.gov/?id=ED598443

Kelderman, E. (2020, January 7). Happy New Year, higher ed: You've missed your completion goal. *Chronicle of Higher Education, 66*(17).

Kuh, G. D., Kinzie, J., Schuh, J. H., & Whitt, E. J. (2011). *Student success in college: Creating conditions that matter.* Wiley.

Li, Q., & Baker, R. (2018). The different relationships between engagement and outcomes across participant subgroups in massive open online courses. *Computers & Education, 127,* 41–65. https://doi.org/10.1016/j.compedu.2018.08.005

Locke, E. A., & Latham, G. P. (2006). New directions in goal-setting theory. *Current Directions in Psychological Science, 15*(5), 265–268.

Logue, A. W., Douglas, D., & Watanabe-Rose, M. (2019). Corequisite mathematics remediation: Results over time and in different contexts. *Educational Evaluation and Policy Analysis, 41*(3), 294–315. https://doi.org/10.3102/0162373719848777

Lumina Foundation. (2020). *A stronger nation.* https://www.luminafoundation.org/our-work/stronger-nation/

McNaughtan, J., García, H. A., & Nehls, K. (2017). Understanding the growth of contingent faculty. In H. A. García, J. McNaughtan, & K. Nehls (Eds.), *Hidden and Visible: The Role and Impact of Contingency Faculty in Higher Education* (New Directions for Institutional Research, no. 176, pp. 9–26). Wiley. https://doi.org/10.1002/ir.20241

Miller, C., Headlam, C., Manno, M., & Cullinan, D. (2020). *Increasing community college graduation rates with a proven model: Three-year results from the Accelerated Study in Associate Programs (ASAP) Ohio demonstration.* MDRC.

Miller, G. N. S., & Morphew, C. C. (2017). Merchants of optimism: Agenda-setting organizations and the framing of performance-based funding for higher education. *Journal of Higher Education, 88*(5), 754–784. https://doi.org/10.1080/00221546.2017.1313084

Moe, T. M. (1984). The new economics of organization. *American Journal of Political Science, 28*(4), 739–777. https://doi.org/10.2307/2110997

Morphew, C., Ward, K., & Wolf-Wendel, L. (2017). Contingent faculty composition and utilization: Perspectives from independent colleges and universities. In H. A. García, J. McNaughtan, & K. Nehls (Eds.), *Hidden and Visible: The Role and Impact of Contingency Faculty in Higher Education* (New Directions for Institutional Research, no. 176, pp. 67–81). Wiley. https://doi.org/10.1002/ir.20245

Murnane, R. J., & Nelson, R. R. (1984). Production and innovation when techniques are tacit: The case of education. *Journal of Economic Behavior & Organization, 5*(3–4), 353–373.

Obama, B. (2009). *Remarks of President Barack Obama—Address to joint session of Congress* [Speech audio recording]. White House Archives. https://obamawhitehouse.archives.gov/the-press-office/remarks-president-barack-obama-address-joint-session-congress

Olsen, D., & Near, J. P. (1994). Role conflict and faculty life satisfaction. *Review of Higher Education, 17*(2), 179–195. https://doi.org/10.1353/rhe.1994.0026

Phillips, J. M., & Gully, S. M. (1997). Role of goal orientation, ability, need for achievement, and locus of control in the self-efficacy and goal-setting process. *Journal of Applied Psychology, 82*(5), 792–802. https://doi.org/10.1037/0021-9010.82.5.792

Rubin, P. G., & Hearn, J. C. (2018). *The policy filtering process: Understanding distinctive state responses to the National College Completion Agenda in the United States.* Education Policy Analysis Archives. https://doi.org/10.14507/epaa.26.3447

Rutherford, A., & Rabovsky, T. (2014). Evaluating impacts of performance funding policies on student outcomes in higher education. *ANNALS of the American Academy of Political and Social Science, 655*(1), 185–208. https://doi.org/10.1177/0002716214541048

Thaler, R. H., & Sunstein, C. R. (2009). *Nudge: Improving decisions about health, wealth, and happiness.* Penguin.

Titus, M. A., Vamosiu, A., & McClure, K. R. (2017). Are public master's institutions cost efficient? A stochastic frontier and spatial analysis. *Research in Higher Education, 58*(5), 469–496.

Treisman, U. (1992). Studying students studying calculus: A look at the lives of minority mathematics students in college. *College Mathematics Journal, 23*(5), 362–372. https://doi.org/10.1080/07468342.1992.11973486

Trow, M. (2007). Reflections on the transition from elite to mass to universal access: Forms and phases of higher education in modern societies since WWII. In J. J. F. Forest & P. G. Altbach (Eds.), *International handbook of higher education* (pp. 243–280). Springer. https://doi.org/10.1007/978-1-4020-4012-2_13

View from the Bridge. (1958). *TIME Magazine, 72*(20), 96.

Waldrop, M. M. (2013). Online learning: Campus 2.0. *Nature News, 495*(7440), 160. https://doi.org/10.1038/495160a

Wang, X. (2017). Toward a holistic theoretical model of momentum for community college student success. In M. B. Paulsen (Ed.), *Higher education: Handbook of theory and research* (Vol. 32, pp. 259–308). Springer.

Weinhardt, J. M., & Sitzmann, T. (2019). Revolutionizing training and education? Three questions regarding massive open online courses (MOOCs). *Human Resource Management Review, 29*(2), 218–225. https://doi.org/10.1016/j.hrmr.2018.06.004

Williams, K. M., Stafford, R. E., Corliss, S. B., & Reilly, E. D. (2018). Examining student characteristics, goals, and engagement in massive open online courses. *Computers & Education, 126,* 433–442. https://doi.org/10.1016/j.compedu.2018.08.014

15

CHARTING FUTURE DIRECTIONS FOR THEORY, RESEARCH, AND PRACTICE OF COLLEGE STUDENT PERSISTENCE

John M. Braxton and Robert D. Reason

We envisioned this edited volume as a place to engage a comprehensive conversation about the current state of our understanding of student persistence. A comprehensive conversation, which leads to a comprehensive understanding, must include discussion of theory, research, and practice related to student persistence. Each of these distinct, but related, topical areas was addressed in a section of this book by some of the most forward-thinking scholars we could identify. In this concluding chapter, we (John and Bob) share our thoughts related to all of the work that went into this volume and suggest some ways to continue the conversation moving forward. In parallel with the book, we start with theory followed by sections on research and practice.

Theory

Over 45 years have transpired since Tinto first published his generative 1975 article, "Drop Outs From Higher Education: A Theoretical Synthesis of Recent Research," in the *Review of Educational Research*. Tinto's article constituted the first theoretical framework in the long scholarly focus on college student retention (Braxton et al., 2004). Braxton et al.'s (2004, 2014) works, we would argue, constituted the next major advance in theorizing about student persistence. Since the publication of *Rethinking College Student Retention* (Braxton et al., 2014), which reported the results of empirical tests of the theory of student persistence in residential colleges and universities and the theory of student persistence in commuter colleges and universities, seven different theories emerged (see chapter 2), indicating that the generation and testing of college student persistence theories continues.

To guide our understanding of the recent theoretical developments, we adapt the framework offered by Merton (1968) to classify the seven theories identified by Jones in chapter 2, according to three levels of theory: grand theories, middle-range theories, and focused theories. Grand theories strive to explain broad, large-scale topics that can be universally applied to a wide range of all types of organizations throughout societies (Merton, 1968). Theories of the middle range have a narrower scope than grand theories. Nevertheless, they can be applied to more than one setting and to groups with shared characteristics such as low-income or minoritized identity status (Hirschy, 2015; Merton, 1968). In sharp contrast to these two levels, focused theories offer explanations for a particular setting or particular group of students (Merton, 1968).

None of the seven more recent theoretical perspectives identified by Jones in chapter 2 fits the category of a grand theory. However, two of these theories stand as middle-range theories: the structural model of predicting undergraduate student retention (Sass et al., 2018) and the theory of planned behavior (Dewberry & Jackson, 2018). We classify these two theories as middle range because they focus on a circumscribed set of constructs but are testable across a range of colleges and universities.

The two newly revised theories of student persistence in residential colleges and universities and in commuter colleges and universities advanced by Reason and Braxton in chapter 4 of this book also fit the category of middle-range theories. These two theories center attention on a clearly delineated set of concepts that are empirically testable across a range of colleges and universities. In the case of the newly revised theory of student persistence in commuter colleges and universities, this theory applies to a range of 2-year and 4-year institutions. Moreover, the newly revised theory of student persistence in residential colleges and universities pertains to a variety of institutions such as research and doctoral universities and liberal arts colleges.

The five other theories identified by Jones in chapter 2 constitute focused theories because they concentrate on a particular type of college or university or on particular groups of students. For example, Wang (2017) posited the theoretical model of momentum for community college student success focused only on students in community colleges, whereas three other theories attend to students with specific social identities: American Indian/

Alaska Native Millennium Falcon persistence model from Lopez (2018), the theoretical model of belonging for college students with a disability by Vaccaro et al. (2015), and the model of college student sense of belonging for privileged and minoritized students forwarded by Vaccaro and Newman (2016). The culturally engaged campus environment (CECE) model of college student success formulated by Museus (2014) centers attention on an array of racially and ethnically diverse students, which also situates this theory as a focused theory.

We note that Jones in chapter 2 regards the seven previously delineated theories as meeting criteria for designation as *good theory* set forth by Patterson (1983). These criteria include testability, parsimony, grounding in previous empirical evidence, and importance and practicality. Importance and practicality constitute a significant consideration for scholars and practitioners and comport with the notion of professional judgment espoused by Hirschy (2015) for the selection of a theory. We assert that these criteria of good theory also apply to the newly revised theory of student persistence in residential colleges and universities and the newly revised theory of student persistence in commuter colleges and universities (see chapter 4). Because these nine theories meet the criteria of "good theory," we echo the recommendation of Jones in chapter 2 that scholars work to further the empirical validity of these theories with particular attention to theories germane to minoritized student groups. These theories are Lopez's (2018) American Indian/Alaska Native Millennium Falcon persistence model, the Vaccaro et al. (2015) theoretical model of belonging for college students with a disability, the Vaccaro and Newman (2016) model of college student sense of belonging for privileged and minoritized students, and Museus's (2014) CECE model.

We add to the recommendation of Jones in chapter 2 by asserting that these theories should be tested in a variety of colleges and universities. For scholars who choose predominantly White colleges and universities (PWI) to conduct such tests, we urge that such scholars take note of the experiences of minoritized students at PWIs to ascertain how their experiences with racist, chilly, or alienating campus climates affect persistence. Reason and Braxton in chapter 4 offer a similar admonition regarding the newly revised theory of student persistence in residential colleges and universities and the newly revised theory of student persistence in commuter institutions. We make this recommendation because of the assertion of Palmer and Walker in chapter 3 that such experiences of African American students render an extant grand theory like Tinto's (1975, 1993) inappropriate for the study of the persistence of African American students attending a PWI. The application of the focused theories delineated in this book should be explored in various institutional contexts, especially PWIs.

Because of their criticism of the applicability of extant theories to African American students attending PWIs, Palmer and Walker in chapter 3 describe three theoretical perspectives to account for African American student persistence in PWIs. Two of the three theories suggested by Palmer and Walker in chapter 3 stand as middle-range theories: Rendón's (1994) validation theory and Schlossberg's (1989) theory of mattering and marginality. We classify them as middle range because their formulations are not restricted to a particular type of college or university or specific groups of students. Although Rendón's (1994) original theory was limited to Latinx students in higher education, its use has been expanded to include students with several other minoritized social identities, which makes classifying it exclusively as middle range or focused very difficult. Yosso's (2005) concept of community cultural wealth (CCW), the third theory identified by Palmer and Walker, we classify as a focused theory because it pertains only to students of color.

Like Palmer and Walker in chapter 3, we assert that additional theoretical work should center attention on studies of Yosso's (2005) CCW concept, Schlossberg's (1989) theory of mattering and marginality, and Rendón's (1994) validation theory in a variety of PWIs. The findings of such theoretically informed studies could guide the development and implementation of policies and practices at PWIs to forge more inclusive environments that support the persistence of African American students and students from other minoritized groups.

Research

The research section of this book reveals an interesting dichotomy. The research into student persistence in college continues, perhaps even at a rapid pace, due presumably to the importance of student persistence to institutional budgets and to the need for a college-educated workforce in a technologically advanced economy. On the other hand, recent research revealed in this volume does not indicate that we have learned much new since Reason's (2009) comprehensive review of persistence literature, except perhaps as it relates to the experiences of minoritized students in higher education.

In chapter 5, Gansemer Topf et al. review 608 empirically based persistence articles published in the last 10 years. The vast majority, over 90%, of the articles focused on student-level variables, with increasing attention paid to the experiences of racially minoritized students in higher education. The authors did conclude, however, White students' experiences were still overrepresented in the persistence literature.

In keeping with the attention on student demographic variables and their effect on persistence, three chapters in this volume focused on recent research findings specific to student characteristics. Means and Kniess in chapter 6 focus specifically on sociodemographic variables and their relationships to persistence, concluding that students from lower socioeconomic backgrounds, those with first-generation status, and those who identify as racially and ethnically minoritized still face barriers to completion of college. Culver and Bowman in chapter 8 explore students' levels of engagement on college campuses, concluding that the campus environment and specific institutional programs that encourage greater engagement can facilitate greater levels of persistence, particularly among those students who face additional barriers because of sociodemographic identities. Finally, Lee in chapter 9 reports both on the persistence experiences of students who swirl between institutions as well as the methodological difficulties in studying students who swirl, concluding that these behaviors are increasingly common among students and that methodological difficulties have kept researchers from fully understanding the effects of swirling on student persistence.

Our understanding of the effects of organizational variables on student persistence is both growing and understudied. Gansemer-Topf et al. in chapter 5 conclude that over 80% of the articles they reviewed focused exclusively on 4-year institutions. Moreover, the vast majority of these articles focused only on public 4-year institutions. Situating research studies exclusively in 4-year public institutions provides only a partial understanding of student persistence, as it does not allow us to explore different experiences in different contexts. These authors echoed calls by Tinto (2006–2007), who concluded that we must study "student retention in different institutional settings" (p. 4), and Reason (2009), who called for "multi-institutional studies . . . [that] include measures related to organizational environments, moving beyond the standard measures of institutions (e.g., size, source of support, selectivity) to include measures of organizational behaviors and contexts" (p. 676). These assertions, in combination with the findings of Gansemer-Topf et al. in chapter 5, strongly suggest that the institutional settings for all future studies of college student persistence should work to include private 4-year colleges and universities and both public and private 2-year colleges.

De los Ríos and Oseguera, in chapter 7 of this volume, address the concern expressed by previous authors about the paucity of understanding of how organizational behavior affects student persistence. Although they acknowledge the research into organizational behavior continues to be lacking, de los Ríos and Oseguera draw connections between organizational behavior and student persistence. Most notably, these contributors conclude that the connection between organizational behavior and persistence is often indirect and related to how well organizational behaviors encourage student engagement, a conclusion reinforced by Culver and Bowman's review in chapter 8 as well.

As we ponder the future of research into college student persistence, we recognize that this future needs two basic strands of research. One strand involves research on topics delineated by the research community. Such topics emerge from gaps in the literature on college student persistence or from the recommendations for further research derived from studies conducted by members of the research community. The topics previously presented in this chapter depict well this strand of research. In contrast, the second strand springs from a scholarship of practice—in this case, a scholarship of practice focused on college student retention. In its most basic form, a scholarship of practice uses findings from empirical research to guide the work of practitioners such as in making decisions or in program development (Braxton, 2017; Kramer & Braxton, 2017).

In addition to our previously stated call for future research in 4-year private colleges and universities and in both public and private 2-year colleges, we delineate two lines of inquiry for future research for the first strand. Two conclusions derived from the research highlighted previously define the first of these two lines of inquiry. Specifically, Means and Kniess in chapter 6 conclude that barriers to the completion of college remain for first-generation students, students from lower socioeconomic backgrounds, or racially and ethnically minoritized students. Moreover, Culver and Bowman in chapter 8 conclude that the campus environment and specific institutional programs that encourage student engagement, in turn, enhance the persistence of these types of students. Taken together, these conclusions outline the first line of future inquiry: factors that either pose barriers to or facilitate the persistence of students with the demographic characteristics of first-generation status, lower socioeconomic backgrounds, or with racially or ethnically minoritized identities. The recommendations advanced in the previous section of this chapter should guide future research pursuant to this first line of inquiry.

As previously asserted our understanding of the influence of organizational behavior on student persistence remains understudied despite growing attention to this topic. De los Ríos and Oseguera in chapter 7 provide guidance on future research on the relationship between organizational behavior and student persistence through their conclusion that this often indirect relationship works through organizational behavior that encourages students' engagement. This conclusion gives rise to the second line of inquiry for future research. This second line of inquiry should focus on the identification of different types of organizational behavior associated with student persistence. For example, the influence of organizational behavior in the form of institutional policies and practices that shape student perceptions of the characteristics of institutional culture constitute such organizational behavior. Because they posit the influence of institutional policies and practices on characteristics of institutional culture, future research should focus on empirical tests of the newly revised theories of student persistence in residential and commuter colleges and universities postulated by Reason and Braxton in chapter 4. In the theory section we offer suggestions, as do Reason and Braxton, for empirical tests of these two newly revised theories.

We next consider the particulars of the second strand of future research on college student persistence. It is important to note that research findings most useful to practitioners often originate from studies identified by practitioners as needed for their work. Put differently, such studies spring from a practitioner-defined research agenda. In this case, enrollment management officers of colleges and universities constitute the practitioners who produce the practitioner-defined research agenda. As Wendt et al. point out in chapter 13 enrollment management involves attention to the retention of enrolled students.

Thus, this second strand entails research conducted on studies delineated in a practitioner-defined research agenda of enrollment management. A first and necessary step for this strand involves the communication of this practitioner-defined research agenda to members of the research community by individuals who study college students. Braxton and Hossler (2019) and Wendt et al. in chapter 13 refer to this step as a loop from practitioners to researchers. Researchers can then select specific studies from the practitioner-defined research to explore more deeply.

We strongly encourage attention to the development of this second strand by presenting to members of the research community studies pertaining to retention or persistence delineated in a practitioner-defined research agenda for enrollment management. Put differently, we are forging the loop from practitioners to researchers.

Wendt et al. in chapter 13 derive a practitioner-defined research agenda for enrollment management that consists of 19 topical areas. Of these 19 topical areas, three pertain to student persistence or retention: efficacy of various retention strategies, financial aid, and attrition. The specific studies included under these three topical areas are as follows:

- the effectiveness of different strategies or interventions on the retention of students of various backgrounds such as student of color, African American males, adults, part-time students, nontraditional students, first-generation students

- studies that focus on the relationship between majors and student persistence as well as possible variability of retention rates across different majors
- the effects of financial aid on student persistence
- the approaches to increasing student retention by different types of colleges and universities

Like Wendt et al. in chapter 13 we recognize that research on some of the previously noted studies may already have been conducted. For example, Kramer et al. (2022) addressed the last of the needed studies listed previously as they concentrated on the approaches to increase student retention used by different colleges and universities. More specifically, Kramer et al. (2022) created a database of 99 institutional student retention efforts profiled by the *Chronicle of Higher Education* and *Inside Higher Education* during a 3-year period from August 2015 to August 2018. These institutional efforts fall into the four categories of academic support, advising, financial supports, and social supports.

However, literature reviews on the availability of extant studies on the other three topics listed previously fall outside the scope of this chapter. Without a knowledge of any research on the first topic listed previously, we view the need for studies on the effectiveness of different retention strategies for various types of students as particularly warranting attention by researchers.

Practice

Future directions for theory and research pertain to efforts to understand or increase our understanding of college student persistence. In sharp contrast, future directions regarding practice should concentrate on efforts to increase student retention. We differentiate between persistence and retention. Hagedorn (2005) put forth this distinction as she stated that students persist and institutions retain students.

As we envision future directions regarding efforts of individual colleges and universities to improve their rates of student retention, we put forth three imperatives. The first imperative for institutional practice entails an active engagement in a scholarship of practice by individual practitioners, who bear the primary responsibility for increasing their institution's student retention rate. By active engagement we mean the intentional use of research findings by institutional practitioners to guide their development of programs and activities designed to increase student retention at their college or university. Practitioners may derive such research findings from either of the two strands previously described. Optimally, the research findings used should involve empirically supported concepts derived from theories of college student persistence. Institutional programs and activities grounded in such concepts offer some degree of fidelity to the implementation of retention initiatives as well as adjustments in retention initiatives congruent with the focal theory (Braxton et al., 2014).

Kimball and Gowen in chapter 11 offer a framework for the translation of theory and research into retention strategies that can guide intentional engagement in a scholarship of practice by institutional practitioners. The Kimball and Gowen framework consists of a set of factors to consider in the development of retention strategies: expert knowledge, institutional contexts, cognitive schema, and retention strategies.

Expert knowledge takes the form of the type of knowledge practitioners should acquire before developing retention strategies. In chapter 11, Kimball and Gowen suggest that practitioners read broadly about the student experience. A particularly valuable suggestion by Kimball and Gowen entails a knowledge of an institution's current students by reviewing social artifacts produced by students such as social media, student-run blogs, student newspapers, and works of student advocacy.

The second factor pertains to the campus learning environments of the institution (see chapter 11). Practitioners need an awareness of the different aspects of institutional context within which retention strategies will take place. These aspects include the classrooms, laboratories, residence halls, student organizations, and on-campus employment. They also assert that practitioners should have a knowledge of institutional assessment data.

As chapter 11 explains, the cognitive schema of the practitioner stands as the third factor. Cognitive schema pertains to the dispositions of the individual practitioner that function as filters through which practitioners view expert knowledge and campus learning environments.

Retention strategies constitute the fourth factor. At base, Kimball and Gowen in chapter 11 suggest that retention strategies result from a careful consideration of expert knowledge, campus learning environments, and the cognitive schema of the practitioner to produce planned institutional behavior to increase student retention. Kimball and Gowen contend that all of the individuals involved in the development of retention strategies must be fully aware of the aspects of the strategies and their effects on students.

The last factor takes the form of a feedback loop that involves an assessment of the effectiveness of the retention strategies to increase student persistence. This loop also can involve modifications to the other factors delineated, especially to the retention strategies. Kimball and Gowen in chapter 11 also posit scholarly engagement as a part of the feedback loop. Their perspective on scholarly engagement closely resembles the loop from practitioners to researchers delineated by Wendt et al. in chapter 13. In this case, the communication of results of retention strategies from practitioners to researchers takes place rather than a practitioner-defined research agenda.

The second imperative for institutional practice stipulates that practitioners should maintain a skeptical view regarding so-called "game changer" initiatives advanced by foundations, policymakers, and thought leaders. This imperative stems from Doyle's assertion in chapter 14 that the various reforms delineated by Complete College America and other reform efforts resulted in little or no impact on college retention and competition. Instead of "magic bullets" or "game-changing" initiatives Doyle suggests that practitioners should embrace the view that it may take much trial and error to identify "multiple policy levers" (Braxton et al., 2004) to increase student persistence.

Colleges and universities should continually monitor the effects of institutional policies and practices on the student retention rate at their college or university. Such monitoring should focus on a wide range of policies and practices that might adversely affect enrolled students. The basis for this third imperative arises from questions that Rine and Brown in chapter 12 put forth regarding changes in institutional enrollment management practices. Such practices include the adoption of a sales approach to student recruitment. Early decision incentives offer an example of a sales approach that might negatively affect the length and nature of the college search process, which in turn, may also adversely shape the students' expectations for college.

Finally, Renn and Smith in chapter 10 provide guidance for institutional leaders who wish to use a data-informed systems perspective to create and sustain organizational change to improve student retention. Using examples from the University Innovation Alliance (UIA), Renn and Smith highlight how the feedback loop between practice and scholarship (and back again) can be used to adapt promising practices from one institution to another in a way that honors the local context of the adapting institution. Sharing successful and unsuccessful interventions with other institutions, encouraging institutional leaders to adapt practices at their own institutions, and assessing the results of those interventions are hallmarks of the UIA and can serve as a framework for other institutions to collaborate for the improvement of student success. A fourth imperative for institutional practice emerges from the guidance offered by Renn and Smith in chapter 10. This imperative asserts that colleges and universities should share their institutional initiatives designed to improve their institutional retention rate with other colleges and universities. In addition to the work of UIA, the database of 99 institutional student retention efforts profiled in the *Chronicle of Higher Education* and *Inside Higher Ed* provides another vehicle for the sharing of institutional retention initiatives (Kramer et al., 2022).

Final Thoughts

Wither scholarly attention to the problem of college student persistence. This heretofore but unstated underlying issue looms in the background of this chapter and to some extent the other chapters of this volume. This issue holds particular significance given its longevity of 95 years as a topic of empirical inquiry. Summerskill (1962) demarcated this longevity through his review of research that noted a study by Johnson published in 1926. We do not view the study of college student persistence as withering but rather as a topic of some vibrancy. To elaborate, in this concluding chapter we summarize and highlight many of the most salient points from the other chapters. In doing so, we also provides readers our perspective on how to make sense of this volume and how to consider using the work presented in this volume to improve student persistence. We also chart future directions for theory, research, and practice regarding college student persistence.

In closing, the focus on minoritized and other previously underserved populations may be the most powerful advancement in the theorizing, researching, and application of interventions related to student persistence in the past decade. The future vibrancy of college student persistence as a topic for theory, research, and practice hinges on the attention of research and practice communities to improvement of the persistence of minoritized student populations.

References

Braxton, J. M. (Ed.). (2017). *Toward a scholarship of practice* (New Directions for Higher Education, no. 178). Jossey-Bass.

Braxton, J. M., Doyle, W. R., Hartley, H. V., III, Hirschy, A. S., Jones, W. A., & McLendon, M. K. (2014). *Rethinking college student retention.* Jossey-Bass.

Braxton, J., Hirschy, A., & McClendon, S. (2004). *Understanding and reducing college student departure.* Jossey-Bass.

Braxton, J. M., & Hossler, D. (2019). Developing the two-way practitioner-researcher loop for enrollment management. *Strategic Enrollment Management Quarterly, 7*(2), 7–12. https://doi.org/info:doi/

Dewberry, C., & Jackson, D. J. (2018). An application of the theory of planned behavior to student retention. *Journal of Vocational Behavior, 107,* 100–110. https://doi.org/10.1016/j.jvb.2018.03.005

Hagedorn, L. S. (2005). How to define retention. In A. Seidman (Ed.), *College student retention formula for student success* (pp. 90–105). Praeger.

Hirschy, A. S. (2015). Models of student retention and persistence. In D. Hossler & B. Bontrager (Eds.), *Handbook of strategic enrollment management* (pp. 268–287). Wiley.

Johnson, J. B. (1926). Predicting success in college at time of entrance. *School and Society, 23,* 82–88.

Kramer, J. W., & Braxton, J. M. (2017). Contributions to types of professional knowledge by higher education journals. In J. M. Braxton (Ed.), *Toward a Scholarship of Practice* (New Directions for Higher Education, no. 178, pp. 9–20). Jossey-Bass.

Kramer, J., Rausch, S., & Braxton, J. M. (2022). Cataloguing institutional retention efforts and their empirical grounding. In N. A. Bowman (Ed), *How college students succeed: Making meaning across disciplinary perspectives* (pp. 6–27). Stylus.

Lopez, J. D. (2018). Factors influencing American Indian and Alaska Native postsecondary persistence: AI/AN Millennium Falcon persistence model. *Research in Higher Education, 59*(6), 792–811. https://doi.org/10.1007/s11162-017-9487-6

Merton, R. K. (1968). *Social theory and social structure.* The Free Press.

Museus, S. D. (2014). The culturally engaging campus environments (CECE) model: A new theory of success among racially diverse college student populations. In M. B. Paulsen (Ed.), *Higher education: Handbook of theory and research* (Vol. 29, pp. 189–227). Springer.

Patterson, C. H. (1983). *Theories of counseling and psychotherapy.* Harper & Row.

Reason, R. D. (2009). An examination of persistence research through the lens of a comprehensive conceptual framework. *Journal of College Student Development, 50*(6). 659–682. https://muse.jhu.edu/article/364959

Rendón, L. I. (1994). Validating culturally diverse students: Toward a new model of learning and student development. *Innovative Higher Education, 19*(1), 33–50. https://doi.org/10.1007/BF01191156

Sass, D. A., Castro-Villarreal, F., Wilkerson, S., Guerra, N., & Sullivan, J. (2018). A structural model for predicting student retention. *Review of Higher Education, 42*(1), 103–135. https://doi.org/10.1353/rhe.2018.0035

Schlossberg, N. K. (1989). Marginality and mattering: Key issues in building community. In D. C. Roberts (Ed.), *Designing Campus Activities to Foster a Sense of Community* (New Directions for Student Services, no. 48, pp. 1–15). Jossey-Bass.

Summerskill, J. (1962). Dropouts from college. In N. Sanford (Ed.), *The American college: A psychological and social interpretation of the higher learning* (pp. 627–657). Wiley.

Tinto, V. (1975). Dropouts from higher education: A theoretical synthesis of the recent literature. *Review of Educational Research, 45*(1), 89–125. https://doi.org/10.3102/00346543045001089

Tinto, V. (1993). *Leaving college: Rethinking the causes and cures of student attrition* (2nd ed.). The University of Chicago Press.

Tinto, V. (2006–2007). Research and practice of student retention: What next? *Journal of College Student Retention, 8*(1), 1–19. https://doi.org/10.2190/4YNU-4TMB-22DJ-AN4W

Vaccaro, A., Daly-Cano, M., & Newman, B. M. (2015). A sense of belonging among college students with disabilities: An emergent theoretical model. *Journal of College Student Development, 56*(7), 670–686. https://muse.jhu.edu/article/638558

Vaccaro, A., & Newman, B. M. (2016). Development of a sense of belonging for privileged and minoritized students: An emergent model. *Journal of College Student Development, 57*(8), 925–942. https://muse.jhu.edu/article/638558

Wang, X. (2017). Toward a holistic theoretical model of momentum for community college student success. In M. B. Paulsen (Ed.), *Higher education: Handbook of theory and research* (Vol. 32, pp. 259–308). Springer.

Yosso, T. J. (2005). Whose culture has capital? A critical race theory discussion of community cultural wealth. *Race Ethnicity and Education, 8*(1), 69–91. https://doi.org/10.4324/9781315709796-10

Maggie Bell received her BA in sociology from Grinnell College and her MEd, with an emphasis in student affairs, from Iowa State University. Prior to her graduate studies, she worked in residence life at Beloit College, where she also ran the Sustained Dialogue program. Maggie currently serves as a residence life coordinator at Grinnell College. Her ongoing professional and research interests center around creating more supportive educational environments and experiences for first-generation, low-income students.

Nicholas A. Bowman is the Mary Louise Petersen Chair in Higher Education, professor of higher education and student affairs, senior research fellow in the Public Policy Center, and director of the Center for Research on Undergraduate Education at the University of Iowa. His work uses a social psychological lens to explore key issues in higher education, including student success, equity and diversity, undergraduate admissions, college rankings, and quantitative research methodology. He has written nearly 100 peer-reviewed journal articles that have appeared in outlets such as *Review of Educational Research, Educational Researcher, Educational Evaluation and Policy Analysis, Journal of Research on Educational Effectiveness, Sociology of Education, Social Psychological and Personality Science*, and *Science Advances*.

John M. Braxton is a professor emeritus in the Higher Education, Education Leadership, and Policy Program, Peabody College of Vanderbilt University. He is also senior associate editor, *Innovative Higher Education*; a resident scholar, Tennessee Independent College and University Association; an affiliate scholar, USC Center for Enrollment Research, Policy and Practice; and a coprincipal, Community College Practice-Research-Policy Exchange. Professor Braxton has two research programs, one of which centers on the construction and testing of theory pertaining to college and university student persistence. He has published numerous publications on this topic in the form of articles, book chapters, and books. Most notable among these publications is his 2014 book with William Doyle and others, *Rethinking College Student Retention* (Jossey-Bass). Professor Braxton is the recipient of two awards for outstanding contributions to knowledge that advance the understanding of higher education: the research Achievement Award bestowed by the Association for the Study of Higher Education and the Contribution to Knowledge Award given by the American College Personnel Association. He is also a past president of the Association for the Study of Higher Education.

Joshua T. Brown is an instructor of higher education in the Department of Educational Leadership, Foundations, and Policy at the University of Virginia. His research focus attempts to understand the strategies colleges and universities develop to sustain their educational missions in complex policy and resource contexts, which has been generously funded through the National Science Foundation and the Association of College and University Housing Officers–International. Brown is the past editor of *Research and Practice in Assessment,* and his work can be found in a diverse array of outlets including the *American Journal of Education, Journal of Student Affairs Research and Practice, Journal of American College Health, Higher Education: Handbook of Theory and Research, Change, American Journal of Economics and Sociology, Teacher's College Record,* and *Journal of College Student Psychotherapy.* His research has received prominent media coverage through NPR On Point, as well as *Times Higher Ed, Inside Higher Ed, Hechinger Report,* and the *Chronicle of Higher Education.*

KC Culver is an assistant professor in the Higher Education Administration program at the University of Alabama. Her research focuses on improving equity in the policies, programs, and practices related to the academic mission of higher education, with a focus on faculty careers, instructional practices, and the impact of students' academic experiences on their outcomes. In the past 6 years, KC has published more than 30 peer-reviewed journal articles, book chapters, and national reports on these topics. Her work is informed by her own career trajectory in academia, including spending more than a decade as a nontenure-track faculty member and administrator in the English department at the University of Miami.

Maria Javiera de los Ríos is a PhD student and graduate research assistant in the Higher Education Program and the Center for the Study of Higher Education in the Department of Education Policy Studies at the Pennsylvania State University, where she also earned her MEd degree in higher education as a Fulbright scholar. Prior to Penn State, she earned a BA in political science at the Pontifical Catholic University of Chile. Her research focuses on campus climate and educational experiences of historically underserved and underrepresented higher education student populations. As a graduate research assistant, she has collaborated in the coevaluation team of the inaugural Howard Hughes Medical Institute–funded Millennium Scholars Program at Penn State, and she also worked in the evaluation of the National Science Foundation–funded National Research Traineeship Computational Materials Education Training Program at Penn State.

William R. Doyle is professor of higher education and public policy in the department of Leadership, Policy, and Organizations at Peabody College of Vanderbilt University. Doyle serves as editor-in-chief of *Research in Higher Education*. His research includes evaluating the impact of higher education policy, the antecedents and outcomes of higher education policy at the state level, and the study of political behavior as it affects higher education.

Ann M. Gansemer-Topf is an associate professor in higher education and student affairs at Iowa State University. Having worked 20 years in various academic and student affairs positions in higher education, she engages in research that has direct implications for research, practice, and policy. She received her BA in psychology from Loras College, her MS in professional studies, and PhD in educational leadership and policy studies from Iowa State University. She has published in over 30 peer-reviewed journals, including *Research in Higher Education, Journal of College Student Development, Journal of College Student Retention, Theory and Practice, Strategic Enrollment Management, Community College Journal of Research and Practice*, and *Research and Practice in Assessment*.

Garrett Gowen is an independent scholar living in New York City. His research focuses on the relationship between student political identity and college pathways and decision-making.

Don Hossler is a senior scholar at the University of Southern California. Hossler is an emeritus in the Department of Educational Leadership and Policy Studies from Indiana University Bloomington where he was named a provost professor and received the Sonneborn Award for Outstanding Research and Teaching from Indiana University in 2015. He has also held leadership roles including the vice chancellor of enrollment management at Indiana University, and is the founding executive director of the National Student Clearinghouse Research Center.

Willis A. Jones is an associate professor of higher education at the Simmons School of Education and Human Development at Southern Methodist University. Jones's research examines the antecedents and outcomes of college/university behavior, strategy, structures, and policies. Within this broad research agenda, his primary area of interest is the study of intercollegiate athletics. Jones has published on topics such as college student retention, college rankings, historically Black colleges and universities, student body racial diversity, the role of nontenure-track faculty in institutional governance, and competency-based education.

Wendy Kilgore has more than 20 years of experience as a higher education administrator, researcher, and consultant in the United States and Canada. She brings expertise in areas related to enrollment management and enrollment services, including the use of technology, organizational restructuring, student-centric business practice development, policy development, and managing comprehensive collaboration to support enrollment efforts.

Ezekiel Kimball is a professor of higher education at the University of Maine, where he also serves as the associate dean for undergraduate and teacher education in the College of Education and Human Development. Kimball's research agenda examines the success trajectories of minoritized student groups—particularly disabled students in higher education—and explores how empirical research on and theories of student development inform practice.

Dena R. Kniess is an associate professor of higher education administration and college student affairs in the College of Education at the University of West Georgia. She currently serves as director of the EdD program in higher education administration at UWG. Kniess studies assessment in higher education, college student access and success, faculty development, and multicultural issues in higher education. Her articles have been published in the *College Student Affairs Journal, Journal of College and University Student Housing*, and *Journal of Leadership Education*. Recently, she coedited a New Directions for Student Services volume on *Managing Career Transitions Throughout the Lifespan of the Student Affairs Practitioner* with Kristin Walker-Donnelly and Tony Cawthon (Jossey-Bass, 2019).

Jungmin Lee is assistant professor of higher education in the Department of Educational Policy Studies and Evaluation at the University of Kentucky. Her research interests include the effect of higher education policies and practices including financial aid policy, dual enrollment, and college transfer.

Darris R. Means is an associate professor of higher education in the School of Education at the University of Pittsburgh. Means studies how social, economic, and educational conditions shape postsecondary education access and success for rural students, Black students, low-income students, and/or first-generation college students. His articles have been published in the *Review of Higher Education, Teachers College Record, Journal of College Student Development,* and *Journal of Diversity in Higher Education.*

Leticia Oseguera is a professor and senior scientist in the Higher Education Program and the Center for the Study of Higher Education in the Department of Education Policy Studies at The Pennsylvania State University. She received her MA and PhD degrees from the Higher Education and Organizational Change Program at UCLA. Oseguera's research focuses on campus climate and understanding college access and educational opportunities for historically underserved and underrepresented student populations. Oseguera's research has been cited in articles in the *Washington Post, The Chronicle of Higher Education,* and *Hispanic Outlook in Higher Education.* Her recent publications include a coedited book, *Educational Policy Goes to School: Case Studies on the Limitations and Possibilities of Educational Innovation* (Routledge, 2019) and a research article on Black student science identity in the *Journal of Negro Education* and two coedited special journal issues on Latinx students in the *Journal of Equity, Leadership, and Research.* She also has extensive program evaluation expertise.

Robert T. Palmer is professor and chair in the Department of Educational Leadership and Policy Studies in the School of Education at Howard University. He is also a faculty affiliate for the Center of Minority Serving Institutions (CMSI) at Rutgers University. Upon arriving to Howard University in 2015, he helped to establish the PhD program in higher education leadership and policy studies. Prior to Howard University, Palmer was on the faculty at Binghamton University in the Department of Student Affairs Administration. His research examines issues of access, equity, retention, persistence, and the college experience of racial and ethnic minorities, particularly within the context of historically Black colleges and universities.

Robert D. Reason is professor of higher education and student affairs in the School of Education (SOE) at Iowa State University. He currently serves as the associate dean for undergraduate academic affairs in the College of Human Science. Prior to joining the faculty at Iowa State in 2011, Reason was on the faculty at Penn State University, where he was also a senior scientist in the Center for the Study of Higher Education. Reason studies how college and university policies, the campus climate, and students' experiences in college interact to influence student outcomes. Along with persistence through college, his research has focused on student learning outcomes during the first year of college. He has written a widely used text with Kristen Renn, titled *College Students in the United States: Characteristics, Experiences, and Outcomes* (Stylus, 2021).

Kristen A. Renn, PhD, is Mildred B. Erickson Distinguished Chair and Professor of Higher, Adult, and Lifelong Education at Michigan State University, where she also serves as associate dean of undergraduate studies for student success research. Renn's research addresses the learning, development, and success of minoritized students in higher education. She is author or coauthor of nine books about higher education, including *Student Development in College: Theory, Research, and Practice* (Jossey-Bass, 2016) and *College Students in the United States: Characteristics, Experiences, and Outcomes* (Stylus, 2021), coauthored with Robert Reason. She is Michigan State University's liaison to the University Innovation Alliance and coprincipal investigator on several grants related to increasing success for low-income and underrepresented students.

P. Jesse Rine is professor of education and director of the EdD Program in Educational Leadership at North Greenville University. Prior to joining the College of Education at North Greenville, Rine was the founding director of the MS Program in Higher Education Administration at Duquesne University. In addition, he previously directed the research programs of two national higher education associations, the Council for Christian Colleges & Universities and the Council of Independent Colleges, and served as assistant provost at Grove City College. Rine's research explores institutional identity, organizational adaptation, and student outcomes in higher education, with a focus on liberal arts colleges and religiously affiliated institutions. His scholarship has been published in several edited volumes, research reports, and academic journals, including the *Journal of College Student Development*, *Journal of College and Character*, *Journal of Academic Ethics*, *American Journal of Economics and Sociology*, *Religion & Education*, and *Christian Higher Education*.

Brandon R. G. Smith is a doctoral student in the Higher, Adult, and Lifelong Education program at Michigan State University and has an MEd in higher education from the University of Toronto–OISE. Prior to beginning doctoral studies, Brandon worked in progressive leadership roles in residence life and student affairs at Mount Royal, McMaster, and Ryerson Universities in Canada. Brandon's research interests focus on student success and professional success of administration working in postsecondary education—specifically, career buoyancy of this population.

Rachel A. Smith is assistant professor of higher education and student affairs in the School of Education at Iowa State University. Her research relies on social network analysis and mixed methods to examine the roles higher educational institutions play in organizing student academic and social relationship patterns and their associations with educational outcomes, particularly for first-year students and students in learning communities. Her work has appeared in the *Journal of College Student Development, Review of Higher Education,* and the *Journal of Higher Education.* She earned her PhD and MS in higher postsecondary education from Syracuse University and holds a BA in history from the University of Wisconsin-Madison.

Larry J. Walker is an assistant professor in the Department of Educational Leadership at the University of Central Florida. His research focuses on race, leadership, and policy.

Alexandra Cannell Wendt recently earned her MEd in higher education administration from Vanderbilt University. Currently, she is a senior project coordinator of executive projects in the Office of the Chancellor at Vanderbilt University. Prior to this role, Wendt served as a graduate assistant in the Office of the Provost and the Chancellor's Office at Vanderbilt. Before coming to Vanderbilt, Wendt served in various roles in Arizona, leading the AmeriCorps Program in the Mary Lou Fulton Teachers College at Arizona State University and, prior to that, leading the nationally recognized Service-Learning Program at Chandler-Gilbert Community College. Wendt also holds an associate degree from Chandler-Gilbert Community College and a BA in human communication with a minor in global studies.

Jodi Wilson is an academic success advisor at Arizona State University. She received a MEd in student affairs and a BS in psychology from Iowa State University.

Heather Zimar is managing editor of the American Association of Collegiate Registrars and Admissions Officers' *College & University Journal* and *SEM Quarterly Journal.* Zimar works with higher education researchers and practitioners across the globe to develop and publish content in the fields of admissions, registration, and enrollment management. She coedited *The SEM Anthology, Leadership Lessons: Visions and Value for a New Generation* and *Mentorship in Higher Education: Practical Advice and Leadership.* She has a BA in print journalism and a MS in communications from Ithaca College.

collegial dimension of organizational
behavior, 126, 130–132
communal potential, as social
integration antecedent, 54
communication, to enrollment
management (EM), 297–301
community colleges
advisor role within, 128
Black students at, 108
bureaucratic structure of, 128
"cooling out" by, 190
counter-momentum friction and, 17
holistic theory regarding, 16–18
learning communities within,
166–167
life responsibilities and, 18
persistence models within, 140
theoretical model of momentum
for, 16–18
transfer from, 193–194
vertical transfer from, 189–191
community cultural wealth (CCW),
44–45, 327
community service, 15
commuter colleges and universities
academic and intellectual
development at, 56
campus environment at, 55–56
characteristics of, 52
external environment and, 55
financial aid at, 55
organizational characteristics of, 55–56
revised theory of student persistence
at, 12, 13
student entry characteristics and, 55
student persistence at, 56
subsequent institutional commitment
at, 56
theory of student persistence in,
54–56, 62–65, 325
competition, 267–268, 273–274
Complete College America, 305, 313
completion grants initiative, 224–226
compositional diversity concept, 62–63

comprehensive level of service, of
online program management
(OPM), 266
comprehensive model of influences on
student learning and persistence,
141
conceptual model of theory-to-practice
translation for retention, 242–249,
250–252
formal theory and, 244–247
informal theory and, 248–249
institutional context and, 247–248
overview of, 242–244
practice of, 250–251
connection, in the living environment,
157
coping, as persistence factor, 111
counseling, within the admissions
office, 260
counter-momentum friction, 17
COVID-19 pandemic, 274
credit transferability, 191, 197
critical perspectives and approaches, 98
critical political approach, 133
critical race theory (CRT), 44
cross-cultural engagement, 15
cross-functional campus teams, 132
cultural capital, 11–12
cultural centers, 167–168
cultural community service, 15
cultural familiarity, 15
culturally engaged campus environment
model (CECE), 14–16, 25, 326
culturally relevant knowledge, 15
culturally validating environments, 15
culture, campus, 155–158
curricular experiences, persistence rate
and, 60–61
curriculum, "60-Second Survey"
responses regarding, 292
customer relationship management
(CRM) software, 261
customer service, within the admissions
office, 260